A Dublin Magdalene Laundry

A Dublin Magdalene Laundry

*Donnybrook and Church-State Power
in Ireland*

Edited by
Mark Coen
Katherine O'Donnell
Maeve O'Rourke

BLOOMSBURY ACADEMIC
LONDON • NEW YORK • OXFORD • NEW DELHI • SYDNEY

BLOOMSBURY ACADEMIC
Bloomsbury Publishing Plc
50 Bedford Square, London, WC1B 3DP, UK
1385 Broadway, New York, NY 10018, USA
29 Earlsfort Terrace, Dublin 2, Ireland

BLOOMSBURY, BLOOMSBURY ACADEMIC and the Diana logo are trademarks
of Bloomsbury Publishing Plc

First published in Great Britain 2023

Cover Design by Toby Way
Cover image © Exterior view of a Magdalene asylum, Donnybrook, reproduced courtesy
of the National Library of Ireland

A catalogue record for this book is available from the British Library.

A catalog record for this book is available from the Library of Congress.

ISBN: HB: 978-1-3502-7905-6
       PB: 978-1-3502-7904-9
       ePDF: 978-1-3502-7907-0
       eBook: 978-1-3502-7906-3

Typeset by RefineCatch Limited, Bungay, Suffolk

To find out more about our authors and books visit www.bloomsbury.com
and sign up for our newsletters.

Contents

Heritage and Memory

Illustrations

Plates

Figures

Tables

Contributors

Lynsey Black is Assistant Professor at the Department of Law, Maynooth University.

Mark Coen is a Lecturer in Law at the Sutherland School of Law, University College Dublin.

Lindsey Earner-Byrne is Professor of Irish Gender History at University College Cork.

Máiréad Enright is Professor of Feminist Legal Studies at Birmingham Law School.

Christopher Hamill is an architect and a PhD student at Queen's University Belfast.

Barry Houlihan is an archivist at the James Hardiman Library at the University of Galway.

Brenda Malone is a curator at the National Museum of Ireland.

Laura McAtackney is Professor at the Radical Humanities Laboratory and the School of Human Environment at University College Cork and Professor in Heritage Studies, Aarhus University.

Claire McGettrick is an Irish Research Council postgraduate scholar at the School of Sociology at University College Dublin and co-founder of Justice for Magdalenes Research.

Brid Murphy is Assistant Professor of Accounting at Dublin City University.

Katherine O'Donnell is Professor, History of Ideas at University College Dublin and a member of Justice for Magdalenes Research.

Maeve O'Rourke is Assistant Professor at the Irish Centre for Human Rights, School of Law, University of Galway, and a member of Justice for Magdalenes Research.

Martin Quinn is Professor of Management Accounting and Accounting History at Queen's University Belfast.

Acknowledgements

This book would not have come to fruition without the help and support of many people and organizations.

We gratefully acknowledge the support of a Publications Grant from the National University of Ireland. We also wish to acknowledge the research and editorial assistance provided by Justice for Magdalenes Research (JFMR). The British Library, the Irish Architectural Archive and the National Library of Ireland kindly gave permission to reproduce images from their collections.

Noelle Dowling, Archivist at the Dublin Diocesan Archives, was patient, good-humoured and generous with her time. Edel Purcell of the Central Catholic Library was always welcoming and interesting. Colum O'Riordan of the Irish Architectural Archive provided great assistance. Sr Mairéad Ní Chuirc kindly facilitated one day of access to the house annals of the Religious Sisters of Charity. Our thanks to Dermot Lacey for providing us with his archive of the *Donnybrook Review*. Stephen Kilroy was courteous and helpful in facilitating access to the remaining laundry buildings on behalf of the current owners.

We would like to thank to all those at Bloomsbury who worked on this book, in particular Tomasz Hoskins, Sophie Campbell, Atifa Jiwa, Nayiri Kendir and Merv Honeywood.

Each of us has benefited from the research culture and support of colleagues at our places of work – the Sutherland School of Law at University College Dublin; UCD Centre for Ethics in Public Life and UCD Newman Centre for the Study of Religions, both housed at the School of Philosophy at University College Dublin, and the Irish Centre for Human Rights and School of Law at the University of Galway.

Sincere thanks to Grace Weber for her assistance in getting the manuscript ready for publication. Max K. Feenan was meticulous and efficient in compiling the select bibliography and index.

We wish to thank Maolíosa Boyle for her wonderful foreword.

The encouragement and support of friends sustained us in editing this collection. In particular we would like to thank Ciarán Ahern, Sheila Ahern, Catherine Blaney, Oonagh Breen, Sarah-Anne Buckley, Hugh Campbell, Rebecca Coen, Elizabeth Coppin, Brendan Curran, Angela Downey, Suzanne Egan, Lisa Foran, Fionna Fox, James Gallen, Mary Harney, Liz Heffernan, Raymond Hill, Carole Holohan, Niamh Howlin, Jonathan Johanssens, Gordon Lynch, Joan McCarthy, Dearbhla MacManus, Mary Merritt, Denise Murray, Franc Myles, Jennifer O'Donnell, Gabrielle O'Gorman, Aoife O'Donoghue, Conall Ó Fátharta, Sinéad Ring, Colin Smith, James M. Smith, Deirdre Somers, Mari Steed and Pádraig Yeates.

Finally, we were very fortunate to work with a group of enthusiastic and dynamic contributors from a variety of backgrounds and disciplines.

Foreword

Derry, 1997. It was my second visit to The Good Shepherd Laundry. The week before I lied to the nun in charge to gain access to a building that I knew was scheduled for demolition. My first visit had led to an encounter with a woman who was polishing the long oak banister that twisted through the convent. As we talked, it became clear that she had always lived there. She had spent a lifetime polishing the lino and bannisters of the stairwells. This time I was greeted with an air of suspicion, the warm welcome was gone and I was chaperoned by a nun through the building. I realized that in conversing with the woman, I had crossed a line. But that is what art does.

I first met Katherine O'Donnell and Maeve O'Rourke in March 2020 in University College Dublin (UCD) when I was invited to view a presentation of students' work on the Sean McDermott Street Laundry. I was asked to attend as I am commissioning and curating a series of exhibitions entitled *The Magdalene Series* which explores the conflicted and mysterious figure of Mary Magdalene, a subject that has fascinated me since I was a child. 'It was the artists who led the way,' Katherine responded when I told her about documenting the Good Shepherd Laundry in Derry in the 1990s, my own experiences as a single young mother and how, twenty-five years later, I was curating *The Magdalene Series* at Rua Red, Dublin.

My upbringing in 1970s Derry was liberal, and while Catholicism defined which 'side of the house' I came from, it did not define me as an individual. I was never judged for being pregnant at 19. My sister and I were raised by our mother following the death of our father when we were very young. Single parenting was my norm. In 1992, the same year the Donnybrook Magdalene Laundry was sold, I arrived in Dublin with my 3-month-old daughter to start a new chapter in my life as a fine art student at the National College of Art and Design (NCAD).

In the early 1990s, the Republic of Ireland was considered another world for someone from the North. The border brought relief. The atmosphere was different and there was a distinct absence of surveillance towers, armoured cars, Saracens, patrols and checkpoints. What I wasn't prepared for was the repression and control that the Catholic Church had over its people in the so-called 'Free State'. A lasting memory was the difficulty I had trying to secure accommodation as a single mother. In 1992, a character reference signed by a priest was required as proof of my virtue in order to get a roof over our heads. I felt ostracized and a long way from my secure, supportive upbringing in Derry.

Mary Magdalene has always intrigued me. As a child, I was fascinated by images of the woman in red who had seven demons driven from her, who used her long hair to dry Jesus' feet after anointing them with spikenard. Unlike the celestial Virgin Mary, she felt closer to the real world. She had emotion and rawness.

In early 1993, I was gifted a book by one of my tutors at NCAD which massively impacted me: *Alone of All Her Sex: The Myth and Cult of the Virgin Mary* by Marina Warner. In the book, Warner writes, 'The Magdalene, like Eve, was brought into existence by the powerful undertow of misogyny in Christianity, which associates women with the dangers and degradations of the flesh.'[1] Warner is referring to Pope Gregory the Great's decision in 591 to label Mary Magdalene a sinful woman. Gregory's amalgamation of three characters all named Mary into one gave rise, in Warner's phrase, to 'a muddle of Marys'.[2] The three figures were the 'unknown sinful woman' who anointed Jesus' feet (Luke 7:36–50), Mary of Bethany who also anointed Jesus' feet (John 12:1–8) and Miriam (Mary) of Magdala who had seven demons driven out of her (Mark 16:9). The unknown sinner and Mary of Bethany both anointed Jesus' feet with spikenard, an alluring and expensive healing balm often associated with sex workers. This act of anointing was similar to Mary of Magdala's anointing of Jesus' body with spices after his death (Mark 16:1).

In 1996, I returned to Derry and started work as an Artist in Residence at a Mental Health Day Care Centre. It was the same year that Sean McDermott Street Magdalene Laundry closed its doors. The Day Care centre was located on the periphery of Derry, in the Waterside area. It was surrounded by the nineteenth-century bleak, grey, workhouse. Not long after I started, I asked what the austere building across the road was. 'The Good Shepherd Laundry,' was the reply, 'where the girls were taken.'

Convents have a distinct smell and colour palette. Furniture polish and clothes starch. Magnolia and pale-green walls, cross-patterned floor tiles and lino of burgundy and brown. Twenty-six years later, I can still walk through the rooms in my head as I did with my camera. Endless corridors of identical cells devoid of any traits of the individuals who once occupied them. Stale still air, dead flies on windowsills, holy-water bottles, a medal, numbered keys to rooms, letters, postcards of someone else's holiday and life pinned to the wall. In the laundry, packets of Reckitt's Blue which had made whites appear whiter. In the communal space, a wheelchair pushed against the wall next to a record player. A reminder of the impossibility of enjoyment and freedom.

In 1997, the third time I returned to the Good Shepherd, the building was in a state of demolition. What remained was a vast landscape of grey masonry rubble against a blue sky, doorways filled with bricks and mortar. Impossible to get in, impossible to get out, the pale green and magnolia walls now exposed to the outside world. I didn't need permission to enter.

In 1999, I exhibited the work publicly. It was entitled 'Fallen from Grace' and displayed at the Orchard Gallery, Derry. It consisted of thirty, 6-by-8-foot images of the interior of the laundry and the building in a state of dereliction. I painted the gallery floor the colour of the cracked brown lino. I wanted the public to witness what I had seen, to experience what I had experienced. A confrontation and unearthing of the truth.

Four years later, I returned. I was asked to facilitate a photography project involving a group of young single mothers from an emergency housing initiative called 'Shepherd's View for Young Parents', which had been built on the former laundry site. Following the demolition, two buildings replaced the barrack-like dormitories that housed the women. These buildings contained 'Shepherd's View for Young Parents' and

'Daleview Nursing Home'. The latter housed many of the women who spent a lifetime working in the laundry. The young mothers were not aware they were living on the site of a Magdalene Laundry. They repositioned themselves within the project after this and became emotionally engaged, drawing similarities between their own lives and their location.

Over three months, the group documented the last 'listed' building on the site. 'The Big House' as it was referred to in Derry, was the austere convent building where the nuns resided. It still stands in 2022, ominous and boarded up at the top of 'Shepherd's View', overshadowing the homes of the young women and the nursing home. A threatening reminder of the past. The young mothers met with the Daleview Residents and they shared personal stories. The audio recordings of these and the photographs informed an exhibition *Behind Closed Doors* in The Women's Centre, Derry, in 2004.

The Good Shepherd Laundry, like many others, may have been demolished, but the researchers of this book afford us another means with which to unearth what happened. They have uncovered the uncomfortable 'material memory'[3] that the Church and State thought they could bury and silently erase. They have given voice to the hundreds of women who were marginalized, imprisoned, treated like slaves, and mentally and physically abused at the hands of those in power. Through analysing architectural drawings, ledgers, electoral registers, machinery, religious books, newspapers, death certificates and personal testimonies, they have highlighted the abject misuse of this power for political and economic gain. They have evidenced how the women went unpaid, were brutally treated, injured by unsafe machinery, kept locked in cells, stripped completely of their identity yet registered to vote in the affluent Dublin 4 constituency. This book evidences that Donnybrook Magdalene Laundry was a corrupt business that made vast profits from the enslavement of women who were controlled and confined in horrendous living and working conditions. The authors highlight how these institutions were deeply embedded in an elite capitalist system that exploited the incarceration of women for their labour. A corrupt system that served renowned schools, famous hospitals, prestigious sports clubs and exclusive businesses. The authors present the unearthed truths, restoring voice to those who were seen as voiceless and power back to those who were rendered powerless.

I feel completely honoured to be part of this publication and would like to thank Katherine, Maeve and Mark for inviting me to contribute.

Maolíosa Boyle

Notes

1   Marina Warner, *Alone of All Her Sex: The Myth and the Cult of the Virgin Mary* (New York: Knopf, 1976).
2   Ibid., 344.
3   See Laura Mc Atackney, Chapter 9, this volume. A term coined by the French archaeologist Laurent Olivier. See Laurent Olivier, *The Dark Abyss of Time: Archaelogy and Memory* (London: AltaMira Press, 2011).

Abbreviations

CICA	Commission to Inquire into Child Abuse
CICA Final Report	*Final Report of the Commission to Inquire into Child Abuse* (2009)
DCC	Dublin City Council
DDA	Dublin Diocesan Archives
DHM	Dublin Honours Magdalenes
DML	Donnybrook Magdalene Laundry
DoEnv	Department of the Environment
DoJ	Department of Justice
DoT	Department of the Taoiseach
FOI	Freedom of Information
Fr	Father, title of a Catholic Priest
GPR	Ground-penetrating radar
IDC	Inter-Departmental Committee to Establish the Facts of State Involvement with the Magdalen Laundries
IDC Report	*Report of the Inter-Departmental Committee to Establish the Facts of State Involvement with the Magdalen Laundries* (2013)
INMH	Irish National Maternity Hospital
IPP	Irish Parliamentary Party
IRC	Irish Research Council
ITPA	Irish Trade Protection Association
JFM	Justice for Magdalenes
JFMR	Justice for Magdalenes Research
MBHCOI	Mother and Baby Homes Commission of Investigation
MMC	Magdalene Memorial Committee
MNP	Magdalene Names Project

MOHP	Magdalene Oral History Project
NAI	National Archives of Ireland
NDU	North Dublin Union
NMH	National Maternity Hospital
NMI	National Museum of Ireland
OLC	Sisters of Our Lady of Charity
Quirke Report	*The Magdalen Commission Report: Report of Mr Justice John Quirke*
RDLA	Richmond District Lunatic Asylum
RIRB	Residential Institutions Redress Board
RSC	Religious Sisters of Charity
RSM	Sisters of Mercy
RTÉ	Raidió Teleifís Éireann
SDU	South Dublin Union
SGS	Sisters of the Good Shepherd
SPG	St Patrick's Guild
Sr	Sister, title of nun or religious woman in a Catholic religious congregation or order
SSAP	Statement of Standard Accounting Practice
SVH	St Vincent's Hospital
SVHG	St Vincent's Healthcare Group
TD	Teachta Dála/Member of Parliament
TJ	Transitional Justice
TUSLA	Child and Family Agency
UCD	University College Dublin
UNCAT	United Nations Committee Against Torture
VAT	Value Added Tax

Introduction

Mark Coen, Katherine O'Donnell, Maeve O'Rourke

By 1922, there were ten Magdalene laundries in operation in the 26 counties of the new Irish Free State.[1] These were convents with large commercial laundry operations and other enterprises such as needlework and dressmaking, which confined women and girls for indefinite durations while forcing them into servitude. The institutions were owned and managed by four Catholic religious congregations of nuns.[2] Two were congregations originally founded in France, which merged in 2014: the Order of Our Lady of Charity of Refuge (OLC) ran Magdalene laundries at High Park and Sean McDermott Street in Dublin, and the Sisters of the Good Shepherd (SGS) owned laundries in Cork city (Sundays Well), Waterford, Limerick, and New Ross, Co. Wexford.[3] The other two were indigenous Irish congregations: the Sisters of Mercy (RSM) operated laundries in Galway and Dún Laoghaire, while the Sisters of Charity (RSC) operated a laundry in Cork (Peacock Lane) and Donnybrook Magdalene Laundry (DML), which is the focus of this book. All four of these religious orders additionally owned and managed teenage 'Training Centres', which were similar to Magdalene laundries – and were often physically attached to laundries – except that their policy appears to have been to release girls upon reaching adulthood. Little is known about these institutions because they and their connections to the Magdalene laundries have not been the subject of any formal investigation, and while financially supported by the State they were not statute-based institutions nor regulated as places of childcare. The RSC ran St Mary's Training Centre, Stanhope Street, in Dublin, now widely recognized as having been a de facto Magdalene and included within the terms of the Irish Government's 'Magdalen Restorative Justice Ex-Gratia Scheme' in 2013.[4] Besides operating Magdalene laundries and a teenage Training Centre, the RSC was also in the business of managing residential schools to which poor and working-class children considered 'neglected' or 'wayward' were committed by judicial order. These institutions were heavily funded but lightly regulated by the State.[5] The RSC ran five industrial schools, two of which were examined by the Commission to Inquire into Child Abuse (CICA) (which focused merely on a selection of institutions). The *Final Report of the Commission to Inquire into Child Abuse* (*CICA Final Report*) published in 2009 found damning evidence of systemic abuse and neglect.[6]

In Northern Ireland, from partition onwards, a network of Magdalene laundries also operated. The SGS (which owned four Magdalene institutions south of the border) ran Magdalene Laundries in Belfast, Derry/Londonderry and Newry.[7] Historians have also classified as a Magdalene laundry a Protestant 'Industrial/Rescue Home' operated by the Salvation Army in Belfast until 1965.[8] As was the case across the border, these locations formed part of a larger network of institutions and practices separating young girls and women from society and from their children. This network, aspects of which have been publicly investigated or designated for upcoming public inquiry,[9] was cross-border in nature. Leanne McCormick and Sean O'Connell have established that Northern Ireland's Magdalene laundries detained significant numbers of girls and women with home addresses in the Free State/Republic of Ireland, and several religious congregations in the Free State/Republic transferred girls and women from their institutions to the SGS-owned Magdalene laundries north of the border.[10]

Magdalene laundries are not an exclusively Irish phenomenon, nor is their history in Ireland confined to the post-independence/partition period. Maria Luddy has noted that the institutions now referred to as Magdalene laundries operated over a number of centuries throughout the United Kingdom, Europe, North America and Australia and that their furthest history in Europe may date back to medieval times.[11] In Ireland, the first such institution was established by Lady Arabella Denny in Leeson Street, Dublin, in 1765. Denny's asylum was specifically for Protestant young women who had 'fallen' into destitution and perhaps prostitution. Her Magdalene Home provided shelter and training for two years: a chance for the innocent victims of poverty to redeem themselves, after which the women would be placed in outside employment as servants. Denny's asylum was not for 'hardened' women who had adapted their lives to squalor and crime and were considered to be beyond moral rehabilitation.[12] According to the *Report of the Inter-Departmental Committee to Establish the Facts of State Involvement with the Magdalen Laundries* (*IDC Report*) published in 2013, it is estimated that by the late 1800s there were more than 300 Magdalene institutions in England alone and at least 41 in Ireland.[13] These early institutions – variously entitled asylums, refuges and penitentiaries – included institutions of all denominations and none. As demonstrated above, they included not only Catholic-operated institutions but also Protestant institutions as well as institutions run by lay Committees.[14] However, as James M. Smith notes, the post-independence Irish Magdalene system 'took on a distinct character' and continued to flourish right to the end of the twentieth century, long after Magdalene institutions had ceased to operate elsewhere.[15] By 1951, about 1 in every 100 Irish citizens was coercively confined in an institution operated collaboratively by the Church/State establishment, including psychiatric hospitals, industrial and reformatory schools, residential schools for disabled children, mother and baby 'homes',[16] county homes and Magdalene institutions.[17] Eoin O'Sullivan and Ian O'Donnell describe the system of institutional 'care' in twentieth-century Ireland as 'coercive confinement' in 'inherited networks of social control'.[18]

While many girls and women were trafficked between the two types of institution,[19] there is some public confusion as to the differences between mother and baby 'homes' and Magdalene laundries.[20] Mother and baby 'homes' were institutions that held unwed pregnant girls and women, and mothers, and subsequently arranged for their babies to be 'boarded out', sent to residential institutions or adopted. The girls and women were expected to pay for their confinement or otherwise work off their 'debt' in the institution. The RSC did not run a mother and baby 'home', however from 1943 the congregation operated St Patrick's Infant and Dietetic Hospital, an institution that is more popularly known as 'Temple Hill', in the salubrious neighbourhood of Blackrock. The RSC's 'hospital' housed in the Georgian villa at Temple Hill was used as a holding stage for babies born to unmarried mothers.[21] Many mothers were middle-class women who could afford to avail of private maternity services and avoid the mother and baby 'home' institutions.[22] Their babies were brought to Temple Hill along with babies from mother and baby 'homes'. The RSC also ran St Patrick's Guild Adoption Society (SPG), which is the agency that exported the most children to America for adoption between the 1940s and 1970s.[23] The agency also facilitated a large number of illegal adoptions.[24]

Many who were held in Magdalene institutions were not mothers, and infants were not held in those institutions. The Magdalene laundries were regarded as places for the containment and punishment of women and girls deemed incorrigible and morally corrupt, a fact which can be discerned from the Irish Catholic Directories of the nineteenth and twentieth centuries. The 1841 *Irish Catholic Directory* contained a table of 'asylums' in Dublin, the top half of which listed 'asylums for aged and virtuous females' while the bottom half detailed 'asylums for penitent Magdalenes'.[25] This distinction, between institutions catering for respectable persons and those targeting supposedly immoral women, may also be seen in a later volume of the *Directory*, which enumerated among the Catholic charities of Dublin 'several Widow's Houses and other Refuges for virtuous women … Night Asylums for the houseless [and] penitentiaries for the depraved'.[26] The Magdalene asylums of Dublin were listed under the heading 'Magdalen Penitentiaries' in the *Directory* until 1971.[27] While these classifications demonstrate that the punitive and containment objectives of the Magdalene laundries were officially endorsed and accepted by the Catholic hierarchy, one did not have to read religious directories to know about the institutions.

The Magdalene laundries occupied a prominent place in Irish public consciousness and discourse. As Fintan Cullen has demonstrated, the towering statue of Cardinal Paul Cullen erected in Dublin's Pro-Cathedral in 1882 incorporates significant Magdalene imagery. The statue sits on a plinth encircled by carved figures, among which is a group of three nuns tending to a woman, '[h]er fallen status … literally represented by her prostrate position'.[28] Using Donnybrook as a case study, the chapters in this book show that the Magdalene laundries had a considerable public profile, at least until 1970. Newspapers carried stories about their work, publicized their appeals for donations and reported on the content of the charity sermons priests preached to raise funds for them. These sermons were broadcast on national radio for several decades. Bequests to the institutions were listed in the press,[29] which also reported on cases where women were sent to the Laundries by the judiciary.[30] The last Magdalene institution in Ireland was the Sean McDermott Street Laundry operated by the OLC congregation in Dublin, which closed in 1996.

Survivors' voices

Over the past thirty years, as those subjected to abuse in Ireland's institutions have spoken increasingly of their experiences, the need to understand the nation's institutional 'care' and family separation system as just that – an integrated system – has become ever clearer. The cooperation of hundreds of institutions and agencies and thousands of state, religious, professional and business personnel, including across the Irish border and the Irish Sea,[31] is a key facet of the power structure which confined and disappeared people from relatives and community and which continues in the form of secrecy today.[32] Survivors of institutionalization and forced family separation consistently draw attention to the re-ostracizing and discriminatory nature of successive governments' limited investigations and redress mechanisms.[33] Demonstrating the interconnected nature of the system and its effects, three adoption rights activists, Mari Steed, Claire McGettrick and Angela Newsome, founded the Justice for Magdalenes (JFM) campaign in 2003. Steed and Newsome are the daughters of women incarcerated in Magdalene laundries for a combined total of approximately sixty years.[34]

JFM grew out of the Magdalene Memorial Committee (MMC), established in 1993 in response to the alarming activity of the OLC sisters at High Park who, in order to clear land to sell to a developer, rapidly exhumed and cremated the bodies of women who had died in the Magdalene Laundry there. The work of JFM gained added urgency when James M. Smith sought to collaborate with Steed and McGettrick in 2009, the year that the *CICA Final Report* was published. Volume 3, chapter 18 of the *CICA Final Report* is entitled 'Residential Laundries, Novitiates, Hostels and other Out-of-home Settings', and while it is clear that the authors realized that girls were sent to work in Magdalene Laundries, the term 'Magdalenes' is never used to describe the institutions. Katherine O'Donnell and Maeve O'Rourke (two of the editors of this volume) were recruited to JFM by Smith. The campaign initially coalesced around Smith's work of building archival evidence of State involvement with the Magdalene institutions throughout the twentieth century which, with O'Rourke's legal analysis, formed the basis of JFM's successful efforts to obtain an official report and recommendations from the Irish Human Rights Commission in 2010.[35] The archival evidence was supplemented with initial witness statements gathered by O'Rourke in 2011[36] and a much larger oral history project capturing the recollections of survivors, former nuns and other witnesses to the activities of the Magdalene laundries, led by O'Donnell.[37] All members of JFM continuously contributed to the archive of evidence and JFM engaged in a wide-ranging political, legal and media campaign which included advocacy at the United Nations. McGettrick developed the 'Magdalene Names Project', revealing how many had died in the institutions yet lay buried in unmarked graves.[38] Steed disseminated all of the research and legal argument via the campaign website, social media platforms and press releases. JFM developed a comprehensive four-part redress and restorative justice scheme which included, as a first step, a State apology to the girls and women who had been held and forced to labour in the Magdalene laundries. JFM worked with NGOs such as Amnesty International, the National Women's Council of Ireland and the Irish Council for Civil Liberties to lobby the Government, raise media interest, inform the public and generate momentum for the justice campaign.

Eventually, the Government established an inquiry, but unlike the earlier CICA or the subsequent Mother and Baby Home Commission of Investigation (MBHCOI), the inter-departmental committee (IDC) was a non-statutory process of inquiry. The IDC comprised civil servants from six government departments which JFM had shown were primarily involved in the Magdalene laundries and the inquiry was chaired by Senator Martin McAleese, a Taoiseach's nominee to the Seanad (Irish Senate). In August 2012, JFM lodged its principal submission with the IDC: a 145-page document collating evidence of State complicity and conveying its legal significance, supported by 796 pages of survivor testimony consistent with 3,707 pages of supporting evidence.[39] JFM's research revealed that the Irish State had been extensively involved with the Magdalene Laundries, through sending girls and women there from county homes, mother and baby 'homes', industrial schools and orphanages, as well as through the courts. The State also supported the Magdalene laundries in awarding them State contracts from various sectors such as hospitals, prisons, schools, the Defence Forces and semi-state bodies such as the national airline. Furthermore, the State did not uphold domestic law, the Irish Constitution nor international treaties in its failure to vindicate the rights of the girls and women who were forced into servitude and if they escaped were subject to Garda (police) searches, capture and return to the institution.

When the IDC finally issued its report in February 2013, it ignored the 796 pages of testimony submitted by JFM and further neglected to report on all the records available to it. The report was egregiously misleading in its account of the duration of time that girls and women spent in the institutions and the IDC failed to adequately investigate deaths that occurred there.[40] The IDC did not merely fail to fully investigate breaches of law and human rights abuses; it did not accurately portray the experience of the girls and women who were held under lock and key and forced to work in Magdalene institutions such as DML. The IDC allowed the nuns to provide their own written critique on drafts of the final report and the nuns' statements were accepted and presented as fact. Furthermore, the IDC decided to step outside the stated remit of its inquiry which was supposed to focus on the Irish State's involvement with the institutions; the members took the opportunity (in spite of evidence to the contrary) to assert that the religious orders made no significant profits from their Magdalene institutions and operated on a 'break-even' basis.[41] Furthermore and astoundingly, in spite of chapter 19 of the *IDC Report* detailing physical punishment, forced labour and unlawful imprisonment, the press statements from the IDC as well as the report itself insisted that 'physical abuse' was not endemic in the Magdalene institutions.[42]

Despite the assertions of the *IDC Report*, the Government issued an apology and appointed a High Court judge, Mr Justice John Quirke, to design a Magdalene Restorative Justice Scheme. JFM published a guide for survivors to engage with Mr Justice Quirke and formally resigned the campaign and reconstituted as Justice for Magdalenes Research (JFMR). The scheme designed by Mr Justice Quirke in many respects mapped the Redress and Restorative Justice scheme proposed by JFM. However, in spite of Government assurances that the scheme would be implemented in full, the promised medical care package, which was supposed to provide excellent care for the survivors, is instead little more than the basic medical card supplied to those in receipt of social welfare.[43] The Department of Justice (DoJ), charged with administering the scheme, has offered an abysmal service to hundreds of Magdalene survivors. At the end of 2017, Ireland's Ombudsman, Peter Tyndall, wrote an extraordinary report, castigating the actions and inaction of the DoJ. He declared the Magdalen Restorative Justice Ex Gratia Scheme 'manifestly unfair',[44] and stated that he had never before in his entire career as Ombudsman in Ireland and abroad encountered civil servants who 'absolutely and categorically refused to engage' with him as the DoJ had.[45] Among other criticisms Mr Tyndall found that: 'There was an over reliance on the records of the congregations and it is not apparent what weight, if any, was afforded to the testimony of the women and/or their relatives.'[46] He revealed that in assessing applications, 'the Department gave undue weight to the evidence supplied by the religious congregations—some of which was requested and received after the decision to exclude the women was made.'[47] Minister for Justice, Charlie Flanagan, appointed Mary O'Toole SC to hear appeals by women forced to work in Magdalene laundries against decisions made by the DoJ. At the time of writing in July 2022, she is finally clearing the backlog of cases.

Donnybrook: A desirable address

The question might be asked why this edited collection concentrates on one institution only: the Magdalene Laundry at Donnybrook, Dublin 4, owned and managed by the RSC from the nineteenth century until sold as a going commercial concern in 1992. It does so because adopting such a focus offers an opportunity to explore deeply and from a range of disciplinary standpoints both the institution and the wider system within which the institution functioned. Elements of that system continue today, such as the ongoing close relationships between departments of government and religious orders as evidenced in Tyndall's 2017 report on the Magdalene redress scheme.

The asylum which was initially located at Townsend Street and moved to Donnybrook in 1837, has a special historical significance within the network of Irish Magdalene institutions. It was the first Magdalene asylum in Ireland to change from being an institution under lay management to one located within, and controlled by, a convent. In pioneering this change, it provided the template for what would become the archetypal Irish Magdalene laundry, owned and overseen by nuns. In the decades that followed, the other Irish Magdalene asylums would undergo a similar transformation.[48] Further, DML was designed to be carceral: the women were locked into small, individual cells. Fanny Taylor, an English visitor to DML in the 1860s, was surprised to find that the 'mode of management' at DML 'differs somewhat from that of the penitentiaries generally known in England. The wish and intention of the Sisters is that their inmates should remain with them for life.'[49] Luddy notes that by 1922, all ten of the Catholic Magdalene Laundries that were to flourish until the closing decades of the twentieth century 'appear to have become much less flexible institutions', and their reputation was that they were long-term carceral institutions rather than temporary asylums.[50]

DML's operation is an exemplar of the nexus between the powerful in Irish religious life and in politics, business, the judiciary, the media, criminal law and broader society which enabled the exploitation of the most vulnerable. The institution's physical location in itself speaks to its cultural and social positioning: it is nestled in the leafy and affluent area of Dublin 4. 'Donnybrook' and 'D4' are common parlance in Ireland to refer to the country's wealthy elite and most important power brokers. DML's site abuts a large Garda (police) station and is within walking distance of the campuses of both RTÉ, the State's public service broadcaster, and University College Dublin (UCD), the country's largest university and alma mater of government ministers, Taoisigh (prime ministers) and many members of the Irish judiciary. The position of DML lies adjacent to the streets where international embassies and ambassadors' residences are located. A large property developer now acts on behalf of the site's current owner, who lives abroad. Planning permission to construct luxury apartments in place of the laundry building and surrounding site was granted by Dublin City Council on 29 January 2020.[51] The RSC, meanwhile, continues to manage state-funded care services. They are at the centre of ongoing public debate regarding a government plan to build a state-of-the-art national maternity hospital on land that the Sisters will continue to own, with the hospital to be managed through a corporate arrangement committed to the values of the RSC's founder, Mother Mary Aikenhead.

Archives of resistance for a resilient future

Accompanying the editors' and several of the other authors' scholarly interest in DML is their personal involvement in the effort to preserve its material history and to ensure respect for human rights in the course of its future development and use. In August 2016, a planning application appeared on the website of Dublin City Council seeking permission for a luxury residential development on the approximately 0.257 hectare site (which is only part of the original laundry site and does not include the convent or the buildings where the women lived). The independent archaeological assessment submitted alongside cautioned that: '[t]here are no clear records as to what happened to some of the women who operated within the laundries once they died. It remains a possibility that some are buried within the area of proposed development.'[52] The assessment further revealed that the building was 'the last Magdalen Laundry building which still contains much of its contents from when it was used as a Magdalen Laundry, much of which is intact'[53] – a fact confirmed by video footage of the interior posted anonymously on YouTube around the same time.[54] Claire McGettrick, (whose essay appears in this collection) wrote with her Justice for Magdalenes Research colleagues, including Katherine O'Donnell and Maeve O'Rourke, to Dublin City Council, arguing in response to the planning application that: (i) survivors of Magdalene Laundries, and of Donnybrook in particular, should be engaged in expertly facilitated consultation regarding the question of memorialization, (ii) women still living on the grounds of the convent at Donnybrook, who were never released, should be offered the opportunity if they so wished to live independently and with all necessary support in any social housing to be included in the proposed development, (iii) subject to survivors' views, the State should in fact purchase the site from its commercial owners in order for it to be preserved as part of the historical record, (iv) every effort must be made to ascertain whether burials had taken place on the site, and (v) because no memorial should ever act as a means to preclude investigation and accountability, any physical memorial should be combined with 'active' memorialization, including the preservation and releasing of records, the gathering of oral histories, the complete identification and marking of burial places and the creation of a museum.[55]

Also in 2016, Mark Coen wrote to the developer acting on behalf of the owner of DML, pointing to evidence which indicated that important contents from the Magdalene period remained on the site. He emphasized the social, cultural and historical importance of the site and drew attention to the fact that one of the laundry baskets, still extant from DML's heyday, was labelled 'Áras an Uachtaráin, Phoenix Park', which is the official residence of the President of Ireland. While the developers appeared receptive to this approach and open to collaboration in safeguarding the contents, it was not until Coen sent a follow-up email in April 2018 that real engagement began to take place. A meeting took place between Coen and the developers in June 2018, in advance of which he liaised with O'Rourke and O'Donnell of JFMR. At the meeting, it was agreed that access to the laundry site would be facilitated so that the buildings and contents could be inspected. The successful meeting followed shortly after the Dublin Honours Magdalene (DHM) event which JFMR had organized with businesswoman Norah Casey.

The DHM event saw over 230 women who had been held in Magdalene Laundries, including DML, come to meet each other. The Minister for Justice, Charlie Flanagan, agreed to fund the event because one of the aspects of the Magdalene Restorative Justice scheme that had not been implemented was that the DoJ were expected to facilitate women from the Magdalene Laundries to meet each other. The women attended a reception hosted by President Michael D. Higgins, and Dublin's Lord Mayor hosted a concert and dinner to honour the women. The convoy of coaches which carried the women and their companions from their hotel through the city had their way cleared by an accompaniment of Garda cars and motorcycle riders (an irony which seemed to delight the women). The event led to a groundswell of emotional public support; as the coaches passed by, they were waved and cheered at by onlookers. Broadcast media captured the warmth of the welcome from members of the public (mainly women) who lined up outside the Lord Mayor's residence as the former Magdalene women arrived for the gala dinner. Signs carried by the crowds who gathered read, 'Welcome Home', 'The Women of Ireland Salute You', 'Mná Mná!' 'Welcome Home, Sisters'. The DHM event also included a 'Listening Exercise', where all three editors of this volume played a role in gathering views from survivors on how the Magdalene Laundries should be remembered by future generations.[56] The Listening Exercise consisted of round-table group discussions with 147 participants. Tables were mediated by 26 volunteer facilitators assisted by scribes who took notes and were responsible for the audio recordings. The DHM event was reported in the Irish national press and internationally as an event of historic significance and its impact was recognized by those who owned and sought to develop the site at DML.

The developers agreed to support the research work of Laura McAtackney, who contributes to this volume. McAtackney arranged for an archaeological survey of the site that included reporting on the extant machinery and she also contacted Brenda Malone (a further contributor to this volume) of the National Museum of Ireland (NMI) and arranged for her to engage with the project. The developers have consented to the NMI acquiring the contents of the site, including religious statues, machinery, domestic artefacts, ledgers and correspondence. The University of Galway, through Barry Houlihan (also a contributor to this volume), has archived the extant documents.

A significant outcome of the involvement of academic researchers, archivists and museum curators with the current owners of DML site has been the creation of a crucial archive – of documents, materials and knowledge. This archive, combined with the transcripts of the DHM listening event (which provide essential evidence of the women's wishes in terms of future education, memorialization and truth-telling), has guided the development of this book project.

The editors actively sought to include the voices and perspectives of the RSC in this book. In September 2020, we wrote to the Leadership Team of the congregation, informing them that we were preparing an edited collection on DML. In the letter, we indicated that we were willing to present our work to the RSC in order to receive feedback on it. We also stated that we were interested in designing an oral history project in collaboration with the congregation, in order to capture the perspectives of the nuns on the operation and legacy of the institution. On 20 November 2020, the three editors had a Zoom meeting with the Leadership Team, during which we had an open discussion about this project and invited their participation as outlined above. Coen had previously been permitted to access the House Annals of St Mary Magdalen's up to the year 1920 for one day only (31 October 2019) at the RSC Archives in Sandymount. At the November 2020 meeting, we asked if we could consult the House Annals up to the closure of the institution and stated that if this was permitted, we would anonymize the names of the sisters that our research had revealed were involved in the running of the institution. The Leadership Team indicated that they would think about our proposals. The RSC subsequently informed us that they were unwilling to collaborate with us or facilitate the research for this book in any way. Even a request to see a copy of the 1941 rules of the congregation was refused on the basis that: 'Our Constitutions are written for members of the Congregation and we do not lend copies of them to anyone unless it is for the purpose of working with the Congregation.' It would appear that a congregation with a long involvement in education is not well disposed towards academic research, a trait it shares with the other congregations who ran Magdalene asylums, mother and baby 'homes', industrial schools, etc. In the course of our contacts with the RSC, we were informed that the congregational archives contain no photographs or building plans of DML, nor do they contain any correspondence with customers, suppliers of machinery or State agencies such as the Department of Justice. It is remarkable that a congregation that managed an institution from 1833 to 1992 has no such archival material. In the meeting with the RSC, the editors invited them to participate in the Magdalene Oral History project, funded by the Irish Research Council, in which over a hundred people have participated. However, the voices of religious sisters are largely absent from that archive. We encouraged them to consider developing their own oral history project, not merely to aid in understanding DML, but to add to the historical record on the experiences of Irish women religious in the twentieth century. We concur with the view of Margaret MacCurtain and Suellen Hoy that: 'we need to hear the voices of women who are nuns, especially the self who is no longer annalist but the subject of the testimony'.[57]

The editors, and the contributors we have gathered in this volume, believe that it is more important than ever to examine Ireland's institutional legacies carefully, from numerous disciplinary perspectives, with survivors' testimony to the forefront. This imperative arises not only from the lack of access to (what we hope are still extant) records held by the RSC and other religious orders but also from the increasing tendency of the State to treat its official inquiries as the one and only 'truth', to shut down access to its archives and to refuse to compel religious orders to release any documents they hold. As recorded in its final report, the IDC declared that it would place its collected copies of official records in the Department of the Taoiseach (DoT) because 'maintenance of these copies together in a single location will be a concrete outcome to the Committee's work and may be a resource for future research'.[58] However, the IDC archive, deposited in the DoT, does not include any of the records which the IDC received from: (i) the religious congregations that operated Magdalene laundries, (ii) the Dioceses in which Magdalene laundries were located, or (iii) the Irish Society for the Prevention of Cruelty to Children.[59] As explained by the IDC in its *Interim Report*, in exchange for access to the nuns' records the IDC agreed that the records and all copies of them would be 'destroyed and/or returned to the relevant Religious Order upon conclusion of the Committee's work and publication of its report'.[60] Moreover, for many years following the conclusion of the IDC's work, the DoT refused all requests, even under the Freedom of Information (FOI) Act, 2014, for access to the IDC archive, including a request solely for the archive's index or finding aid. The DoT insisted that: 'these records are stored in this Department for the purpose of safe keeping in a central location and are not held nor within the control of the Department for the purposes of the FOI Act. They cannot therefore be released by this Department.'[61]

The Information Commissioner upheld an appeal by a Magdalene survivor with the assistance of pro bono lawyers and JFMR, finding that the archive in the DoT *can* be accessed under the FOI Act. Following this decision, Maeve O'Rourke requested all records relating to DML to assist with our book. The Taoiseach's office responded by saying that searching through the archive for certain records would be so expensive that it could not be countenanced under FOI, and that the editors should make individual requests of all the government departments that originally gave their records to the IDC. O'Rourke requested and received the index to the archive and Sheila Ahern, a greatly experienced researcher whose work includes contributing to Mary Raftery's 1999 documentary for RTÉ, *States of Fear*, attempted to piece together the collection of documents, making FOI requests of all of the original sources as instructed by the Taoiseach's department and at significant cost. Ahern summarizes the results of her efforts thus:

> All (except one) of the FOI requests were refused. Among the grounds given for refusal were that the scale of the request was too big, that there was insufficient data from the Index to identify the records or that the information requested was otherwise available and didn't come under FOI legislation. In one case, Revenue, they said they couldn't find any correspondence between Revenue and the IDC despite the fact that the IDC listed correspondence with Revenue in their Index.[62]

Ahern decided also to search publicly available records, visiting the Valuation Office in the Irish Life Centre (which holds the rates and valuation archives), the Military Archives in Rathmines (because the Department of Defence was one of the customers for Magdalene laundry services) and the National Archives, where Ahern was informed that most of the files she was seeking were 'closed files' and that special permission from individual government departments was required to access them. Despite devoting numerous days and weeks to this task and having the assistance of archivists at each location, she concludes that: 'the task of trying to recreate the archive that the IDC relied on for its Report is, I believe, impossible without the resources and access that was given to McAleese and the Committee'.[63]

Donnybrook Magdalene Laundry and Church-State power: A multidisciplinary focus

The first four chapters in this volume discuss the political, cultural and social contexts of DML. Chapter 1, by Mark Coen, traces the history of the RSC from its foundation in 1815 and compares its structures, governance and objectives to those of other religious congregations of the period. This chapter also discusses the formation of RSC sisters, the major works of the congregation and the myriad controversies in which it has been embroiled since the early 1990s. Lindsey Earner-Byrne's essay (Chapter 2) examines the historical role of respectability as a social norm, highlighting its influence on the policing of class and gender both before and after Irish independence. Earner-Byrne argues that the quest for respectability was one of the key factors that was regarded as justifying and indeed requiring the institutionalization of women at DML and other similar sites of incarceration. Chapter 3, by Mark Coen, presents an institutional history of DML, drawing on sources including RSC publications, newspapers, the letters of Mary Aikenhead and material from the Dublin Diocesan Archives. The fact that DML was highly visible as both a commercial laundry and a penitentiary until an apparent retreat from publicity in the 1960s is a strong theme in this chapter. The chapter also discusses in detail the withdrawal of a State laundry contract from DML in the 1940s, on the basis that it violated the fair wages clause contained in all government contracts. Katherine O'Donnell's essay, Chapter 4, argues that the distinct character of the Irish Magdalene institutions is best understood not merely as an exemplum of the kind of 'voluntary' organization advocated in Catholic social doctrine but also as a neocolonial construct. The chapter draws heavily on the testimony offered by survivors of DML, describing myriad aspects of their lives and their unpaid work in the institution. The accounts reveal the catastrophic impact of institutionalization on those who lived, worked and – in some cases – died behind DML walls.

The next four chapters analyse discrete aspects of DML during its time as a functioning Magdalene institution. The architecture of the site is the focus of Chapter 5, written by Chris Hamill. Using archival architects' drawings to recreate the buildings of DML, Hamill demonstrates their ad hoc development and their internal configuration. The essay also serves as a reminder that while significant elements of the site remain, much has been demolished. Two chapters consider the income-generating activities of DML. Máiréad Enright, in Chapter 6, analyses the status of DML as a charity in law and highlights the important contribution donations and bequests made to its economic power. Enright considers the motivations of donors and testators and argues convincingly that charitable giving of this kind served to perpetuate social and gender inequalities. The operation of a commercial laundry was also income-generating, and Chapter 7, written by Brid Murphy and Martin Quinn, makes an important contribution in this regard. The *IDC Report*, which was published in 2013, stated that the financial records of DML did not survive. It also found that the Magdalene Laundries operated on a subsistence or close to break-even basis (*IDC Report*, Chapter 20, p993). Chapter 7 disproves these findings by demonstrating that significant accounting records from DML exist and, furthermore, that they reveal a very lucrative commercial laundry business made possible by the non-payment of wages. Lynsey Black in Chapter 8 considers the role of DML within what she terms 'a shadow penal system'. Using case studies, the chapter illustrates the various pathways by which women were committed to the institution by the State's criminal justice system. Black demonstrates that detention in DML entailed many disadvantages that a sentence of imprisonment did not, including the lack of any oversight of conditions and, most crucially, the absence of a release date.

The final three chapters address the themes of heritage and memory. The importance of preserving the material culture of Ireland's institutional past has only come to be appreciated in recent years. It is important now because of the refusal of religious congregations to permit access to their archives, and the related concern that archival materials may have been knowingly destroyed in an effort to erase the past. It will become even more important in the future when survivors of institutional abuse are no longer alive to speak of their experiences. In Chapter 9, Laura McAtackney explores the potential of archaeological approaches to DML, situating her study within the subfield of contemporary archaeology. She gives special consideration to how we can use the privileged position of archaeology to include survivors' perspectives. Through broadening the form of archaeological interventions, McAtackney demonstrates how the material world of Donnybrook can yield revealing insights.

The role of museums and archives in evidencing the Magdalene system and educating future generations is to the fore in Chapter 10. Brenda Malone locates the acquisition of objects from DML by the NMI within the museum's emerging interest in recording and exhibiting post-independence Ireland, including its institutional and coercive dimensions. Archivist Barry Houlihan discusses the documents relating to DML that have been acquired by the archives of the University of Galway. The possibility that both the objects and the documents may be located in a National Centre for Research and Remembrance located on the publicly owned site of the former Sean McDermott Street Magdalene Laundry is an undercurrent in this chapter.

The final chapter of the collection, by Claire McGettrick, reveals the uniquely innovative research underpinning the Magdalene Names Project. It is a case study in how creative methods, painstakingly deployed, can generate very rich data. McGettrick has unearthed a wealth of information on the women of DML and their length of stay in the institution by comparing the grave markers in the convent cemetery with electoral registers and death certificates. The chapter also interrogates the burial and memorial practices of DML.

The chapters in this volume demonstrate how much knowledge can be acquired about an institution and its practices even without direct access to the particular archives of that institution. The essays draw on a wide range of sources: newspapers, planning files, architectural drawings, books about religious congregations, memoirs of religious life, biographies of influential religious figures, oral histories, archaeological surveys, commercial registers and financial accounts, reports of commissions of inquiry, electoral rolls, legislation, photographs, the National Archives, Dublin Diocesan Archives, parliamentary speeches, court records, annual *Irish Catholic Directories*, death certificates, grave markers; all can illuminate a recent history that religious and secular authorities might still wish to conceal. The authors bring a wide array of disciplinary expertise to bear on analysing and understanding the workings, significance, impact and legacy of DML. The following essays are written by lawyers, historians, accountants, an archaeologist, an archivist, an architect, a museum curator, a philosopher, a criminologist and a sociologist. In focusing on one key institution, we have been able to reveal a great deal about its establishment, consolidation and operation. The cumulative effect of our work is that we have written a book by which the reader will be able to appreciate how religious, cultural, political and economic power was exercised in nineteenth- and twentieth-century Ireland. It is a multilayered story of gender and class, vulnerability, labour exploitation and coercion.

Notes

1 Throughout this book, we spell Magdalene with a final 'e' as this is the spelling used by survivors, journalists and more recent academic collections such as: Chloe K. Gott, *Experience, Identity & Epistemic Injustice within Ireland's Magdalene Laundries* (London: Bloomsbury, 2022); Claire McGettrick, Katherine O'Donnell, Maeve O'Rourke, James. M. Smith and Mari Steed, *Ireland and the Magdalene Laundries: A Campaign for Justice* (London: I.B. Tauris, 2021); Nathalie Sebbane, *Memorialising the Magdalene Laundries: From Story to History* (Oxford: Peter Lang, 2021). A departure from this usage is the collection by Miriam Haughton, Mary McAuliffe and Emilie Pine (eds), *Legacies of the Magdalen Laundries* (Manchester: Manchester University Press, 2021). Many older official documents spell the term 'Magdalen' without a final 'e'.

2 In the strict ecclesiastical sense, the term 'nun' is used only to refer to members of an enclosed order and a woman who has taken vows in an active congregation is referred to as a 'sister'. Both groups are referenced by the term 'women religious'. However, in everyday speech, the term 'nun' is generally used to refer to women in both active and enclosed congregations, so the terms 'nun' and 'sister' are used interchangeably throughout this book. Furthermore, the canons of the Catholic Church distinguish between Congregations and Orders to dictate how women religious (that is, both nuns and sisters) operate in the world and in their own communities. The RSC is a religious congregation but it is common to find the RSC also being popularly described as a religious order.

3 For a history of the OLC, see Jacinta Prunty, *The Monasteries, Magdalen Asylums and Reformatory Schools of Our Lady of Charity in Ireland 1853–1973* (Dublin: Columba Press, 2017).

4 The OLC operated the An Grianán Training Centre and Martanna House Hostel on the same grounds as its High Park Magdalene Laundry; it also operated St Anne's Hostel at the Sean McDermott Street Magdalene Laundry site. The SGS ran teenage

Training Centres on its Waterford, Cork and Limerick Magdalene Laundry sites. The RSM operated a Training Centre at Summerhill, Wexford. Department of Children, Equality, Disability, Integration and Youth, 'Application Form: Magdalen Restorative Justice Ex-Gratia Scheme (Adjoining Institutions), Appendix A'.

5   Alison Healy, 'The 18 Orders: What They Do Now', *The Irish Times*, 30 May 2009.

6   See *Final Report of the Commission to Inquire into Child Abuse* (Dublin: Stationery Office, 2009, aka *The Ryan Report*, hereinafter *CICA Final Report*), vol. 2, chs 12, 13, 14. See also *Report on the Inquiry into the Operation of Madonna House* (Dublin: Stationery Office, 1996). Three lay male staff, employed by the RSC (one in Madonna House and two in St Joseph's, Kilkenny), received criminal convictions for child sexual abuse.

7   Leanne McCormick, Sean O'Connell, Olivia Dee and John Privilege, *Mother and Baby Homes and Magdalene Laundries in Northern Ireland, 1922–1990: A Report for the Inter Departmental Working Group on Mother and Baby Homes, Magdalene Laundries and Historical Clerical Child Abuse* (Coleraine and Belfast: Ulster University and Queen's University Belfast, January 2021), 21.

8   Ibid.

9   See *Report of the Historical Institutional Abuse Inquiry* (2017, aka *Hart Report*), available online: https://www.hiainquiry.org/ (accessed 11 September 2022); Northern Ireland Executive Office, Press Release, 'Executive announces major steps forward on mother and baby institutions and Magdalene Laundries', 15 November 2021, available online: https://www.executiveoffice-ni.gov.uk/news/executive-announces-major-steps-forward-mother-and-baby-institutions-and-magdalene-laundries (accessed 1 August 2022).

10   McCormick and O'Connell, *Mother and Baby Homes*, 34, 282, 294, 297.

11   Department of Justice, *Report of the Inter-Departmental Committee to Establish the Facts of State Involvement with the Magdalen Laundries* (Dublin, January 2013, aka *McAleese Report*, hereinafter *IDC Report*), ch. 3, pp. 15–16.

12   James M. Smith, *Ireland's Magdalen Laundries and the Nation's Architecture of Containment* (South Bend, IN: Notre Dame Press, 2007, and Manchester: Manchester University Press, 2008), 25.

13   *IDC Report*, ch. 3, p. 16.

14   Ibid.

15   Smith, *Ireland's Magdalen Laundries*, xiv.

16   Survivors object to the use of the word 'home' in the name of these institutions, hence the use of quote marks.

17   Eoin O'Sullivan and Ian O'Donnell (eds), *Coercive Confinement in Post-Independent Ireland: Patients, Prisoners and Penitents* (Manchester: Manchester University Press, 2012).

18   Ibid., 7.

19   See, for example, Maeve O'Rourke, Claire McGettrick, Rod Baker, Raymond Hill et al., *Clann: Ireland's Unmarried Mothers and Their Children: Gathering the Data: Principal Submissions to the Commission of Investigation into Mother and Baby Homes* (Dublin: Justice for Magdalenes Research, Adoption Rights Alliance, Hogan Lovells, 15 October 2018, hereinafter *Clann Report*), 19–21.

20   See, for example, the popular film, *Philomena*, directed by Stephen Frears (Pathé, 2013), closely based on the real-life experiences of the unwed mother Philomena Lee's efforts to find her son Anthony. In the film's dialogue, Sean Ross Abbey Mother and Baby 'Home' is referred to as a 'Magdalene'.

21 Caitriona Palmer, *An Affair with My Mother* (Dublin: Penguin Ireland, 2016).

22 See closing remarks of Professor Daly, recorded in *Transcript: Dr Deirdre Foley and Professor Ian McBride in conversation with Professor Mary Daly 2nd June 2021* (Clann Project, 2021), available online: http://clannproject.org/commission-report/oxfordtranscript/ (accessed 10 August 2022). Professor Daly was one of three Commissioners in the Commission of Investigation into Mother and Baby Homes and Certain Related Matters which published its controversial report in January 2021. The final question at the online seminar hosted by Hertford College, Oxford University, asked Professor Daly what it was that she still did not know about Irish mother and baby 'homes' that she would most like to have answers to as an historian. Her reply revealed that she understood that the eighteen-institution investigation by the Commission was a class-based inquiry that focused on poor, working-class and lower-middle-class women and did not capture the experience of unwed middle class mothers:

> Oh, where would you begin? What happened all the women who weren't in Mother and Baby Homes? I mean there's a good comment by Pat Thane at the beginning of her history of the National Association for the Unmarried Mother and Child that the history of middle-class women who gave birth outside marriage is almost missing. And as I said I think in answer to one of Deirdre's questions, that those homes only at their maximum had about half, in a couple of years, half of the mothers. The majority of these children were born elsewhere. So what about their stories?

23 Mike Milotte, *Banished Babies: The Secret History of Ireland's Baby Export Business* (Dublin: New Island, 2012).

24 Marion Reynolds, *A Shadow Cast Long: Independent Review Report into Incorrect Birth Registrations*, Commissioned by the Minister for Children and Youth Affairs [Government of Ireland], May 2019, available online: https://opac.oireachtas.ie/Data/Library3/Documents%20Laid/2021/pdf/CEDIYdocslaid090321_090321_155657.pdf (accessed 21 August 2022). See also Mark Coen, Chapter 3, this volume.

25 *Irish Catholic Directory, 1841*, 282.

26 *Irish Catholic Directory, 1876*, 159.

27 *Irish Catholic Directory, 1971*, 142.

28 Fintan Cullen, 'Visualising Ireland's First Cardinal', in *Cardinal Paul Cullen and His World*, ed. Dáire Keogh and Albert McDonnell (Dublin: Four Courts Press, 2011) 401, 410.

29 See Máiréad Enright, Chapter 6, this volume.

30 See Lynsey Black, Chapter 8, this volume.

31 For discussion of the forced repatriation of unmarried Irish pregnant girls and women from England, see *Clann Report*, 22–3; Paul Michael Garrett, 'The Hidden History of the PFIs: The Repatriation of Unmarried Mothers and their Children from England to Ireland in the 1950s and 1960s', *Immigrants & Minorities* 19, no. 3 (2000): 25–44; Jennifer Redmond, *Moving Histories: Irish Women's Emigration to Britain from Independence to Republic* (Liverpool: Liverpool University Press, 2018); Maria Luddy, 'Moral Rescue and Unmarried Mothers in Ireland in the 1920s', *Women's Studies: An Interdisciplinary Journal* 30, no. 6 (2001): 797–817; Louise Ryan, 'Sexualizing Emigration: Discourses of Irish Female Emigration in the 1930s', *Women's Studies International Forum* 25, no. 1 (2002): 51–65.

32 In relation to adoption alone, the Clann Project has counted at least 182 agencies, individuals and institutions directly involved in separating unmarried mothers and

their children from 1922 onwards in the Irish Free State/Republic, see online: http://
clannproject.org/wp-content/uploads/Institutions-agencies-personnel_
Redacted_27-01-2022.pdf (accessed 13 August 2022).

33 See Katherine O'Donnell, Maeve O'Rourke and James M. Smith (eds), *Redress: Ireland's
Institutions and Transitional Justice* (Dublin: University College Dublin Press, 2022).

34 McGettrick et al., *Ireland and the Magdalene Laundries*, 43.

35 See Justice for Magdalenes Research, 'JFM Political Campaign 2009–2013', available
online: http://jfmresearch.com/home/jfm-political-campaign-2009-2013/ (accessed
17 August 2022).

36 Maeve O'Rourke, *Justice for Magdalenes Ireland, Submission to the United Nations
Committee Against Torture*, Justice for Magdalenes Research, May 2011, available
online: https://aran.library.nuigalway.ie/bitstream/handle/10379/15323/JFM_report_
to_UNCAT_2011.pdf?sequence=1&isAllowed=y (accessed 31 August 2022); Maeve
O'Rourke, *Justice for Magdalenes Ireland: Submission to the United Nations Universal
Periodic Review*, Justice for Magdalenes, 6 October 2011, available online: https://aran.
library.nuigalway.ie/bitstream/handle/10379/15325/JFM_Report_to_UPR_2011.
pdf?sequence=1&isAllowed=y (accessed 19 August 2022).

37 See Justice for Magdalenes Research, 'Magdalene Oral History Project', available
online: http://jfmresearch.com/home/oralhistoryproject/ (accessed 21 August 2022).

38 See Justice for Magdalenes Research, 'Magdalene Names Project', available online:
http://jfmresearch.com/home/magdalene-names-project/ (accessed 21 August 2022).
See also Claire McGettrick, Chapter 11, this volume.

39 James M. Smith, Maeve O'Rourke, Raymond Hill, Claire McGettrick et al., *JFM's
Principal Submissions to the Inter-Departmental Committee to Establish the Facts of
State Involvement with the Magdalene Laundries* (Dublin: Justice for Magdalenes,
18 September 2012, hereinafter *Principal Submission*).

40 See McGettrick et al., *Ireland and the Magdalene Laundries*, 115–16.

41 *IDC Report*, Executive Summary, XIII. See also McGettrick et al., *Ireland and the
Magdalene Laundries*, 102.

42 *IDC Report*, 'Introduction', para. 17, vi, and ch. 19, para. 33, 932. See also McGettrick et
al., *Ireland and the Magdalene Laundries*, 101–2, 105–7, 117–19, 139.

43 See McGettrick et al., *Ireland and the Magdalene Laundries*, 154–61.

44 Ombudsman, *Opportunity Lost: An Investigation by the Ombudsman into the
Administration of the Magdalen Restorative Justice Scheme* (Dublin: November 2107), 34.

45 *Dáil Éireann Debate*, Oireachtas Committee on Justice, Defence and Equality,
Administration of Magdalen Restorative Justice Scheme: Report of Ombudsman, 31
January 2018, available online: https://www.kildarestreet.com/committees/?id=2018-
01-31a.563 (accessed 2 May 2022).

46 Ibid., 8.

47 Press Release statement available at: https://www.ombudsman.ie/news/ombudsman-
investigation-f/ (accessed 12 May 2022).

48 Maria Luddy, *Prostitution in Irish Society 1800–1940* (Cambridge; Cambridge University
Press 2007), 78–80, discusses RSM involvement in Galway which started in 1840.
Luddy differentiates between the RSM's 'assistance' from 1840 and their taking over the
Magdalene asylum between 1845 and 1847. Religious running of the other Dublin
asylums came later: Dún Laoghaire was taken over by the RSM in 1865; the Magdalene
Laundry in Drumcondra was taken over by the OLC in 1853, moving to High Park in
1858; and the Magdalene in Gloucester Street (later renamed Sean McDermott Street)
came under RSM control in 1873 before transferring to the OLC in 1887.

49 Fanny Taylor, *Irish Homes and Irish Hearts* (London: Longmans, Green and Co. 1867), 28.

50 Maria Luddy, 'Magdalen Asylums in Ireland, 1880–1930: Welfare, Reform, Incarceration?', in *Armenfursorge und Wohltatigkeit. Landliche Gesellschaften in Europa, 1850–1930*, ed. Inga Brandes and Katrin Marx-Jaskulski (Berlin: Peter Lang, 2008), 293.

51 An Bord Pleanála, Case reference 305475: The former Donnybrook Laundry at The Crescent, Donnybrook, Dublin 4, D04 R856 and No. 17 The Crescent, Donnybrook Road, Dublin 4 D04 A6Y7, available online: https://www.pleanala.ie/en-ie/case/305475 (accessed 20 May 2022); Dublin City Council Application reference 2412/19.

52 Faith Bailey and Brenda Fuller, *Archaeological Assessment at The Crescent, Donnybrook, Dublin 4* (Kilcoole, Co. Wicklow: [Irish Archaeological Consultancy] IAC Ltd, July 2016), 19–20.

53 Ibid., 11.

54 *Abandoned Magdalene Laundry in Donnybrook, Dublin, Ireland*, YouTube, 26 April 2016, available online: https://www.youtube.com/watch?v=YETH7W0yCBg&t=168s (accessed 24 May 2022).

55 Claire McGettrick et al., *Justice for Magdalenes Research Submission to Dublin City Council Redevelopment at Donnybrook* (Dublin: Justice for Magdalenes Research, 4 October 2016).

56 Katherine O'Donnell and Claire McGettrick et al., *Dublin Honours Magdalenes: Listening Exercise, Vol. 1: Report on Key Findings* (Dublin: Justice for Magdalenes Research, 2020).

57 Margaret MacCurtain and Suellen Hoy (eds), *From Dublin to New Orleans: The Journey of Nora and Alice* (Dublin: Attic Press Dublin, 1994), 131–9.

58 *IDC Report*, ch. 6, para. 7.

59 Department of the Taoiseach, Index to the Archive of the Inter-Departmental Committee to Establish the Facts of State Involvement with the Magdalen Laundries, on file with authors.

60 *Inter-Departmental Committee to Establish the Facts of State Involvement with the Magdalen Laundries, Interim Progress Report* (20 October 2011), 7, available online: http://www.justice.ie/en/JELR/Appendix%201.pdf/Files/Appendix%201.pdf (accessed 12 May 2022).

61 Letter from Cillian Doyle, Department of the Taoiseach, to Maeve O'Rourke, dated 25 September 2018; Letter from Eamonn Molloy, Assistant Secretary General, Department of the Taoiseach, to Maeve O'Rourke, dated 13 November 2018, on file with the editors.

62 Sheila Ahern, correspondence with Maeve O'Rourke and Claire McGettrick, on file with the authors, 31 March 2022. Ahern notes that: 'I did receive some material from the Department of Rural and Community Affairs under FOI which is very useful but was only a part of what I had requested.'

63 Ibid.

Political, Cultural and Social Contexts of Donnybrook Magdalene Laundry

1

The Religious Sisters of Charity

Origins, Development and Controversies

Mark Coen

At the annual dinner of the Clinical Association attended by members of the medical staff, the important toast of the evening is the 'Irish Sisters of Charity.'[1]

This quote, from a book published in 1994 to mark 160 years of St Vincent's Hospital (SVH), one of Dublin's best known institutions, exemplifies the prominent position that the Religious Sisters of Charity (RSC) secured in Irish life. The congregation, though smaller in size than many other Irish orders of nuns, achieved a profile and influence to rival them, particularly in the capital. The theme of class is discussed in a number of chapters in this collection[2] and it arises squarely in relation to the RSC, because its avowed purpose was to serve the poor. A diverse portfolio of projects and institutions brought the congregation into contact with the socioeconomically deprived at every conceivable stage of life, from the cradle to the grave. The class dimension is further apparent when one considers that the nuns who directed and engaged in the public activities of the order came from middle- and upper-class backgrounds. In addition, they were supported financially by people from that milieu.[3] As the congregation expanded, it began to serve the needs of the more prosperous, notably in the field of healthcare.

The fact that Donnybrook Magdalene Laundry (DML) was an institution owned and managed by a particular religious congregation is key to understanding its ethos and operation. As will be seen in Chapter 3, the foundress of the RSC, Mary Aikenhead, was highly influential in shaping DML in its first twenty years, and the nuns who came after her were very conscious of continuing the model she had put in place. Most of the other Magdalene Laundries on the island of Ireland were managed by religious orders that were established specifically to run such asylums, namely the Good Shepherd Sisters and the Sisters of Our Lady of Charity of Refuge.[4] By contrast, the RSC was a generalist order that involved itself in a broad range of activities in the fields of education, healthcare, welfare and 'rescue'.

Origins of the RSC

Mary Aikenhead was born in Cork city in 1787. She was the daughter of a Protestant Scottish doctor and a Catholic Irish mother. Her parents agreed that she would be raised in the Protestant religion.[5] The infant Mary was entrusted to a Catholic nurse and her husband and lived in their house until she was 6.[6] According to Aikenhead's chief biographer, Sarah Atkinson, they had the child baptized a Catholic without her parents' knowledge.[7] When Mary returned to the Aikenhead family home, the couple who had nursed her came with her.[8] She was undoubtedly influenced by their Catholic faith and that of her maternal aunt, Mrs Gorman. The latter was on friendly terms with Bishop Moylan of Cork and many priests and nuns.[9] In 1801, Mary Aikenhead's father died, converting to Catholicism on his deathbed.[10] His daughter formally adopted that religion in 1802, at the age of 16.[11]

Aikenhead visited the poor of Cork with her friend Cecilia Lynch,[12] who ultimately entered the Poor Clare Convent in Harold's Cross, Dublin.[13] Through Lynch, Aikenhead became acquainted with Fr Daniel Murray and a friendship was born that would set in train the creation of RSC.[14] In 1809, Murray was appointed Coadjutor Archbishop of Dublin.[15] He harboured the ambition of establishing an order of female religious devoted to the needs of the poor and identified Aikenhead as the person who should lead it. He was aware that she had considered joining a number of existing religious congregations but had rejected them because they were not concerned with the poor (for example, the Ursulines) or could not leave their convents because they were enclosed (as was the case with the Presentation Sisters).[16]

Murray and Aikenhead discussed the idea of bringing a French order, the Daughters of Charity of St Vincent de Paul, to Ireland. This congregation appealed to them because its focus was on serving the poor and its nuns were permitted to undertake activities outside convent walls.[17] However, ultimately it was considered unsuitable for two reasons; its members took temporary vows that were renewed annually, and any Irish branch would be under French control.[18] Aikenhead thus decided to found her own order with the support and help of Archbishop Murray. In May 1812, she and a companion travelled to Bar Convent in York, where they completed a three-year novitiate.[19] On their return in 1815, they took charge of an orphanage in North William Street, Dublin, which was the first foundation of the RSC.[20] The congregation's constitutions were modelled on those of St Ignatius Loyola for the Jesuit order.[21] The motto of the congregation is 'Caritas Christi Urget Nos,' meaning 'The Charity of Christ presses us on.'[22]

Innovative features of the RSC

At the time of its creation, the RSC was radically different to the orders of nuns then present in Ireland. The most novel feature of the new congregation was that it was not enclosed. Visiting the poor and the sick in their homes was to be a central task of the sisters. They also engaged in the public collection of money for their charitable endeavours, including going from house to house seeking funds.[23] However, their freedom of movement was limited and did not extend to leaving the convent for recreational purposes.[24] Because of the emphasis on works of mercy in the community, RSC members did not gather together at various points of the day to recite prayers together, as enclosed congregations such as the Poor Clares did.[25]

In addition to the novelty of working outside their convents, which earned them the epithet 'the walking nuns',[26] the RSC was generalist in its objectives. It was not confined to a particular field of activity, such as education or care of the sick. This was unusual; the non-contemplative orders that existed in Ireland at the time of the creation of the RSC (most notably the Presentation Sisters, the Ursulines and the Dominicans) focused almost exclusively on education. The RSC wasted no time in availing of its non-enclosed status, and soon acquired a reputation for energetically pursuing diverse works. *The Times* of London observed of Dublin in 1829: 'You meet the sisters of charity in every lane and alley, muffled in their veils, and bearing their baskets of provisions to the wretched inmates of the garret or the cellar.'[27] The *Catholic Directory* of 1836–7 (an admittedly partial source) reported a remarkable range of activities:

[I]nstructing hundreds of poor children in the rudiments of religion and education … forwarding the interests of industrious and virtuous servants … [visiting] the abodes of wretchedness … [attending] the bed of the dying destitute … Their charity knows no exception; it is found in our gaols and penitentiaries, and is exercised on the scaffold in favour of the dying malefactor … [T]hey day and night, remained in our hospitals, during the dreadful cholera.[28]

Clearly most of these endeavours would not have been possible if the congregation had been bound by the rule of enclosure. At the time of this account the RSC had only four convents. The range of its works was a recurring feature in commendations of the congregation. In 1867, Fanny Taylor observed of the RSC: '[T]he institutions under their care in Ireland evidence that almost every form of human misery has found a helping hand from them.'[29] In similar vein, 'Eithne', writing in the Jesuit periodical the *Irish Monthly* in 1927, stated:

One only has to know these magnificent women to be convinced of their abounding zeal. Nothing is too small to be noticed, nothing too great to be attempted for His sake: an unmarried mother is picked out of the gutter, a little child is instructed in the Faith, a job is found for some unfortunate, rent is supplied in order to hold an orphaned family together …[30]

It is interesting that in an article primarily about St Mary's Blind Asylum, Merrion, the first example provided of the other varied works of the RSC is the 'rescue' of the unmarried mother, with a pointed reference to the gutter. The implication of moral as well as physical poverty is clear.

Another noteworthy feature of the RSC was its centralized structure, which apparently was influenced by Archbishop Murray.[31] Centralization meant that individual convents were not independent but were subject to the authority of the

Mother House.[32] It also meant that novices were received and trained at one novitiate, instead of joining any convent of the congregation and undergoing formation there, as was the practice in other congregations.[33] The centralized structures of the RSC were in harmony with the personality of the foundress, whose correspondence was filled with 'ceaseless instructions and recommendations'[34] to her subordinates. From the early 1830s, Aikenhead became increasingly invalided, confined to her room at the convent in Sandymount, Dublin.[35] In Atkinson's words, she 'began to direct and govern by the pen',[36] writing at length to her nuns about all practical, organizational and spiritual matters affecting the congregation. No detail was too small for inclusion in her missives, not even the merits of 'simple whitewash'.[37] While centralized orders appear to have been less prone to interference by bishops,[38] they also did not grow at anything like the same pace as those that were more localized in their operation, particularly the Presentation Sisters and the Sisters of Mercy.[39]

The RSC was further distinguished from other congregations of female religious by the fourth vow taken by its sisters, namely 'to devote themselves perpetually to the service of the poor'.[40] In interacting with the poor, the sisters should 'avoid ... all haughtiness and coldness of manner'[41] but equally 'too great freedom and familiarity'.[42] In 1837, Aikenhead dismissed a Sister Mary Ignatius (formerly Miss Bodenham) from the congregation, on the basis that she had attempted to subvert its emphasis on service to the poor.[43] She had become influential as novice mistress and was apparently planning to take some of her charges to England to set up a convent to educate the upper classes.[44] According to Prunty:

> Her forcible removal caused havoc in the community, with some believing Aikenhead's handling of the situation unjust and sympathising with the undoubtedly accomplished and attractive mistress of novices.[45]

In a real setback for the fledgling congregation, 13 novices and two nuns left with her.[46] One of those who left in solidarity with Bodenham was Margaret Aylward, the future foundress of the Holy Faith Sisters.[47]

A rival congregation?

The Sisters of Mercy, founded by Catherine McCauley in 1828, also adopted the fourth vow of serving the poor. McCauley did not intend to establish an order of nuns but was instructed by the religious authorities to either stop her charitable activities with fellow 'pious ladies'[48] or bring them within the confines of a formal religious congregation. In eventually deciding to found the Sisters of Mercy, a generalist order, she faced much hostility from the clergy for adopting a course that was considered to pose a threat to the growth of the RSC.[49] Some perceived 'a spirit of rivalry and partisanship between the two Institutes'.[50] Indeed, the RSC often found itself being compared to the soon numerically stronger Sisters of Mercy. A nineteenth-century priest commentator wrote of the two congregations:

[B]oth the Sisters of Charity and Mercy are noble institutions, an honour to our native land … We hope that for many a year it may be difficult to decide which is the best, the most useful, or the most meritorious; and that both may continue that heroic mission to which they have devoted themselves in generous emulation of each other's excellence.[51]

The RSC and the Sisters of Mercy were involved in a wide range of work in schools, orphanages, industrial schools, hospitals and Magdalene asylums, which contrasted with other orders that focused on specific fields of endeavour. However, the RSC arguably punched above its weight in terms of public profile. One reason for this was the concentration of its institutions in Dublin. In 1922, the RSC had 16 convents in the Diocese of Dublin, compared to 15 convents of the Mercy order.[52] By 1960, there were 21 RSC convents in Dublin and 17 Mercy convents.[53] Ownership and management of prominent Dublin institutions (including St Vincent's Hospital;[54] St Joseph's Children's Hospital, Temple Street; Our Lady's Hospice for the Dying, Harold's Cross; St Mary's Blind Asylum, Merrion; St Mary's Orthopaedic Hospital at Cappagh and DML), conferred on the congregation a status greater than an exclusive focus on its number of convents nationally would suggest. The RSC also had a significant presence in Cork city, with schools, a hospital and a Magdalene laundry under its management there. Ultimately the Sisters of Mercy had many more convents across the country than the RSC, but the major Dublin institutions controlled by the latter gave it a stature and prominence out of proportion to its size.

Internal structures and governance

The RSC was a profoundly hierarchical organization, with 'supreme authority'[55] vested in the head of the order, known as the Mother General. She appointed the superiors of convents, could transfer nuns from one convent to another, assign sisters to particular roles and dismiss novices without giving a reason.[56] In order to be eligible for election to the position of Mother General, a member of the RSC had to be 'of legitimate birth, at least forty years of age, and have been professed for ten years'.[57] The Mother General was elected by the General Assembly (composed of delegates from each convent) for a term of six years, which could be renewed.[58] At the election, presided over by the Archbishop of Dublin, the new Mother General received obeisance from the delegates, who 'with bended knee, kiss her hand'.[59]

Each convent had a Superior or Rectress, appointed by the Mother General for a three-year term.[60] In the closed world of the convent, the Superior was extremely powerful. Her sphere of influence and authority extended beyond the lives of the nuns in her community to the institutions under their control, potentially affecting large numbers of people. The Constitutions of the congregation emphasized the obedience due to the Superior: 'Each must obey the voice of the Superior as readily as if it were the voice of Jesus Christ Our Lord, leaving everything in order to follow it.'[61]

As in most other congregations of female religious, the RSC distinguished between choir sisters and lay sisters (referred to as 'Domestic Sisters' in the RSC Constitutions).[62]

The choir sisters were drawn from more prosperous and better-educated backgrounds and 'carried out the public work for which the convent had been established'.[63] They were expected to bring a sum of money known as a dowry with them on joining the convent. In the early years of the RSC, a number of entrants brought substantial dowries of between £600 and £1,000.[64] By contrast, lay sisters did not bring a dowry and undertook the convent 'cooking, scrubbing, serving, gardening [and] washing'.[65] They had no vote in community or congregational affairs and could not be elected to positions of leadership.[66] They did not take the fourth vow of service to the poor; by undertaking the domestic tasks of the convent they enabled the choir nuns to pursue the core objective of the congregation. A former member of the RSC has written that she was unaware of the distinction between choir nuns and lay sisters until she entered the congregation: 'I was quite taken aback when I discovered there was a two-tier system ... It was during our noviceship that it was decided to change the title [of lay/domestic sister] to "second degree sister." I thought that was even worse.'[67]

The difference between choir nuns and domestic sisters in the RSC was reflected in the habits they wore. Some elements were common to both; a habit of black serge with a white collar, a brass crucifix hung from the neck and a rosary suspended from the waist.[68] However, the habit worn by lay sisters differed in two important respects; their veil was white (in contrast to the black veil of the choir sisters)[69] and they also wore 'a blue and white check apron'[70] at all times other than when they were at chapel. The hierarchical structure of religious communities thus 'mirrored wider social divisions',[71] with the distinctive habit worn by lay sisters bearing a resemblance to 'the uniforms worn by domestic servants in big houses'.[72] Between 1812 and 1900, lay sisters accounted for almost 30 per cent of the membership of the RSC.[73] The subservient position of lay sisters could give rise to conventual tensions and the RSC Archives contain evidence of this phenomenon.[74]

The internal rules of the congregation made clear the strictures within which professed sisters must live. Both incoming and outgoing mail was to be read by the Superior of the convent.[75] No sister could lock her door or 'keep a trunk or anything else locked'[76] without permission. The taking of medicine or the consulting of a doctor was also prohibited unless approved by the Superior.[77] One's lips 'must not be too much compressed, nor too open',[78] and one's hands 'if not duly engaged, must be kept modestly quiet'.[79] Silence was imposed outside of recreation time,[80] which in the words of the foundress 'should never be entirely given to idle, frivolous, and unprofitable chit chat'.[81]

The Constitutions of the RSC required the Mother General (or her nominee) to conduct a visitation of each house of the congregation every three years.[82] The purpose of the visitation was to determine that the house in question was operating in accordance with the rules of the order. The sister conducting the visitation should 'inspect all the apartments of the house, the schools, and institution [*sic*], and in particular the chapel and sacristy, to satisfy herself that the neatness and order becoming a religious house are everywhere in evidence'.[83] Each sister in the convent was to be interviewed and the financial accounts inspected.[84] It is worth reflecting on the fact that the Magdalene Laundries operated by the RSC were subject to this requirement of regular inspection by the head of the congregation.

Expansion of the RSC

The congregation expanded slowly but steadily from its beginnings in North William Street, Dublin, in 1815. By 1900, there were 19 convents of the order in Ireland,[85] 11 of which were in Dublin.[86] The foundations outside the capital at that time were scattered across the country and were located in Cork (two convents), Waterford, Kilkenny, Clonmel in County Tipperary, Clarinbridge in County Galway, Tramore in County Waterford and Benada in County Sligo. Subsequent expansion within Ireland occurred largely, but not exclusively, in Dublin.[87]

However, the influence of the RSC has not been confined to Ireland. In 1838, five members of the congregation sailed to Sydney (a four-month voyage from Gravesend) and set to work in the penal colony in Paramatta.[88] The Australian branch became a separate congregation in 1842.[89] An initial attempt to make an RSC foundation in England was not a success; sisters sent to Preston in 1840 at the behest of the Jesuits there were withdrawn by Aikenhead in 1848[90] after some tensions between the two religious communities.[91] A major point of disagreement arose from the desire of the Jesuits that the RSC would become involved in the 'secondary education of well-to-do children'[92] which conflicted with the congregation's vow to serve the poor. The first English foundation that endured was St Margaret's Home in Rockferry, Cheshire, described in 1924 as 'an asylum for penitents'.[93] The women there worked in a laundry which presumably operated in a similar way to that at DML.[94] An RSC publication of 1941 outlined the difficulties of this kind of 'rescue work' for the nuns:

> [T]he Sisters must bear with and manage the undisciplined temper, rough ways, foolish fancies, and sometimes dull intellects of those poor girls and women, victims – some of bad homes, of drink, of a hundred evil influences and impulses; bear with them, and train them to order, to industry, to piety, purity, and truth.[95]

It will be seen in Chapter 3 that similar statements about the difficulties – from the nuns' perspective – of managing a Magdalene institution exist regarding DML. Several other RSC foundations were subsequently made in Britain, including St Joseph's Hospice, Hackney, founded in 1905, and St Margaret of Scotland Hospice, Glasgow, which opened in 1950. By 1958, there were 25 convents in Ireland, 13 in Britain, 3 in California and 3 in what was then called Rhodesia.[96] The congregation's global reach subsequently extended to Nigeria,[97] Zambia and Malawi.

Mary Aikenhead and sainthood

The canonization of the foundress of the RSC has been under consideration by the Vatican for the past one hundred years. Pope Benedict XV signed the 'decree for the introduction of the Cause of Mary Aikenhead'[98] in March 1921. In the 1930s, a 'great Crusade of Masses and Prayers'[99] in support of the cause was endorsed by Cardinal Pacelli, the future Pope Pius XII, and annual pilgrimages were made to Aikenhead's tomb in the grounds of DML. The *Irish Independent* described the 1933 pilgrimage as follows:

> A wonderful manifestation of the strength of the Faith in Dublin City and County was given yesterday on the occasion of the first public pilgrimage to the tomb of Mother Mary Aikenhead, Foundress of the Irish Sisters of Charity, at St Mary Magdalen's Asylum, Donnybrook. About 3,000 people took part in the pilgrimage and prayed for the Beatification of Mother Mary Aikenhead.[100]

The casual reference to the Magdalene Laundry touches on a theme that comes through strongly in Chapter 3, namely that DML was not hidden from public view but was in fact highly visible for most of its existence. According to press reports, '[u]pwards of 50,000 people'[101] visited Aikenhead's grave during a nine-day Novena to mark the 148th anniversary of her death in 1935. In 1940, the Catholic newspaper *The Standard* reported:

> Devotion to the Beatification Cause is widespread, extending not only throughout Ireland and Britain, but also to the United States and Australasia, as well as Mexico, China, India, and many parts of Africa. The most prodigious favours have been attributed to her intercession; and these have now assumed a total of several thousands – from cases of employment secured to remarkable cures from obstinate and often declared Incurable maladies.[102]

The centenary of Aikenhead's death in 1958 involved a flurry of commemorative activity, including public lectures on her life and performances of a three-act play ('Vision Splendid' by Sister Mary Alphonsus).[103] RSC convents throughout Ireland organized celebrations presided over by the local bishop.[104] An open-air pageant depicting the life of the foundress, with a cast of 500 people and music by the No. 1 Army Band was performed in front of thousands of people in Dublin.[105] A postage stamp bearing Aikenhead's image was released to commemorate the centenary, the first time an Irish stamp bore the image of a woman.[106] A breakthrough in the campaign to have Mary Aikenhead made a saint occurred in 2015, the 200th anniversary of the foundation of the RSC, when Pope Francis declared her Venerable. The next step would be a declaration that she is Blessed, for which proof of a miracle attributable to her is necessary. One can only speculate what the effect on vocations to the congregation would have been if the foundress had been canonized decades ago, particularly in 1958.

Recruitment and training

Consideration of the recruitment and training of RSC members is an important dimension of seeking to understand how sisters of that order approached their work in a Magdalene laundry. Oral histories of RSC members would be particularly valuable in illuminating these issues. However, in the absence of such material, this section analyses the available documentary sources.

Joining the RSC

Without access to the records of the RSC, it is impossible to thoroughly analyse trends or patterns in relation to the women who joined the congregation. Luddy notes that 1,348 women joined between 1812 and 1900. Of this number, 535 were either dismissed or left of their own volition.[107] Figures for the twentieth century are not in the public domain, but some information about entrants to the congregation is available.

Middle-class women who joined the congregation may not have been overly familiar with its spirit and conventions prior to entry, a fact alluded to in a biography of Mary Aikenhead published in 1924:

> [Recruits] have not been educated in secondary schools conducted by the Sisters of Charity, where they would know the sisters and be known by them, for the Congregation being devoted exclusively to the service of the poor, has no such schools.[108]

In the absence of secondary schools – at least until the late 1950s, when the RSC started opening them – the idea of joining the congregation must have been derived from other sources, such as advice from priests to young girls who expressed an interest in religious life, or family links to women who were already members of the congregation. There is evidence that the presence of an RSC convent in the prosperous neighbourhood of Donnybrook was helpful in ensuring that the congregation featured in the deliberations of local girls who were discerning vocations.[109]

Over the course of its history, the RSC attracted several entrants from the upper echelons of society. Writing in 1867, Fanny Taylor observed of the congregation: '[S]uperior, refined and intelligent ladies ... fill its ranks.'[110] Sister (Sr) Lucy Clifford, the daughter of the Hon. Thomas Clifford and Baroness de Lutzow, provided the dowry that bought 57 St Stephen's Green, where St Vincent's Hospital was established.[111] Sr Phillipa Morris, a young nursing sister who died in 1889, was the daughter of Sir Michael Morris, the Lord Chief Justice of the King's Bench for Ireland.[112] Sr Benedict Joseph Constable Maxwell was the aunt of the Duchess of Norfolk.[113] Mother Canisius Cullen, who would go on to become Mother General of the congregation, was the niece of Cardinal Cullen and was encouraged to join the congregation by him.[114] Women from privileged backgrounds also entered the order in the twentieth century. Katherine Bayley Butler, who joined the RSC in 1936 and later wrote a biography of Mary Aikenhead, was the daughter of a professor of zoology at University College Dublin.[115] She took private flying lessons and acquired a pilot's licence before entering the congregation. The McCann sisters, Catherine and Elizabeth, became Sisters of Charity in the 1950s. Their upbringing was especially elite. They grew up in a Dublin mansion called Simmonscourt, located on an 18-acre site in salubrious Ballsbridge, which was staffed by eight indoor servants and seven outdoor staff.[116] Despite the large domestic staff, the laundry was sent weekly to DML.[117] In a further indication of the family's social position, Catherine was sent to an English boarding school to be educated by the Society of the Holy Child Jesus.[118]

McCann's account of joining the RSC in the 1950s describes her fellow recruits as mostly 'around seventeen, having come straight from school'.[119] While this is no doubt accurate, women with significant life experience and academic qualifications also joined the order. The RSC website provides some interesting examples. Sr Rose Murphy was born in 1924 and entered the RSC in 1956. She qualified and worked as a pharmacist before joining the congregation.[120] Sr Catherine Patricia Renahan qualified as a radiographer in 1946 and entered the RSC aged 33 in 1959.[121] Sr Francis Catherine Barrett taught in a primary school for eight years prior to joining in 1955 aged 30. Sr Mary Daniel McCarry was a hotel manageress aged 39 when she entered.[122]

Religious formation in the RSC

For most of the period under discussion in this chapter, recruits to religious life entered a strict, regimented existence in which they were to unquestioningly follow the commands of their superiors. Their religious formation was thus of great importance. The RSC novitiate was initially located in Stanhope Street, Dublin, but in 1845 was moved to Our Lady's Mount, Harold's Cross. In 1879, it moved again to Mount St Anne's, Milltown, which was the Mother House of the Congregation until it was sold in 1995.[123]

An account entitled 'The Making of a Sister of Charity' from 1958 describes 'Entrance Day', a triannual occasion when groups of aspirants arrived at Mount St Anne's to begin their formation. Addressing the position of the entrant, the writer is unequivocal: 'No desires, no bargains, she has come to be used.'[124] Women who joined the order embarked at first upon a six-month postulancy. As was the norm in pre-Vatican II religious congregations,[125] obedience was greatly emphasized:

> Obedience must be solid for the work of a Sister of Charity; her duties will not always be among the innocent, she will be thrown among seculars good and bad; she will need the strength and courage that obedience gives.[126]

Fuller observes that religious training of this nature sought to achieve 'discipline [and] docility . . . but was less successful in developing a sense of initiative and personal responsibility'.[127] Withdrawal from the affairs of the world was also a feature of religious formation. An anonymous RSC commentator writing in 1958 expressed it thus:

> Monarchies may tumble, war clouds gather, politicians tear one another's throats, royal romances set the nations' pulses throbbing, but not a breath of this penetrates the 'garden enclosed' where every hour is occupied and there is never an idle second. Duty succeeds duty – manual work, sewing, meals, recreations, choir practice, study, with Spiritual exercises woven all through so that it is true to say that there is not a moment that is not lived for God and in union with Him.[128]

Lest the reader be concerned that religious formation entailed no gaiety, they were assured that concert rehearsals and preparation for religious ceremonies gave rise to 'a pleasurable buzz of excitement'.[129] Recreation was marked by 'peals of laughter'[130] and lively discussion, but a wide variety of conversational topics were banned: '[O]ne may not gossip or indulge in family chit-chat, nor criticize films, books or plays, nor mention where she spent the holidays last year, or the people she met . . .'[131] While most of their time was spent at the Novitiate, sometimes postulants experienced a few weeks in another convent of the congregation.[132]

After six months of postulancy, the recruits participated in a clothing ceremony in which they made temporary vows, took a religious name and received the habit of a white-veiled novice.[133] A two-year novitiate constituted the remaining period of formation.[134] The first year was known as 'the Spiritual Year' and involved even greater seclusion: 'Parlour visits are limited to the immediate members of her family so that there will be nothing to distract each one from the great work on hands [sic], her personal sanctification.'[135] This year was followed by six months in convents of the congregation, not necessarily in Ireland.[136] At the end of this period, the novice returned to Mount St Anne's for the final months of their novitiate. During this time, the novices were referred to as 'Brides', a reference to the fact that they were preparing for the ceremony of final profession, which 'followed the ritual of a wedding ceremony'.[137] The 'Brides' wore a wedding dress and professed their final, permanent vows in the presence of their family and friends.[138] Each newly professed sister was presented with 'a plain gold ring worn on the third finger of the right hand, and a brass crucifix peculiar to themselves, both cross and figure made of brass'.[139] This crucifix was substantial in size and was worn at all times on a chain from the neck. A two-day silent retreat followed profession and the newly professed nuns were then dispatched to their new destinations and tasks.[140]

Looking back on her training to become a Sister of Charity in the late 1950s, Sr Stanislaus Kennedy reflected that 'there was no emphasis on relationships, or human growth and development'.[141] She also stated that she did not get to know her fellow novices well, 'as we were discouraged from talking about our families and friends'.[142] Catherine McCann, a former Sister of Charity, echoed this sentiment, remarking that 'we knew very little about each other'[143] at the end of the two and a half years of formation. According to McCann, there was 'no input on scripture or theology'.[144] She also describes being given two devices for engaging in private physical penances (a chain with spikes and a small rope with knots).[145] Meetings were held at which each novice was expected to ask her assembled peers to publicly identify her faults.[146] Acts of mortification like kissing the floor and eating meals while sitting on the floor also occurred.[147] Manual work, obedience and conformity appear to have been prioritized. McCann identifies a connection between the regime for novices and the conduct of nuns in institutions, stating that: '[t]he rigidity and at times harshness of the routine, the silence, the prayers, and the minute methods of cleaning and washing'[148] they experienced in the Novitiate 'most likely influenced the way of life that was set up in industrial schools, orphanages and Magdalen laundries'.[149]

Major works of the RSC

As a generalist order, the RSC has been – and remains – involved in a wide variety of work. This section outlines three areas of the congregation's endeavours that have both historical and contemporary significance, namely healthcare, education and social justice.

Healthcare

Of all the institutions the RSC came to establish and manage, SVH in Dublin was – and is – the most high profile. When opened in 1834 to care for 'the Sick Poor',[150] it was pioneering in many ways. It was the first Catholic hospital in Dublin.[151] It also holds the distinction of being 'the first hospital in these islands to be founded, administered and staffed by women'.[152] It was located in an elegant mansion on St Stephen's Green formerly occupied by the Earl of Meath. The adjoining building, previously the residence of the Marquess of Westmeath, was acquired later.[153] In 1934, the hospital celebrated its centenary, and *The Standard* stated triumphantly:

> St Vincent's Hospital has not only been the welcoming refuge of the stricken poor of Dublin, but also a great school of Medical and Surgical Science. It is a monument of what the energy and intelligence of a Catholic Sisterhood can accomplish in the creation and control of an institution that some would pretend is exclusively within the province of masculine initiative.[154]

St Vincent's grew exponentially and, in 1970, it moved from its city-centre location to a new 455 bed facility on a greenfield site at Elm Park in Donnybrook. A description of the funding arrangements for the new hospital captures the Irish model of the State paying voluntary – invariably religious – bodies to provide essential services: 'This ... was to be a marriage of resources, money from the State, land from the Sisters and the University and Department of Education looking after the medical teaching side.'[155] St Vincent's is now known as St Vincent's University Hospital and is a major teaching hospital affiliated with University College Dublin.

Healthcare became a core focus of the RSC as it expanded. In Dublin, the congregation came to control Linden Convalescent Home, Blackrock (established in 1865), St Joseph's Children's Hospital, Temple Street (1876), Our Lady's Hospice for the Dying, Harold's Cross (1879), St Mary's Orthopaedic Hospital, Cappagh (1908), St Patrick's Infant Hospital, Temple Hill (1943) and St Mary's Orthopaedic Hospital, Baldoyle (1943). St Patrick's Hospital for Incurables was established in Cork in 1870. In 2001, the RSC bought St Michael's Hospital in Dún Laoghaire from the Sisters of Mercy.

Despite its central mission of serving the poor, the RSC did not confine itself to public healthcare provision. When St Vincent's was located on St Stephen's Green, the RSC operated two private facilities nearby: St Vincent's Private Nursing Home at 96 Lower Leeson Street and the Pembroke Private Nursing Home on Upper Pembroke Street.[156] In 1974, these nursing homes relocated to Elm Park and became St Vincent's Private Hospital.[157] Nor are these the only instances of the RSC caring for the wealthy; Ireland's longest-serving Taoiseach (Prime Minister) and former President of Ireland, Eamon de Valera, spent the final two years of his life at Talbot Lodge, 'a home for private patients'[158] in the grounds of the Linden Convalescent Home.[159] Sr Sister Stanislaus Kennedy has queried if RSC involvement in St Vincent's Private Hospital is consistent with the charism of the congregation and the values of Mary Aikenhead.[160]

Education

The provision of elementary education has always been an important aspect of the work of the RSC, and schools were established at most of its convents in Ireland. Writing in 1840, Aikenhead stated: 'It is obvious that we shall always have a greater number of schools than any other institution for the poor.'[161] The historical educational objectives of the congregation may be discerned from its reflections on almost 80 years of instruction in Tramore, County Waterford, in 1941:

> In the course of years pupils became proficient, not alone in the ordinary subjects of education, but also in such accomplishments as music, instrumental and vocal, painting, drawing, needlework and cookery. Many entered convents and are doing splendid work for God, at home and abroad; others became trained teachers, more are a credit in business occupations, whilst the majority settled down as good wives and mothers.[162]

When in 1939 the congregation opened the enormous St Agnes' Convent Schools in Crumlin, Dublin, 3,000 pupils presented at buildings designed for 2,000.[163] Some RSC convents conducted multiple educational projects; for example, in 1943, the Convent of Our Lady of Benada, County Sligo, had 'an elementary school, an Industrial School and Orphanage, an Agricultural School with courses of [sic] Dairying, Poultry Keeping, etc., a Lace School, and a Workroom'.[164] From 1858 onwards, the RSC also educated visually impaired girls at St Mary's Asylum for the Blind (later St Mary's School for the Blind), Merrion Road, Dublin 4.

Past pupils of the RSC nuns have differing memories of the experience. Mary Gallagher, who attended their school in Ballaghaderreen, County Roscommon, recalled a school 'full of earnestness and orderliness' run by 'dedicated and self-sacrificing women, ahead of their time in the spirit of true education'.[165] The journalist Nuala O'Faolain remembered performing in a school play and later being beaten by a nun with the leg of a chair for waving to someone she recognized in the audience.[166] Broadcaster Miriam O'Callaghan has also referred to being slapped by the nuns in their school at Milltown, Dublin.[167] The stories of O'Faolain and O'Callaghan are at odds with a 1943 statement of the congregation that 'no restraint arising from fear'[168] was used in their schools. The Commission to Inquire into Child Abuse (CICA) found that children 'were severely physically punished'[169] at St Joseph's Industrial School, Kilkenny, which opened in 1873 and closed in 1999. In relation to St Patrick's Industrial School, also located in Kilkenny, the report of the Commission stated: 'The Sisters of Charity accept that some excessive punishments were inevitable over the years, but no record of them exists.'[170]

While the education of children – especially girls – under fourteen years of age was the focus of the RSC for its first 140 years, an expansion into secondary education occurred from the late 1950s onwards. Secondary schools were opened alongside existing RSC primary schools in places including Benada, County Sligo; Foxford, County Mayo; Blarney, County Cork and Walkinstown, Dublin. The congregation's involvement in education remained true to the vision of its foundress; no boarding schools were established, in contrast to the Mercy and Presentation Orders.

Social justice

As has been discussed above, the primary purpose of the RSC was to serve the poor, and, St Vincent's Private Hospital aside, its activities in education and healthcare were predominantly directed to the achievement of that purpose. Members of the congregation also engaged in work to alleviate poverty, such as the provision of hot meals and the collection of clothes for distribution to the needy.[171] House visitation was an important RSC activity and where that work was undertaken by a particular convent it was assigned to a nun called the Missioner.[172] Prison visitation, including visits to persons sentenced to death,[173] was another field of endeavour. The famous Providence Woollen Mills in Foxford, County Mayo, was one of the more unusual RSC foundations and in 1943 employed 200 people in a rural area where employment opportunities were very scarce.[174] In more modern times, the RSC has made a number of its properties available for social justice projects, particularly housing.[175]

The most famous member of the RSC in Ireland today is the social justice campaigner Sr Stanislaus Kennedy, known universally as Sr Stan. She is the founder of a number of voluntary organizations, most notably the homeless charity Focus Ireland, with which she is strongly associated. She has featured in the Irish media for decades as an outspoken advocate for the marginalized. While generally a recipient of positive media coverage for her social justice work,[176] she has also faced questions about her knowledge of abuse in an RSC institution with which she was associated.[177] She said that she was 'ashamed, shocked and horrified'[178] as a member of the RSC by the findings of the CICA in relation to institutions managed by the order. Most recently she has described public criticism of the RSC, particularly in relation to the new National Maternity Hospital (NMH) controversy,[179] as 'elder abuse'.[180]

Controversy and the RSC

The overall reputation of the RSC in Ireland is now tainted, largely because of a litany of revelations about historic abuses in the areas of adoption, childcare and Magdalene asylums. In addition, the congregation's lucrative property transactions and its abrupt closure of several facilities have attracted negative publicity. The organization has essentially lurched from one controversy to the next from the early 1990s to the present day. An overview of these controversies is provided below, with the exception of the ongoing and highly charged saga about ownership of the proposed NMH, which is discussed in Chapter 6.

Madonna House

In 1993, the media reported that allegations of sexual abuse had been made by former residents of Madonna House, a home for children in State care owned and managed by the RSC.[181] The RSC closed the facility in 1994. In the same year, a former maintenance man, Frank Griffin, was convicted of sexually assaulting five girls at Madonna House between the years 1987 and 1991.[182] A report commissioned by the congregation was published in 1996 in highly redacted form. It stated that of the nine former long-stay residents interviewed for the inquiry, all but one alleged that they were sexually abused.[183] The Report also emphasized that 'the Sisters of Charity were at all times concerned to try to provide a warm and caring setting for any child in need' and 'though the allegations described are very serious they nonetheless relate to a relatively small number of children'.[184] Such an attempt to minimize the gravity of the failings at Madonna House is perhaps not surprising, when one considers the composition of the inquiry team – four representatives from Health Boards (the State bodies sending children to Madonna House) and one member of the RSC. In 1999, the 'States of Fear' television programme revealed the redacted content of the report. It stated that management had repeatedly ignored information it had received about physical violence and sexual abuse against children over many years, allowing the abuse to continue. It also noted that in 1976, a member of staff abducted and killed a child who was a former resident.[185] The Madonna House story has the unhappy distinction of being the first in a long line of institutional abuse disclosures involving Catholic religious, and the first major controversy involving the RSC.

School closure

In March 1994, the congregation announced the closure of St Anne's Primary School in Milltown, Dublin.[186] The order had indicated previously that it would sell the 12-acre site behind the school buildings, where the Novitiate and Generalate of the order had been located for over a century.[187] The decision to close the school without consultation angered the parents and teaching staff and the episode became a lightning rod for a broader discussion of the role of the Catholic Church in education.[188] The fact that the school was located on very valuable land with development potential was identified as the underlying rationale of the decision by those who campaigned against it. Raising the matter in the Dáil, Frances Fitzgerald TD asked if the RSC 'wish to withdraw from education for commercial rather than educational reasons?'[189] In an interview in the *Irish Times*, Sr Marie Carroll stated: 'We want to refute absolutely allegations that we are property speculators.'[190] While the RSC was keen to emphasize that enrolment had fallen from 450 pupils in 1982 to 158 in 1994, it did not engage with arguments that this was still a relatively large primary school by Irish standards, or reveal if it had tried to transfer the school to an alternative trustee. Headlines such as 'Nuns in boycott of meeting to discuss closure of their school'[191] and 'Anger over nuns' plan to close school is growing'[192] capture the conflict generated by the episode. The school ultimately closed. Although the RSC stated at the time that there were no plans to close the adjoining secondary school, its closure was announced in 1998, with the earlier decision to close the feeder primary school blamed for falling student numbers.[193] The secondary school building was donated by the RSC to the Society of St Vincent de Paul, who redeveloped it as sheltered housing.

St Mary's, Merrion Road

There have been a number of controversies relating to the former St Mary's School for the Blind and its associated valuable lands. When the RSC announced its intention to sell 14.5 acres attached to the facility in 2001, the Chief Executive of the National Council for the Blind of Ireland (NCBI) accused the congregation of 'turning their backs on the blind'[194] because none of the proceeds of the sale were earmarked for services for the visually impaired. Sr Una O'Neill replied on behalf of the congregation:

> There is no trust which says that the sisters cannot sell the land at Merrion. The sisters own the land freehold. The annals of the congregation confirm that the £2,000 to buy Merrion was raised by holding bazaars and sales of work.[195]

The RSC also threatened to sue the NCBI if it continued to allege that the nuns were acting improperly.[196] The land ultimately sold for €45.7 million.[197] Part of the congregation's defence that it was not abandoning its work with the visually impaired was that it had built two nursing homes and housing on the Merrion site to cater for 70 visually impaired women who had attended St Mary's School.[198] However, in October 2020, these facilities – owned by the RSC but operated by a separate company – were closed. Visually impaired people living in supported accommodation on the site expressed their shock at losing their homes, as did the relatives of people in the nursing homes.[199] At the same time, staff at the Merrion site received unwelcome news; first, that they would only receive the minimum statutory redundancy payment, and subsequently, that the company employing them would not be able to meet even that basic level of payment. The congregation stated that it was 'extremely disappointed to learn that there may not be enough funds to pay statutory redundancy payments to the staff'.[200] This episode, which coincided with the closure in similar circumstances of St Monica's Nursing Home at Belvedere Place, Dublin, attracted much negative publicity for the RSC.[201] In February 2022, it was reported that the RSC were seeking to have the Merrion Road lands on which the former facilities for the visually impaired stand rezoned for residential use. This would substantially increase their value and potentially realize €50 million for the congregation.[202]

Adoption

In 1997, the RSC admitted that it had deliberately provided false and misleading information to people adopted through St Patrick's Guild (SPG), an adoption society it controlled.[203] Adopted people who asked SPG for information regarding their birth mothers were given erroneous and fabricated details that they then used in fruitless searches. Sr Francis Ignatius, the director of SPG, stated that this was 'in part'[204] because some women who availed of its services used a false name. This was a classic deflection strategy; the issue was not that some birth mothers had concealed their identities, but that the RSC had knowingly supplied incorrect information, rather than the actual information they held. Instead of stating that all details were confidential, a religious congregation told lies and gave adopted people false information and thus false hope, frustrating searches to discern their identity and any possibility of making contact with their families.[205]

Damaging disclosures involving SPG have continued. It was involved in an unknown number of illegal adoptions in which births were falsely registered in the names of adoptive parents.[206] In 2021, a television programme revealed historical correspondence from the RSC to a woman who had placed her baby for adoption with SPG. The letter stated that if the woman did not pay the adoption fee, the nuns would get their debt collector to call on her at her place of work in Arnotts Department Store. Having threatened public exposure of the woman in a society that regarded extramarital pregnancy as a scandal, the note concluded: 'We have not failed you; you have failed us.'[207] The RSC stated that it was 'deeply saddened'[208] by the revelations.

Institutional abuse and redress

As was noted above, two industrial schools operated by the congregation were the subject of adverse findings by the CICA. A number of industrial schools and hospitals, as well as Madonna House and St Mary's School for the Visually Impaired, were included in the Residential Institutions Redress Scheme, which paid compensation to survivors of institutional abuse. The Scheme was operated and overwhelmingly paid for by the State, with a controversial indemnity deal limiting the financial contribution of the religious orders. The RSC pledged to contribute €5 million towards the costs of the Scheme but contributed just €2 million.[209] Three of the congregation's institutions came within the terms of the Magdalen Restorative Justice Ex-Gratia Scheme,[210] to which the congregation refused to contribute any money.[211] Between 1999 and 2009, the RSC sold property worth over €63 million.[212]

Conclusion

The RSC was a pioneering Irish religious order of women, founded to serve the poor in all circumstances and at all stages of life. Its foundress, Mary Aikenhead, was ambitious for her organization and lived to oversee its early endeavours in the fields of education, healthcare and Magdalene asylums. Moreover, the sisters who came after her were highly conscious of her legacy and keen to act in accordance with what they perceived to be her priorities. Indeed, the RSC observed 100 years after Mary Aikenhead's death: '[T]he spirit of the Congregation remaining unchanged, anything she said regarding it is as true today as in her lifetime.'[213]

This chapter has provided an overview of the RSC in an effort to contextualize its management of DML from 1837 to 1992. When one knows the origins and ethos of the order, its internal structures, its approach to the formation of its members and the extent of its other activities, one can begin to appreciate how the Donnybrook convent and Magdalene laundry fitted into the overall congregational picture. The young woman joining the RSC from a comfortably off background rolled a dice in relation to the type of work she would be instructed to undertake by her superiors. She might find herself nursing the dying in a hospice, visiting the poor in their homes, teaching children in a school or supervising 'penitents' undertaking laundry work.

The chapter has also demonstrated the power and prominence the RSC achieved in Ireland, largely by virtue of the concentration of its activities in Dublin.[214] It owned and managed several major institutions in the capital, particularly in healthcare. In common with other religious congregations, the past thirty years have seen a decline in the size of the RSC, the closure of some institutions and a withdrawal from day-to-day involvement in those that remain. A religious sister teaching or nursing, or managing others undertaking those roles, has ceased to be the norm in a relatively short period. The RSC has disposed of a considerable amount of its property in lucrative sales in the past three decades. In spite of reduced numbers and a rapidly ageing profile,[215] the congregation remains powerful. Its ownership of St Vincent's public and private hospitals alone ensures this.

Finally, as this chapter has illustrated, the congregation has been embroiled in a wide variety of controversies since the early 1990s. These have related to its activities in childcare, education, adoption, industrial schools and nursing-home provision. The long-running controversy about the ownership of the new NMH is discussed elsewhere in this volume. Recent scrutiny of RSC involvement in Magdalene Laundries at Donnybrook, Cork, and a de facto Magdalene institution at Stanhope Street in Dublin, combine to reveal a religious congregation with a very damaged reputation. It has not faced up to its failings. In a speech to mark 200 years of the RSC in 2015, Sr Mary Christian stated:

> Following in the footsteps of our foundress, the sisters have for the last two hundred years brought comfort and consolation to people who are poor, marginalized, imprisoned, homeless, in need of education or medical care.[216]

The speech contained no reference to the shortcomings of the congregation, presumably because its leadership believes it has none.

Notes

1   F. O. C. Meenan, *St Vincent's Hospital, 1834–1994: An Historical and Social Portrait* (Dublin: Gill and Macmillan, 1994), 123.
2   See Katherine O'Donnell, Chapter 4, and Lindsey Earner-Byrne, Chapter 2, this volume.
3   See Máiréad Enright, Chapter 6, this volume.
4   The Good Shepherd Sisters were in charge of Magdalene institutions at Waterford, New Ross, Limerick, Cork, Belfast, Derry and Newry. The Sisters of Our Lady of Charity of Refuge operated laundries at High Park and Seán McDermott Street in Dublin. The Sisters of Mercy, a generalist order like the RSC, ran Magdalene Laundries in Dún Laoghaire and Galway.
5   Sarah Atkinson, *Mary Aikenhead: Her Life, Her Work and Her Friends* (Dublin: M. H. Gill & Son, 1879), 72.
6   Ibid., 72–6.

7 Ibid., 74.

8 Ibid., 76.

9 Ibid., 82–3.

10 Ibid., 86.

11 Ibid., 87.

12 Ibid., 109.

13 Ibid., 111.

14 Ibid., 120.

15 Thomas J. Morrissey, *The Life and Times of Daniel Murray: Archbishop of Dublin 1823–1852* (Dublin: Messenger Publications, 2018), 58.

16 Atkinson, *Mary Aikenhead*, 111.

17 Mary Peckham Magray, *The Transforming Power of the Nuns* (Oxford: Oxford University Press, 1998), 18.

18 Ibid., 19.

19 Morrissey, *The Life and Times of Daniel Murray*, 58–9.

20 A Member of the Congregation, *The Life and Work of Mary Aikenhead* (London: Longmans, Green & Co., 1924, hereinafter *Life and Work*), 37. The convent at North William Street moved to Upper Gardiner Street in 1830. See Atkinson, *Mary Aikenhead*, 499.

21 H. Hohn, *"Vocations": Conditions of Admission, etc., into the Convents, Congregations, Societies, Religious Institutes, etc., According to Authentical Information and the Latest Regulations* (London: R. & T. Washbourne, 1912), 243.

22 *Life and Work*, 47.

23 Ciarán McCabe, *Begging, Charity and Religion in Pre-Famine Ireland* (Liverpool: Liverpool University Press, 2018), 208. Sr Stanislaus Kennedy recalls 'begging from door to door' in late 1950s Dublin. See Stanislaus Kennedy, *The Road Home* (Dublin: Transworld Ireland, 2011), 28.

24 Caitriona Clear, *Nuns in Nineteenth-Century Ireland* (Dublin: Gill and Macmillan, 1987), 78.

25 Francesca M. Steele, *The Convents of Great Britain and Ireland* (London: Sands & Co., 1925), 200.

26 Clear, *Nuns*, 78.

27 'Ireland', *The Times*, 23 June 1829, 3.

28 *Irish Catholic Directory 1836–37*, 87.

29 Fanny Taylor, *Irish Homes and Irish Hearts* (London: Longmans, Green & Co., 1867), 21. I am grateful to Maria Luddy for drawing this source to my attention.

30 Eithne, 'Unwanted Ones – V', *Irish Monthly* 55, no. 647 (1927): 235, 240.

31 Clear, *Nuns*, 52.

32 Dominick Murphy, *Sketches of Irish Nunneries* (Dublin: James Duffy, 1865), 163–4.

33 Ibid.

34 Clear, *Nuns*, 102.

35 Atkinson, *Mary Aikenhead*, 213.

36 Ibid.

37 *Letters of Mary Aikenhead* (Dublin: M. H. Gill & Son, 1914, hereinafter *Letters*), 369.

38 Peckham Magray, *The Transforming Power*, 54, 109.

39 Clear, *Nuns*, 52–3. Peckham Magray, *The Transforming Power*, 122, refers to the 'almost uncontrollable growth' of the Mercy order.

40 *Life and Work*, 41.

41 Ibid., 142–3.

42 Ibid., 143.
43 Margery Bayley Butler, *A Candle was Lit: The Life of Mother M. Aikenhead* (Dublin: Clonmore & Reynolds, 1954), 104–11.
44 Ibid., 109.
45 Jacinta Prunty, 'Margaret Louisa Aylward', in *Women, Power and Consciousness in 19th Century Ireland*, ed. Mary Cullen and Maria Luddy (Dublin: Attic Press, 1995), 55, 58.
46 Ibid.
47 Ibid.
48 Peckham Magray, *The Transforming Power*, 20.
49 Maria Luddy, *Women and Philanthropy in Nineteenth-Century Ireland* (Cambridge: Cambridge University Press, 1995), 25; Peckham Magray, *The Transforming Power*, 21.
50 *Life and Work*, 141.
51 Murphy, *Sketches*, 165.
52 *Irish Catholic Directory 1922*, 196–8.
53 *Irish Catholic Directory 1960*, 113–15.
54 On the establishment and early years of St Vincent's Hospital, see Helen Burke, *The People and the Poor Law in 19th Century Ireland* (Littlehampton, West Sussex: WEB, 1987), 5–6.
55 *Constitutions of the Pious Congregation of the Religious Sisters of Charity of Ireland* (Dublin: Browne & Nolan, 1927, hereinafter *Constitutions*), 69. This document is contained in the papers of Archbishop Byrne in the Dublin Diocesan Archives (DDA).
56 Ibid., 63.
57 Ibid., 70.
58 Ibid. The number of delegates a convent could send to the General Assembly depended on its size, ibid., 95.
59 Ibid., 104–5.
60 Ibid., 86.
61 Ibid., 31.
62 Ibid., 3.
63 Luddy, *Women and Philanthropy*, 32.
64 Ibid., 33. Such sums would have been unusually high. The size of dowries declined over the course of the nineteenth century. See Peckham Magray, *The Transforming*, 37. An extraordinary dowry of £3,000 provided the money to establish St Vincent's Hospital. See Atkinson, *Mary Aikenhead*, 227.
65 Prunty, 'Margaret Louisa', 79.
66 Margaret MacCurtain, 'Godly Burden: Catholic Sisterhoods in Twentieth-Century Ireland', in *Gender and Sexuality in Modern Ireland*, ed. Anthony Bradley and Maryann Gialanella Valiulis (Amherst, MA: University of Massachusetts Press, 1997), 245, 250.
67 Catherine McCann, *In Gratitude: The Story of a Gift-Filled Life* (Dublin: Orpen Press, 2015), 57.
68 *Constitutions*, 5.
69 Ibid. See also Peter Anson, *The Religious Orders and Congregations of Great Britain and Ireland* (Worcester: Stanbrook Abbey, 1949), 227–8.
70 Steele, *The Convents*, 200.
71 McCabe, *Begging, Charity*, 208.
72 Clear, *Nuns*, 94.
73 Luddy, *Women and Philanthropy*, 30.
74 Peckham Magray, *The Transforming Power*, 43–4.

75   *Rules of the Religious Sisters of Charity* (Dublin: Mount St Anne's Milltown, 1941), 35–6. I am grateful to Maria Luddy for sharing her copy of the *Rules* with me.

76   Ibid., 52.

77   Ibid., 54.

78   Ibid., 76.

79   Ibid., 77.

80   Ibid., 59. See also Kennedy, *The Road Home*, 30, who states that in the late 1950s, silence was observed in the Novitiate except for one hour of recreation daily.

81   *Letters*, 469.

82   *Constitutions*, 71.

83   Ibid., 118.

84   Ibid., 118–19.

85   *Life and Work*, 464. Many of these convents had large institutions attached to them, such as orphanages, hospitals, schools and Magdalene Laundries.

86   Ibid.

87   For example, convents were subsequently founded outside Dublin at Ballaghaderreen, County Roscommon (1877) Foxford, County Mayo (1891) and Blarney, County Cork (1892). See *Life and Work*, 465.

88   Ibid., 209.

89   Ibid., 208. See also John Hugh Cullen, *The Australian Daughters of Mary Aikenhead* (Sydney: Pellegrini & Co., 1938).

90   *Life and Work*, 252–3.

91   Ibid., 235–6.

92   Ibid., 236.

93   Ibid., 452.

94   In 1947, St Margaret's was 'converted to a Residential Home for elderly ladies'. See *The Irish Sisters of Charity: Centenary Brochure* (Dublin: Mount Saint Anne's, 1958, hereinafter *Centenary Brochure*), 109. St Margaret's closed in 2004.

95   *The Irish Sisters of Charity: Giving a Brief Sketch of the Foundations of the Congregation* (Dublin: Anthonian Press, 1941, hereinafter *Brief Sketch of the Foundations*), 94.

96   'Mother Mary's Centenary', *Irish Press*, 7 June 1958, 7.

97   Ibid., 73–89. See further Anne Lally, *History of the Religious Sisters of Charity in Nigeria (1961–2011)* (Dublin: Speciality Printing, 2011). Nigeria has been a major source of vocations for the RSC.

98   'The History of the Cause of Mary Aikenhead', Religious Sisters of Charity, available online: rsccaritas.com/96-uncategorised/487-history-of-the-cause (accessed 7 September 2022).

99   'Mother Mary Aikenhead: Progress of Cause', *Irish Independent*, 1 May 1934, 8.

100 'Venerable Nun's Tomb: A Great Pilgrimage', *Irish Independent*, 11 September 1933, 8.

101 'Mother Aikenhead's Cause', *Irish Independent*, 22 January 1935, 10.

102 'Drive for Irish Nun's Beatification', *The Standard*, 5 January 1940, 3.

103 'Play on Life of Irish Nun', *Irish Press*, 5 December 1958, 3.

104 See, for example, 'Centenary Celebrations at Clarenbridge', *Connacht Sentinel*, 8 July 1958, 2.

105 'Pageant Tribute to Irish Nun', *Irish Press*, 6 October 1958, 3.

106 'First Stamp to Honour Irishwoman', *Tuam Herald*, 11 October 1958, 2.

107 Luddy, *Women and Philanthropy*, 29.

108 *Life and Work*, 432.

109 Fr Crean, the parish priest of Donnybrook, suggested the RSC to Catherine McCann when she went to him for advice about which order of nuns to join, see McCann, *In Gratitude*, 47. Fr Crean was parish priest of Donnybrook from 1953 to 1955 and again from 1962 to 1973, see J. Anthony Gaughan, *The Archbishops, Bishops and Priests Who Served in the Archdiocese of Dublin 1900 to 2011* (Dublin: Kingdom Books, 2012), 69.

110 Taylor, *Irish Homes*, 21.

111 Meenan, *St Vincent's*, 124.

112 Ibid.

113 Ibid.

114 Ibid., 125.

115 'Sr Katherine Butler: Unconventional, Forward-thinking Nun Who had a Pilot's Licence', *Irish Times*, 26 August 2000, 16.

116 McCann, *In Gratitude*, 3, 13.

117 Ibid., 61.

118 Ibid., 33. The Society of the Holy Child was subsequently invited to set up a fee-paying school in Dublin by Archbishop McQuaid, who was concerned that too many Irish families were sending their daughters to be educated in England. The order established a school in the affluent suburb of Killiney in 1947.

119 McCann, *In Gratitude*, 52.

120 See 'Sister Rose Murphy', Religious Sisters of Charity, available online: www.rsccaritas. com/we-remember/809-sister-rose-murphy (accessed 7 September 2022). As Sr Gabriel Murphy, she was in charge of St Patrick's Guild adoption society and provided false information to adopted people seeking to know about their birth mothers. See Padraig O'Morain, 'Adoption Society Admits Supplying False Information to Shield Mothers' Identities', *Irish Times*, 7 April 1997, 1.

121 'Sister Catherine Patricia Renahan', Religious Sisters of Charity, available online: rsccaritas.com/index.php/we-remember/1119-sister-catherine-patricia-renahan (accessed 7 September 2022).

122 'Sister Mary Daniel McCarry', Religious Sisters of Charity, rsccaritas.com/index.php/ we-remember/1149-sister-mary-daniel-mccarry (accessed 7 September 2022).

123 *Letters*, 521; Jack Fagan, 'Housebuilder Pays over £8m for Milltown Convent Site', *Irish Times*, 6 April 1995, 29.

124 *Centenary Brochure*, 142.

125 Yvonne McKenna, *Made Holy: Irish Women Religious at Home and Abroad* (Dublin: Irish Academic Press, 2006), 86–8.

126 *Brief Sketch of the Foundations*, 159. See also *Centenary Brochure*, 144.

127 Louise Fuller, *Irish Catholicism since 1950: The Undoing of a Culture* (Dublin: Gill and Macmillan, 2022), 166.

128 *Centenary Brochure*, 144.

129 Ibid., 145.

130 Ibid.

131 Ibid.

132 Ibid.

133 Hohn, "*Vocations*", 244. See also *Centenary Brochure*, 145.

134 *Centenary Brochure*.

135 Ibid.

136 Ibid., 146.

137 Luddy, *Women and Philanthropy*, 28.

138 Clear, *Nuns*, 69.

139 Steele, *The Convents*, 200–1.

140 *Brief Sketch of the Foundations*, 160.

141 Kennedy, *The Road Home*, 31.

142 Ibid.

143 McCann, *In Gratitude*, 52.

144 Ibid., 57.

145 Ibid., 59.

146 Ibid.

147 Ibid., 60.

148 Ibid., 64.

149 Ibid.

150 'St Vincent's Hospital', *Freeman's Journal*, 13 January 1844, 1.

151 Taylor, *Irish Homes*, 21.

152 Moira Lysaght, 'Daniel Murray: Archbishop of Dublin 1823–1852', *Dublin Historical Record*, 27, no. 3 (1974): 101, 105.

153 'St Vincent's Hospital', *Irish Society*, 5 December 1891, 1161. This was an early Irish example of the acquisition and repurposing of an aristocratic residence by a religious order, something that would be replicated all over the country hundreds of times. See G. L. MacD., 'The Old Order Changeth: Irish Castles and Mansions Become Religious Sanctuaries', *Sunday Independent*, 22 March 1931, 4.

154 'Next Week's Centenary Event: Saint Vincent's Hospital's Century of Service for the People', *The Standard*, 19 January 1934, 3.

155 Hylda J. Beckett, 'St Vincent's Hospital, Dublin: 1834–1984', *Dublin Historical Record*, 37, nos 3–4 (1984): 137, 141.

156 'A Hospital of Which the Nation Can Feel Proud', *Irish Independent*, 26 November 1970, 12.

157 'Our History', St Vincent's Private Hospital, available online: https://svph.ie/about/our-history/ (accessed 7 September 2022).

158 *Centenary Brochure*, 153.

159 John Cowell, *Where They Lived in Dublin* (Dublin: O'Brien Press, 1980), 33. See also *St Vincent's Hospital Annual 1975*, 7.

160 Patsy McGarry, 'Sister Stan Apologises for Abuse by Her Order', *Irish Times*, 1 July 2009, 8.

161 *Letters*, 319.

162 *Brief Sketch of the Foundations*, 67.

163 Ibid., 155.

164 *Irish Sisters of Charity 1843–1943: Souvenir Book* (Dublin: Annesley Press, 1943, hereinafter *Souvenir Book*), 93. This book commemorated the centenary of the appointment of Mary Aikenhead as Superior General of the congregation for life by Pope Gregory XVI.

165 Mary Gallagher, 'An Irishwoman's Diary', *Irish Times*, 6 June 1995, 11.

166 Nuala O'Faolain, 'Sadism of Religious Reflected Values of Society', *Irish Times*, 4 March 1996, 12.

167 'Mum's the Word: Miriam O'Callaghan, Louise Duffy and Georgie Crawford on What Their Mothers Taught Them', *Independent.ie*, 30 March 2019.

168 *Souvenir Book*, 85.

169 Commission to Inquire into Child Abuse, *Final Report of the Commission to Inquire into Child Abuse* (Dublin Stationery Office, 2009, hereinafter *Final Report CICA*), vol. 2, 545.

170 Ibid., 485.

171 See, for example, the notice soliciting 'alms, contributions of wearing apparel, bed covering [*sic*] etc, which will find their way to the really deserving poor', contained on the front page of *The Standard*, 18 December 1942.

172 See further McCann, *In Gratitude*, 54.

173 *Life and Work*, 459.

174 *Souvenir Book*, 147.

175 See, for example, Frank McDonald, 'New Life Injected into Old Convent', *Irish Times*, 12 March 1992, 5; Patsy McGarry, 'Sisters Give Corporation Gift of Land', *Irish Times*, 18 January 2001, 8.

176 See, for example, Eileen Battersby, 'Friend of the Homeless and Invisible Poor', *Irish Times*, 24 December 1998, 6; Marjorie Brennan, 'The Power of Peace', The Weekend, *Irish Examiner*, 24 December 2021, 13.

177 See, for example, Carol Coulter, 'Questions about Kilkenny Scandal Have Not Been Answered Convincingly', *Irish Times*, 15 May 1999, 8.

178 Patsy McGarry, 'Sr Stan Apologises for Abuse by Her Order', *Irish Times*, 1 July 2009, 8.

179 See further Máiréad Enright, Chapter 6, this volume.

180 Paul Cullen, 'Sr Stan Hurt by Depiction of Sisters of Charity', *Irish Times*, 3 June 2017, 8.

181 Padraig Yeates, 'Gardaí to Examine Claims of Abuse at Home', *Irish Times*, 24 August 1993.

182 'Children's Home Worker Jailed for 13 Sex Offences', *Irish Times*, 28 June 1994, 4.

183 Department of Health, *Report on the Inquiry into the Operation of Madonna House* (Dublin: Government of Ireland, 1996), 94.

184 Ibid., 6.

185 Padraig O'Morain, 'Child Abuse Scandal', *Irish Times*, 13 May 1999, 7.

186 'Pickets Put on Dublin School Facing Closure', *Irish Times*, 15 March 1994, 5.

187 Nuala O'Faolain, 'Last Orders?', *Irish Times*, 13 November 1993, 40.

188 See, for example, Fintan O'Toole, 'Heavenly Inspiration Casts Aside Need for Consistency', *Irish Times*, 13 April 1994, 12.

189 *Dáil Éireann Debate*, 22 March 1994, vol. 440, col. 1059.

190 Frank McNally, 'The Nuns' Story', *Irish Times*, 26 April 1994, 8.

191 *Irish Times*, 24 May 1994, 2.

192 *Irish Times*, 11 June 1994, 10.

193 'Dublin Secondary School to Close', *Irish Times*, 14 March 1998, 6.

194 Gillian Ní Cheallaigh, 'Nuns Reject Charge of "Turning Their Backs on the Blind" as Outrageous', *Irish Times*, 26 January 2001, 4.

195 Ibid.

196 'Nuns in Warning to Blind Council', *Sunday Independent*, 28 January 2001, 3.

197 Jack Fagan, 'Dublin 4 Site Sold for Record Price', *Irish Times*, 30 March 2001, 1.

198 Martha Kearns, '"Uncaring" Nuns Face Law Threat over £35m Land Sale', *Irish Independent*, 24 January 2001, 45.

199 Kitty Holland, 'Families and Staff to Protest Closure of South Dublin Nursing Home', *Irish Times*, 12 June 2020, 6; Kitty Holland, 'Residents "Very Angry" over Liquidation of Dublin Facility', *Irish Times*, 31 August 2020, 4.

200 Patsy McGarry, 'Nursing Homes "Lack Funds" for Redundancies', *Irish Times*, 31 July 2020, 5.

201 See, for example, Anne-Marie Walshe, 'Nuns Urged to "Pay Up" as Staff at Three Nursing Homes Face Redundancy', *Irish Independent*, 13 August 2020, 27.

202 Arthur Beesley and Patsy McGarry, 'Move by Sisters of Charity to Rezone Merrion Road Land Could Boost Its Value to €50m', *Irish Times*, 22 February 2022.

203 Padraig O'Morain, 'Adoption Society Admits Supplying False Information to Shield Mothers' Identities', *Irish Times*, 7 April 1997, 1. The RSC took over the guild and the St Patrick's Infant Hospital at Temple Hill, Blackrock, Dublin, in 1943. See John MacSheahan, 'St Patrick's Guild', *Irish Monthly* 71, no. 843 (1943): 357.

204 Ibid.

205 Padraig O'Morain, 'Adoption Agency's Misinformation is Blamed for Years of Fruitless Searching', *Irish Times*, 8 April 1997, 3.

206 Cormac McQuinn, 'Illegal Adoptions: Government to Consider Review of St Patrick's Guild Files', *Irish Times*, 9 March 2021.

207 Patsy McGarry, 'Sisters of Charity Saddened by Disclosures and Calls for Inquiry', *Irish Times*, 5 March 2021, 7.

208 Ibid.

209 Beesley and McGarry, 'Move by Sisters of Charity'.

210 The institutions are St Mary Magdalen's, Donnybrook, Dublin, St Vincent's, Peacock Lane, Cork, and St Mary's Training Centre, Stanhope Street, Dublin.

211 Conall Ó Fátharta, 'Orders Rebuffed Request for Money', *Irish Examiner*, 14 March 2017, 13.

212 Conall Ó Fátharta, 'Counting the Cost of Broken Lives', *Irish Examiner*, 6 July 2011, 7.

213 *Centenary Brochure*, 140.

214 The strong personality of its foundress, which seems to have exerted a remarkable influence over her successors, even after her death, was an additional factor.

215 In 2015, there were 213 Sisters of Charity in Ireland, with a median age of 76. See *Review of Child Safeguarding Practice in the Religious Congregation of the Religious Sisters of Charity* (Maynooth, Co. Kildare: National Board for Safeguarding Children in the Catholic Church in Ireland, 2015).

216 Sr Mary Christian, RSC, '200 Years Celebrations from Donnybook', Welcome Address, available online: www.sistersofcharity.org.au/wp-content/uploads/2017/02/200-years-celebrations-from-Donnybook.pdf (accessed 7 September 2022).

2

Donnybrook Magdalene Asylum and the Priorities of a Nation

A History of Respectability

Lindsey Earner-Byrne

This chapter contextualizes Donnybrook Magdalene Laundry (DML) in the history of Irish modernization and nation-building, one in which Irish women paid a high price for 'threatening' the emerging social order. This order was founded on the premise that respectability was the route to legitimacy and ownership: ownership of status, of land, and of the bricks and mortar of Empire and, eventually, of an Irish nation. The respectability project was an international phenomenon, which Mary Evans notes was such a 'powerful concept' that it could be used to convince people 'to behave in ways more aligned to the interests of others rather than their own'.[1] In Ireland, the colonial and nationalist contexts operated as twin impulses to reinforce the power of respectability as a mechanism of ordering and licensing considerable self-sacrifice, social control and violence. Consequently, respectability became a key element in defining and deciding moral and social worth.[2]

Morality and female social power

In convents throughout Ireland and elsewhere, written records of life were kept by nuns in the form of annals.[3] Similar to journals of convent and local community life, the annals were a genre of writing which recorded the social memory of an order, reinforced its values, and performed its anxieties and priorities.[4] The parable of a 'good death', for example, recurs in these annals, in which the passing of members, including inhabitants such as penitent women and orphaned children, were recorded as epitomes of virtue or as examples of redemption through suffering and/or prayer.[5] In the early twentieth century, the annals of DML recorded a death that underscored the religious, gender and class sensibilities of respectable Ireland. In the 1890s, when Mary Fleming sought rescue from the Sisters of Charity (RSC), she was a 'sweet looking girl ... but alas! It was the old story, so old, and so often told it is hardly interesting now.'[6] Her parents were 'poor but very respectable' – clearly, the annal keeper believed respectability was an attribute that could traverse class lines, if one knew how to behave. Unfortunately, Mary ran away from that respectable home when a rich doctor from out of town asked her to marry him:

> he would make a lady of her, and he would provide for her mother, there would be no more hard work for her, or days of anxiety and worry about the ways and means, and the young brothers and sisters would all be sent to good schools, it just seemed like a wonderful fairy-tale to Mary, and she never doubted when he said, that it would be better for them to be married in Dublin . . .

The marriage never materialized, instead Mary found herself 'broken-hearted' in a big city. She yielded to the temptation of drink and 'became reckless', but only for a short period before 'her natural piety saved her'. When the man in question 'suggested that they were both in the wrong, and that she should go to a convent, to a Magdalen asylum she consented at once. He brought her to the gate and left her.' She 'was from the first a most fervent Penitent', but her health began to fail, and she was sent to hospital. However, she immediately requested to return to the asylum because the 'cause of all her sorrow' was working in the hospital as 'an honoured and respected surgeon'. She was so anxious to prevent him seeing her that she denied herself medical care and returned to the nuns to die. Her one wish was that her mother would be told what had happened to her and this the nuns duly did. The mother, the annals record, was told that her daughter, despite her fall, had become a saint and her example was of 'untold good . . . to the other Penitents'. Her mother forgave her and asked the Mother Rectress to tell Mary that 'she would meet her "Molly Bawn" in heaven'.[7] It appears that Mary died in DML in 1914 of bronchitis.[8]

Mary Fleming's story, as recounted by the annal keeper, reinforced the moral universe the nuns were building and protecting, one in which some women carried the burden of moral sanction, some the power of rescue and all women were defined in relation to this moral spectrum. Cara Delay notes that during the late nineteenth and early twentieth centuries, with growing literacy rates, Catholic girls and women were 'bombarded with messages on Catholic womanhood',[9] which sought to sell morality as a social power that all women could exercise if self-sacrifice was their guiding light. Indeed, the reference by Mary's mother to 'Molly Bawn' roots this story in the romantic fiction of the era, as it was the title of Margaret Wolfe Hungerford's hugely popular novel, published in 1878. Furthermore, the 'innocent' dying of consumption, as Mary did, was a recurring trope in Victorian literature as was moral fall and spiritual redemption.[10] Mary's death reaffirmed the class and gender principles of modern Ireland, which were informed by Victorian sensibilities and sanctified by Catholicism. The world that condemned the naive Mary to social ruin and physical death for trusting a wealthy stranger, even an honourable doctor, provided a purpose for the Magdalene asylum and, in turn, the asylum served that world. When the doctor decided they had both done wrong, he knew just where to dispose of Mary, although in the annalist's telling no blame was apportioned to the good doctor, because he was of a superior gender and class to Mary. It is instructive of the values of the putative Catholic nation that the lesson of Mary's story, as crafted by another woman, the nun keeping the annals, was that violating the class order was as deadly as transgressing the moral one and only by sacrificing the body could women find redemption. The dynamic of this annual entry reveals much about the centrality of sexual politics to the Ireland being forged from the mid-nineteenth century, an Ireland which would fortify its grip throughout much of the twentieth century. Mary Fleming's life and death, as conjured by a nun, was an exemplum of the emerging moral order.

Class relations and the policing of sexuality and gender

Sexuality and appropriate gender behaviour were central parameters of respectability, and women were portrayed as both the guardians of and biggest potential threat to this project.[11] From the outset, class and the sexual politics of gender were pivotal. In many respects, the Magdalene asylum-laundry system was symbolic of this emerging order: it contained the hierarchies of both class and gender and its relationship with religion reflected the fact that notions of moral worth, reform and sexuality, crossed religious lines for much of the history of these institutions. The Irish Magdalene asylum system began in Leeson Street in Dublin, in 1766, as a lay Protestant endeavour of 'moral reform'; it provided a model for philanthropy which appealed to a growing number of middle-class Irish women eager to contribute to the changing society around them.[12] By the early nineteenth century, there were multiple, relatively small, Magdalene asylums operating in Dublin under both Protestant and Catholic female management. Among these was the Donnybrook Magdalene Asylum, run by the RSC; it had opened in 1798 on Townsend Street before moving in 1837 to the site at Donnybrook.[13] In the emerging religious and welfare landscape of nineteenth-century Ireland, the relationship constructed between the nuns and their female penitents took on heightened significance.

The 1830s, when the RSC's Magdalene Laundry was establishing itself in Donnybrook, were crucial in Ireland's welfare history. The concepts of poverty, dependence and the relationship between the state (in the guise of relief/welfare) and religion (in the form of charity) were being renegotiated. Notions of the 'deserving' and 'undeserving' became widely accepted moral divisions upon which to decide who qualified for relief (welfare subsidized by taxpayers or charity) underwritten by the respectable middle classes.[14] As both poor relief and charity were understood to come with conditions attached, the opportunity for religious pressure or proselytism grew. It was in this context that non-denominational reform work became difficult and controversial. The Roman Catholic Church looked to a growing reserve of young men and women to populate various religious orders and congregations and dedicate their lives to 'protecting' the Catholic poor from the pressure/temptation of proselytism. There was a lot more than souls at stake; this was about ensuring religious dominion over Ireland, whether it remained a colony or became an independent nation. In the case of the Magdalene asylums, it was regarded as crucial that Catholic 'penitents' attend those run by Catholic women and Protestant 'penitents' rely on those run by women of their religious profession.

This hardening of the religious lines occurred during a period of drastic economic change, resulting in, among other things, a collapse in the linen industry and a growth in female unemployment and destitution. The cities of Ireland, in particular Dublin, Belfast, Cork and Limerick, became hosts to impoverished women and girls who, for various reasons, had fallen beyond the pale of the peasant economy and were destitute. Thus, gender-based moral reform became a significant industry in which the single mother came increasingly into focus. In the evolving nineteenth-century economy, all women had less financial purchase, but single destitute mothers and/or prostitutes had the least economic opportunities and, consequently, virtually no social capital.[15] They were the proverbial weak link in the economics of patriarchy, placing them outside the limits of respectability. As Arlette Farge observed, 'deviance and marginality are powerfully indicative of political authority and of norms'.[16]

Indeed, it is no accident that it was in the ecosystem of the poor law that 'the unmarried mother' began to appear as a social category, as opposed to the more general discussions regarding illegitimacy. This shift in emphasis aligns with Virginia Crossman's observation that during the same period, within English welfare institutions, there was a shift in emphasis from the care of the 'illegitimate' to the reform of the 'unmarried mother'.[17] The Irish poor law of the 1830s, and the thinking it generated, proved crucial in defining social and moral worth, in deciding who belonged and had value for the greater whole and who needed to be excised. Catholic Archbishop Paul Cullen was a key driver of a campaign to have 'unmarried mothers' segregated from the 'respectable poor' in the workhouse in the 1860s, declaring 'the presence and mixture of women with illegitimate children among young girls must tend to lower their idea of female modesty and purity'.[18] Note the hierarchy of women, those that are pure and those that corrupt, those that might reform and those who were irredeemable. This is not to suggest that prior to the 1860s single mothers did not encounter prejudice or harsh treatment, but it was a crucial historical moment when this treatment became integral to a system of structural violence that limited the lives of all women. Indeed, Crossman makes this connection, noting that the introduction of the poor law in Ireland 'increased the stigma attached to illegitimacy by forcing single mothers into workhouses in order to receive relief and placing the major share of responsibility on the mothers rather than fathers of illegitimate children'.[19] This intersection of sexual morality and entitlement – or deservingness – was to become an integral feature of welfare throughout the twentieth century. The other element of the narrative that was established by the turn of the century and would inform all future treatment of single mothers, was the idea that to help them demeaned and punished 'legitimate mothers'. Compassion was not just misplaced, it was dangerous as it encouraged vice and harmed good women. This was key in silencing any counter-narrative or familial support.

In her recent study of the creation of Catholic girlhood, Cara Delay points to the Catholic Church's sustained attempts to define the 'ideal woman' as linked to the evolution of Catholicism and the creation of the modern Irish nation. The idea that mass literacy was the handmaiden of the nineteenth-century economic development and 'modernization' of Ireland is not a new insight.[20] The first generations of literate Irish boys and girls were reading both British colonial norms of their gendered identities through the national school system and, as Delay notes, a literal flood of 'Church-sanctioned respectable literature'.[21] Crucially, Delay highlights the tradeoff involved in increased literacy for women, noting that while this literature 'increased pressures on Irish women to conform to gender norms', it also 'afforded women the opportunity to increase their literacy, manage consumerism, and even write'.[22] Lisa Godson's work confirms not just the connection between literacy and consumption but the role of religious objects in this mix highlighting 'the interrelationship between capitalism, mechanization and the material culture of ultramontane Catholicism'.[23] This served to create a middle-class consumer culture founded on rigid moral sensibilities. In 1863, the *Freeman's Journal* reported that pupils of the Loreto Convent school in Omagh were addressed by Reverend O'Kane who told them: 'you now assume a new, a high position ... You have received favours beyond the reach of many who will scan with jealous eye your every act, your every word, your whole demeanour'.[24] Mary Hatfield and Ciaran O'Neill point out that these women were being 'empowered by the women who taught them, in accordance with the power structures of the society they lived in, and in ways that were complementary to parallel elite education for male elites'.[25] Indeed they were, and stitched into this empowering was the implicit acceptance of its elitism, an awareness not only that it rested on social inequality, but that it relied upon it. Respectability licensed these young women as the hegemonic version of femininity inhibiting any disruptive gender alliance across the classes.

Protecting ideal women

Of course, that all this certainty about what constituted the masculine and the feminine was founded on uncertainty is not as counterintuitive as it sounds. By the 1880s, Delay observes, 'the ideal of womanhood was pervasive but essentially fragile'.[26] Crucially, the idea of this fragility, while real, was also doing important work in stabilizing gender norms and enforcing certain behaviour: no one was ever denying that being the 'right type' of woman or man required work, sacrifice and vigilance.[27] Hence, the contemporary talk about the threats to ideal womanhood and the emergence of so-called 'masculine women',[28] was as much a reflection of this anxiety as it was a conscious performance and stoking of those very fears. The constant discussion of the threat posed by bad women to all other men and women helped to establish communal boundaries of belonging. This was reflected in the increased focus on the so-called 'unmarried mother problem' in the years preceding and following the foundation of the Irish Free State in 1922: it formed a foundational part of the reasoning and ordering of Irish independence. This can literally be read in newspapers, journals, commissions of inquiry, religious literature (and annals) and political debates of the period. For example, a series of articles in the *Irish Ecclesiastical Record* between 1921 and 1922 established 'The Unmarried Mother Problem' as an urgent issue of 'national significance'.[29] As one article in the series declared: 'This whole subject is of extreme importance, concerning as it does the preservation of a strict standard of moral life in the nation, and the saving from utter ruin of the faith and the morality of so many Catholic girls.'[30] However, this was not just a Catholic consensus: the *Irish Times*, aimed primarily at the Protestant middle class, believed its readers shared the values of this nation, noting in 1929 that Ireland 'was famous for her men's chivalry and for her women's modesty. To-day every honest Irishman must admit that this reputation is in danger.'[31]

The single mother was proof of this moral decline, the paper declared: 'cases in which unmarried mothers have been brought to trial for infanticide indicate a general looseness of manners, a contempt of moral decencies, that are a wholly new feature of Irish life'.[32] The newspaper traced this to 'the downfall of parental responsibility and the disregard of religious teaching that are producing the present harvest of sexual looseness and crime'.[33] The focus on parental discipline, which was ubiquitous in newspapers, commissions of inquiry and political debates, was a reflection of an anxiety that the institution of the family was failing in its duty to maintain social order. If the family disregarded this role, contemporaries feared social chaos would ensue, a fear linked to the experience of violence and war on the island since the mid-1910s. If the 'unmarried mother' was the moral watermark of the nation, the family was seen as the frontline of defence. All social forces were focused on preventing any understanding of the family as a potential refuge for these daughters. The institutionalization of these women was vital to this worldview and the existing Magdalene system served a valuable function in terms of moral reform and the affirmation of the hierarchies of femininity: the nuns were the ideal, their charges were the warning to all other women of how easy it was to fall and how serious the consequences were. The ghost of Mary Fleming haunted the streets of the Irish Free State.

Rejecting that 'class of girl'

In 1925, the murder of a young single mother gripped the new state. On the 2 February 1925, the *Irish Times* announced to its readers: 'The courthouse at Green St, Dublin, was crowded yesterday morning, when Patrick Purcell, a medical doctor practicing in Co Wicklow, and Leopold Dillon, an ex-superintendent of the Civic Guard, were put on trial .... for the murder of Elizabeth O'Neill (known as "Honour Bright" [*sic*]) on the morning of the 9th June, 1925.'[34] Shot in the chest, her body was found in Ticknock in the Dublin mountains. While not the first female body left in the cold for the new nation to stumble over, this case generated particular interest because the accused, a doctor and a policeman, were supposedly members of respectable society.[35] Lizzie O'Neill was not the focus of attention. It was the story spun around her murder that captured the nation's attention because it portrayed apparent pillars of society galivanting around Dublin in a 'little grey two-seater car' engaging in excessive drinking and general debauchery.[36] The irrelevance of the woman at the centre of the narrative is noteworthy. In the newspaper coverage and throughout the trial, she was referred to as Elizabeth O'Neill, Lizzie O'Neill, Mary Kate O'Neill, Mary Kate Neill, Lily O'Neill and Honour Bright, the latter name the court referred to as a pseudonym used in her life of prostitution. In fact, like many other women working as prostitutes, she used multiple names, probably to both distance herself from a way of life almost universally condemned by her contemporaries and to help evade arrest and prosecution.[37]

It is important to pause a moment over what we do know of this woman because the purpose of the system of incarceration, in which the DML played a crucial role, was to obscure these women, to render their names and lives irrelevant. She appeared in the 1901 census as Mary Kate Neill, the youngest of five children born to a blacksmith and his wife. She was orphaned at 8 years of age and relocated to Dublin in 1918, when the last of her siblings had emigrated. She gained employment at Pim Brothers & Co. department store, known as Pim's or the Stores, on South Great George's Street, Dublin.[38] Within two years of arriving in the capital, on 9 November 1920, she gave birth to a baby boy in the Coombe maternity hospital. She named her son, as did quite a few others at that time, after the young medical student and Irish volunteer Kevin Barry,[39] executed by the British eight days before her son's birth.[40] There is something incredibly poignant about this choice of name for her son as it indicates that she identified with the Irish nation being forged around her, a nation that explicitly rejected her 'class of girl'. During the trial, counsel for the prosecution, William Carrigan, QC,[41] described the accused, Dr Purcell and Supt. Dillon, as 'a pair of moral degenerates who quitted their families and their responsibilities to spend a night of debauchery in the City of Dublin' and 'murdered this unhappy girl of the unfortunate class'.[42] Women like Lizzie O'Neill were a class unto themselves. They were, as the defence explained, 'doubtful women'.[43]

Despite the weight of evidence against the accused, 'the jury, after a few minutes' absence, returned a verdict of "Not guilty" and both men were discharged'.[44] With the acquittal, the Irish Free State was off the hook; the respectable had been legally acquitted, but effectively expelled for their anti-social/anti-Irish behaviour, and the 'unmarried mother' represented only as a prostitute of various names, was dead. As Maria Luddy argues, 'the Church and State constructed the sexuality of young women as dangerous' in order to control 'the sexuality of all women', so the unsolved murder of a prostitute represented a deadly warning to all women.[45] Lizzie O'Neill was potentially every and any woman, while 'Honor Bright' embodied the 'fallen woman' – her fate a literal dramatization of the price paid for living outside the embrace of the nation. Her death certificate inscribed her tenuous place in the new state: 'Lizzie O'Neill Alias Lil O'Neill Alias Honor Bright', whose age was 'unknown', dead '[F]rom Bullet Fired at her by some person or persons at present not made amenable [?] and that such person or persons were guilty of wilful murder.'[46]

For many in Ireland, Honour Bright's fate reinforced the need for institutions of reform. The following year, when issuing an appeal for the RSC Magdalene asylum in Cork, Reverend Father Philip, OFM, explained that these institutions offered asylum to rejected girls: 'the Sisters would share with them the home that they had built for themselves out of their dowries'. The newspaper reported that Fr Philip had known 'those poor outcasts in Dublin even that poor girl who was found [murdered] on Ticknock hill, with her Rosary beads in her pocket, and a badge of the Sacred Heart he had given to her'.[47] The reference to Lizzie O'Neill indicates the resonance this story had for the Irish public and the role it played in reinforcing the need for Magdalene asylums.[48] In his 1926 appeal for DML, Reverend James McCann declared that: 'but for the work continuously carried out by the Sisters of Charity there would be such a flood of immorality and distress all over the country that in a very few years it would shake the very foundations of society and plunge it in despair'.[49] These appeals enabled the rehearsal of the moral arguments of respectability in the public arena (both in churches and reproduced in newspapers) *and* provided a way to reinforce the system of incarceration by continuously reiterating the idea of moral contamination. In this context, the transfer of money from the people of Ireland to the Magdalene asylums was an important process in reaffirming the connection between respectability, charity and belonging.[50] In 1929, Reverend P. Gannon, S.J., informed his flock that DML worked 'towards the eradication of immorality'. Appealing, no doubt, to the parents in his audience, he noted the need for 'a higher standard of conduct all round. This meant religious principles carried into effect, the awakening of conscience on the part of both sexes, and a careful watch over their minds and hearts.'[51] Stressing the hierarchies of femininity, the *Irish Independent* noted that Reverend Gannon had portrayed the nuns as exemplars of self-sacrifice, while also calling on all women to do the work of moral enforcement, if for no other reason than for the safety of their own families:

> The good nuns surely did their part under great difficulties, for the inmates must be treated with tact and sympathy, and yet with a degree of firmness – qualities not easily combined. In appealing for support he particularly addressed himself to the women, for a variety of reasons, the lowest of which he put at conscience and self-interest – the interest of the husband, the brother, and the son, which was bound up in the elimination of the evil.[52]

In this narrative, Magdalen asylums were bulwarks of respectable family life, preventing moral corrosion. In all these appeals, the single mother was an abstraction and rarely considered in human terms: she was a prototype of immorality that risked contaminating other women, men and the family.

Official policy and single mothers

In spite of all this talk and angst, the new Irish state, and the various local authorities, were distinctly reluctant to take responsibility for the care of single mothers and, while this reluctance was couched in moral terms, it was motivated by financial concerns.[53] The general sentiment was perfectly summed up by the chairman of the Ballina local authority, in Co. Mayo, during a discussion about having local single mothers transferred to the Bon Secours' Tuam Mother and Baby Home in Galway: 'For a long time,' he lamented, 'there has been a loud cry to have the unmarried mothers taken somewhere else.'[54] Throughout the 1920s and 1930s, the local authorities of the country grumbled and waged a consistent campaign to have 'the unmarried mother' removed from 'their' remit. Lest we be in any doubt, money was intimately connected to the sexual politics of all of this; one only has to consult the minutes of the regional Boards of Health which were all pushing for action 'against putative fathers' to recoup the cost of maintaining these women and their children.[55] In County Meath, the Board of Health advocated the use of abandoned workhouses to isolate these women 'in two divisions, one for the habituals and the other for girls whose first fall it was'. It called for 'the habituals' (those 'habitual offenders' who had more than one child outside marriage) to 'be sent to industrial homes for whatever time the magistrate might deem necessary'.[56] The official was referring to women who had had children outside marriage, i.e. who had committed no indictable offence, thus the mention of a magistrate was indicative of a contemporary tendency to conflate morality and crime. This conflation was both assisted and reflected by the fact that some women convicted of other crimes ranging from petty theft to infanticide and/or concealment of birth were sent to Magdalene asylums and other religious-run 'industrial homes' rather than prison.[57] However, most women found themselves in Ireland's Magdalene system for no legal or criminal reasons.

In 1925, the new State had begun a consultation process with local authorities, religious and lay leaders and members of the general public on what kind of a welfare system the new nation wished to create. The Commission on the Relief of the Sick and Destitute Poor, including the Insane Poor, sat between 1925 and 1926 and heard from witnesses from all over the country.[58] The tone of the evidence provided was representative of a general desire to have the issue of single mothers considered primarily as one of morality and, thus, an issue for religious groups. On 25 May 1925, when Mr Thomas McArdle of the Department of Local Government and Public Health, was questioned by the Commission about the State's policy in relation to this group, he explained:

> The whole question of the unmarried mothers is one of the most difficult problems we have got to deal with. We have not thought out any settled policy, but we think it unwise to congregate them in large numbers in big institutions where first offenders would be associating with hardened cases.[59]

Sir Joseph Glynn, a senior figure in the philanthropic world of 1920s Ireland, responded to McArdle by wondering if: 'You ... get a large number of young girls, fallen for the first time ... will they not lose the sense of shame by being congregated in the one building?'[60] He asked if the government had considered allowing the baby to be sent out to nurse, so that the mother could work, which elicited the most definite response thus far from Mr McArdle: 'No. This is a policy that we oppose strongly. Some County Boards of Health are inclined to support that policy, but we hold that it relieves the mother of responsibility.' However, within a few minutes, even this certainty had evaporated and McArdle was back to reiterating, 'we haven't made up our minds'.[61]

The State's policy became effectively one born of avoidance and amounting to little more than the extension of the existing system. At the dawn of the Irish Free State, the majority of single mothers were accommodated in poor law institutions – former Work Houses renamed County Homes. Many of these continued to have mixed populations, but a few were given over entirely to the institutionalization of single mothers, for example the Tuam Work House was handed over to the Bon Secours Sisters to become a mother and baby 'home'.[62] Magdalene asylums like Donnybrook, were co-opted into the service of the State to take the more 'intractable cases', a term that implied a particularly poor moral status, but, in fact, covered anything from very poor women to those with more than one child outside marriage, those born in institutions themselves, and many who were the victims of sexual assault or some who had worked as prostitutes.[63]

In the late 1920s and 1930s, the Irish government actively sought to place the responsibility for single mothers on the shoulders of the Catholic Church. Indeed, there was some criticism within government that the Irish Catholic Church was failing to 'imitate the zeal' of its English counterpart in this regard.[64] The Secretary of the Department of External Affairs, Joseph Walshe, explained that the 'unmarried mother problem' had particular features that made it best suited to religious oversight: 'Its moral and religious aspects and the extreme care and delicacy required for handling it point inevitably to a Church organisation of some kind.'[65] It was this logic that enabled the government to turn to specific religious orders to create institutions to cater for the 'respectable class of girl'.[66] As a result, between 1922 and 1933, the Sisters of the Sacred Hearts of Jesus and Mary opened three maternity homes in Cork, Galway and Westmeath, respectively: 'for the reception and reformation of girls who for the first time have had illegitimate offspring, or as they are usually designated – first offenders'.[67] These homes accepted private cases and referrals from local authorities or from one of the three poor-law mother-and-baby homes as well as private cases.[68] Within this system, women could be held for as long as a matron desired. For example, in 1930, the matron of the Bessboro Mother and Baby Home in Cork, explained: 'a number of girls are weak willed and have to be maintained in the home for a long period to safeguard against a second lapse'.[69] It is little wonder so many women left each year to the relative anonymity of Britain, where there were better (though far from perfect) supports for maternity care, adoption and, on occasion, abortion.[70]

Legislative initiatives were all relatively tame and largely about minimizing the financial burden of the single mother and her child on the rate payers. The Illegitimate Children (Affiliation Orders) Act, 1930,[71] enabled the mother of a child born outside of marriage to sue the 'putative father', via the district court system, for maintenance of the child.[72] A successful prosecution was very difficult to achieve because corroborating evidence of the sexual relationship with the putative father was required. For example, in 1933, a mother of fourteen wrote to the Archbishop of Dublin for assistance after her daughter's case floundered 'for the Lack of Witness to prove she was seen in His Company which the young woman who was to come Died and the case was put out of the court'.[73] In reality, cases were usually taken by County Home authorities in a bid to recoup costs of housing the mother and her child. The Legitimacy Act, 1931,[74] considered to be a 'very uncontroversial measure' by one of its political sponsors, allowed for the legitimation of a child born to unwed parents who subsequently married.[75] While supporters of this legislation may have hoped that it would result in less children and mothers becoming reliant on the State, the main focus was on inheritance and property rights. The Act meant that a previously 'illegitimate' child was considered to have been born on the day it was legitimized and entitled to inherit the property of its parents on that basis. In this regard, legislators considered it important that the Act did nothing to legitimate, and thus render entitled to inherit, any child conceived as a result of adultery.[76] For many social workers, charitable and religious campaigners concerned with the welfare of women and children, this Act was regarded as part of an agenda to bring Free State legislation in line with Great Britain and Northern Ireland in relation to the protection of women and girls.[77]

The piece of legislation with the greatest relevance to the institutions within which single mothers and their children were held was the Registration of Maternity Homes Act, 1934.[78] It was introduced in response to recommendations made by the aforementioned Commission on the Relief of the Sick and Destitute Poor. The

Commission had argued that the extremely high mortality rate among infants born outside marriage was at least in part due to a number of 'poor class maternity homes' which boarded children out with little care.[79] During the Dáil readings of the bill, the Parliamentary Secretary to the Minister for Local Government and Public Health, Dr Con Ward, cited paragraph 268 of Commission's report regarding the mortality rate of infants born outside marriage:

> It is high for many reasons, but there is one to which we wish specially to refer. The illegitimate child being proof to the mother's shame is, in most cases, sought to be hidden at all costs. What frequently happens is that the mother, or the mother's family, at the time the mother leaves the hospital or home, make arrangements with someone to take the child, either paying a lump sum down or undertaking to pay something from time to time.[80]

Undoubtedly there were unscrupulous maternity homes and agencies that took advantage of terrified women to charge exorbitant rates to take their children and then boarded them out to unsafe homes.[81] However, quite apart from the desire to consider the mother's sense of shame as the cause of all harm, what is significant is the lack of focus on the County Homes and religious-run mother and baby 'homes' and Magdalene asylums, where the death rates were as high and higher. It is also notable that the mother herself was not the primary focus of concern in introducing this piece of legislation. We now know that the Act failed to protect either women or children from harm and, where the infants were concerned, death.[82] The 2021 *Final Report of the Commission of Investigation into Mother and Baby Homes* noted that:

> Although the DLGPH/Department of Health received regular inspection reports on mother and baby homes, which were often critical of conditions, the evidence suggests that the department preferred to use persuasion, not compulsion to implement improvements. The department's main interest appears to have been the occupancy figures, and the rising cost of maintaining women and children in these homes.[83]

This Act did not apply to the Magdalene system.[84]

Conclusion

A notice which appeared in the *Connacht Tribune* on 25 August 1928 tells us much about the status of women in Ireland and makes it clear that so much of Ireland's brutal treatment of women and children was carried out in plain sight:

> On Thursday morning a young woman inmate of the Magdalen Asylum, Galway, whose name was stated to be unknown, escaped from the institution. She is described as being aged about 25 years, wearing a black skirt, and had a slight stoppage in her speech.[85]

The strange breed of 'young woman inmate' did not even warrant the very basic ingredients of biography, the only distinguishing feature of certainty was her 'slight stoppage' of speech. However, in making a run for it, she pierced, briefly, the sanctimonious world of moral certainty Ireland was building on the backs of women such as her. The notice was presumably placed to aid in the woman's capture, thus enlisting broader society in the system of incarceration, while also offering an implicit warning to all women. While it is possible that the woman in question had been placed in the Galway Asylum by the courts,[86] it is equally possible that she had been referred there from an industrial school by her local priest due to what he considered to be an inappropriate family situation, or because she had survived sexual assault. Whatever the reason for her detention, it was not deemed necessary to reassure the Irish reading public that there was a legal basis for her recapture. The repeated use of criminal language in relation to single mothers may well have led many in Ireland, including women who became pregnant outside marriage, to believe that there was a legal basis for detaining single mothers who had not actually been convicted of anything.

If you Google Donnybrook Magdalene Asylum, the first site you encounter is that of the Justice for Magdalenes Research (JFMR) resource:[87] all subsequent sites on the first search page relate to plans to demolish the old laundry-asylum and build apartments in its stead.[88] It is fitting that the most immediate contemporary record of DML is a resource generated for and with the survivors of the asylum, by the group most active in attempting to have the historical record corrected, retained and augmented.[89] JFMR's site is followed in quick succession by numerous accounts of the capitalist pressures of modern Ireland, in which property is, and always has been, king. This is symbolic not just of twenty-first-century Ireland's obsession with property, but of the eighteenth-century origins of the Magdalene system itself, which was rooted in the concrete of modernity and a world vision moulded to contain certain populations and, thus, define the limits of social power. This was an inherently hierarchical system which created some forms of power for some women while limiting it for many others. It is important, too, that among the remnants of the Donnybrook site, photographed for an article on its possible future, there was casual evidence of the Irish State's involvement and use of the laundry system – one of the remaining laundry baskets was labelled 'Áras an Úachtaráin, Phoenix Park', that is the residence of the President of Ireland.[90] Far from disbanding an 'alien and degrading' system, the new Irish dispensation fortified and extended it. In fact, the role of the Irish State in folding the Magdalene system, including its ethos, into a wider panoply of institutions to contain Irish women, is a central feature of this history.

Contemporary Ireland first registered the asylum system, and its endurance into the 1990s, as a result of the controversy generated by the sale of High Park Magdalene asylum in Drumcondra, Dublin, in 1993, by the Sisters of Our Lady of Charity (OLC). The main basis for disquiet on that occasion was that the sale of High Park had resulted in the exhumation of the women buried on the site, so that it could be readied for redevelopment. As the journalist Fintan O'Toole put it in his characteristically perceptive way:

> The image of the Magdalen women being unable to rest in peace in the Ireland of global capital, stock markets and business heroes we are trying to construct is, or

at least should be, a haunting one. The past is full of unfinished business. It will not be finished until it is acknowledged and given its due.[91]

This was 'a history of chosen forgetfulness',[92] in which the contemporary exhumation and reinternment of Irish women, who had died in an institution created to obscure their lives, was emblematic of the continuance of the very power structures underpinning contemporary Irish patriarchal capitalism.[93]

Notes

1   Mary Evans and Kimberley Beach, *Making Respectable Women: Changing Moralities, Changing Times* (London: Palgrave Macmillan, 2020), 96. The link with sexuality, respectability and the building of nations and nationalisms was, of course, first comprehensively outlined by George Lachmann Mosse in *Nationalism and Sexuality: Respectability and Abnormal Sexuality in Modern Europe* (New York: Howard Fertig, 1985).

2   James M. Smith, *Ireland's Magdalen Laundries and the Nation's Architecture of Containment* (Manchester: Manchester University Press, 2008); ibid., 'The Politics of Sexual Knowledge: The Origins of Ireland's Containment Culture and the Carrigan Report (1931)', *Journal of the History of Sexuality* 13, no. 2 (2004): 208–33; Eoin O'Sullivan and Ian O'Donnell, 'Coercive Confinement in the Republic of Ireland', *Punishment and Society* 9, no. 1 (24 January 2007): 27–48.

3   Maria Luddy, 'Convent Archives as Sources for Irish History', in *Religious Women and their History: Breaking the Silence*, ed. Rosemary Raughter (Dublin: Irish Academic Press, 2005), 98–115.

4   For a history of Irish Catholic nuns, see Caitriona Clear, *Nuns in Nineteenth-Century Ireland* (Dublin: Gill and Macmillan, 1988); Mary Peckham Magray, *The Transforming Power of the Nuns: Women, Religion and Cultural Change in Ireland, 1750–1900* (Oxford: Oxford University Press, 1998).

5   There were multiple formulations, but the common trait was the centrality of a moral lesson.

6   The House Annals of St Mary Magdalen's 1909 to 1915, RSC Archives. See Introduction, this volume, for an explanation of access to this source.

7   Ibid.

8   Mary Fleming, death certificate, 4 January 1914 (General Register Office, Dublin). My thanks to Claire McGettrick for supplying this information.

9   Cara Delay, *Irish Women and the Creation of Modern Catholicism, 1850–1950* (Manchester: Manchester University Press, 2019), 31–47.

10 Katherine Byrne, *Tuberculosis and the Victorian Literary Imagination* (Cambridge: Cambridge University Press, 2011).

11 Mosse, *Nationalism and Sexuality*.

12 Maria Luddy, 'Prostitution and Rescue Work in Nineteenth-Century Ireland', in *Studies in Irish Women's History in the 19th and 20th Centuries*, ed. Maria Luddy and Clíona Murphy (Swords, Co. Dublin: Poolbeg, 1989), 51–84; Maria Luddy, 'Moral Rescue and Unmarried Mothers in Ireland in the 1920s', *Women's Studies* 30, no. 6 (November 2001): 797–817; Maria Luddy, *Prostitution and Irish Society, 1800–1940* (Cambridge: Cambridge University Press, 2007); Rebecca Lea McCarthy, *Origins of the Magdalene Laundries: An Analytical History* (Jefferson, NC: McFarland & Co., 2010).

13 Jacinta Prunty, *The Monasteries, Magdalen Asylums and Reformatory Schools of Our Lady of Charity in Ireland 1853–1973* (Dublin: Columba Press, 2017), 105; McCarthy, *Origins of the Magdalene*, 148. See also Mark Coen, Chapter 3, this volume.

14 Virginia Crossman, 'Middle-Class Attitudes to Poverty and Welfare in Post-Famine Ireland', in *Politics, Society and the Middle Class in Modern Ireland*, ed. Fintan Lane (Basingstoke: Palgrave Macmillan, 2010), 130–47.

15 Luddy notes that single mothers and prostitutes were often conflated by contemporaries. See Luddy, *Prostitution and Irish Society*, 195.

16 Arlette Farge, *The Allure of the Archives* (New Haven, CT: Yale University Press, 2013), 27.

17 Virginia Crossman, *Poverty and the Poor Law in Ireland, 1850–1914* (Liverpool: Liverpool University Press, 2013), 181.

18 Ibid., 173.

19 Ibid., 181.

20 Ó Ciosáin notes this association was made in Ireland as early as 1841. See, Niall Ó Ciosáin, 'Varieties of Literacy in Nineteenth-Century Ireland: Gender, Religion and Language', in *Literacy, Language and Reading in Nineteenth-Century Ireland*, ed. Rebecca Anne Barr, Sarah-Anne Buckley and Muireann Ó'Cinnéide, Society for the Study of Nineteenth-Century Ireland (Liverpool: Liverpool University Press, 2019), 16.

21 Delay, *Irish Women and the Creation of Modern Catholicism*, 31.

22 Ibid.

23 Lisa Godson, 'Charting the Material Culture of the "Devotional Revolution": The Advertising Register of the *Irish Catholic Directory*, 1837–96', *Proceedings of the Royal Irish Academy: Archaeology, Culture, History, Literature* 116C (2016): 293.

24 'Loretto Convent, Omagh', *Freeman's Journal*, 13 August 1863, cited in Mary Hatfield and Ciaran O'Neill, 'Education and Empowerment: Cosmopolitan Education and Irish Women in the Early Nineteenth Century', *Gender and History* 30, no. 1 (2018): 194.

25 Ibid.

26 Delay, *Irish Women and the Creation of Modern Catholicism*, 7.

27 Mary Louise Roberts, 'Beyond "Crisis" in Understanding Gender Transformation', *Gender and History* 28, no. 2 (12 July 2016): 357–8.

28 For a typical iteration of these fears see, Senex, 'The New Girl', *Irish Monthly* 54, no. 632 (February 1926): 738–44. The idea of women becoming masculine was often raised in relation to the suffrage movement in the late nineteenth and early twentieth century, see, for example, Nora Tynan O'Mahony's accusation that modern women (and suffragists) wore 'mannish' clothing and adopted an 'entirely masculine and (in a woman) ugly stride'. See, O'Mahony, 'The Mother', *Irish Monthly* 41, no. 484 (1913): 529–32. However, there is a definite increase in the articulation of this fear in the post-war world. See, A. F. Timm and J. A. Sanborn, *Gender, Sex and the Shaping of Modern Europe: A History from the French Revolution to the Present Day* (New York: Bloomsbury Academic, 2016), 96–112.

29 Sagart, 'How to Deal with the Unmarried Mother', *Irish Ecclesiastical Record: A Monthly Journal under Episcopal Sanction* 20, no. 5 (1922): 145–53.

30 Ibid., 145.

31 'Irish Morals', *Irish Times*, 2 March 1929.

32 Ibid.

33 Ibid.

34 *Irish Times*, 2 February 1926.

35 For example, in November 1922, the body of Lily Johnston was found in a field, having been brutally assaulted in the course of an attempted rape. 'Kicked to Death: Woman's

Long Struggle with Assailant', *Irish Times*, 3 November 1922, cited in Lindsey Earner-Byrne, 'The Rape of Mary M.: A Microhistory of Sexual Violence and Moral Redemption in 1920s Ireland', *Journal of the History of Sexuality* 24, no. 1 (2015): 75–98, 84.

36 'The Little Grey Motor Car: Evidence in Ticknock Murder Charge Cab-Driver's Story', *Irish Times*, 20 July 1925.

37 It appears she identified most with the name Lizzie O'Neill, which is the name she used when registering her son's name and the name most commonly used in relation to her. For the most detailed study of prostitution in Ireland, see Luddy, *Prostitution and Irish Society, 1800–1940*.

38 Jasmine Mulliken, 'The Stores (Pim's)', The Mapping Dubliners Project, available online: mappingdubliners.org/the-stores/ (accessed 4 July 2021).

39 Barry had been a member of the Irish Volunteer Force and was executed for a capital offence under the Restoration of Order in Ireland Act, 1920. For further details, see Richard Hawkins, 'Barry, Kevin Gerard', *Dictionary of Irish Biography*, available online: https://www.dib.ie/biography/barry-kevin-gerard-a0451 (accessed 10 September 2022).

40 According to Kevin Barry O'Neill's birth certificate, he was born to Lizzie O'Neill in the Coombe Maternity Hospital on 9 November 1921. Lizzie O'Neill was listed as resident at 2 Catherine's St. 'Kevin Barry O'Neill', no. 221, *Registrar's Book of Births for the City of Dublin*.

41 William Carrigan chaired the influential Committee on Criminal Law Amendment Acts of 1880 and 1885, between June 1930 and August 1931, often referred to as the Carrigan Committee. The committee dealt with a range of issues, from the age of sexual consent to contraception and censorship. See, Mark Finnane, 'The Carrigan Committee of 1930–31 and the "Moral Condition of the Saorstát"', *Irish Historical Studies* 23, no. 128 (2001): 519–36; Finola Kennedy, 'The Suppression of the Carrigan Report: A Historical Perspective on Child Abuse', *Studies: An Irish Quarterly Review* 89, no. 356 (2000): 354–63; Smith, 'The Politics'.

42 *Irish Times*, 2 February 1926.

43 Ibid., 3 February 1926.

44 Ibid.

45 Luddy, *Prostitution and Irish Society*, 195.

46 'Lizzie O'Neill', no. 372, 9 June 1925, *Registrar's Book of Deaths District of Dundrum*.

47 'Magdalen Asylum', *Cork Evening Echo*, 8 February 1926.

48 Cara Diver noted that in 1950, a woman alleged her violent husband had threatened to kill her in the same way as Honour Bright. This implies that the Bright murder lasted long in the social memory and was understood as an act of gender-based murder even if no one was ever convicted. Cara Diver, *Marital Violence in Post-Independence Ireland, 1922–96: 'A Living Tomb for Women'* (Manchester: Manchester University Press, 2019), 81.

49 'Magdalen Home, Dublin', *Irish Independent*, 15 February 1926.

50 See Máiréad Enright, Chapter 6, this volume.

51 'Great Social Problem: Aid Sought for Nobel Work', *Irish Independent*, 11 February 1929.

52 Ibid.

53 Miss Emily Buchanan of the Protestant Magdalen asylum on Lower Leeson Street, also advocated that all these homes should be under religious control. See 'Unmarried Mothers', *Irish Independent*, 24 September 1925.

54 'More County Institutions: Unmarried Others and Imbeciles', *Connaught Telegraph*, 27 September 1930.

55 'Board and Unmarried Mothers', *Irish Independent*, 26 August 1931.

56 *Meath Chronicle*, 25 October 1924; see also, 'Unmarried Mothers in County Homes', *Longford Leader*, 13 April 1929.

57 Clíona Rattigan, '"Half Mad at the Time": Unmarried Mothers and Infanticide in Ireland, 1922–1950', in *Cultures of Care in Irish Medical History, 1750–1970*, ed. Catherine Cox and Maria Luddy (Basingstoke: Palgrave Macmillan, 2010), 168–90; Clíona Rattigan, *What Else Could I Do?: Single Mothers and Infanticide, Ireland 1900–1950* (Dublin: Irish Academic Press, 2012). See also Lynsey Black, Chapter 8, this volume.

58 See, *Report of the Commission on the Relief of the Sick and Destitute Poor*, including the *Insane Poor Minutes of Evidence 1925* (Dublin).

59 *Minutes of Evidence 1925*, 14.

60 Ibid., 15.

61 Ibid.

62 Similarly, the Dublin Poor Law Union Workhouse on the Navan Road became St Patrick's Mother and Baby Home in 1919 (frequently referred to as Pelletstown) and was run by the Daughters of Charity of Saint Vincent de Paul. It was also a national school and orphanage and often catered for sick children or the children of sick parents. It closed in 1985.

63 The State's rationale for the use of the Magdalene system is articulated in *Annual Report of the Department of Local Government and Public Health, 1930–1* (Dublin, 1931), 129.

64 Memo from Department of External Affairs, Joseph Walshe to the Secretary of the Department of Local Government and Public Health, James Hurson, 'Letters/Reports Setting up of Repatriation Scheme UK/Ireland, 1939–50', 15 December 1936, cited in Lindsey Earner-Byrne, *Mother and Child: Maternity and Child Welfare in Dublin, 1922–60* (Manchester: Manchester University Press, 2017), 193.

65 Ibid. He made this observation in relation to the emigration of pregnant single Irish women to the UK; he wished to see the churches take control of the issue in Ireland, thus preventing this kind of prenatal emigration.

66 See this intention articulated in *Annual Report of the Department of Local Government and Public Health, 1927–8* (Dublin, 1928), 86; *Annual Report of the Department of Local Government and Public Health, 1928–9* (Dublin, 1929), 114; *Annual Report of the Department of Local Government and Public Health, 1930–1* (Dublin, 1931), 129; *Annual Report of the Department of Local Government and Public Health, 1931–2* (Dublin, 1932), 129.

67 *Report of the Local Government and Public Health, 1922–1925* (Dublin, 1926), 56.

68 The cost of three shillings a day for mother and child; there was no charge if the infant died. See *Annual Report of the Department of Local Government and Public Health, 1928–9*, 112.

69 *Annual Report of the Department of Local Government and Public Health, 1930–1* (Dublin, 1931), 130. The following year, the matron claimed that some 'girls first received into the Home are still there and have no desire to leave it. These girls have a great influence for good over the newcomers', *Annual Report of the Department of Local Government and Public Health, 1932–3* (Dublin, 1933), 55.

70 Britain was no utopia for single mothers but there was greater state support, earlier legal adoption and women were not required to stay long term in institutions after

giving birth. See, Pat Thane and Tanya Evans, *Sinners? Scroungers? Saints? Unmarried Motherhood in Twentieth-Century England* (Oxford: Oxford University Press, 2012).

71 'Illegitimate Children (Affiliation Orders) Act ,1930', Irish Statute Book, available online: www.irishstatutebook.ie/eli/1930/act/17/enacted/en/html (accessed 11 April 2021).

72 It resulted in the repeal of the Bastardy (Ireland) Act, 1863, which had allowed putative fathers to be sued for the maintenance of a child during the time that such child was in receipt of relief from the poor rates and while under the age of 14.

73 Mrs Mary B., X Tolka Road, Ballybough, (north-east Dublin city), 21 July 1937. Dublin Diocesan Archives, Byrne Papers, Charity cases Box 7: May 1937–Dec. 1939.

74 'Legitimacy Act, 1931', Irish Statute Book, available online: www.irishstatutebook.ie/eli/1931/act/13/enacted/en/html (accessed 11 April 2021).

75 Houses of Oireachtas, 'Legitimacy Bill, 1929—Second Stage', *Dáil Éireann Debate*, Thursday, 27 March 1930, vol. 34, no. 2, available online: www.oireachtas.ie/en/debates/debate/dail/1930-03-27/16?highlight%5B0%5D=law&highlight%5B1%5D=bill (accessed 9 April 2021). See also, 'Legitimacy Bill', *Irish Times*, 22 February 1930. 'Legitimacy Bill', *Irish Times*, 22 February 1930.

76 This was discussed during the readings of the bill and is reflected in section 1.2 of the Act which states: 'Nothing in this Act shall operate to legitimate a person unless the father and mother of such person could have been lawfully married to one another at the time of birth of such person or at some time during the period of ten months preceding such birth.'

77 Richard Devane S.J., a regular commentator on such issues, believed that this Asct was a necessary corollary of the Affiliation Orders Act and would bring the State's law in line with Canon Law, which regarded such children as legitimate. He considered this legislation to be part of a panoply of issues that required attention, including, for example, raising the age of sexual consent and amending the Criminal Law Amendment Act, 1885, to 'bring our legislation in relation to the protection of women and girls in line with that of Great Britain (1922) and Northern Ireland (1923)'. See Richard Devane, 'The Illegitimate Children Bill', letter to the editor, *Irish Times*, 6 November 1929. This view was broadly shared among social workers and charitable organizations involved with families and children, see, 'Protecting Children', *Irish Times*, 9 November 1934; 'Women Citizens Association: The Criminal Law Amendment Bill', *Irish Times*, 13 November 1934.

78 See 'Registration of Maternity Homes Act, 1934', Irish Statute Book, available online: www.irishstatutebook.ie/eli/1934/act/14/enacted/en/print.html (accessed 9 April 2021).

79 See, for example, 'Maternity Homes', *Irish Times*, 8 February 1934.

80 *Dáil Éireann Debates*, 7 February 1934, vol. 50, col. 1214.

81 The Saint Patrick's Guild, a Roman Catholic rescue society, run until 1943 by Mary Josephine Cruice, was one such agency which took in vulnerable, often 'illegitimate', children and baptized them. The children were then either temporarily housed at the guild's own home, placed in other institutions, boarded out in 'homes of respectable families' or offered for adoption. For example, in 1923, the guild interviewed 2,247 women seeking its services and received 2,007 letters. In that year, it admitted 143 children, discharged 98, while 32 died and 18 remained in the home. See *Annual Report of the Saint Patrick's Guild, 1923–24*, 8, 10. Dublin Diocesan Archives, Byrne Papers, Lay Organisations (2). Cruice charged mothers 25/- a month for keeping their children and £20 for arranging an adoption. See, Earner-Byrne, 'The Rape of Mary M.'.

By the mid-1930s, a birth mother could be charged up to £50 for the adoption of her child. See, Rattigan, *What Else Could I Do?*, 62; Sarah-Anne Buckley, 'Found in a "Dying" Condition: Nurse-Children in Ireland, 1872–1952', in *'She Said She Was in the Family Way': Pregnancy and Infancy in Modern Ireland*, ed. Elaine Farrell (London: Institute of Historical Research, 2012), 145–52. In 1943, the Guild was taken over by the Irish Sisters of Charity and Ms Cruice was given fulsome praise for her life's work. See, J. J. MacSheahan, S.J., 'St Patrick's Guild', *Irish Monthly* 71, no. 843 (1943): 357–65.

82 Earner-Byrne, *Mother and Child*, 200–2.

83 'Executive Summary', *Final Report of the Commission of Investigation into Mother and Baby Homes and Certain Related Matters* (Dublin: Department of Children, Equality, Disability, Integration and Youth, 2021), 8–9. The Commission's report notes that some homes were either not registered under the Act or registered late/many years after opening, for example, Dunboyne (ch. 24, p. 8), Regina Coeli (ch. 21, p. 36), Denny House (ch. 23, p. 20) and in other cases, e.g. the Bon Secours Mother and Baby Home in Tuam; it only had access to a small number of related inspection reports (ch. 15, p. 3).

84 The Act is not considered by the report that inquired into the running of these homes. See, Department of Justice, *Report of the Inter-Departmental Committee to Establish the Facts of State Involvement with the Magdalen Laundries* (Dublin, January 2013, aka *McAleese Report*, hereinafter *IDC Report*), 72–3.

85 'Patient's Escape Magdalen Asylum', *Connaught Tribune*, 25 August 1928.

86 For a range of offences from petty theft to infanticide. See *IDC Report*, 204–324.

87 This was the result of a Google search carried out on 1 August 2021: 'Justice for Magdalenes, Justice for Magdalenes Research: A Resource for People Affected by and Interested in Ireland's Magdalene Institutions', available online: http://jfmresearch. com/home/preserving-magdalene-history/donnybrook/.

88 Based on a Google search carried out in November 2021. For example: Gordon Deegan, 'Permission Granted for Apartments on Donnybrook Magdalene Site', *Irish Times*, 6 February 2020; Olivia Kelly, 'Donnybrook Magdalene Laundry Demolition Proposal Scrapped', *Irish Times*, 8 April 2017; 'Plans for Donnybrook Magdalene Laundry Development Gets Approval', *RTÉ*, 5 February 2020; Louisa McGrath, 'In Donnybrook, Future of Crumbling Magdalene Laundry is Uncertain', *Dublin InQuirer*, 9 March 2020.

89 For a thorough account, see Claire McGettrick, Katherine O'Donnell, Maeve O'Rourke, James M. Smith and Mari Steed, *Ireland and the Magdalene Laundries: A Campaign for Justice* (London: I.B. Tauris, 2021).

90 McGrath, 'In Donnybrook'.

91 Fintan O'Toole, 'GPA, Magdalen Women and the Underground Connection', *Irish Times*, 8 September 1993.

92 Ibid.

93 See Carol A. Brown, 'Patriarchal Capitalism and the Female-Headed Family', in 'Special Number on Women', special issue, *Social Scientist* 4, nos 4–5 (1975): 28–39.

3

'Cheap in the End'

A History of Donnybrook Magdalene Laundry

Mark Coen

It has been practically established that sin cannot be legislated out of existence, nor can the vicious be dragooned into virtue. But the grace of God can do all things. It is the grace of God that runs the Refuge at Donnybrook.[1]

In October 1837, a group of nuns took possession of Donnybrook Castle, a mansion on five acres outside the city of Dublin.[2] Queen Victoria had ascended the throne of the United Kingdom of Great Britain and Ireland at the age of 18, four months earlier. Donnybrook was one of the earliest foundations of the Religious Sisters of Charity (RSC), a pioneering order of Irish nuns founded by Mary Aikenhead in 1815.[3] The castle was renamed St Mary Magdalen's, in reference to the follower of Jesus wrongly described for centuries as a prostitute. For over 150 years, this saintly yet foreboding title would be accompanied by one of a series of words descriptive of the institution's function, most usually 'penitentiary', 'asylum', 'refuge', 'laundry' or, in later years, 'home'. In 1992, the nuns sold part of the laundry premises, accounting for a small proportion of the overall Donnybrook site. An early Victorian institution had remained operational for the first two years of Mary Robinson's term as President of Ireland.

This chapter provides an institutional history of Donnybrook Magdalene Laundry (DML), drawing on a variety of sources. These include biographies of Mary Aikenhead, her published letters,[4] books published by the RSC describing the congregation's varied works, material held at the Dublin Diocesan Archives (DDA), religious directories and periodicals, newspapers, memoirs of religious life, applications for planning permission and general histories. The RSC provided one day of access to the House Annals contained in their archives.[5] The Annals had to be transcribed rather than photographed, so this chapter provides only glimpses of an important source that is not in the public domain. Some correspondence was found on the laundry site and is now held at the University of Galway Archives.[6] The oral testimonies of survivors of Donnybrook, so crucial in understanding its operation and effect on the lives of women, are analysed in other chapters in this book.[7] The voices of nuns who worked in the institution are also of importance in telling the Donnybrook story, but such accounts are not available.[8]

The chapter sketches the outline history of the institution from its establishment in an earlier location in 1798 to its closure in 1992, highlighting key themes present in material that is predominantly publicly available. It also discusses some developments in the DML story that occurred after 1992. The chapter highlights how Donnybrook was presented to the world by the RSC and its supporters and emphasizes just how visible the institution was to the wider public. The infantilization of the women held in the institution and the RSC emphasis on the importance of the commercial laundry work are also recurrent themes. The chapter discusses in detail the withdrawal of a commercial laundry contract from DML by the Department of Defence, on the basis that the nuns were in violation of the fair wages clause contained in all State contracts. This episode illustrates concern about the *modus operandi* of the Magdalene laundries in some official circles in the 1940s and challenges our understanding of how those institutions were perceived, even when the power of the Catholic Church was at its height.

Origins

The institution known as St Mary Magdalen's was established in Donnybrook by the RSC in 1837. However, its origins are to be found in the endeavours of lay people almost 40 years earlier. The General Magdalen Asylum was established in 1798 by a Mr Quarterman and a Mrs Burke, 'two humble individuals engaged in domestic service'.[9] They raised sufficient funds by means of a penny collection to lease premises in Townsend Street, Dublin, for the reform of women involved in prostitution.[10] Management of the institution later passed to a Mrs Ryan, who was the niece of Dr Troy, the Archbishop of Dublin.[11] She is said to have established for the institution 'a high reputation'[12] in laundry and needlework. However, her health declined and the RSC took over the asylum in January 1833. It was their fifth foundation.[13] Mother Francis Magdalen McCarthy (who would become Superior General of the congregation after Mary Aikenhead's death) was put in charge and according to an official account, '[i]n her efficient hands the place was in a short time brought to a state of great perfection'.[14] In contrast, Aikenhead admitted in private correspondence that 'more sin than virtue progressed [there] for years after'.[15]

The inner-city conditions of Townsend Street were not regarded as suitable and by August 1835, Aikenhead was writing that she hoped Donnybrook Castle would soon be acquired by the congregation.[16] While in charge of the asylum, Mrs Ryan had accumulated the substantial sum of £1,500 and this enabled the RSC to buy the castle and fit up a laundry there.[17] The grounds also provided a new burial ground for the congregation.[18] In May 1836, Aikenhead recounted a visit to the property:

> I was at Donnybrook last Friday ... I am more than ever pleased with the place, it is well calculated for the purpose ... we shall have months of repairing and a new wash-house to build; but the place will be cheap in the end.[19]

An advertisement on the front page of the *Freeman's Journal* of 13 October 1837 advised the public that Townsend Street Asylum had relocated to Donnybrook, 'where the different branches of Washing, Making-up Family and Fine Linen, Mangling, Glazing and Needle Work, will be carried on with the strictest attention and punctuality'.[20] The notice expressed the hope that the change in premises would see an increase in the work given to the institution, all of which was completed 'by the labour and industry of the Penitent Inmates of the Asylum'.[21] Considerable thought had clearly been put into ensuring that no business would be lost in the move, as 'a confidential person'[22] remained in Townsend Street to receive business during the transitional period. In December of that year there were 36 women in the asylum,[23] increasing to 40 in 1839[24] and 50 by 1843.[25] Early notices seeking funds emphasized that the asylum would accept inmates of all religious denominations.[26]

In the early 1840s, the energetic Carmelite priest Fr John Spratt planned to establish, in his words, 'a new institution for the reception of unfortunate females'.[27] Spratt was a prominent temperance campaigner and the taking of a pledge of total abstinence from alcohol would have been a condition of admission to his proposed asylum. He envisaged that it would be called 'The House of the Good Shepherd' and would be under the management of the Good Shepherd Sisters. However, Archbishop Murray 'convinced'[28] him that women already in his charge should be transferred to DML and that all funds collected by Spratt for his project should be given to the RSC. It would seem that Murray was concerned that Spratt's initiative might detract from the endeavours of his friend Mary Aikenhead. Spratt was thereafter listed as a guardian of DML, which seems to have been a purely honorific title.[29]

Donnybrook and the foundress

Mary Aikenhead mentioned Donnybrook in her letters on a regular basis. She sought prayers from her correspondents for women who died or were ill. Of Peggy Barrett, who died in 1848, she stated:

> Thanks be to God, she was a true penitent. She is a very serious loss in every sense. Most important was the really good example of her steady pious conduct, she was very clever at all the laundry business, and so virtuously laborious, that really one might take her for a nun.[30]

Aikenhead also regularly discussed financial aspects of Donnybrook in her correspondence. In 1842, she recounted the 'curious' fact that the amount of money received from private benefactors in donations and bequests in the previous year was £1,700 – the same as the profit from laundry, needlework and bazaars in the same period.[31] On other occasions, she reported 'rather a falling off in the washing',[32] and lamented the effect on profit of paying for the men and horses necessitated by keeping two laundry carts on the road.[33]

Aikenhead took a keen interest in the buildings and architecture of all of her foundations, and Donnybrook was no exception. For example, in February 1845, she reported as follows to a correspondent:

At St Mary Magdalen's yesterday our dear and venerated Archbishop consecrated the really fine church bell, 'Mary Refuge of Sinners,' weight 550 lbs., and a smaller bell, 'St Mary Magdalen.'[34]

The absence of a proper drying room in the laundry caused her concern and she was pleased to report the commencement of its construction in June 1854.[35] On another occasion, she expressed the hope that 'separate sleeping places' would, in the future, be created at Donnybrook, in order to achieve 'entire separation at night for the penitents.'[36] Aikenhead often referred to Donnybrook anniversaries in her letters, noting that it was a certain number of years since the RSC had taken over the asylum, or since it had been founded in Townsend Street 'by pious individuals.'[37]

After many years of declining health, Mary Aikenhead died at the RSC convent at Harold's Cross on 22 July 1858. It was the feast day of St Mary Magdalen, a day of special significance at DML. The last words attributed to her were reputedly said the day before: 'If I die tomorrow, do not tell the poor penitents until the day after, as it would spoil their pleasure.'[38] Her funeral in the chapel of St Mary Magdalen's was attended by a 'crowded assemblage of Clergy', 'lay gentry' and 'interesting groups of inmates' from each of the Dublin institutions of the congregation, including women from Donnybrook.[39] The feast day on which Aikenhead died and her burial at Donnybrook were regarded as auguring well for the institution: 'With such holy omens ... how could the refuge for Magdalens at Donnybrook do aught but prosper in its holy work?'[40]

The women of Donnybrook

(i) Occupancy and admission routes

The typical number of women in Donnybrook at any one time was 100, after significant building works in the 1870s allowed for an increase. A slight rise in numbers occurred again in the 1930s (for example, there were 108 women in 1937)[41] and once more in the 1940s (115 women in 1943),[42] reaching a peak of 120 women in the 1960s.[43] Donnybrook was thus smaller than the other Dublin Magdalene asylums at Lower Gloucester Street (which housed 140 women in 1950) and High Park, Drumcondra (where there were 220 women in the same year),[44] but larger than St Patrick's Refuge in Dún Laoghaire where occupancy was 'typically 50 women at any one time.'[45]

Without access to the administrative records of DML, it is impossible to construct a full picture of the admission routes of the women who entered the institution. However, Luddy was permitted to view the nineteenth-century records a number of years ago and analysed the entry pathways. According to her research, the most common routes of entry between 1833 and 1899 were 'voluntary' (almost 40.95%) and 'religious referrals' (37.49%).[46] The latter involved referral by a member of the clergy. Referrals from the police and prisons accounted for a very low percentage (2.52%). According to Luddy's figures, 1,387 women entered DML during this period. A high proportion also left, with voluntary exits (44.48%) and expulsions (24.24%) accounting for the main reasons. These patterns cannot be taken as representative of entries and exits at Donnybrook in the twentieth century. Indeed, it has been observed that Magdalene institutions became more coercive and punitive after Irish independence in 1922.[47]

Some departures of women from DML were the result of interventions by outsiders. In the twentieth century, this could arise if a woman was deemed suitable for external work and a 'situation' could be found for her. For example, a priest called Father (Fr) Celestine Kelly resided in Donnybrook (in a Carmelite house and seminary called Gaybrook) in the 1950s and 1960s. He secured a position in domestic service for at least one woman held at DML.[48] Domestic work in private houses and religious-run schools and hospitals generally came with live-in accommodation, making it suitable as an exit job for the more fortunate women.

Some admission and occupancy information relating to DML in the 1970s exists in the public domain. Writing to Archbishop McQuaid in 1971, the Donnybrook nuns stated:

> The pattern is changing – many of the inmates are ex-psychiatric patients from St Brendan's Hospital, Grangegorman. These get a minimum measure of rehabilitation. They help in the laundry. Our own old penitents are beyond work – we feel we should keep them on. There are some, though not many, brought in 'off the street.'[49]

The language here is cold and dehumanizing, referring to 'these' and 'some' while omitting the word 'women'. Not every admission involved an adult; in 1976, a 16-year-old girl was taken to DML by a Garda in circumstances that are unclear. She spent two months there.[50]

(ii) Duration of stay

The typical duration of the women's stay arises repeatedly in the RSC literature. Aikenhead, in one of her letters, remarked that she hoped the women in the congregation's Magdalene asylum in Cork would:

> tend to make the asylum a place of permanent abode in the same way as ours in Donnybrook; felt by themselves to be voluntary, but too much valued to allow any temptation to leave the place to take possession of their minds.[51]

The Centenary Brochure of 1958 would have pleased the foundress, as it observed in relation to DML:'Although, there is no obligation on them to do so, most of the inmates remain for life.'[52] This is particularly interesting in light of the finding of the *Report of the Inter-Departmental Committee to Establish the Facts of State Involvement with the Magdalen Laundries* (*IDC Report*, 2013) that the median stay of women in Donnybrook was 20.3 weeks and the average was 61.8 weeks.[53]

A number of sources refer to women who had spent several decades in DML. An RSC book from the 1940s enthused:

Fifty years, sixty years – proudly they count out the years of their service spent in laborious, prayerful days and nights of glad rest after labour. There are young heads here too – heads as bright as Magdalen's when she spread the glory of her hair to wipe the Master's feet.[54]

This is confirmed by the account of the chaplain to Donnybrook in the early 1960s, who recalled that while a majority of the women 'were in their sixties, seventies and eighties', about one-fifth of the women were younger and 'came and went every two or three months'.[55] A retired member of the Factories Inspectorate recalled inspecting the laundry equipment in the mid-1980s and noticing very old women working: 'There were women of 70 plus years there with white hair.'[56]

The RSC's own publications, as well as the eyewitness accounts of third parties who had access to the institution, reveal that very elderly women who spent most of their adult lives there were a prominent feature of DML. This evidence, when combined with Claire McGettrick's findings from her research on the institution's burial ground (Chapter 11) raises serious questions about the accuracy of the duration of stay data contained in the *IDC Report*.

(iii) Involuntary detention

There is a large body of evidence that women were detained in Donnybrook against their will in both centuries of its existence. In the late nineteenth century, women who asked to leave encountered procedures designed to frustrate their wishes. The Reverend Mother of the period was quoted in an article explaining her system:

'[I]f I carried the keys of the big gate in my pocket, well' – with a meaning smile – 'there would be considerably more traffic in that direction than there is. But you see, when an inmate demands instant release, the key has to be fetched with some official formula from another part of the building, the girl's clothes have to be taken from a certain cupboard and identified, and by the time this has been done, as a rule, she has changed her mind.'[57]

Several accounts written by authors sympathetic to the RSC also allude to involuntary detention. Bayley Butler, an RSC sister, explained the challenging behaviour of some of the women by stating that they found 'their captivity irksome'.[58] A book about Mary Aikenhead published in 1979 observed:

Not all the penitents were there because of their eagerness to atone for their sins. Many of them had been sent by parents or guardians who had found them unmanageable, and they often continued to be troublesome in the asylum ... Their were others who came of their own will ...[59]

Catherine Rynne, writing in 1980, stated: 'Most of the girls were living with the nuns against their own wishes: caring for them, therefore, was no easy task.'[60] There are hints of preventative detention also, such as the statement in a 1956 charity sermon that some of the Donnybrook women were 'unfit to face the moral dangers of life'.[61] It is unlikely that the determination of fitness to engage with the sinful world was made individually and freely by the women involved.

A book about the RSC published in 1941 stated: 'There may be people even to-day who do not realize that these girls and women are free to go at any time. Nobody can detain them.'[62] The fact that the congregation felt the need to clarify that no laws confined the women to the institution suggests that there was a public perception of their involuntary detention. If such an external perception prevailed then it would not be surprising if it was also shared by the women within, with serious implications for their legal rights. The reverence with which nuns were treated in Irish society and knowledge that some of the women living and working with them were sent to the institution by the criminal justice arm of the State[63] may also have deterred some women from reflecting on the legitimacy and voluntariness – or otherwise – of their time at DML.

(iv) Redemption narratives

Many of the books about Mary Aikenhead published in the century after her death celebrated what they regarded as the redemptive work of DML, extolling a place 'of very wonderful conversions and very beautiful deaths'.[64] Tales of specific women were invoked to demonstrate the success of the asylum in its sacred mission. Women who had stayed in the institution for several decades, those whose characters had been dramatically reformed, those who worked hard and those who exhibited strong religious faith during a final illness featured prominently in these narratives of redemption. The life of Mary Gibbons, who died in 1848 after 17 years in DML, is discussed in a number of books. While working as a prostitute, she experienced a vision of hell, in which she believed God told her to pull out her eyes. She complied with the instruction and after a year in hospital, she entered DML where 'she was always gentle, silent, patient, and wonderfully industrious'.[65] Her story is described in one book as 'strange and wonderful'.[66]

Aikenhead's biographer, Sarah Atkinson, praises a number of unnamed Donnybrook women in her book, pointing to them as living lives of example and, as a consequence, having holy deaths. She emphasizes particular characteristics of these notable women, including kindness, helpfulness and encouragement of 'the ignorant young penitents'.[67] She mentions a woman who spent almost 50 years as a Magdalene, living a life 'of humble, unostentatious virtue, practical faith, sweet patience, and simple obedience'.[68]

The annals held by the RSC also recall individual women who died. For example, the annals for the years 1909 to 1915 discuss seven penitents whose deaths occurred in that period. A commitment to hard work was obviously greatly valued by the annalist, as the level of industry of six of the seven women is commented upon.[69] Biddy Judge 'came to the Institution at a very early age 17 or 18 and lived to an advanced old age, she was most laborious'. Margaret Maguire 'had a very hot temper' but was 'laborious and hard-working'. Fanny Martin 'continued her work as long as possible and when she could no longer work, edified all by her quiet endurance of pain and suffering'. Martha Fitzpatrick 'was a most earnest Penitent, very laborious and her example was an encouragement to all to work'. Katie Mahony 'did most beautiful embroidery, it was marvellous the amount of work she got through'. An adverse comment was made in relation to the working habits of the sixth woman, Katie Legget: '[S]he was inclined to be lazy and inert, but that was probably caused by delicacy'.

Atkinson is quite explicit in stating that many penitents died as saints and were recognized as such by the priest, nuns and women gathered around their deathbed. This image evokes a sense of community and care that may or may not accurately depict attitudes to dying women (or dying women regarded as worthy) at DML in the nineteenth century. But there is also a darker subtext – their heavenly reward is anticipated because they entered into complete self-abnegation, accepting the regime of hard work and total obedience prescribed by the religious authorities. In Atkinson's words, such women had 'found an outlet for their energy in toilsome manual work ... persevered to the end and won the crown'.[70] Analysing similar accounts of the deaths of women at High Park Magdalene Asylum in Drumcondra, Smith observes: 'the penitents are significant in death because they validate normative discourses of social and spiritual responsibility'.[71] The women who conformed and 'died in harness' were celebrated as success stories and held up as models for others to emulate. Their stories were misappropriated to lend credence to a system that viewed 'the washtub as the basis of sainthood for the Magdalen'.[72]

(v) Recreation

Some fleeting references to the lives of the women outside the working hours of the laundry can be gleaned from documentary sources. In 1935, a company performed 'The Pirates of Penzance' at DML, and also at the High Park and Gloucester Street Magdalene Laundries.[73] There are references to the performance of a variety show,[74] concert[75] and play[76] for the women in newspaper reports from 1965 to 1970. The women also appear to have taken part in some productions. An RSC publication of 1941 alluded to this aspect of life at DML:

> In this pleasant big room there is a piano, and an animated discussion, to which everybody contributes, nuns and layfolk, and the question at issue is the most attractive colour for the stage fittings, for this is a hall of music and drama.[77]

Fr Gaughan, who was chaplain at St Mary Magdalen's in the 1960s, remembers an annual Christmas show at the institution:

> The women, both those on stage and in front of it, would be at their most glamorous. On one occasion I congratulated one of the young women a Marilyn Monroe lookalike as quite a few of them were on her appearance. She replied good naturedly: 'Father, I would not do any business, if I had not my war paint on!'[78]

There is evidence of some recreational activity outside the walls of the institution in its later decades. An account in the *Irish Press* of a pilgrimage to the Marian shrine at Knock in 1961 noted that 'inmates' from DML were in attendance.[79] In the 1980s, and possibly earlier, there was an annual holiday to Skerries with Sister (Sr) Bernardine.[80] The surviving sources capture the exceptional rather than the routine in relation to the recreation time of the women. An annual show by a touring company or a trip to the seaside is worth recording, but it does not reflect the daily reality of life outside working hours, which must have been monotonous.

The religious community at Donnybrook

The number of nuns living in the convent at St Mary Magdalen's increased over time. Ten nuns were resident in 1860,[81] 12 in 1877,[82] 16 in 1890[83] and 19 in 1900.[84] For most of the twentieth century, the number was about 20, although it reached 26 in the late 1950s and early 1960s.[85] In the absence of access to records held by the RSC – if they still exist – it is impossible to ascertain how many nuns were involved in the day-to-day running of the laundry. However, it is clear that a significant proportion of the Donnybrook religious community were not actively engaged in its operation, although it was the dominant activity on the site.

A number of choir nuns[86] would have undertaken the other public activities of the convent, which, depending on the time period under consideration, included teaching in 'poor schools',[87] the organization of several sodalities for girls and women, 'visitation of the poor and sick in their homes' and the provision of meals to unemployed men.[88] In later years, a residential nursing home, Maryville, and a day centre for senior citizens, the Mary Aikenhead Centre, were established. Donnybrook was thus a 'multiple-project convent'[89] rather than solely a Magdalene institution, and this must have had implications for how its religious personnel were deployed. In addition to those employed in activities unrelated to the laundry, some nuns of the community may have been elderly or infirm. Others were lay (or domestic) sisters engaged in cooking and housework in the convent. Sacristan, portress (answering the convent door) and responsibility for the grounds and farm would likely have been other areas of responsibility.[90]

Mother Rectress presided over the entire convent establishment, aided by a deputy known as the Ministress and a local council of senior nuns. Under the Constitutions of the RSC, the Rectress was appointed by the Mother General of the congregation. A list of the women who occupied the position of Rectress at DML is contained in the Appendix to this book. In the early years, when there were fewer nuns in the community, it seems that the Rectress was heavily involved in the running of DML. However, it is probable that as the number of nuns and projects increased, the Rectress would have delegated charge of the laundry and the women to other nuns. Bearing in mind all of the above considerations, it seems unlikely that the number of nuns engaged in 'superintending labour'[91] in the laundry or being responsible for the women outside work hours ever exceeded 10. At times, particularly in the first forty and final twenty years of the institution, the number was probably considerably lower.

Nineteenth-century Donnybrook nuns

For over thirty years, until her death in 1870, Mother Mary Elizabeth Knaresborough was Rectress of Donnybrook. Atkinson attributed to Knaresborough 'a natural capacity for business'[92] and the achievement of getting the institution 'to a state of admirable efficiency'.[93] Atkinson continued:

> In her government of the penitents she was strict, and very exact with regard to regularity and industry; also endeavouring earnestly to maintain a spirit of charity among them. Insight and penetration she possessed in a remarkable degree.[94]

An anonymous Sister of Charity stated that Knaresborough was 'a strict disciplinarian' and that some of her nuns 'found her code of perfection fairly strenuous'.[95] Around 1884, Sr Mary Baptist Delany was appointed sister in charge of the penitents, a post she held for 28 years. The House Annals of Donnybrook recall her as follows:

> She governed the Penitents with a very firm hand, and they respected, and had the utmost confidence in her. They felt she acted from the very highest motives in this regard, that her one anxiety was for their souls' welfare: no one could ever say that she showed any partiality, all had to own that she was absolutely just. When she had to correct them, she did so when possible in private, and no one knew anything she said to them, unless as she expressed it, 'they were fools enough to tell themselves.'[96]

The descriptions of Knaresborough and Delany emphasize qualities that one might expect to find in accounts of schoolteachers from the same period, with their emphasis on maintaining order and not exhibiting favouritism. The grown women in their charge were infantilized. Indeed, a late Victorian article about Donnybrook in the Irish periodical *The Lady of the House* quoted the Reverend Mother (who is unnamed but was, according to the *Irish Catholic Directory* of 1897, Mother Peter Synnott) as saying:

> They are children in temperament the majority that come to us, creatures of impulse, who live in the world immediately about them, who are urged by gusts of longing and desire, which subside almost as quickly as they arise.[97]

Sr Baptist Delaney died aged 55 and the annalist took the opportunity of considering her character in some detail. While incorporating the expected tributes, including that Delany was the 'most perfect model of a Religious',[98] the writer also made a somewhat frank disclosure:

> [S]he found the Penitents faults particularly trying, but no one ever guessed how distasteful she felt her duties, until some chance words she let fall a few years before her death, showed her feelings on the subject.[99]

This sentence prompts one to consider how some nuns assigned to Donnybrook and institutions like it must have struggled with the work they were assigned. For many, it must have been very different to the duties they had expected to undertake as Sisters of Charity, a generalist congregation with a wide range of potential postings. However, their training had emphasized unquestioning obedience and like Delaney they saw no alternative.

Twentieth-century Donnybrook nuns

Given the refusal of the RSC to permit further access to the Donnybrook Annals and to participate in an oral history project,[100] our knowledge of individual nuns involved in the laundry after the death of Sr Baptist Delaney in 1912 is very incomplete. A letter written by a Monsignor Walsh to Archbishop McQuaid in 1941 described the then Rectress of Donnybrook, Mother Frances Eucharia Greer, as 'quite a competent and experienced person, of long laundry experience' and also 'thoroughly alert and resourceful'.[101] There is more than a trace in these comments of Clear's observation: 'Nuns ... had a reputation as good economic managers.'[102]

Sr Teresa Bernardine Keane was an important individual in the Donnybrook story from the early 1940s to the late 1980s. A native of Claremorris, County Mayo, she was a nun at Stanhope Street Convent in the early 1940s[103] before moving to Donnybrook, where she registered the death of one of the women who died there in December 1943.[104] She regularly performed this function over the next forty years and seems to have been in overall charge of the women. She was described as the 'guiding genius' behind a two-day garden fête held as a fundraiser in 1968.[105] This was an elaborate event opened by the popular singer Dickie Rock. A committee called the Friends of St Mary Magdalen's was chaired by local Fianna Fáil TD Seán Moore who explained the object of the fête:

> For many years the Sisters of Charity have been running a laundry. Their plant is, to say the least, antiquated and they are losing business to the launderettes. A new plant is needed here and it will cost £5,000. The convent buildings also need renovation.[106]

The same event took place in the following year, with Sr Bernardine described as director of fundraising.[107] It is probable that the funds raised at these events were spent on the erection of a strikingly modern building at the laundry in the 1970s or 1980s, consisting of a large packing room and offices.[108] Sr Bernardine's name is included in the surviving expenditure books; it appears that the monthly pocket money for the women was given to her for distribution.[109] It is unclear if she was ever engaged in the practical side of the laundry business; the remaining sources indicate a senior administrative role. She remained involved in DML in the late 1980s, organizing an annual holiday to the seaside for the women.[110] She died in 1996.[111]

Some sisters spent a relatively short time working in Donnybrook. Sr Margaret Andrew Meade did so in the late 1940s, prior to attending teacher training college.[112] Sr Teresa Martin Hopkins (later known as Sr Catherine/Kit) did likewise at roughly the same time. The tribute written at the time of her death in 2012 recalled: 'She became very proficient in laundry work and this proved to be a valuable asset later on when she shared her skills with many sisters.'[113] Sr Mary Daniel McCarry was attached to Donnybrook from 1969 to 1977. On her death in 2020, the RSC noted: '[S]he worked with the residents and helped out in the laundry. She was noted for her kindness to the residents and kept up with many of them throughout the years.'[114]

Sr Peter Ignatius Stoker and Sr Lucy O'Sullivan were in charge of running the laundry in its final two decades. Correspondence between them and large institutional customers survives. A polite but firm exchange of letters occurred between Sr Peter Ignatius and Sr Mary Magdalen, the Secretary/Manager of St Vincent's Hospital (SVH) in the 1980s. Sr Mary Magdalen informed her counterpart in Donnybrook that the laundering of staff uniforms from SVH was moved to another RSC laundry at Stanhope Street Convent because of dissatisfaction with the results achieved at DML.[115] Conversely, Sr Peter Ignatius wrote on a number of occasions to Sr Mary Magdalen expressing concern about the condition of the laundry being received from the hospital. She pointed out that it contained inappropriate items, including paper and 'every imaginable kind of disposables', and that 'foul' laundry was not being submitted in sealed, soluble bags as agreed.[116]

The surviving correspondence indicates that Sr Peter was in charge in 1985 but that by 1988 Sr Lucy O'Sullivan had replaced her as Laundry Manager.[117] Whereas Sr Peter Ignatius' tone in correspondence was somewhat apologetic, one gets the impression that Sr Lucy was altogether more assertive and unflappable. In response to a query (in September 1992) from the National Maternity Hospital (NMH) about whether cot blankets were being damaged by 'bad handling or faulty equipment', Sr Lucy replied robustly, stating that the cause 'of what you term "tearing" . . . is a manufacturing fault and not in any way due to maltreatment in the washing process'.[118] O'Sullivan's brusque style is also evident in a report published in a local newspaper in 1987, where she stated that DML provided 'a good home' for women who would otherwise be homeless or in St Brendan's Psychiatric Hospital.[119]

A difficult station for sisters

Mary Aikenhead observed that 'the care of penitents' was the most difficult task entrusted to the congregation, giving rise to 'much anxiety' and fewer 'desirable results' than in any other of our holy functions'.[120] Those who have written about the foundress and the RSC have tended to parrot these sentiments, referring sympathetically to the trials the nuns were exposed to by the women. Atkinson described the situation thus:

> Though more withdrawn from public observation than most of the institutions under the care of the Sisters of Charity, the work of the Penitents' Asylum at Donnybrook was perhaps in some respects the most onerous and difficult of all. It needed unusual tact and prudence to carry on the daily routine of labour and to maintain order in an establishment whose inmates, varying in age and circumstances as well as in character, were as a rule naturally wayward, and not unfrequently turbulent.[121]

Similarly, Bayley Butler referred to women 'refusing to work, feigning illness and, in general, making life hard for those around them'.[122] As recently as 2001, a commentator stated: '[M]any of the inmates were unstable and not noted for gratitude.'[123]

Atkinson recounts acts of defiance among the women in the nineteenth century. One woman, instructed by Mother Rectress to adjust her cap, instead flung it on the floor and left the room. Atkinson characterized this as 'a humiliation for the mother',[124] particularly as it occurred in front of visitors to the laundry. She also describes women fighting amongst themselves as to who would do particular work, 'in such a state of excitement as to be almost ready to fall to blows'.[125] While such stories are recounted to illustrate the saintly patience of the nuns or the ultimate redemption of the women involved, they also suggest acts of resistance by the women and a more disrupted environment than might be expected. Whether acts of defiance were a common feature of the laundry in the twentieth century is less clear. The House Annals for the period 1909 to 1915 give the following report:

> The conduct of the Penitents continued uniformly good, this was largely due to the effect of Daily Communion, which had become an almost universal practice among the Penitents, and many a rising quarrel was checked by the 'fear of losing the Altar' as they expressed it.[126]

The Annals for the period up to 1921 again attested to the positive effects of daily Communion, adding: 'though they can be troublesome from time to time, the wild scenes of the past are D.G. quite unknown'.[127] While convent annals should be treated with caution as they are created by insiders with a view to posterity, the reference to 'the wild scenes of the past' is noteworthy.

When Sr Peter Ignatius wrote to the RSC manager of St Vincent's Hospital in 1984 to complain that 'foul' laundry was not being packaged properly, she referred to the potential for discord: 'Our girls are by no means fastidious, but one man complained that union workers would refuse to handle this laundry and I fear this spirit might spread.'[128] This correspondence provides an insight into the management of potential dissent by the nuns in the final decade of DML.

The laundry operation

The running of a large public laundry was a major undertaking requiring considerable organizational and administrative skill. Laundering to a standard acceptable to customers was obviously crucial to the success of the business and entailed departments devoted to specific tasks such as sorting, marking, washing, drying, ironing, folding and packing. Ensuring that the rightful owners received their laundry back from the large volume of items being processed at any one time and that meticulous records were kept of payments due and received were among the other imperatives. Complaints from customers, particularly those with lucrative commercial contracts, had to be carefully investigated and resolved.

The division of the labour force into different departments or sections, each performing specialized tasks, is captured in a description of DML from an RSC publication of 1941:

> [H]ere they are sorting the clothes, here marking, here the big machines plunge blankets down and up again, down and up again; in this room the whole care is to put just that perfection of finish to our fine linen; this department is packing; out

here in the sunlight are socks and shirts and towels in serried ranks, each of its kind.[129]

A sheet of paper found affixed to the wall on the Donnybrook site provides evidence of the division of the women into sections. It outlines the membership of 'Section C: Folding Department of Packing Room', apparently for fire evacuation purposes. The section consisted of twelve members, including the 'Section Leader' Sr Maura.[130] Eleven women are named, with one designated 'Assistant Leader' of the section. There may also have been dedicated departments within the laundry for certain types of clothing. For example, one commercial laundry had a shirt department with women working on the ironing and finishing of different parts of each shirt.[131]

For most of the life of DML, clothing and domestic habits were quite different to those of today. Mother Peter Synnott is quoted in an article from 1897 referring to 'the miles of frills and flounces which we have to stiffen and puff out, and which are yearly growing more elaborate, more intricate and luxurious'.[132] Tablecloths, napkins and blankets were used extensively in hotels and middle-class households up to the later decades of the twentieth century. Until the 1930s, men's shirts had separate collars that required starching.[133] Handkerchiefs and shop coats were among the other common items that have since fallen out of fashion.[134]

Contracts for institutional laundry were an important aspect of DML's business, particularly in the twentieth century. In the 1920s and 1930s, the laundry secured contracts to do the laundry from a number of Dublin teacher training colleges[135] and the British and Irish Steam Packet Company.[136] A receipts book from 1978–80 reveals a wide variety of contract customers at DML, including hotels (the Royal Dublin Hotel, Power's Hotel, the Grey Door Hotel); hospitals (the NMH, the Mater Private, St Vincent's Hospital); restaurants (Captain America's, Grundy's, University College Dublin Restaurant); public bodies (the Blood Transfusion Service Board, State transport company CIE, the Commissioners of Irish Lights), the upmarket Switzers Department Store and exclusive private sports clubs (Fitzwilliam Lawn Tennis Club, Elm Park Golf Club).[137] The elite boys' boarding and day school Blackrock College was an important customer in this period also.[138]

In addition to these large contract customers, DML also received a large amount of business from religious communities of priests, nuns and brothers across Dublin.[139] Business from private houses came from customers living at Dublin's most prestigious addresses. The location of DML in upmarket Dublin 4 was helpful in this respect, with houses on nearby roads including Eglington Road, Burlington Road, Wellington Road and Shrewsbury Road featuring in typed customer lists.[140] Other prestigious locations where DML customers lived included Sandymount, Blackrock and Foxrock.[141] The proximity of DML to Dublin's leafy 'embassy belt' also ensured diplomatic business. The Argentine, Japanese, Canadian and French embassies are listed in surviving documents.[142] Laundry from Áras an Uachtaráin, the official residence of the President of Ireland, was also sent to DML.

Laundry work was physically demanding and repetitive. Even when performed for pay in privately owned laundries, it was 'drudgery' akin to domestic service.[143] In the 1940s, the Irish Women Workers' Union stated: 'Laundry work is performed in a heated atmosphere causing, in hot weather especially, great fatigue, excessive perspiration and blistered feet.'[144] Workers who participated in the 1945 Laundresses' Strike (which did not affect the Magdalene laundries) recalled the laundries of the time as very noisy, sweaty environments. Burns from feeding sheets and tablecloths into calenders – enormous, heated rollers that dried and pressed large items – were common. A hand becoming caught and burned was also a real risk. The unloading of heavy, wet washing and its separation after it was squeezed in a spin-dryer were also described as physically demanding by these women.[145] There were other hazards, too: in 1983, Sr Mary Magdalen of SVH wrote to Sr Peter Ignatius to apologize that razor blades were found in sheets sent from the hospital to DML.[146] In earlier periods, prior to mechanization, all washing would have been done by hand by women standing at rows of sinks. It is difficult to discern the level of mechanization at Donnybrook at different times, but one gets a sense that the manual washing of most items was conducted well into the twentieth century, until modernization became unavoidable. The annalist recorded:

> This year 1920 it was thought advisable to get some machinery into the Laundry in order to compete with the Public Laundries which were so well-equipped in this respect, so a Hydro-Wringer and a Washing Machine were put up and the electric power for both was installed.[147]

A letter from Mother Rectress to a civil servant in 1941 refuted an assertion made at a public meeting that convent laundries started work at 6 am, stating: 'Our penitents are never at work before 9 O'C [sic] and it is generally 9.30 as we often have 2nd Mass and they are at it.'[148] She added that the women had lunch at 11 am, dinner at 2 pm for an hour and tea at 6pm when the laundry was closed. A former Factories Inspector who visited the DML premises in the 1980s described them as 'Dickensian' but added that they were typical enough of 'laundries run by nuns, health boards, etc. at the time'.[149]

While the women worked in the laundry for no pay, there were some paid, generally male, employees. Men who drove carts and later vans were employed to conduct the laundry collections and deliveries. The boiler house probably required a male attendant for at least some of the laundry's existence. There may also have been a maintenance man who had knowledge of all the laundry equipment and could effect minor repairs to machinery. The surviving financial records indicate that a bookkeeper was employed and in later years there appear to have been a number of male employees, some of whom were supervisors.

In addition to laundry work, there is evidence of other labour being engaged in by the women of DML. The institution had a commercial relationship with Walpole Brothers of Suffolk Street, a high-class purveyor of Irish damask and linen, hosiery and wedding trousseaux.[150] Sales of work were also held on the premises; at one such sale in 1925, 'there was a large collection of very beautiful needlework, embroidered linen and hand-made lingerie trimmed with Irish lace'.[151] A 1956 charity appeal by the Carmelite priest Fr Hugh Byrne broadcast on national radio referred to leather craft and rug-making as activities engaged in by the women.[152] It is possible that such products were made during 'recreation' periods in the evenings, when the laundry was closed.

The military contract

Labour historian Marie Jones notes that in 1941, a contract for Defence Forces laundry was secured by DML, resulting in a commercial laundry laying off 25 paid female employees.[153] The *IDC Report* stated that it had been unable to verify if DML had been awarded such a military contract.[154] However, documents contained in the Dublin Diocesan Archives reveal that such a contract did indeed exist. More significantly, it was subsequently revoked by the Department of Defence on the basis that the RSC were in violation of the fair wages clause, which was a standard term in all State contracts. The episode reveals Church–State interactions of an unexpected nature for the period, with the religious authorities on the back foot. The correspondence also demonstrates the unshakeable conviction of the RSC in the legitimacy of their business model, a core element of which was the non-payment of wages.

On 23 May 1941, an official in the Department of Defence wrote to Mother Frances Eucharia Greer at Donnybrook. He stated that 'representations' had been received by the Department that DML was in breach of the fair wages clause contained in the contract for the laundry of a number of Dublin military barracks and invited her to respond.[155] In her reply, Mother Frances Eucharia stated that she had 'gone into the matter with our van-men and found all satisfied and in order'.[156] Moving on to the women, whom she referred to alternately as 'inmates' and 'penitents', she explained that there were 115 of them and that all kinds of expenses were incurred by the institution on their behalf:

> We have to find them in everything, pay a Doctor for weekly attendance, supply all medicines etc, Food bedding [sic], and clothes, are a big item these times. Then there is the upkeep of their larger establishment necessary to house so many, this needs repairs of all kinds ...

She then referred to the cost of running the actual laundry, mentioning the purchase of two boilers in 1939 and 'heavy rent and taxes'. The reference to rent and taxes is curious; the laundry premises was owned by the RSC and no taxes were payable on the laundry profits because of its designation as a charity. Unable to rebut the allegation that fair wages were not being paid, Mother Frances Eucharia instead emphasized the charitable nature of the enterprise:

> In a Public laundry if the work gets light the workers are dismissed, here no matter how light the work gets we keep our Penitents ... As we support more girls than any public laundry, I cannot see why ther [sic] is any objection raised to our securing work for them, all they earn is spent on them and a good deal more. We the Sisters who actually work with them doing what they do, give our services gratis for the salvation of these poor girls.

The letter also contains an argument that it is not reasonable to apply the same rules to the women at DML as those in paid employment in non-convent laundries; whereas the latter employ 'only efficient workers', at DML 'many of them are mentally deficient.'

If the institution did not exist, 'many of them would be in the County Home or on the Streets'. A short reply from the Department of Defence advised Mother Frances Eucharia that the contract would be terminated on 31 July.[157] Evidently annoyed by the fact that the Department had not engaged with the points she had made, she replied on 8 June 1941:

> There is no use seemingly of stating our cause, as I have already written all about our inmates-Penitents [sic] and the expense of their upkeep and got no reply … Surely it is not too much to expect our own Catholic Government will give some helping hand to a charitable Institution.[158]

Two months later, Mother Frances Eucharia decided to raise the matter with Archbishop McQuaid. She explained the delay in contacting him by saying that the Mother General of the RSC had told her not to bother him about it, but two priests had since told her that she should. The letter reveals the lobbying engaged in by the RSC in an effort to retain the military contract, the political pressure that had defeated them and their concern that Magdalene laundries would no longer receive State work:

> We got friends to speak to the Authorities on our behalf, but the answer given was that nothing could be done as a promise had been given to the Labour Party that the contract would be taken from us and given back to a Public Laundry. There is nothing now to prevent the Labour Party from taking all the contract work from Convent Laundries all over the country, in fact two years ago it was taken from the Good Shepherd Sisters in Cork and given to a Protestant Laundry, and now from us![159]

In subsequent correspondence, Mother Frances Eucharia informed Archbishop McQuaid that the RSC were having a Novena of Masses offered for the intention of a good outcome to the military contract episode.[160] In a note to a Monsignor Walsh who met with Mother Frances about the issue, McQuaid wrote: 'It is a strange procedure on the part of this good woman to approach me, after five months of negotiations and after a final decision of the Department.'[161] The implication appears to be that if he had been informed about the issue before the contract was terminated he could have brought his considerable influence to bear. However, it was now impossible for him to do so. There is no evidence in the Dublin Diocesan Archives of what happened next, but it appears that the military contract was not restored to DML.

Donnybrook and the Archbishops of Dublin

The Archbishop of Dublin was an important figure in relation to all religious institutions within his archdiocese, and DML was no exception. One of the powers of the Archbishop was the appointment of the priest who would act as chaplain. Sometimes there was a dedicated chaplain, while in other periods the priests of Donnybrook parish took on the responsibilities in addition to their parish work. In 1907 the Rectress of DML, Mother Gonzaga Keating, wrote an eight-page letter to Archbishop Walsh complaining in the most forthright terms about Fr James Williams, who had been appointed to Donnybrook parish the year before. It is clear that Mother Gonzaga regarded Fr Williams as a disruptive influence on the women. She alleged that he insisted on hearing the confession of a woman who wanted to wait until her usual confessor came. She further alleged that on a subsequent occasion when he asked to see this woman again and was refused by the sister in charge:

> he rang the hall door bell + asked the portress to send him the Penitent which of course she could not do without telling the sister in charge, who came to tell me about it. I then had a very unpleasant interview with Father Williams in the parlour.[162]

One reason Mother Gonzaga gave for limiting the access the priest had to the women was that he had previously advised women to leave the institution. She argued that this was inappropriate because in one case the woman was an alcoholic and in another the woman would be returning to a husband 'who had nearly killed her by ill treatment'. An alternative reason is perhaps discernible in the correspondence. The Rectress alluded to the fact that the priest 'spent a remarkably long time' with one of the women and 'had the effect of upsetting others in whom he seemed to take this special kind of interest'. While her concern may have been limited to the advice he was giving women to leave, there is potential for a darker reading relating to sexual misconduct also. Whether this was justifiable based on Fr Williams' conduct or merely a tactic by Mother Gonzaga to ensure his removal by the Archbishop is impossible to know. One thing is clear; she wanted him gone:

> I am sorry to trouble your Grace with all these details but in the interest of this Institute (sic) under my charge I feel it my duty to do so. We find it hard enough to manage the Penitents + if the priests who hear their confessions are in opposition to us, it would make it almost impossible.

While the reply of the archbishop does not survive, Father Williams was moved to Howth, a coastal town on the other side of County Dublin, in the same year. He had spent only one year in Donnybrook.[163] The Williams episode reveals a Rectress of strong views and forceful expression, and a pragmatic approach by Archbishop's House.

A different dynamic between the Donnybrook nuns and the Archbishop of Dublin emerges from the period when Archbishop McQuaid was in office. During that time, a number of proposals to change the nature of the activities undertaken on the DML site were submitted to the Archbishop for his approval. In June 1965 Mother Teresa Anthony Heskin, the Mother General of the RSC, wrote seeking endorsement of a proposal that St Mary Magdalen's would become 'a training centre for mentally handicapped persons, male and female, over 16 years of age'.[164] In reply, McQuaid described the proposal as 'cloudy'.[165] He was concerned about the combination of men and women 'in the same narrow surroundings'. He also objected to the inclusion of the words 'possibly' and 'probably' to describe how various aspects of the training centre would operate, noting acidly: 'This is very amateur phrasing indeed.' Mother Teresa Anthony sent a gushing reply, expressing her gratitude for 'Your Grace's excellent letter.'[166] She continued: 'I know I should feel very much ashamed of the document I sent to Your Grace.' Then, misremembering McQuaid's characterization of the phrasing, she stated: 'Immature is the word for it!' She promised to rework the proposal having sought legal advice. A letter from the Archbishop dated October 1965 indicated that he was satisfied that the proposal had been clarified. He stated that he approved it in principle but enjoined the Mother General to ensure 'that you may be protected in regard to the Ministry and the National Rehabilitation'.[167] This appeared to be a concern relating to the role of the State in the proposed scheme. It seems that no such training centre was ever established.

In 1971, the RSC sought the Archbishop's 'sanction and blessing . . . to erect a Home for the Aged Poor' at Donnybrook and to avail of a substantial grant from the Dublin Health Authority for that purpose.[168] A reply indicated that McQuaid saw merit in such an institution but directed the RSC 'to examine very closely the implication of receiving a grant from the Dublin Health Authority'.[169] As with the training centre proposal in the 1960s, McQuaid appeared to be troubled by the potential for state interference where public monies were accepted by a church institution. This proposal also does not seem to have borne fruit.

Another point of contact between the Archbishop and the Donnybrook nuns arose in respect of the annual radio charity sermon, for which the Rectress of Donnybrook had to obtain permission. Thanking Archbishop McQuaid for his permission in July 1952, Mother Frances Eucharia Greer wrote:

> The Appeal is a great help to the Home where we have at the moment one hundred and fifteen Penitents. I would ask Your Grace's blessing for them, as they are in retreat for St Mary Magdalens Day.[170]

In her 1956 correspondence on the radio appeal, she wrote: 'Our home thank God is full 118 so we know Divine Providence will not fail to supply their needs.'[171] Overall, the surviving correspondence between the RSC at Donnybrook and the Archbishop of Dublin is businesslike in tone and concerned issues that required his resolution or permission. Occasionally there were letters of thanks, as when Mother Peter Synnott acknowledged a donation by cheque of £50 from Archbishop Walsh in December 1900.[172]

Donnybrook and the Gardaí

One of the most striking features of the DML premises is its proximity to Donnybrook Garda Station. It is possible to walk from the laundry to the rear of the Garda station in half a minute. This physical proximity appears to have underpinned close personal relationships between the nuns and the Donnybrook Gardaí (police). The use of the institution as a place where women were sent by the courts, both on probation and in lieu of imprisonment,[173] presumably also gave rise to considerable contact with the

Gardaí. In February 1952, one Martin Maher was jailed for six months for obtaining £3 from the Reverend Mother at Donnybrook by falsely claiming that he was a Guard in need of a loan until pay day.[174] Fr Anthony Vaughan, who was chaplain at St Mary Magdalen's in the early 1960s, recounted that the Mother Superior arranged accommodation for him with a Garda Superintendent's widow.[175]

Visibility

Donnybrook was not a secret, known only to the few who gained entry, local people who passed its high walls or those who consumed the RSC publications discussed in the next section of this chapter. Friends and allies of the institution ensured that it featured regularly in newspapers and charity sermons (which were broadcast on national radio for many years, ending in 1970).[176] The women performed for a select audience in an annual Christmas concert: 'Local dignitaries and especially those who supported St Mary's throughout the year would be honoured guests.'[177] They were also highly visible at the annual local Corpus Christi procession.[178]

The *Freeman's Journal* was a great supporter and advocate of the institution in the nineteenth century. A journalist who visited the premises in the 1850s stated: 'The modest demeanour, cheerful looks, and evident unaffected piety of the poor inmates, were most cheering to contemplate.'[179] The importance of the asylum was emphasized by spelling out for the reader the perils from which the women had been saved. They had been 'snatched not only from a life of infamy and sin, but also rescued from the deeper degradation of becoming renegades to their faith and hypocrites in religion'.[180] The newspaper resorted to even more denigratory language later in the century, when it praised Donnybrook for 'making out of those who were noxious pests, a disgrace and an insult to humanity, and a shame and a scorn to life, honest, virtuous, patient, industrious, pious, penitent, and practically good women'.[181] Nor did the piece end there, referring to the salvation by the asylum of 'outcast wanderers' living 'lives of the blackest infamy' who had been exercising a 'poisonous influence' on others.[182] This language was not only condemnatory and dehumanizing but also created the misleading impression that all the women admitted to the asylum were engaged in prostitution.

In the twentieth century, paid advertisements seeking donations to DML appeared to become more common. An *Irish Times* notice seeking funds expressed satisfaction that many of the women 'have been of their own free will more than fifty years in rigorous penance'.[183] During the First World War, an appeal for funds drew a direct analogy between the international conflict and the mission of DML:

> At present men are called to the Front to fight for their country but at home there is a far more serious warfare going on around in which all are asked to fight – namely, to aid the Sisters of Charity, Donnybrook, to fight for souls against Satan.[184]

The centenary of Catholic Emancipation occurred in 1929 and was marked with a commemorative programme organized by the Catholic Truth Society,[185] culminating in a Mass in the Phoenix Park attended by half a million people.[186] The official *Catholic Emancipation Centenary Record* contained adverts for all four Magdalene convents in Dublin.[187] The one for Donnybrook stated that it was 'badly in want of Funds owing to the unavoidable additional expenses which had to be incurred in the upkeep and repair of the Institution during the year.'[188]

Accounts of charity sermons preached to raise funds for Donnybrook were a staple of newspaper reporting in both centuries of the institution's existence. A common feature of these was an allusion to the fact that the ability of the nuns to accept new entrants would be dependent on the success or otherwise of the appeal. A failure of the collection would have a direct impact on the salvation of souls:

> How sad it would be if, through lack of funds, the Sisters were forced either to reduce the number of their penitents, or to refuse admission to some poor sinner, touched by grace and seeking ... shelter.[189]

Bequests left to the institution were also reported in newspapers, reinforcing its existence and operation in the public eye.[190]

In addition to advertisements seeking charitable donations, discussed below, others were solely commercial, soliciting business for the laundry. Religious publications such as *The Standard, Irish Jesuit Directory, The Irish Rosary, The Capuchin Annual* and *St Anthony's Annals*[191] featured adverts emphasizing various features of the laundry service. The claim that no chemicals were used and that van collections and deliveries occurred on a daily basis were emphasized.[192] 'All work under personal supervision'[193] was included on occasion. The college annuals of prestigious Catholic schools in the Dublin area were another favoured outlet for advertising. The wording of the *Blackrock College Annual* advertisement remained constant over several decades. It invited comfortably off suburban parents to 'entrust your laundry with comfort to St Mary Magdalen's Laundry Donnybrook'[194] and occupied either a full or half page. A quarter-page advert with the same wording appeared in the annual of another school operated by the Holy Ghost Fathers, St Mary's College, for many years.[195] These advertisements made no direct reference to the penitential dimension of the laundry; their message was solely directed to attracting custom for an enterprise '[u]nder the care of the Sisters of Charity'.

Presenting Donnybrook to the world

In the twentieth century, the RSC produced three publications showcasing their institutions: one in 1941, another in 1943 (marking the centenary of the appointment of Mary Aikenhead as Superior General for life) and the third in 1958 (marking the centenary of her death). These books describe the purpose and merits of each foundation of the congregation, accompanied by photographs. Their tone is triumphalist. For example, the 1941 book says of Donnybrook: 'What a work is this! – what a social service! – done for the greater glory of God, and so social service on the highest plane.'[196] In similar vein, the writer enthuses: 'And some of the penitents have seen sixty years of that work. Wonderful record!'[197] The piece is quite explicit in describing the laundry operation and emphasizes that the women stay voluntarily. However, it is rather less clear in explaining why a woman would come to enter the institution in the first place. St Mary Magdalen's is described as catering for the 'wayward, hurt, sinful or sinned-against soul'[198] who will be 'served and assisted by the spiritual daughters of Mother Mary Aikenhead, whose joy was to serve the lowly'.[199] There is a veiled reference to prostitution: 'The wayward girl, especially when she is at the mercy of economic circumstances, has been a problem in many climes, for many ages.'[200] The opacity reaches its zenith in a patronizing pen picture:

> Look at this placid, fair, old face. She has not a care in the world, as she explains just how the electric washing-machine operates. Yet, there must be a story behind the old unwrinkled forehead. Somewhere, sometime, someone blundered. Perhaps of her own free will she came here to the quiet arms of Charity. Perhaps she was gently led here. We will never know. The old hurt, whatever it was, is now God's secret.[201]

The references here and earlier to 'sinned against' women coming to DML is interesting. One could speculate about whether their inclusion in accounts of the institution was motivated by a desire to seem non-judgemental, not to unduly restrict the categories of women who might be committed, or both. If the former, it jars with the continuous references to 'penitents' and 'inmates'. Equally, there is a concerted attempt to evoke a sense of peace, serenity and calm, which sits uneasily with our knowledge of the harsh working conditions of laundries generally in the 1940s and with the complaints of the nuns about the challenges of maintaining order in the institution.

The publications of 1943 and 1958 outlined the work of Donnybrook in much less detail and used the same text. The key passage reads:

> Founded in 1833, for those who, like Magdalen, have turned from evil surroundings to a life of peace and prayer ... A public laundry gives them occupation and helps towards their upkeep.[202]

The comparison with Mary Magdalen and the reference to 'evil surroundings' once again evoke prostitution. It is interesting that this narrow description of the women was chosen, in contrast to the much broader one in the 1941 volume. DML was also featured in books published by Donnybrook parish. A book to mark the blessing of a new church in 1957 was keen to emphasize that not all the women were penitents, 'but all are souls who, for one reason or another, need the safeguard of an institution such as this'.[203]

From the beginning of the 1960s, a change in nomenclature is evident, with the term 'penitents' falling out of favour and being replaced by 'girls'. Pejorative adjectives like 'wayward' and 'fallen' and comparisons to Mary Magdalen also disappeared. 'Asylum' and 'refuge' were also dropped in favour of 'home'. In 1961, the RSC produced a slim volume, rather oddly entitled a 'Yearbook' of St Mary Magdalen's. Mostly consisting of advertisements, photographs of religious paintings and information about how to say the Rosary, the first page explains the institution:

Since [1833] it has been carrying out its mission of providing a home for young girls who found it difficult to save their souls in the world outside and who spend their lives in a peaceful, happy and spiritual atmosphere.[204]

With an echo of the 1941 book, triumphalism is evident: 'How wonderful it is to note the success of our mission.'[205] There is also an interesting reference to religious and moral decline:

In these times of irreligion and forgetfulness of God, the Home in Donnybrook forms an oasis of prayerful work – done for God and for souls. Here lives are lived in reparation – some going on for forty and fifty years. Here we strive to make atonement for the forgetfulness and carelessness of others.

The dire assessment of the status of religion in Ireland in 1961 can only be read as a rhetorical ploy to focus and rally the faithful, considering that the power of the Catholic Church reached its apogee in the 1960s.[206] The language is also euphemistic and once more seeks to paint an idealized picture of serene surroundings. A book to mark the 100th anniversary of Donnybrook Parish in 1966 took a largely historical approach to St Mary Magdalen's, only briefly mentioning its current status as a 'home' for 'girls', made comfortable by electricity and central heating.[207]

Changing terminology relating to the institution at Donnybrook is also evident in other publications in the 1960s, in particular in the *Irish Catholic Directory*. From 1932 onwards, the following advertisement appeared annually:

St Mary Magdalen's
DONNYBROOK, DUBLIN
UNDER THE CARE OF THE SISTERS OF CHARITY
Your kind patronage for the Laundry department attached to the Institution – to enable the Sisters to carry on this work of redeeming charity – will entitle you to a share in the prayers of the Penitents.

However, in 1962, this advertisement appeared for the last time. The use of the word 'penitent' was going out of fashion for the RSC, at least in public. The *Directory* listed each religious institution in the Diocese of Dublin, naming its Superior, specifying its number of religious and outlining the works in which it was involved. In 1959, the Donnybrook entry stated:

ST. MARY MAGDALEN'S ASYLUM, Donnybrook. Founded 1833. *Rectress*, Mother Mary Senan. Community, 26. Penitents, 115. *Chaplains*, Parochial Clergy.[208]

The word 'asylum' was removed from the entry from 1961 onwards. In 1964, 'Penitents' was excised in favour of 'Girls'. In 1970, the reference to St Mary Magdalen disappeared, the institution being described merely as Donnybrook. The entry changed substantially in 1977, with the institution named as 'St Magdalen's Home for Girls' and the women also referred to as 'residents'. Finally, in 1990, the institution was renamed in the

Directory as a 'Residential Centre for Women', which was accompanied by the addition to the entry of 'Public Laundry'.[209]

The adoption of the term 'girls' in the 1960s to describe the women was very deliberate. It made the institution sound less punitive and implied that those detained there were young and helpless. It provided a justification for infantilization. It was also highly inaccurate, because the women were adults. Indeed, many were well advanced in years, a fact to which RSC publications frequently alluded. As the decades passed, vagueness regarding the function and status of the institution increased. In 1979, Sr Bernardine Keane wrote to a newspaper to draw attention to 'a sale of work and super wheel-of-fortune to raise funds for a new building for girls attached to the convent'.[210] Community charity groups donated money to 'Mary Magdalen Home, Donnybrook (for [the] aged and destitute)'.[211]

The language of 'mental handicap' was also used to explain the presence of the women and the purpose of Donnybrook. A former Sister of Charity recalled attending a Christmas concert put on by the Donnybrook women when she was a novice and being surprised 'that several of them were intellectually disabled'.[212] A letter submitted as part of a planning application on behalf of the RSC in 1994 – a year after the exhumation of Magdalene graves at High Park Convent in Dublin caused controversy – seemed to deliberately obscure the origins of the women and the reason for their presence on the site. The application sought permission to demolish the old accommodation block, which had been replaced by a nursing home for the surviving women. However, in describing the structure, no reference was made to the fact that it had housed women associated with a Magdalene laundry. Rather, '[t]he building was used as a residential block in recent years for the mildly mentally incapable ladies including some adult Downes Syndrome [sic] ladies in the care of the Sisters of Charity'.[213] The Magdalene story was thus concealed (a mere two years after the closure of the laundry) and the erroneous impression was given that all residents had an intellectual disability. It must be asked if this was a convenient, blanket label to apply to women who were suffering the effects of institutionalization and possibly medicalization. It may have also been partly influenced by the fact that the RSC received grants from the state on the basis that some of the women were 'permanently disabled or subnormal unemployable females'.[214]

Controversy and criticism

While criticism of the Magdalene system was relatively muted until the 1990s, it did exist. Michael John Fitzgerald McCarthy, in his famous polemic of 1902, *Priests and People in Ireland*,[215] discussed DML specifically. Outlining the various institutions operated by the RSC and their sources of income, he continued:

> They also conduct a Magdalene Penitentiary at Donnybrook, in which they do a large laundry business, and get the free labour of a hundred penitents. The bedroom doors of the poor penitents are locked at night, and they are bound to stay in that penitentiary at the hard work of laundry for the best years of their lives;

and should they ever leave it, they find themselves in a world in which they are more helpless than they were on the day of their birth.[216]

It is interesting that Fitzgerald Murphy highlighted not only labour exploitation and deprivation of liberty but also the long-term effects of institutionalization. Referring to the women as 'poor galley-slaves', he stated that Jesus imposed no such life on 'the original Magdalene'.[217] Murphy was highly unusual in the unflinching terms in which he discussed Catholic-controlled institutions. A softer tone was felt necessary eight decades later in the 1980s, when a local newspaper investigated DML. The investigative article was prompted by unspecified 'adverse criticism of the working conditions'[218] there. While the journalist put allegations of unfair treatment and exploitation to the nun in charge, he was disarmed by her interaction with him:

> Certainly there is nothing underhand in their methods. The nuns answered all my questions courteously and frankly and allowed me access to the laundry and to the workers. 'We have nothing to hide' says Sister Lucy [O'Sullivan]. 'We are not riding around in big limousines or drinking champagne.'[219]

The reporter acknowledged that none of the women voiced any complaints during his visit. With its conclusion about the 'much appreciated role' of the RSC, the article appears to acquiesce in the redemption narratives of the RSC. However, it is important for a number of reasons. First, it suggests that there was at least some public disquiet about DML in the 1980s. Second, although the article is superficially deferential to the nuns, it makes connections between the laundry and – for the RSC – unwelcome terms including 'profit' and 'exploitation'. Third, it permitted the reader to draw their own conclusions on a range of issues, including why there were 'no complaints' from the women in circumstances where they could be overheard by the nuns on whom they were completely reliant for food and shelter. Information provided in the piece (the recent sale of RSC land in Donnybrook for over £1 million; the fact that the RSC received a Health Board grant for each woman and part of the old age pensions of the older women) publicized significant sources of income additional to the laundry revenue. Fourth, the piece records a time when the nuns were sufficiently confident in what they were doing to answer queries robustly and directly. It predates their vow of silence regarding the institution they ran at Donnybrook for 155 years.

Sale of the laundry business and its aftermath

Donnybrook was one of the last Magdalene laundries to close, which it did in 1992, with only the Sean McDermott Street Magdalene Laundry in Dublin remaining open thereafter.[220] The Magdalene Laundries at Peacock Lane, Cork (also owned by the RSC), and High Park in Drumcondra had closed in 1991 and a number of others, including those at Limerick, Waterford and Galway, had closed in the 1980s.[221] The closure of Donnybrook as a Magdalene laundry appears to have attracted no media attention, in contrast to the closure of the final such institution at Sean McDermott Street in 1996, which received some coverage.[222]

The RSC sold part of the laundry buildings to a private operator. The sale related to a very limited part of the Donnybrook site, containing only part of the original laundry, and the price was £200,000.[223] The RSC had already received approximately £1.5 million for the sale of eight acres of the Donnybrook Convent lands to a developer in 1986.[224] According to the *IDC Report*, two women who lived in St Mary Magdalen's were employed by the new owner of the laundry.[225] No further detail is supplied in relation to this arrangement and it is thus unclear if and how they were paid and if they continued to live on the Donnybrook Convent site. The enterprise was being advertised as 'The Sisters of Charity Laundry' as late as September 1993, with the slogan 'Continuing over 150 years of traditional quality laundry'. Evidently the association with the standards of the former Magdalene Laundry was of importance to its new management.[226]

Meanwhile, the residential dimension of St Mary Magdalen's, containing the women who had worked in the laundry, was renamed St Margaret's. Modern living quarters in the style of a nursing home were erected in 1992, replacing the large barrack-style accommodation block from the nineteenth century. The kitchen, dining room and sitting room in the old building remained in use until the building of a replacement structure around 1994. A planning application to demolish the accommodation block submitted in 1993 described the former sleeping quarters of the women as 'in very poor structural repair' and 'infected by dry and wet rot'.[227] Permission was subsequently granted for the demolition of that large building, in which generations of DML women had slept. In addition to women who had worked in the laundry, St Margaret's also admitted women with intellectual disabilities who had no affiliation with DML.[228] In May 2019, St Margaret's closed its residential centre and the residents moved into their own homes in the community. A Health Service Executive newsletter that featured this development stated: 'This event marked the last day in the chapter of the lives of the 70 women who had lived most or all of their lives in institutions.'[229] St Margaret's has been reimagined as 'a not-for-profit service, supporting people with intellectual disability (to move) (in their journey) from residential services to a life of their own choosing in their own homes'.[230] Its relationship with the RSC is not clear from its website and although 'Donnybrook' features in the site's domain name, its physical address is given as Stillorgan, Dublin. The building which previously housed St Margaret's has been refurbished and in July 2021, was inaugurated as a new community of RSC sisters called Rosemount.[231] Meanwhile, at the time of writing in 2022, the part of the DML site sold in 1992 has not yet been redeveloped. Important contents and documents found on the site from summer 2018 onwards have been acquired by the National Museum of Ireland and the University of Galway Archives.[232]

After the publication of the *IDC Report* in 2013, the four congregations that owned and operated the ten Magdalene laundries in the Republic of Ireland issued statements. The RSC statement was noteworthy because it contained an apology, whereas the other three religious orders confined themselves to expressions of regret. The RSC stated:

> We apologise unreservedly to any woman who experienced hurt while in our care. In good faith we provided refuge for women at our Magdalene homes in

Donnybrook and Peacock Lane. Some of the women spent a short time with us; some left, returned and left again and some still live with us.[233]

While the unreserved nature of the apology is welcome, there are notable omissions. There is no reference to the laundry and the unpaid labour carried out there. Nor is there any reflection on whether the treatment visited upon women within the institution accorded with Christian values or the teachings of Christ, which are supposed to inform the actions and activities of members of Catholic religious congregations.

Conclusion

Donnybrook Magdalene Laundry was the creation of an eminent nineteenth-century Irishwoman, Mary Aikenhead. Her burial in its grounds is deeply symbolic of how central the institution was to the mission of the congregation she founded. Its ethos of redemption through constant prayer, unrelenting labour and removal 'from the snares of the world'[234] persisted for well over a century after her death in 1858. Only as the 1960s progressed can one discern a shift in style in RSC representations of the place. It is doubtful if the regime within changed very much in that decade, but there was a growing realization that references to 'penitents' and the satisfaction of reforming them were becoming less publicly acceptable. From that time on, the institution retreated more and more from public view, mentioned euphemistically as a 'home' for 'girls' or the intellectually disabled, with a laundry of high reputation attached.

The refusal of the RSC to permit researchers to access their archives in an open and meaningful way is a hindrance to research, but this chapter demonstrates that much material is publicly available. In turn, these sources serve as a reminder that Donnybrook and institutions like it were not hidden from public view. On the contrary, they were highly visible in newspapers, religious magazines, directories, school annuals, church sermons and radio appeals until 1970. They were a source of pride for many Catholics and attracted their enthusiastic support in donations, bequests and laundry business. There are some things that only RSC records could tell us; for example, the admission circumstances of women and the degree to which factors such as prostitution, pregnancy outside marriage, rape and sexual assault, and rebellion against familial and religious authority were involved. However, the telling of the institutional story is not dependent on the cooperation of the RSC; even information about key nuns and major customers can be unearthed in its absence.

The removal of the military contract from DML in the 1940s, told in detail in this chapter for the first time, reveals not only an awareness on the part of the State that the labour exploitation inherent in the Magdalene system was problematic, but also a decision to deprive the institution of publicly funded business on that basis. The episode is arresting for a number of reasons. In particular, it highlights deficiencies in the *IDC Report*, which asserted that it was unable to verify if DML had been awarded a military contract. If the Committee had conducted appropriate research, it would have discovered that at least some elements of the Irish government, at certain periods, were prepared to acknowledge that there were serious breaches of law at DML and were prepared to take action. The episode also offers a glimpse of how the entire Magdalene system might have been deprived of government contracts and perhaps ultimately been rendered unviable, fifty years before DML actually closed. Unfortunately, it is most noteworthy for its exceptionality. The revocation of the military contract was atypical in a state built on deference to the Catholic Church.

Donnybrook is in many ways emblematic of what has been termed 'the long nineteenth century of Irish Catholicism', which Tom Inglis defines as beginning in 1850 and ending in 1970.[235] However, a case can be made that the Catholic Church in Ireland had an even longer nineteenth century, opening in 1829 with Catholic Emancipation and closing in 1995 with the passage of the divorce referendum by a tiny margin. The Donnybrook story fits perfectly into this revised timeline, beginning with the RSC takeover of the Townsend Street Asylum in 1833 and ending with the closure of the laundry in 1992. Nor was DML an insignificant outpost in this long nineteenth century of church-state entanglement. Mother Senan Mulcahy became Superior of the Donnybrook convent in the late 1950s, at a time when her brother Richard was leader of the Fine Gael party and a government minister. Garret FitzGerald, a later leader of Fine Gael who twice served as Taoiseach, recalled 'canvassing the nuns and residents in the Donnybrook Magdalene Asylum'.[236] The grounds of the institution were visible to the aspiring young politician from the upper windows of his house on Eglington Road, which he purchased in 1959.[237]

Notes

1   *The Irish Sisters of Charity: Giving a Brief Sketch of the Foundations of the Congregation* (Dublin: Anthonian Press, 1941, hereinafter *Brief Sketch of the Foundations*), 26.
2   In later years, the RSC enlarged their landholding in Donnybrook. See Nicholas Donnelly, *A Short History of Some Dublin Parishes* (Dublin: Catholic Truth Society of Ireland, 1905), vol. 1, 44.
3   See Mark Coen, Chapter 1, this volume.
4   *Letters of Mary Aikenhead* (Dublin: M. H. Gill & Son, Dublin, 1914, hereinafter *Letters*). This volume runs to over 550 pages.
5   A request for further access was refused on the basis that access had already been provided.
6   See Barry Houlihan, Chapter 10, this volume.
7   See Katherine O'Donnell, Chapter 4, this volume; Chris Hamill, Chapter 5, this volume.
8   The RSC declined an invitation from the editors to engage in an oral history project with nuns who had links with DML. See the Introduction to this volume.
9   Sarah Atkinson, *Mary Aikenhead: Her Life, Her Work and Her Friends* (Dublin: M. H. Gill & Son, 1879), 222.
10 Margery Bayley Butler, *A Candle Was Lit: The Life of Mother M. Aikenhead* (Dublin: Clonmore & Reynolds), 147.
11 Archbishop John Troy died in 1823 and was succeeded by Archbishop Daniel Murray.
12 Atkinson, *Mary Aikenhead*, 222.
13 The previous foundations were located at Upper Gardiner Street, Dublin; Stanhope Street, Dublin; Cork City and Sandymount, Dublin. See ibid., 499–500.
14 A Member of the Congregation, *The Life and Work of Mary Aikenhead* (London: Longmans, Green & Co., 1924, hereinafter *Life and Work*), 138.

15 *Letters*, 185.
16 Ibid., 62.
17 Atkinson, *Mary Aikenhead*, 281–2.
18 Ibid. The cemetery at Donnybrook is the focus of Claire McGettrick, Chapter 11, this volume.
19 *Letters*, 68.
20 'The General Magdalen Asylum', *Freeman's Journal*, 13 October 1837, 1.
21 Ibid.
22 Ibid.
23 'General Magdalen Asylum, Donnybrook', *Freeman's Journal*, 28 December 1837, 1.
24 'General Magdalen Asylum, Donnybrook', *Freeman's Journal*, 27 December 1839, 1.
25 'General Magdalen Asylum, Donnybrook', *Dublin Evening Post*, 28 December 1843, 1.
26 Ibid. See also 'Magdalen Asylum, Donnybrook', *Dublin Morning Register*, 30 December 1837, 1.
27 'Letter to the Editor', *Freeman's Journal*, 29 November 1843, 3.
28 A. E. Farrington, *Rev. Dr Spratt, O.C.C.: His Life and Times* (Dublin: James Duffy and Co., 1893), 153.
29 *Irish Catholic Directory 1860*, 169.
30 *Letters*, 191. In relation to the illness of Catherine Murphy, see ibid., 220. On the death of Elizabeth Leeson, see ibid., 224. Regarding the death of Anne Curran, see ibid., 235.
31 Ibid., 126. On bequests, see Máiréad Enright, Chapter 6, this volume.
32 *Letters*, 228. See also ibid., 198.
33 Ibid., 224.
34 Ibid., 165.
35 Ibid., 238, 272.
36 Ibid., 224.
37 Ibid., 199, 205, 451.
38 *Life and Work*, 428.
39 'The Late Mother Augustine Aikenhead', *The Tablet*, 31 July 1858, 490.
40 *Brief Sketch of the Foundations*, 26.
41 *Irish Catholic Directory 1937*, 209.
42 *Irish Catholic Directory 1943*, 179.
43 *Irish Catholic Directory 1960*, 115.
44 *Irish Catholic Directory 1950*, 233–4. No figure is provided in the 1950 Directory for the number of women present in St Patrick's Refuge, Dún Laoghaire, County Dublin.
45 Department of Justice, *Report of the Inter-Departmental Committee to Establish the Facts of State Involvement with the Magdalen Laundries* (Dublin, January 2013, hereinafter *IDC Report*), 25.
46 Maria Luddy, *Women and Philanthropy in Nineteenth-Century Ireland* (Cambridge: Cambridge University Press, 2009), 128.
47 James M. Smith, *Ireland's Magdalen Laundries and the Nation's Architecture of Containment* (Manchester: Manchester University Press, 2007), 81.
48 Information provided to the author. Fr Kelly was the Superior of Gaybrook in the 1960s. See 'New Superiors for Carmelites', *Sunday Independent*, 12 May 1963, 5. One of his brothers was a missionary bishop in Sierra Leone and another was President of Clonliffe College, the seminary where priests were trained for the Archdiocese of Dublin. See 'Missionary Bishop Dies', *Irish Press*, 13 February 1952, 7. Fr Kelly died in 1986: 'Father Celestine Kelly, ODC: An Appreciation', *Irish Times*, 23 April 1986, 11.

49 Typed memorandum entitled 'St Mary's Donnybrook' with an annotation in Archbishop McQuaid's handwriting dated February 14, 1971, Dublin Diocesan Archives (DDA), McQuaid Papers, Religious Orders (Female).

50 *IDC Report*, 320.

51 *Letters*, 254–5.

52 *The Irish Sisters of Charity: Centenary Brochure* (Dublin: Mount Saint Anne's, 1958, hereinafter *Centenary Brochure*), 151.

53 *IDC Report*, 170.

54 *Brief Sketch of the Foundations*, 27.

55 J. Anthony Gaughan, *At the Coalface: Recollections of a City and Country Priest* (Dublin: Columba Press, 2000), 72.

56 Ibid., 572.

57 'The Sisterhood of Sorrow No. II – The Magdalens', *The Lady of the House*, 15 March 1897, 7, 8 (hereinafter, 'The Sisterhood').

58 Bayley Butler, *A Candle*, 148.

59 Margaret Donovan, *Apostolate of Love: Mary Aikenhead 1787–1858* (Melbourne: The Polding Press, 1979) 98.

60 Catherine Rynne, *Mother Mary Aikenhead* (Dublin: Veritas Publications, 1980), 23.

61 '£14,000 Debt on Magdalen Home', *Irish Independent*, 23 July 1956, 9.

62 *Brief Sketch of the Foundations*, 29.

63 See Lynsey Black, Chapter 8, this volume.

64 *Life and Work*, 200.

65 Ibid., 202. See also Bayley Butler, *A Candle*, 143–7.

66 *Life and Work*, 201.

67 Ibid.

68 Ibid.

69 The seventh and most dramatic account of a woman in the Annals of that period relates to Mary Fleming. Her story is discussed in Lindsey Earner-Byrne, Chapter 2, this volume.

70 Ibid.

71 Smith, *Ireland's Magdalen Laundries*, 41.

72 'Prostitution: Its Nature and Cure', *The Irish Citizen*, 22 February 1922, 315.

73 'Gilbert and Sullivan', *The Standard*, 25 October 1935, 6.

74 'Show at Asylum', *Evening Herald*, 26 April 1965, 7.

75 'Gave Enjoyable Concert', *Evening Herald*, 30 April 1968, 5.

76 'The Press Diary', *Irish Press*, 22 January 1970, 8.

77 *Brief Sketch of the Foundations*, 27.

78 Gaughan, *At the Coalface*, 73.

79 'Many Irish Exiles Abandon the Faith', *Irish Press*, 22 May 1961, 3.

80 Alan Sinclair, 'Penitents' Laundry Work – "Therapy"', *Donnybrook Review*, June 1987, 11. My thanks to Dermot Lacey for bringing this article to my attention and providing me with a copy.

81 *Irish Catholic Directory 1860*, 166.

82 *Irish Catholic Directory 1877*, 153.

83 *Irish Catholic Directory 1890*, 154.

84 *Irish Catholic Directory 1900*, 119.

85 See, for example, *Irish Catholic Directory 1959*, 115; *Irish Catholic Directory 1962*, 115.

86 The distinction between choir nuns and lay sisters is discussed by Mark Coen, Chapter 1, this volume.

87 *The Religious Houses of the United Kingdom Containing a Short History of Every Order and House* (London: Burns & Oates, 1887), 139. The school was on Belmont Avenue and the RSC taught there until 1912. See *Parish of the Sacred Heart Donnybrook* (Dublin: John T. Drought, 1966), 49.

88 Ibid., 102.

89 Caitriona Clear, *Nuns in Nineteenth-Century Ireland* (Dublin: Gill & Macmillan, 1987), 111.

90 A list of the areas of responsibility of particular nuns in Mount St Anne's Convent, Milltown, is contained in the papers of Archbishop Byrne. See DDA, Byrne Papers (Nuns) – Sisters of Charity.

91 *Letters*, 126.

92 Atkinson, *Mary Aikenhead*, 470.

93 Ibid.

94 Ibid.

95 *Life and Work*, 195.

96 The House Annals of St Mary Magdalen's 1909 to 1915, RSC Archives.

97 'The Sisterhood', 8.

98 Ibid.

99 Ibid.

100 See the Introduction to this volume.

101 Letter from Monsignor P. J. Walsh to Archbishop McQuaid, 15 August 1941, DDA, McQuaid Papers, Religious Orders (Female).

102 Clear, *Nuns*, 130.

103 'Births, Marriages and Deaths', *Irish Press*, 8 December 1943, 3.

104 Rose Dowdall, death certificate, 18 December 1943 (General Register Office, Dublin). My thanks to Claire McGettrick for supplying this information.

105 'From Garden Fete to Garden Fete . . .!', *Evening Herald*, 10 June 1968, 10.

106 Ibid.

107 'Going Places', *Evening Herald*, 16 June 1969, 9.

108 A search for the planning file for this substantial addition to the laundry in the Dublin City Archives yielded no results. Subsequent correspondence with the officials there also revealed nothing.

109 St Mary Magdalen's Expenditure Book Jan 1962–Dec 1976, entry for November 1976. Multiple references of this nature occur in St Mary Magdalen's Expenditure Account Jan 1977–Oct 1987. This document is deposited in the University of Galway Archives.

110 Sinclair, 'Penitents' Laundry', 11.

111 Her grave marker in the cemetery at DML gives 1996 as the year of her death. It also states that she was born in 1915 and entered religion in 1933. My thanks to Claire McGettrick for supplying this information.

112 'Sister Margaret Andrew Meade', Religious Sisters of Charity, available online: www.rsccaritas.org/index.php/we-remember/399-sister-margaret-andrew-meade (accessed 7 September 2022).

113 'Sister Catherine (Kit) Hopkins', Religious Sisters of Charity, www.rsccaritas.org/index.php/we-remember/405-sister-catherine-hopkins (accessed 7 September 2022).

114 'Sister Mary Daniel McCarry', Religious Sisters of Charity, available online: www.rsccaritas.com/index.php/we-remember/1149-sister-mary-daniel-mccarry (accessed 7 September 2022).

115 Letter from Sr Mary Magdalen of St Vincent's Hospital to Sr Peter Ignatius of DML, 9 December 1983, deposited in the University of Galway Archives.

116 Letter from Sr Peter Ignatius of DML to Sr Mary Magdalen of St Vincent's Hospital, 27 August 1985. See also, on the same subject, letter from Sr Peter Ignatius of DML to Sr Mary Magdalen of St Vincent's Hospital, 20 July 1984. These documents are deposited in the University of Galway Archives.

117 Letter from Sr Mary Magdalen of St Vincent's Hospital to Sr Lucy O'Sullivan of DML regarding a price increase, 8 July 1988, deposited in the University of Galway Archives. Sr Peter Ignatius died in 1989. See 'Family Announcements', *Evening Herald*, 19 June 1989, 30.

118 Letter from Sr Lucy O'Sullivan to Martin Hughes, Laundry Manager, National Maternity Hospital, September 1992 (precise date not included), deposited in the University of Galway Archives.

119 Sinclair, 'Penitents' Laundry', 11.

120 *Letters*, 170.

121 Atkinson, *Mary Aikenhead*, 466.

122 Bayley Butler, *A Candle*, 148.

123 Donal Blake, *Mary Aikenhead: Servant of the Poor* (Dublin: Caritas, 2001), 53.

124 Atkinson, *Mary Aikenhead*, 470.

125 Ibid., 472.

126 The House Annals of St Mary Magdalen's 1909 to 1915, RSC Archives.

127 Ibid.

128 Letter from Sr Peter Ignatius of DML to Sr Mary Magdalen of St Vincent's Hospital, 20 July 1984, deposited in the University of Galway Archives.

129 *Brief Sketch of the Foundations*, 27.

130 Efforts to identify this nun have been unsuccessful.

131 See the radio documentary *Blue Rinse and Starch – 1945 Laundress Strike*, available online: www.rte.ie/radio/doconone/757882-blue-rinse-and-starch-1945-laundress-strike (accessed 7 September 2022).

132 'The Sisterhood', 8.

133 Robert Tweedy, *The Story of the Court Laundry* (Dublin: Wolfhound Press, 1999), 16–17, 54.

134 Ibid., 16.

135 *IDC Report*, 681.

136 Letter from Mother Frances Eucharia Greer to the Secretary of the Department of Defence, 8 June 1941, DDA, McQuaid Papers, Religious Orders (Female).

137 General and Contract Receipts Ledger 1978–1980, deposited in the University of Galway Archives.

138 Document entitled 'Estimate of Weekly Usage of Linen', deposited in the University of Galway Archives.

139 Religious Accounts Book 1978–1984, deposited in the University of Galway Archives.

140 Typed customer list (no date), deposited in the University of Galway Archives.

141 Ibid.

142 Ibid.

143 Mary Daly, 'Women in the Irish Workforce from Pre-Industrial to Modern Times', *Saothar* 7, (1981): 74, 78.

144 Mary Jones, *These Obstreperous Lassies: A History of the Irish Women Workers' Union* (Dublin: Gill & Macmillan, 1988), 176.

145 See the radio documentary *Blue Rinse and Starch*.

146 Letter from Sr Mary Magdalen of St Vincent's Hospital to Sr Peter Ignatius of DML, 29 September 1983, deposited in the University of Galway Archives.

147 The House Annals of St Mary Magdalen's 1909 to 1915, RSC Archives.
148 Letter from Mother Frances Eucharia Greer to the Secretary of the Department of Defence, 8 June 1941, DDA, McQuaid Papers, Religious Orders (Female).
149 *IDC Report*, 573.
150 'The Sisterhood', 8. Walpole Brothers was the holder of a royal warrant.
151 'St Mary Magdalen's Home: Sale of Work', *Irish Times*, 28 November 1925, 10.
152 '£14,000 Debt on Magdalen Home', *Irish Independent*, 23 July 1956, 9.
153 Jones, *These Obstreperous Lassies*, 176.
154 *IDC Report*, 704.
155 Letter to Mother Frances Eucharia Greer from the Department of Defence, 23 May 1941, DDA, McQuaid Papers, Religious Orders (Female).
156 Letter from Mother Frances Eucharia Greer to the Department of Defence, 26 May 1941, DDA, McQuaid Papers, Religious Orders (Female).
157 Letter to Mother Frances Eucharia Greer from the Department of Defence, 30 June 1941, DDA, McQuaid Papers, Religious Orders (Female).
158 Letter from Mother Frances Eucharia Greer to the Department of Defence, 8 June 1941, DDA, McQuaid Papers, Religious Orders (Female). The date on the letter seems to be a mistake and should probably be July 1941.
159 Letter from Mother Frances Eucharia Greer to Archbishop McQuaid, 7 August 1941, DDA, McQuaid Papers, Religious Orders (Female).
160 Ibid., 26 August 1941, DDA, McQuaid Papers, Religious Orders (Female).
161 Letter from Archbishop McQuaid to Monsignor P. J. Walsh, 13 September 1941, DDA, McQuaid Papers, Religious Orders (Female), emphasis in original.
162 Letter from Mother Gonzaga Keating to Archbishop Walsh, 2 November 1907, DDA, Walsh Papers (Nuns).
163 J. Anthony Gaughan, *The Archbishops, Bishops and Priests Who Served in the Archdiocese of Dublin in the Nineteenth Century* (Dublin: Kingdom Books, 2013), 167.
164 Letter from Mother Teresa Anthony Heskin to Archbishop McQuaid, 23 June 1965, DDA, McQuaid Papers, Religious Orders (Female).
165 Letter from Archbishop McQuaid to Mother Teresa Anthony Heskin, 26 June 1965, DDA, McQuaid Papers, Religious Orders (Female).
166 Letter from Mother Teresa Anthony Heskin to Archbishop McQuaid, 29 June 1965, DDA, McQuaid Papers, Religious Orders (Female).
167 Letter from Archbishop McQuaid to Mother Teresa Anthony Heskin, 23 October 1963, DDA, McQuaid Papers, Religious Orders (Female).
168 Typed memorandum entitled 'St Mary's Donnybrook' with an annotation in Archbishop McQuaid's handwriting dated 14 February 1971, DDA, McQuaid Papers, Religious Orders (Female).
169 Undated copy of a letter from Archbishop McQuaid to Mother Teresa Anthony Heskin, DDA, McQuaid Papers, Religious Orders (Female).
170 Letter from Mother Frances Eucharia Greer to Archbishop McQuaid, 16 July 1952, DDA, McQuaid Papers, Religious Orders (Female).
171 Ibid., 5 March 1956, DDA, McQuaid Papers, Religious Orders (Female).
172 Letter from Mother Peter Synnott to Archbishop Walsh, 17 December 1900, DDA, Walsh Papers (Nuns).
173 See Lynsey Black, Chapter 8, this volume.
174 'Obtained Cash by Trick', *Irish Times*, 19 February 1952, 7.
175 Gaughan, *At the Coalface*, 72–3.

176 See 'Radio Eireann', *Irish Press*, 13 October 1970, 19. See also Máiréad Enright, Chapter 6, this volume.

177 Gaughan, *At the Coalface*, 73.

178 Information provided to the author.

179 'Magdalen Asylum, Donnybrook', *Evening Freeman*, 31 December 1859, 3.

180 Ibid.

181 Ibid., 31 December 1870, 2.

182 Ibid.

183 'Magdalen Asylum, Donnybrook', *Irish Times*, 11 December 1903, 4.

184 'Saint Mary Magdalen's Asylum, Donnybrook', *Irish Independent*, 11 December 1915, 8.

185 Miriam Moffitt, '"Ireland's Destiny is in the Making": The Impact of the Anniversary Celebrations of 1929 and 1932 on the Religious Character of Ireland', in *A Formative Decade: Ireland in the 1920s*, ed. Mel Farrell, Jason Knirck and Ciara Meehan (Kildare: Irish Academic Press, 2015), 225–6.

186 Dermot Keogh, *The Vatican, the Bishops and Irish Politics 1919–1939* (Cambridge: Cambridge University Press, 2004), 153.

187 Adverts for the Good Shepherd Magdalene Laundries in Cork and Belfast were also included.

188 *Catholic Emancipation Centenary Record* (Dublin, 1929), 31.

189 'Charity Sermon', *Irish Times*, 8 February 1937, 8.

190 See Máiréad Enright, Chapter 6, this volume.

191 This was a religious magazine produced by the RSC to raise funds for Temple Street Hospital. See Barry Kennerk, *Temple Street Children's Hospital: An Illustrated History* (Dublin: New Island, 2014), 45.

192 See, for example, *The Standard*, 21 January 1933, 8; *Irish Jesuit Directory* 1928, xlix; *The Capuchin Annual* 1936, 324; *The Irish Rosary*, March 1941, iv; *St Anthony's Annals*, March 1951, 73. It is difficult to definitively chart the extent of advertising by Magdalene laundries in periodicals like *The Irish Rosary*, as surviving copies in libraries were often bound with the advertisements at the beginning and end of each issue removed.

193 *The Standard*, 21 January 1933, 8.

194 See, for example, *Blackrock College Annual 1937*, iv; *Blackrock College Annual 1945*, xx; *Blackrock College Annual Centenary 1860–1960*, iv; *Blackrock College Annual 1970*, x.

195 See, for example, *St Mary's College Annual 1958*; *St Mary's College Annual 1963*, iv; *St Mary's College Annual 1967*, xiii.

196 *Brief Sketch of the Foundations*, 26–7.

197 Ibid., 29.

198 Ibid., 26.

199 Ibid., 29.

200 Ibid., 26.

201 Ibid., 27.

202 *Irish Sisters of Charity 1843–1943: Souvenir Book* (Dublin: Annesley Press, 1943), 89; *Centenary Brochure*, 151.

203 *Souvenir of the Blessing and Dedication of the Church of the Immaculate Virgin Mary of the Miraculous Medal Clonskeagh* (1957).

204 Sisters of Charity, *St Mary Magdalen's Donnybrook: Yearbook* (Shannon Publication, 1961).

205 Ibid.

206 Mary Daly, *Sixties Ireland: Reshaping the Economy, State and Society, 1957–1973* (Cambridge: Cambridge University Press, 2016), 192–3.

207 *Parish of the Sacred Heart Donnybrook* (Dublin: John T. Drought, 1966), 102.

208 *Irish Catholic Directory 1959*, 115.

209 *Irish Catholic Directory 1990*, 137.

210 'Letter to the Editor', *Evening Press*, 28 November 1979, 23.

211 'Cecil is over Sixty Years on the Road', *Wicklow People*, 16 January 1987, 17.

212 Catherine McCann, *In Gratitude: The Story of a Gift-Filled Life* (Dublin: Orpen Press, 2016), 61.

213 Planning Application No. 2212/93, Dublin City Council. The letter containing the quote is dated 23 March 1994. The application was originally submitted in December 1993.

214 *IDC Report*, 615.

215 Michael John Fitzgerald McCarthy, *Priests and People in Ireland* (Dublin: Hodges, Figgis & Co., 1902). Over 60,000 copies of the book were sold.

216 Ibid., 420–1.

217 Ibid., 421.

218 Sinclair, 'Penitents' Laundry', 11.

219 Ibid.

220 It closed in 1996.

221 St Patrick's Refuge, Dún Laoghaire, County Dublin, closed in 1963; the Good Shepherd in New Ross in 1967 and the Good Shepherd, Sundays Well, Cork, in 1977.

222 See, for example, Gary Culliton, 'Last Days of a Laundry', *Irish Times*, 25 September 1996, 15.

223 Information provided by the current owners of DML. The author of this chapter has seen the contract of sale.

224 'Nuns Sell Eight-Acre Site for Around £1.5 Million', *Irish Times*, 18 April 1986, 21.

225 *IDC Report*, 27.

226 'Advertisement', *Irish Times*, 8 September 1993, 19.

227 Letters submitted on behalf of the RSC contained in Planning Application No. 2212/93, Dublin City Council.

228 See, for example, Mary Carolan, 'Disabled Woman Awarded €40,000 over Treatment at Centre', *Irish Times*, 26 July 2018.

229 HSE [Health Service Executive, Ireland], '*Time to Move on from Congregated Settings – A Strategy for Community Inclusion*', *Time to Move on Newsletter*, January 2020, available online: www.hse.ie/eng/services/list/4/disability/congregatedsettings/time-to-move-on-newsletter-january-2020.pdf (accessed 7 September 2022).

230 See St Margaret's Donnybrook, available online: www.stmargaretsdonnybrook.ie/ (accessed 7 September 2022).

231 See 'A New Community in Donnybrook', Religious Sisters of Charity, available online: www.rsccaritas.com/index.php/rscnews/1200-rosemount (accessed 7 September 2022).

232 See Brenda Malone and Barry Houlihan, Chapter 10, this volume.

233 Conall Ó Fátharta, 'Just One Religious Order Apologises', *Irish Examiner*, 6 February 2013.

234 Advertisement for Donnybrook contained in the *Capuchin Annual 1941*, 442.

235 Tom Inglis, *Moral Monopoly: The Rise and Fall of the Catholic Church in Modern Ireland* (Dublin: University College Dublin Press, 1998), 98.

236 Garret FitzGerald, *Just Garret: Tales from the Political Front Line* (Dublin: Liberties Press, 2010), 151.

237 Ibid.

4

'Magdalene'

Testimony from the Donnybrook Laundry[1]

Katherine O'Donnell

As modern democratic and nationalist states came to be established throughout Europe in the nineteenth century, and as European capitalist imperialism expanded globally, threatened only it seemed by Marxist movements, Pope Leo XIII set himself the task of articulating the position and relevance of the Catholic Church within the dominant political structures and social forces. Pope Leo's remarkable document *Rerum Novarum*, published in 1891, is considered a foundational text of modern Catholic social and political theory. Translated into English as *Duties of Capital and Labour*, the work remains firmly entrenched as the urtext of Catholic social doctrine. Pope Leo XIII elaborated a middle course between laissez-faire capitalism and the various forms of socialism which subordinate the individual to the state. He discussed the relationships and mutual duties between labour and capital, as well as government and its citizens. One of his primary concerns was the need for some amelioration of 'the misery and wretchedness pressing so unjustly on the majority of the working class'. He asserted his support for the rights of labour to form unions, and rejected socialism and unrestricted capitalism, while affirming the right to private property. Pope Leo XIII strongly criticized socialism for seeking to replace the rights and duties of parents, families and communities with the supervision of the state. The civil government should not intrude into and exercise control over the family, the basic building block of society. His encyclical elaborated on this point by using the term 'subsidiarity', which has now become an integral principle in Catholic social doctrine. Pope Leo called for harmony between the social classes in order to defeat the spread of socialism. He argued against a strong state and big government in favour of subsidiarity, claiming that it was a disturbance of Natural Law to assign to a higher association (government) what lesser and subordinate organizations can do. The Pope recommended that the state should merely regulate subsidiary organizations to provide social services.

This text provided a clear manifesto and rationale for the Catholic Church's practice of establishing 'voluntary' bodies to run educational, health, social welfare and carceral institutions. What the Pope proposed was already the *modus operandi* of the hierarchy of the Catholic Church in Ireland which under the leadership of Cardinal Paul Cullen, was masterful at harnessing state resources to fund social and educational initiatives run by clergy, Catholic religious orders or lay Catholic organizations. Cullen was created a Cardinal in 1866 and his opposition to leftist movements and secret revolutionary societies meant that he was more amenable to the British colonial establishment than he otherwise might have been. The growing Catholic Irish middle class generously funded their Church, which was also adept at seizing state-funding opportunities. British establishment interests were also served through outreach by Catholic religious orders to contain the legions of Irish poor (even if much diminished by the Great Famine of 1845–9 and emigration) and the British Exchequer funded many of the Victorian institutions run by these orders. For instance, the Religious Sisters of Charity's (RSC) industrial and reformatory schools were able to benefit from British government funding through the Reformatory Schools Act, 1858, and the Industrial Schools Act, 1868.[2] As James M. Smith describes it:

> The governing burden of the British colonial administration was lightened as it increasingly ceded responsibility to the Catholic Church for areas of social welfare including education, health care, and institutional provision. Irish society in general, especially the emerging Catholic middle class, strengthened its identity as a nation; its sense of modernization and progress was increasingly vested in notions of social and moral respectability.[3]

This chapter looks at the cultural, social and political contexts of the Donnybrook Magdalene as it came to be established in nineteenth-century Ireland and argues that the colonial framework in which it developed had a decisive 'neocolonial' imprint that continued throughout the twentieth century. The RSC and its institutions were founded during a period of intense growth and consolidation by the Irish Catholic Church, and served as the cultural wing of a political movement that protested the oppression of Irish Catholics in the British Empire. This chapter argues that the Donnybrook Magdalene is best understood as a neocolonial institution and closes with the testimony of women who were formerly held there. The neocolonial aspects of the Donnybrook Magdalene Laundry (DML) is brought into relief through the light of survivor testimony. The experiences of the inmates who were held in DML and which are recorded in oral histories and focus groups are shown here to reveal the class dynamics of a regime designed during a movement when the Irish Catholic middle class sought to prove themselves worthy of self-governance to the British colonial power. Through the generosity and insight of Magdalene survivors who have testified on their time in DML, we can begin to understand the ideologies that infused the power structures of Ireland's recent past.

The Donnybrook Magdalene and Home Rule

As the nineteenth century turned into the twentieth, the vast majority of the Catholic middle classes supported the Irish Parliamentary Party (IPP) which argued that they were capable of devolved powers of self-governance or 'Home Rule' within the British

Empire. The IPP was most amenable to lobbies from Catholic religious orders. Bridget Harrison says that:

> as more middle-class Catholic women entered religious congregations, family and social ties bonded women religious and the Catholic political class, many of whom were constitutional nationalists. Meanwhile, the rise of institutions and concern for the socially vulnerable, including so-called 'fallen women', meant that reformatories were universally accepted as a public service. These factors coalesced into a situation where Irish nationalist M.P.s argued simultaneously that Magdalene asylums served the state, but that the state had no right to monitor or influence their work.[4]

These MPs successfully represented the views of the Catholic nuns to ensure that businesses run by religious sisters such as Laundries and needlework enterprises would not be subject to state regulation and oversight. The leader of the party, John Redmond, sought to exclude Magdalene Laundries from the Factory and Workshop Act, 1901, explaining that their mission was to prevent 'fallen women ... from continuing with their evil courses' and that 'the great object [of the religious orders] was to keep these girls in those institutions'. He continued, that the sisters 'are unanimously of the opinion that the introduction into their institutions of an outside authority in the shape of Government inspectors would completely destroy the discipline of their institutions, and make their already almost impossible task absolutely impossible'.[5] Irish MPs remained steadfast in their opposition to state oversight even when English MPs presented evidence of serious abuses involving hard labour in Laundries run by Catholic sisters in France. Edmund Leamy, author of *Irish Fairy Tales* and MP for Kildare, protested:

> There was hardly one of the Nationalist Members who had not a relative a nun, and they would be the most dishonest men in the world if they allowed their friends to remain in these institutions if there was anything wrong ... It was esteemed a miracle if a fallen woman turned round and altered her life, but that work of reform was being carried out week after week in the Irish convents ... He did ask that the Legislature would not interfere with the work of the nuns who, day after day and night after night, bestowed constant care, anxiety, and affection on these miserable creatures. He knew that some of these poor girls were the victims of men's passions, and some of their own folly; but could there be any more beautiful or touching sight than that of these women, who had been in the convent since they were only ten or eleven years of age, taking to their hearts women from the streets who came to them for help. He could not conceive of anyone not respecting a beautiful and holy charity like that. He appealed to the House not to make this a Catholic or Irish question. He was not pleading for the nuns, but for the poor girls under their charge.[6]

In a hard-fought debate, the IPP argument that the religious sisters needed free rein in operating their institutions and should not be subject to inspection, finally won the day. Even in 1907, when amending legislation sought to bring religious-run Laundries within the scope of the Factory and Workshop Act, 1901, the application of the Act was subject to broad exceptions, allowing the nuns to set their own 'scheme for the regulation of the hours of employment, intervals for meals, and holidays of the workers' and to give notice that no factory inspector could 'examine an inmate of the institution save in the presence of one of the managers'. Leamy's declaration that there 'was hardly one of the Nationalist Members who had not a relative a nun' (and his patriarchal assertion that the men of the family would not allow their friends to remain in a place 'if there was anything wrong') reveals how in the early years of the twentieth century, the Irish Catholic middle class had become consolidated as the established power, not merely in representing Irish nationalist aspirations but also as brokers in the provision of social welfare services.

The establishment of the RSC convent and Magdalene in Donnybrook was part of a successful wave of prosperous Catholic social reformers who were active in the eradication of public vice. Donnybrook Green had been licensed for a festival since the thirteenth century and over the centuries had become a place for horse trading, public drinking and entertainment, earning a reputation for bawdy debauchery. 'Donnybrook' is still used in American slang as a term for a riot or brawl. In 1855, the Committee for the Abolition of Donnybrook Fair was established to acquire the licence in order to put an end to it. Dr Paul Cullen, then Archbishop of Dublin, issued a letter to the clergy expressing his 'sincere delight' at the 'measures adopted to suppress the Fair': 'Everyone acquainted with the city is aware that that Fair, to say nothing of the loss of time and other temporal considerations, was the occasion of innumerable offences against God: that riotousness, drunkenness, debauchery and profligacy of every kind prevailed to an awful extent and seemed to walk in it in triumph.'[7] The Committee raised the substantial sum of £3,000 to successfully buy out the licensees. When an English convert to Catholicism, Fanny Taylor, visited the Magdalene at Donnybrook in the mid-1860s, she noted that 'after a long struggle with custom', Donnybrook Fair had recently been abolished. 'On the green now stands a new and handsome church, dedicated to the Sacred Heart, and at a little distance is a convent and Magdalene asylum of the Sisters of Charity.'[8]

The previous chapter revealed that references to women staying for life at Donnybrook were frequent in RSC literature. This was also evident to outside observers. Taylor is surprised to find that the 'mode of management' at DML 'differs somewhat from that of the penitentiaries generally known in England. The wish and intention of the Sisters is that their inmates should remain with them for life.' The English Magdalene movement worked to rehabilitate those 'fallen women' who were considered redeemable. The redeemable or 'non-hardened' were those considered to be innocent victims of seducers or those who had 'fallen into sin' merely due to hard luck and the exigencies of poverty, yet who wished to live as respectable servants. Magdalene institutions were to provide temporary asylums for women who wished to reform, redeem their characters, rehabilitate their lives, and re-enter into a better place in society. The British Victorian idealization of women in nineteenth-century Ireland meant that the nuns of the Magdalene institutions were understood to be part of the 'rescue' movement so evident throughout the nineteenth-century British Empire.[9] The rescuers were often women of status, keen to exercise their philanthropic powers and the object of 'rescue' was the prostitute or 'wayward' female who was regarded as 'fallen' even from the status of 'woman', that idealized paragon who was without sexual drive or sexual experience apart from a dutiful response to facilitating her husband's desire.

The sisters who ran DML came from upper- and middle-class families who could pay the required dowry to the Convent and they played their part in confining the disreputable women (or the daughters of disreputable women).[10] According to the final report of the Commission to Inquire into Child Abuse (CICA) which is more popularly known as *The Ryan Report*, they were known as the 'superior degree Sisters'. The congregation also recruited nuns to serve the superior degree Sisters, these were described in the Congregation Rules as 'Second Degree Sisters' and were confined to 'domestic employment suitable to their vocation'. According to the *CICA Final Report*, the Second Degree Sisters were required to be 'content with the occupations of Martha' and interiorly to 'esteem all as being superior to themselves, and, with religious simplicity and modesty, to give each one exteriorly the honour and reverence which her station requires'.[11] The religious sisters were universally admired for embodying sexual chastity, a 'purity' essential to idealized womanhood, and the religious sisters of the Magdalene institutions were further admired for sacrificing their 'unblemished' lives to rescue the 'impure' and trying to elevate the 'fallen woman' to a respectable standard of womanhood. Given the mores of British Victorian imperial ideology, even if the woman was not a prostitute and merely had no option but the streets or the Magdalene, the 'penitent' Magdalenes were disreputable due to the intersection of two social characteristics: poverty and Irish ethnicity.

As David Nally has illustrated when it came to the impoverished condition of the nineteenth-century Irish both at home and abroad their poverty was understood as a racial characteristic: a natural product of their culture and race.[12] The penitential hard labour of the Magdalene institution would be a place where the 'fallen' could atone for their sins. Moreover, according to Catholic doctrine, the merit accrued by the penance of the Magdalenes might be offered up by them so that they could redeem not only their own shame, but the dishonour of their families. The devoutly penitential might accumulate divine indulgences that could be bestowed across their entire ethnicity.

Taylor cautiously deliberates on the merits and demerits of the RSC's wish that 'their inmates should remain with them for life':

> Of course no coercion is used; every one is free to go when she likes, and a certain number always do leave, but the Sisters believe that very few of those who have lost their good name, and generally speaking, have contracted habits of intemperance, idleness, and other vices, will be able to resist temptation if exposed to the rough contact of the world again. There is much to be said on both sides of the question. If such a plan be adopted, the difficulty of rescuing these poor creatures would be increased, for the number of refuges for them must be multiplied. On the other hand, no means to attain a perfect reformation should be thought too costly. It is certain, however, that both systems should be in operation; for many characters among this class of unhappy women could neither brook a life-long restraint, nor even the idea of it, and would do far better in an asylum where they knew a certain time of probation only was required.[13]

The RSC and DML are a manifestation of a distinct post-Famine Catholic socioeconomic transition – what historians describe as a 'Catholic embourgeoisement' – that is an 'upward' social mobility, where an increasing number of Catholics entered the culturally respectable and economically secure ranks of the middle class.[14] The rise of the Catholic middle classes was most evident from the 1860s and is indivisible from the expansion of Catholic religious orders. A feature of this embourgeoisement is the supports the religious orders are able to offer the aspiring Catholic middle class through the provision of education and an affirmation of respectability.

The Donnybrook Magdalene and the Free State

Maria Luddy remarks that in the first decade of the twentieth century, most of the ten Irish Magdalene institutions still functioned as refuges, which the majority of the women could leave if they wished to do so, but that 'between the years 1912 and the 1920s these asylums appear to have become much less flexible institutions', or at least their reputation was that they were more carceral than temporary asylums.[15] That the eight other Irish Magdalene institutions appear to have more closely followed the aims of the RSC and became increasingly more carceral from 1912 might be understood as being part of context of the revolutionary period, 1912–23, when Irish nationalism was on the march. The nationalists in the IPP had successfully defended the Magdalene institutions from state oversight and there was an increased spirit of independence allied to a nationalist purity cause. These years saw the arming of both nationalist militia: pro-Union British and Irish separatist; followed by an armed uprising by Irish nationalists in 1916, and a guerrilla War of Independence from 1919 to 1921. The conclusion of the War of Independence led to the end of British rule in twenty-six of the island's thirty-two counties and the establishment of the Irish Free State/Saorstát Éireann there. The remaining six counties were established as the British-controlled territory of Northern Ireland.

In newly independent Ireland, the now defunct IPP's position of supporting the Catholic religious orders was to become official Irish Free State policy and the ten Magdalene Laundries were about to receive a renewed lease of life. Irish patriots, with the support of the newly empowered Catholic hierarchy, were eager to establish control in symbolic and material terms. Maternity and social reproduction became significant territory on which to assert an Irish national patriarchal discourse of moral probity and purity. The assertion of national pride was an answer to the culture of the former colonizer who had not merely exploited Ireland economically, extracting wealth and dominating it in political terms but had also asserted a cultural supremacy that extended into psychological categorization and racial terms. The British Empire might possess vast wealth and political power, but the fledging Irish State would cultivate supremacy on the moral high ground – or so the argument ran. Ireland would be triumphantly Catholic above all else. As Luddy explains:

> Representing possible immorality, a drain on public finances and someone in need
> not only of rescue, but also of institutionalisation, the unmarried mother had

become, by the foundation of the Irish Free State in 1922, a symbol of unacceptable sexual activity and a problem that had the potential to blight the reputation not only of the family but of the nation.[16]

Olivier Coquelin points out that the Sinn Féin Party that ultimately led the Irish revolution had set itself the goal of winning over the international community to its cause by demonstrating to the world that the Irish people was 'capable of governing itself both responsibly and respectably'.[17] Sinn Féin also appealed to the middle-class and conservative sections of Irish society whose financial support was essential to the nationalist cause. The Irish revolution, then, did not adhere to a radical socioeconomic programme. As Coquelin remarks: 'the aim of this revolution was merely to change the national identity of the rulers in Ireland with a native government liberated from the imperial authority'.[18] Speaking in the Dáil (the Irish Parliament) within the early months of the first Free State government, the Minister for Justice Kevin O'Higgins boasted: 'I think that we were probably the most conservative-minded revolutionaries that ever put through a successful revolution.'[19]

Yet, O'Higgins' claim for the exceptionalism of the Irish revolutionaries is undermined when we consider the successful anti-imperial uprisings that took place throughout the twentieth century. As Kwame Nkrumah notes, even when radical revolutionary forces depose colonizers, this can result in merely a nominal independence to the dominated people. Nkrumah argues that colonialism in Africa was succeeded by neocolonialism: colonizers' cultures had set the standards for the norms and models of behaviour of the territories and societies over which they ruled and the hegemony of those dominant norms was still evident even after revolutionary freedom movements gained power.[20] To quote Walter Mignolo, we invariably discover in postcolonial societies that 'independence changed the actors but not the script'.[21] Neocolonialism, or 'coloniality' to use the concept developed by Anibal Quijano, continues after the official end of colonialism in the form of covert control of the minds of the dominated people who are still trying to prove themselves as undeserving of the racist stereotyping by the colonizer and deserving of the status of respectability again according to the dominant mores of the (former) colonizer.[22] Nelson Maldonado-Torres, usefully elaborates how coloniality is different from colonialism.[23] Colonialism denotes a political and economic relationship in which the sovereignty of a nation or a people is suppressed by the power of another nation, which makes such a nation an empire. Coloniality, instead, refers to long-standing patterns of power that emerged as a result of colonialism, but that define culture, labour, intersubjective relations and knowledge production well beyond the strict limits of colonial administrations: colonialism mutates into coloniality and continues replicating the cultural, social dynamics of colonialism long after the rather deceptive end of the colonial political era.

We can see in the treatment of the girls and women held in the Magdalene institutions, even after independence, a colonial view being continued: that the Irish poor were inherently defective and best contained within a carceral environment. The colonial view of the dangerous prostitute who spread contagion and vitiated the morals of those young men who protected the empire militarily, was now securely projected onto the 'wayward' or 'fallen' woman who must be held in the Magdalene institutions as she endangered the physical and spiritual health of the young nation. The leaders of the fledgling Irish state wished to show the world, that contrary to customary racial profiling, the Irish would prove to be respectable and responsible. As John Banville notes, 'The doctrine of original sin was ingrained in us from our earliest years, and we borrowed from Protestantism the concepts of the elect and the unelect.'[24] Irish upper- and middle-class women who joined the RSC would answer that call to be, as Coen has demonstrated, 'an honour to [their] native land'.[25] They would devote their lives to containment of the fallen woman, so that she would not contaminate society.

Throughout the twentieth century, the Irish state strengthened the hand of the religious orders by deliberately excluding the Magdalene Laundries' commercial operations from the Census of Production after the 1926 Preliminary Report on Laundry, Dyeing and Cleaning Trades revealed that nearly half (thirty-seven) of the eighty returns for commercial laundry work were from religious institutions ('Convents, Penitentiaries, Female Industrial Schools, etc.'). The Report states that: 'The amounts charged to customers in 1926 for laundry work done by such institutions amounted to £97,325.' It further acknowledges that the workers (referred to as 'inmates') engaged in this commercial laundry work were not paid for their labour.[26] After 1926, the Census of Production no longer included commercial businesses operated by the religious sisters and consequently their financial turnover is no longer a matter of public record. Paul Michael Garrett has detailed how policy recommendations relating to 'unmarried mothers' outlined in *The Irish Ecclesiastical Record* in 1921 quickly became law and formal government policy in the newly independent Irish Free State, first under the Local Government (Temporary Provisions) Act, 1923, later in the recommendations of the *Report of the Commission on the Relief of the Sick and Destitute Poor* in1927 and finally in the Registration of Maternity Homes Act, 1934.[27] Each 'first offender' would be admitted to a mother and baby 'home' and would be forced to contribute towards their confinement by way of domestic labour. The second type of woman, the 'less hopeful case' as described in the 1927 Report, was however relegated to one of the completely Church-controlled Magdalene Asylums, in which they would be provided with 'special provision'.[28] The law offered no further detail on these institutions or the nature of this 'special provision'.

In 1936, the Conditions of Employment Act exempted all institutions 'carried on for charitable or reformatory purposes' from the requirement to pay wages to their industrial workers.[29] While this legislation otherwise applied to the Magdalene Laundries, as did the Factories Act, 1955, and subsequent regulations, State records show that only piecemeal inspections of Magdalene Laundries took place from 1957 onwards. The records also show that the Factory Inspectors merely ensured that the machines and processes of production met health and safety regulations, and none spoke to the incarcerated workforce or inquired into their living conditions, or lack of wages and social security payments.[30] The archives show State officials were involved in directing and escorting girls and women to the convents, in particular Court Probation Officers, but there is not one instance recorded of State officials ensuring their release at the end of the appointed sentences.[31]

Although the 1936 *Cussen Report* into Reformatories and Industrial Schools briefly suggested that it was a less than ideal system, the use of Magdalene Laundries as places of arbitrary detention was not subjected to public and official critique until 1970 with the publication of *The Reformatory and Industrial Schools Systems Report* (known as the *Kennedy Report*). The *Report* stated that 'at least 70 girls between the ages of 13 and 19 years' were confined in the laundries when they 'should properly be dealt with under the Reformatory Schools system'. It concluded:

> This method of voluntary arrangement for placement can be criticized on a number of grounds. It is a haphazard system, its legal validity is doubtful and the girls admitted in this irregular way and not being aware of their rights, may remain for long periods and become, in the process, unfit for re-emergence into society. In the past, many girls have been taken into these convents and remained there all their lives.[32]

The *Kennedy Report* did not result in any official remedial action.

In these contexts, Ireland's Magdalene institutions are best understood not as an aberration but as a logical function within the ideology of the Irish establishment whereby law and policy have purposefully and systematically controlled and exploited women's sexuality, labour and bodies. The function of these institutions impacted poor and vulnerable women disproportionately, the population deemed most threatening to establishment sensibilities. The new Free State, with its emphasis on ensuring social purity and sexual respectability, maintained a system of incarcerating vulnerable women and children for most of twentieth-century Ireland. It did so by utilizing the system, inherited from the British colonial era, which had provided basic levels of relief to the Irish poor where massive Victorian institutions were funded by the state and managed by Catholic religious orders.

Carceral welfare in the Irish twentieth century

The Irish establishment which emerged from the symbiotic dyad of Catholic Church and State bodies that combined to copper-fasten a monopoly on power in the new country, gained even more momentum from 1931 with the publication of a papal encyclical by Pope Pius XI entitled *Quadragesimo Anno* (*The Fortieth Year*). This celebrated the fortieth anniversary of Pope Leo's *Rerum Novarum* and restated its central tenets, arguing again for 'subsidiarity' and that it contravened Natural Law to assign to a higher association (government) what lesser and subordinate organizations can do. John Charles McQuaid, who was the Archbishop of Dublin from 1940 to 1972, was particularly adept at persuading successive Irish governments to finance Church involvement in a large 'voluntary sector', while retaining ecclesiastical control of these projects.[33] Lindsey Earner-Byrne has examined how McQuaid insisted that agents of the Catholic Church would decide on the form of services to be provided utterly independent of State control and gives a detailed analysis of how he sought to ensure that Catholic organizations provided welfare services, undercutting the work of non-Catholic service providers.[34] The Catholic Church's preeminent political and cultural position in mid-twentieth-century Ireland can be seen most clearly in its resounding defeat of Dr Noël Browne's 'Mother and Child Scheme' which was rejected because it was a plan for socialized medicine.[35]

The industrial and reformatory schools as well as the Magdalene institutions that the RSC ran were part of a system of the mass institutionalization of the socially and economically vulnerable (particularly women and children) that was maintained by a system of capitation payments to the religious orders from the Irish Exchequer for most of the twentieth century. Ireland's prison population was a relatively negligible percentage of the population; by mid-century, there was an average of just fifty women annually held in Irish prisons, yet by 1951, about 1 in every 100 Irish citizens was coercively confined in an institution operated collaboratively by the Church/State establishment, including psychiatric hospitals, industrial and reformatory schools, residential schools for disabled children, mother and baby 'homes', county homes and Magdalene institutions.[36] Scholars such as Smith refer to this coercive confinement as Ireland's 'architecture of containment', and we can see that its policing had a gender, class, ethnic and disability focus that upheld patriarchal, married, middle-class, white, settled and able-bodied norms.[37] Norms that had been formed in and with resistance to colonization. Eoin O'Sullivan and Ian O'Donnell describe the system of institutional 'care' in twentieth-century Ireland as 'inherited networks of social control'.[38] Harry Ferguson describes how the mentality of those running residential institutions in the Irish Free State and mid-twentieth-century Ireland was still a colonial mindset: the thinking being that unless poor and working-class children were reformed and moulded by the institutions they were considered a 'moral dirt' and a significant threat to the social order.[39] Earner-Byrne has analysed Dáil Debates and describes how 'contemporary welfare debates reveal a deep-rooted distrust of the working class family'.[40] She demonstrates that speeches by Irish politicians reveal that Irish society was always aware that the system was intrinsically class based and biased and she further demonstrates how poverty was often conflated with criminality and the poor were regarded as culpable for their own destitution.[41] Ireland's architecture of containment concentrated on the surveillance and monitoring of all girls and women and, where considered necessary, the incarceration of poorer women and their children; but, it also contained a high proportion of Travellers, as well as so-called 'illegitimate' children, children designated as 'mixed race', and children and adults with disabilities. Carole Holohan analysed the reports generated by the Commission to Inquire into Child Abuse as well as reports following inquiries into clerical sexual abuse of children and found that 'children could be considered corrupted by virtue of their being born out of wedlock or having been sexually abused by an adult'.[42] She also found systematic and long-established negative attitudes towards poverty which deprived poor and working-class children of the rights afforded their middle-class counterparts.[43]

Legacy issues stemming from this system of surveillance, punishment and incarceration are still manifest in twenty-first-century Ireland: one prime example being that adopted people are denied their rights to their birth certificates and other personal data from their adoption files. Other examples include the continuing institutionalization (with capitation payments from the State to private commercial enterprises providing institutional care) of older people, people with disabilities, homeless families and people seeking asylum.

Voices from Donnybrook Magdalene Laundry

In March 2012, I piloted a project to collect oral histories of women who had been held in Magdalene institutions as a Justice for Magdalenes (JFM) exercise which would record survivor testimony to submit to the Irish civil service Inter-Departmental Committee (IDC) which was then investigating State involvement with the Magdalene institutions. In drawing up the questions, I expanded the focus of the initial JFM approach from concentrating on what would be important to know from a legal point of view to taking the opportunity to elicit life stories from the women. Yet, during the oral history gathering we still ensured to ask all legally relevant questions so that the testimonies would also serve the campaign for justice.[44] The ensuing oral histories were gathered through a long list of questions which had benefitted from rigorous critiques by University College Dublin's (UCD) College of Human Science's Ethics Committee before they ultimately gave their sanction to the work. In considering what questions to ask, I aimed to collect as full a life-story as possible and so each interview began with: 'Where were you born and who raised you?' Early in the pilot phase (funded by *The Feminist Review* Trust), I added closing questions that focused on the women's sense of accomplishment and pride both to end the interview with a recollection of positive achievements and also to capture the remarkable generosity and resilience of these women. A few of the questions on daily life within the Magdalene institutions were very specific, such whether they remembered washing any kinds of uniforms (in order to ascertain if they recalled laundry that could be tied to State contracts given to the religious orders). However, most of the questions were open-ended and chronological in terms of charting a life story. The aim was to capture as rich an experience as possible of the former the survivor's life even if a central focus was the years of her incarceration. By aiming to collect life histories, I sought to generate a rich collection of narratives that would inform future generations, inspire artists, and provide enough material for the work of historians and social scientists in their analyses of the interviews. While I understood that a collection of the oral histories of former Magdalene survivors would be of immense benefit to researchers and the heritage of the wider Irish public, I am not by training or inclination a social scientist and I was sceptical that there would be any benefit to the women themselves in having their histories recorded and disseminated. It seemed that I was inviting them to give the precious gift of their life story to a culture and society which had consistently degraded them; it was asking an enormous generosity on their part.

I became Principal Investigator of the Magdalene Institutions: Recording an Oral and Archival History when the project was funded by the Irish Research Council in 2012. I gathered further testimony through the Dublin Honours Magdalenes (DHM) Listening Exercise (funded by the Department of Justice and Equality when Charlie Flanagan was minister). The historic two-day DHM event was an held in June 2018. The event fulfilled two key aspects of the Irish State's Magdalen Restorative Justice Ex-Gratia Scheme: to bring together those women seeking to meet others who also spent time in the Magdalene Laundries, and to provide an opportunity for a listening exercise to gather views from survivors on how the Magdalene Laundries should be remembered by future generations.[45]

A number of insights regarding practices at DML are evident in the interviews. Survivors who gave their testimony to these projects say the girls and women incarcerated in DML were generally young and motherless, and in a relatively small number of cases they may have given birth outside wedlock.[46] Testimony reveals that other women were intellectually disabled; some had committed misdemeanours such as 'stealing trinkets'.[47] Many were raised as children in industrial schools and transferred to DML when they were sill teenagers. As the *IDC Report* euphemistically describes it, these children were 'released on licence from Industrial or Reformatory Schools to the Magdalen Laundries before they reached 16 years of age'.[48] These were understood by the authorities to be 'preventative cases', that is they were incarcerated in the Magdalene to prevent them from 'falling into sin'. Some were released in their early or mid-twenties and sent to work in menial jobs in other religious-run institutions, but their release was neither assured nor systematically applied. Invariably, these girls were not informed that they were being placed 'on licence' and transferred to a Magdalene institution for their own 'protection'; nor were they informed how long they were to remain there.[49] Moreover, in spite of the assertive legal terminology of the use of 'licence' in the *IDC Report*, there was no clear statutory basis for this summary removal of girls from industrial or reformatory schools and incarceration in Magdalene institutions.[50] Survivors were ignorant of the policy underpinning such arrangements, which also stipulated their release on or before their twenty-first birthday.[51] Some of those committed as girls remained in DML until they were past childbearing age and some remained there for their lifetime.[52] Most striking are the girls who were committed to DML who were victims of incest, sexual assault and rape.[53]

The RSC held the girls and women in Donnybrook under lock and key.[54] Once inside the convent, the girls and women were imprisoned behind locked doors, barred or unreachable windows and high walls.[55] The gates to the street at the end of the avenue were locked. Internal doors were also locked, at night-time. Nancy Shannon, a young unmarried mother of two sons was told by her aunt, who was a leading member of the Legion of Mary in her district, that she had secured paid work for Nancy looking after children. Nancy's mother did not want her to leave home but Nancy reasoned with her that the money would be useful. However, she was lured from home under false pretences and found herself incarcerated in DML. As Nancy describes it:

> They took me off and locked me into the convent. They wouldn't let me out. (*Voice breaking*) They wouldn't even let me see me Mammy . . . or they wouldn't let me see . . . didn't want me to see me two sons. They said, 'You don't want to see your sons.' Says I, '*I do*'.[56]

The girls and women held at DML experienced the institution as a prison. Upon entry, they had to strip, and their clothes were taken away and replaced with work uniforms.[57] The uniform at DML in some respects mirrored the habits of the nuns in that they were antiquated uniforms: long dark dresses, aprons and caps, and very heavy boots. One survivor described how the bloomers she was given were Victorian in style with no gusset.[58] The Sisters gave the inmates a number or a house name on entry by which they were identified inside DML. Testimony survivors repeatedly mention how their long hair was cut short and kept crudely chopped. The women and girls in DML slept in very small, individual cells, with just enough room for a narrow iron bed and a slops bucket.[59] As Winifred describes it: 'So it was about six foot in length and maybe three foot in width, do you know what I mean? So that was your room. So you were kept like a prisoner.'[60] Sarah Williams says: 'the doors were locked every night – the room door was locked . . . – and the windows used to be up very high, like a small little window . . . and I used to climb up the top of the bed to look out the window.'[61] Sarah was born outside wedlock and in the 1950s when she was 15, she worked as a servant in a Dublin B&B. However, one Sunday evening when the landlady was out, Sarah was 'kidnapped' by the Legion of Mary and brought to DML.[62] She spent the night crying in the small cell into which she was locked. On the next morning she was given her uniform and told: 'You're number 100 and don't you forget it.'[63] The sisters at DML sought to erase the identities of the girls and women and insisted on treating them as 'penitents'.[64] As Nancy Shannon describes it: 'One of the nuns said that, "Look it, you had children outside, and that's why you're here," (*bangs table*) and she says, "Don't look to get out."'[65]

Sister Stanislaus Kennedy RSC (who is best known as Sr Stan, a household name in Ireland) collected data relating to the three Dublin Magdalene convents at the end of 1983. Her study reveals that nearly a quarter of the women confined had not seen their siblings since entering the institution; most had not seen other relatives or friends, and while just over half of the women had children, approximately 6 per cent of those women who were held in the Magdalenes and were mothers got to see their children after incarceration.[66] Visits to DML by friends or family were not encouraged and were strictly monitored when they did occur. There are repeated testimonies of how difficult it was to contact the world outside DML. Two women recount how their teenage foster sister who was sent to DML when she was found to have stolen a pencil and an orange, managed eventually to sneak a letter out via a man who delivered bread to the convent.[67] Sarah Williams describes how:

> If a letter came for you, you would be called up to the office. It was read out for you then torn up in front of you. If anyone wrote a letter to anyone it had to be read first. I often and often wrote to my auntie asking if she knew why I was here etc. etc. but I got no reply. I wrote to my mother every week but got no reply.

Sarah's aunt had phoned and written to DML to let them know that Sarah's mother was dying from cancer but it was three years after her mother's funeral that Sarah first learned that her mother had died: 'It was like someone putting a knife through me, I'll never forget it, you know.'[68] Sarah's mother was the only person in her life who had shown her kindness and the news of her mother's death led her to the first of many subsequent mental health breakdowns. Nancy Shannon describes how on the rare occasions that her mother and sons were allowed to visit: 'they . . . they were let in, the door was barred when they were in with me, and the nun sat with us in that room, and I couldn't talk what I wanted to say, because she wouldn't let me . . . Wouldn't let me talk.' Nancy says: 'It was in a room . . . like an office. In a room and the door was locked. I wasn't let on me own with me mother or me sons.'[69] Her son Brian describes visiting his mother when he was very young, about 5 or 6 and he did not like how dark the convent was, it seemed like prison. He also remembered: 'we used be in the grounds, we could walk around the grounds. But there was always nuns either side of you . . . and in front of you when you used to walk around.'[70] Letters to inmates at DML were censored or undelivered. As Nancy says:

> I couldn't even write, couldn't even get me . . . any letters that came, they wouldn't let me have them. My step-brother came one Christmas, gave me a letter with money in it for myself. They took the money off me. I haven't even seen it, I never got a penny from them.[71]

Survivors repeat the same story: the ringing of a bell woke them at five or six in the morning, they stood outside their cells to pray, they then washed themselves from the bucket in their room (or slopped it out if they had to use it during the night), went to Mass, had breakfast and then worked without pay, usually six full days a week at laundry from 8:30 am until 6.00 pm with a short half-hour break for dinner in the middle of the day. They also had general chores relating to the running of the institution. At night they did needlework such as crochet, rug making, embroidery, handbags and decorating holy pictures which were all presumed to be sold by the nuns.[72] All the survivors describe how the work was endless, repetitive, compulsory, forced and unpaid. As Nancy Shannon describes her years spent in DML:

> The first thing you do in the morning, you go to say your prayers, outside your bedroom door. Then you come down, get your breakfast. Then you have your breakfast, you go to the chapel . . . Then you come back, you do your room, then you go down to the laundry . . . and do the laundry, I had to do the big sheets . . . and when I had that done, I had to do the big loads of. . .all for the priests in the convent. Then you . . . you have that done, you have to go back and say a prayer in the church. The same when you have your meals. You must say your prayers, if you didn't say your prayers you'd be punished.[73]

Winifred is one of many survivors who report that there were no breaks allowed at DML. Many speak about how they were expected to hurry at the work: 'Because there was a deadline for those sheets and all of that stuff, you know. So they had to be done in time.'[74] Repeated testimony recounts how hot, sweaty and heavy the work was, and also how dangerous it was: 'You could stand in half a foot of water sometimes down in the laundry all day, when I started there first –.'[75] Multiple witnesses speak about accidents they endured or witnessed, some of them very traumatic such as seeing girls or women lose fingers and hands in the machines.[76] When Nuala Lyons was asked about a scar on her hand she replied:

> In the laundry, I cut that, and not a plaster, or nothing. A bit of rag, and you put it round you, and hold right there then. I caught it in the machine in the laundries. You know, dragging down the . . . when you're wringing the clothes. Lucky I didn't get all my hand, but they never. No medication. No nothing. 'Get on with the work.'[77]

One of the striking features of survivor testimony relating to DML is the level of physical violence experienced by the inmates; the violence coming from nuns and also other inmates.[78] Content in the *IDC Report* also corroborates endemic physical punishment in the Magdalene institutions while insisting that it does not make any findings relating physical abuse, yet also making contradictory statements such as: 'The vast majority [of "the very small sample of women"] also told the Committee that the ill-treatment, physical punishment and abuse that was prevalent in the Industrial School system was not something they experienced in the Magdalen Laundries.'[79] On the day that the report was released, initial media headlines ran with the statement that there was no physical abuse in the Magdalene institutions, until journalists had more time to read the report.[80] Survivors describe being beaten and regularly being threatened with beatings by the RSC.[81] Being hit on top of the head with 'belts with of the keys' was a frequent occurrence in DML.[82] On one occasion, Nancy was hit with a set of big keys that left her permanently scarred.[83] Sarah says that some of the nuns:

> were alright you know. And more were horrid like, you'd get the belt of the keys on the top of the head you would, the big heavy keys. They had them here on their side all the time and if you didn't do – they'd have me up in the ironing room then where I was doing all the shirts and everything and if there was a tiny bit of a crease it would be thrown into my face and I would get a belt of the keys if you didn't do a thing right.[84]

A usual punishment for insubordination was to be locked in a cell for days and fed dry bread and tea, or locked in a cell without any food for a day or two.[85] Bridget O'Donnell is typical of the teenage 'preventative cases' in DML, in that she had been raised in an orphanage run by the RSC.[86] She says, 'They would always stop food if you were in trouble.'[87] Sarah concurs:

> But if you done anything wrong now, just say now I got a bit lazy and decided 'I'm not going to do that today', you'd be taken up to your room, up to your cell and you'd get a glass of water and that's all you'd get all day, and the doors would be locked all day. You would get nothing to eat. So you soon come to your senses and say I want something to eat don't you? You'd get the few belts to the top of the head as well, always on the head you know with the keys.[88]

Nancy remembers some punishments in detail: 'they hit me with the keys. They locked me in ... it's like a cellar, they locked me in and gave me tea and dried bread for two days.'[89] Nancy says that the reason she had been punished on that particular occasion was she had shown a son the grave of his mother who had been held in DML:

> they should have told this gentleman that his mother was buried ... in the graveyard, but they didn't. I showed him where the grave ... I had to show him where his mother was buried. (*Crying*) I say a prayer for that woman every single day ... Even [when] I'm knitting I say the prayer for her. I'll never forget ... She was my friend, she looked after me when I was there ... and she told me, 'Be careful

what you say.' And I said, 'I'll tell the truth, I'm not going to tell a lie because it's a sin to tell a lie.'[90]

In addition to the enduring physical violence, the girls and women were also targets of sexual violence. At the Dublin Honours Magdalenes (DHM) Listening Event, Edith recounted:

> [**Edith**]   Of course, you know yourself, that a lot of them men that worked in the laundries were very cruel to the women. What they did to the women in the back of the vans. And I experienced it.
> **Joanne**   I never heard of that.
> **Edith**   Oh, they did. That definitely went on. I know . . . I'm speaking from experience. And when you're trying to get out of the van from the laundry men, they'd touch you up and ask you for favours . . . they'd get their favours and then drop you off at the gate and the gates would shut behind you.
> **Alice**   I never knew that happened.
> **Edith**   Yeah, it did. I experienced it.[91]

Edith's testimony is corroborated by Sharon who was a young teenager when she managed to run away from DML with two other girls:

> And we jumped over a wall about that high, as high . . . very high. I don't know how we did it, but we did. And we're still in our uniform and that, and the lady let us go through her house to get to the bus stop. And we got to the bus stop in Bray, still in uniform, and we spent the night walking around Bray, eating fruit from the gardens and that. And then Monday morning, we met the laundry men, and of course, we were delighted to meet the laundry men, but of course, you know what they wanted . . . Yeah. I mean I was a virgin. We were scared, but we were hungry and we had sandwiches and everything, you know. And anyway, they drove us back to Dublin again and left us in Stephen's Green. And from there, the police picked me up. I don't know what happened to the other girls. I never saw them again. And they took me back to Donnybrook where I was locked up again for two or three days.[92]

Also at the DHM Listening Event, Doreen (who spent thirty years in DML) told how she had become pregnant at the age of 30 while being held there.[93] She focused on the fact that she had no records in her file of the birth of her baby girl in the National Maternity Hospital in Holles Street and : 'they brought it down, let me hold her for a few minutes, and they said I have to bring her to the incubator. About 10 minutes later, they came up and said, "Doreen, the baby died." . . . I screamed the hospital down.'[94]

A priest who regularly visited DML and befriended Nancy Shannon realized that she was being physically beaten when he saw her face was bruised. He arranged for her to leave DML.[95] Bridget O'Donnell tells a similar story:

> So he [the priest] couldn't take me out completely, so he begged could I be moved because he used to say to me, 'what happened your face today?' Well, I might have

got a hiding from them or I'd be black and blue and I used to say, 'I fell, I fell,' because I was afraid I was going to get another beating.[96]

In time,, the priest was able to arrange for Bridget to leave for employment outside the Magdalene institutions. In answer to a question as to whether she was often beaten, Bridget answered: 'Oh yeah, just nonstop, for God's sake. There was only a few of them. It wasn't . . . there was some very good nuns there, but their hands were tied. They could not interfere. It had nothing got to do with them. They all had their own individual jobs.'[97] Winifred also reports:

But there were some nice nuns which I . . . there was a nice nun that . . . in the area where I was and she got on with the girls, but then she was shifted out of there. She was shifted because I asked about her after, I said, 'Where did she go?' You know what I mean because she became a good friend of mine. And to this day, I don't know where she went.[98]

Survivors generally report that there were just three nuns assigned to oversee work in the laundry and they were generally unkind and frequently abusive. Other nuns who lived in the Donnybrook Convent seemed, according to survivor accounts, to be teachers and those who wore white habits were presumed to work in the hospitals.[99]

The rule of silence and prayer was strictly applied at DML. As Nancy relates: 'No, you weren't allowed to talk when you were working.'[100] She further attests that: 'No, you couldn't talk when you were having your meals. You had to keep silent . . . If you opened your mouth you'd be punished.'[101] The diet was very repetitive and food was plain but sufficient. Bread, porridge and tea were the staples for breakfast and teatime and the typical dinner in the middle of the day was: 'mashed potatoes and sausage, mashed potatoes and sausage, potatoes and sausage for everyone.'[102]

The women held in DML knew that if they attempted to escape, the police (known in Ireland as the Gardaí) would search for them, and if captured they would be returned to DML to awaiting punishment. The grandly imposing Donnybrook Garda Station is mere metres from the gates of DML, so it should not be a surprise that successful escapes seem to have been rare.[103] When there was building work on site at the Convent,, Sarah and two other girls seized an opportunity to escape:

And when I think about it now, we went off in our uniforms and then we'll see, I don't know where we went, we were seen in Donnybrook I know, we were going around in circles. And this woman took us in and she changed all our clothes and gave us all new clothes – the following morning – not new clothes, old clothes, she had daughters – the following morning then the squad car came. I'd say she rang the convent myself, when she found out where we were. So they brought us back anyway to the convent – brought me back – and one of the policemen, there was two policemen in the car, two guards, and one of them went in and brought me out a cone, an ice-cream - to tell you now, I was so childish – brought me out an ice-cream – they took me back to the convent and I don't know where the other two went. I never seen them no more.[104]

Survivors report being moved to or from the other RSC Magdalene institution in Peacock Lane, Cork, as well as being moved to Magdalene Laundries run by other religious orders. The moves were often as a direct result of trouble they had caused (such as attempting to escape). They were moved suddenly without a chance to tell others they were being moved. As Ellen Murphy explains it: 'Like when I got so sick then, they shift you from one convent to the other. They didn't want no one being sick.'[105] Sinead Pembroke asked Nancy Shannon why she did not try and escape when she was taken for a week's retreat to a convent in her home town. Nancy replied:

NS   I had the chance [to escape] but I didn't, because they'd have the guards looking for you and all that. Was just …

SP   So you knew that there was that threat?

NS   … yes.

SP   Okay.

NS   Oh, they threatened me before I came out to [interviewee's home town removed] on me holiday. They said, 'If you go up near your mother,' she said, 'you won't be able to walk.'[106]

Speaking at the DHM Listening event, Joanne recounted that:

I remember there was two girls … there was two girls with me in Donnybrook and the vans would come and collect the laundry for the hospitals and the hotels. And these two young girls wanted to leave, and went into the baskets … They went into the baskets and they covered over them. The drivers didn't even know they were there! They were caught. And Jesus help us …[107]

Perhaps the most disturbing aspects of testimony from those who were held at DML are the long-term adverse effects on their physical and mental health. Sarah's words are typical:

I had been so ashamed of being in the place, no I don't know why, I could not tell anyone, I took a long time to get my life together. I have had hang ups all my life. I tried to make something of a life for myself. I always felt the odd one out. Then people did not understand what I had been through all my life, I tried to take my own life several times.[108]

Some survivors also speak of the women who were never released from DML. Sinead, who was a teenager there in the 1970s, describes the long-term inmates:

They were elderly you know and some of them could hardly walk and they tried to go down and I used to feel sorry for them. And there was, there was I think up there then some of them then had a thing where they had to go to the toilet; some of them weren't able to come out and they'd have to go to the toilet in the pot and you'd see them going out in the morning to empty the pot. You know it was very sad, very degrading for them, God help us you know.[109]

Sinead described how she seized on an opportunity to speak to the older woman who slept in the cell next to her:

And there was nobody watching and I says to her 'You were crying last night.' I said 'I often hear you crying before I go to sleep there'. She said: 'I was.' And then she told me then, I was asking her: 'Why are you upset?' Then she told me then she says: 'I often think, when I see you walking down I'd be thinking about my daughter,' she said. God help her! 'And she'd be around your age now,' she said. You know after a while now she said, 'That will go out of my head again, it's just when I see any new person, a new young person coming in that I'd be thinking about her.'[110]

Maria remembers being taken by her grandmother to visit an inmate in DML who was in her late 30s but looked a lot older:

Her hair was cut, exactly what you saw in the Magdalene's, the film. It's exactly, that's exactly how she looked, and you know . . . With a clip and all in her hair, and, there was no, . . . I'll be honest with you. I couldn't even tell you what she done. I could not tell you, I'd be telling you a lie if I told you, because I don't know, but I can still see her face. It was a face that frightened me. She was just staring all the time. Her head down. When she came walking down you could see her walking, and to see her anyway you'd know that she was disturbed in some way, and frightened.[111]

Once the visit was over and as they were leaving DML grounds, Maria's grandmother told Maria that she had just met her mother:

her little hands were like that, (*clenched hands*) and she just, her head down. She had her head down the whole time. She never looked up, and my mother had a terrible stare, you'd know that my mother was depressed. You'd know that she was disturbed . . . You'd know she was in, you know, a person that was locked up . . . She was so frightened looking. To me she was very frightened looking.
  All I know is we never spoke.[112]

In the study that Sr Stan made of three Dublin Magdalene institutions (including DML), she asserts that DML and the other Magdalene Laundries 'provide employment and occupational therapy' and she uses this shorthand reference – 'providing employment and occupational therapy' – or 'therapeutic rehabilitation' throughout her book to distinguish the three Magdalene institutions from other 'hostels' in her study.[113] Sr Stan provides us with stark insights into the effects of institutionalization through her discussion of a census she undertook on 1 December 1983; she found that there were 241 women in the three Dublin Magdalene institutions.[114] She provides alarmingly high figures for mental and physical illness and 'handicap' among the women: only 5 per cent of the observed population do not have any.[115] The study reveals that 17 per cent of these women had a mental illness, yet only 1 per cent were recorded with a mental illness upon entry. An astonishing 80 per cent of the women are 'deemed mentally handicapped', yet only 4 per cent were considered 'mentally handicapped' on entry.[116] Sr Stan acknowledges that the 'very large discrepancy' between the mental health of the women on entry and their current state might 'be explained by the fact that the staff in these hostels [*sic*] may have defined mental handicap in a much broader sense than is normally the case. They may use the term "mental handicap" to describe symptoms of severe institutionalisation'.[117]

Conclusion

As the vast majority (over 90 per cent) of primary schools in Ireland and over 50 per cent of secondary schools are still run under the patronage of the Catholic Church, it is perhaps not surprising that Ireland's recent history of institutional abuse is not taught on the State curriculum.[118] Marie Griffin notes that while the Irish state has provided full funding for school buildings in the twenty-first century, 'most Catholic schools are still on church or congregational lands in buildings that are at least partially funded by Catholic resources'.[119] Griffin illustrates that the status quo in Ireland exists because of at least some partial funding from the Catholic Church:

> Catholic schools are private establishments, in receipt of state funding because of a need for school places and because of their contribution to society in educating its young people. Catholic schools are in the voluntary sector and are not state entities. This difference between being a state school and a private school in receipt of state funding is not always fully appreciated.[120]

Twentieth-century Irish history can be comprehensively recounted as a collusion where the State's public purse funded the Catholic Church to provide education, healthcare and social services. This arrangement of State-funded but religious-run services is still generally referred to in Ireland as the 'voluntary sector'. The existing social contract allows Catholic religious orders, Catholic charities and dioceses to operate as private entities in the dual sense of both being free from monitoring as well as being commercial enterprises. Conforming to the social norms of an orthodox Catholicism provided the most obvious route in twentieth-century Ireland to securing the cultural capital of 'respectability' (exceedingly precious in a country that was so economically poor), and so there were real incentives 'not to know'. Making a critique of Catholic Church hierarchy and doctrine would entail a risk of losing cultural and social capital (which might often translate into economic opportunities) for you and your extended family. Acknowledging how abusive the institutions were would have entailed making a profound moral criticism of the religious orders, congregations and hierarchy of the Catholic Church which was the most powerful hegemonic force in the land.[121]

The experiences of the inmates at DML reveal the cruelty of a regime founded during the rise of a Catholic middle-class cultural and political movement to resist the inequities of British colonization. The neocolonial aspects of the institutions are revealed in survivor testimony and from the perspective of a twenty-first-century Ireland that is more economically and politically secure than at any other time in the past three centuries. Through the resilience, generosity and insight of Magdalene survivors we can begin to understand the ideologies that infused the power structures of Ireland's recent past. When Vicky Conway, one of the facilitators at the DHM Listening Event, asked the women seated at her roundtable: 'What are the lessons that you think as a country, or as a society we need to learn from this?' Penny and Louise who were held at DML joined in the response, and it is their perspectives that provide a fitting conclusion to this chapter:

Penny   Not to have any more Magdalenas [*sic*] or cruel regimental institutions.
Cora   Not to have any more institutions of Magdalenes anywhere.
Penny   Never, ever bring them back, yeah. They won't, but never.
Audrey   It's all gone, never again.
Penny   They won't. Ireland has woken up. Ireland was asleep. I can't think of a better word. All of us were there and outside Ireland, not in the institutions we were locked in but the world outside those four walls, those big walls, they didn't know, they didn't know, and some of them did know but just that Ireland I think was ... it was a different country back then. That's all I can say. It was like it was in the nineteenth century. Dickens' times, wasn't it?

[*Crosstalk in agreement*]

Penny   Yeah. Now we're in the ... we've joined the twenty-first century, haven't we really? We're part of the big world. Whereas we were like that. It was like you were in the nineteenth century world of Dickens. When you look back and that's what ... but now I think we're a big country, cosmopolitan as well. I've seen the differences now.
Vera   In the freedom we are now in the moment. Ireland has woken up at long last, which is a good thing. No more hidden secrets.
Louise   No more hidden secrets. I like that. I do.[122]

Notes

1   A number of the survivors of the Magdalene institutions object to being described as 'Magdalenes' or 'Magdalene women' (and most object to being called 'Maggies'). In this chapter, I am careful not to refer to survivors as such, to the extent possible. Occasionally I use the term 'Magdalenes' to refer to how these women and girls were labelled and hence treated as deserving incarceration and forced labour.
2   Caitriona Clear, *Nuns in Nineteenth-Century Ireland* (Dublin: Gill and Macmillan,1987).
3   James M. Smith, *Ireland's Magdalen Laundries and the Nation's Architecture of Containment* (South Bend, IN: Notre Dame Press, 2007, and Manchester: Manchester University Press, 2008), 24.
4   Bridget Harrison, 'Factory and Workshop Legislation and Convent Laundries, 1895–1907: Campaigning for a Catholic Exception', *Irish Historical Studies* 45, no. 168 (2021): 224–5.

5   Factory and Workshop Acts Amendment Bill, House of Commons Debate, 11 June 1901, vol. 95, cc. 109–42, Mr. John Redmond (Waterford) §.133–138.

6   Factory and Workshop Acts Amendment and Consolidation Bill, House of Commons Debate, 13 August 1901, vol. 99, cc. 649–723, Mr. Leamy (Kildare, N.) §.665–667.

7   Quoted by Fergus A. D'Arcy, 'The Decline and Fall of Donnybrook Fair: Moral Reform and Social Control in Nineteenth Century Dublin', *Saothar* 13 (1988): 10.

8   Fanny Taylor, *Irish Homes and Irish Hearts* (London: Longmans, Green & Co., 1867) 28.

9   For example, see Deborah Logan, 'An "Outstretched Hand to the Fallen": The Magdalen's Friend and the Victorian Reclamation Movement: Part I. "Much More Sinned against than Sinning"', *Victorian Periodicals Review* 30, no. 4 (1997): 368–87; and ibid., 'Part II. "Go, and Sin No More"', *Victorian Periodicals Review* 31, no. 2 (1998): 125–41.

10 Fanny Taylor, who visited the convents of the RSC between 1865 and 1866, attested that: 'no one can visit that convents of this order without being struck by the number of superior, refined, and intelligent sisters who fill its ranks', *Irish Homes and Irish Herts*, 21. See also Mark Coen, Chapter 3 this volume.

11 Quoted in *Final Report of the Commission to Inquire into Child Abuse* (Dublin: Stationery Office, 2009, aka *The Ryan Report*, hereinafter *Final Report CICA*), vol. 2, 12:15.

12 David Nally, *Human Encumbrances: Political Violence and the Great Irish Famine* (Notre Dame, IN: University of Notre Dame Press 2011).

13 Taylor, *Irish Homes and Irish Hearts*, 28.

14 Stuart Henderson, 'Religion and Development in Post-Famine Ireland', *Economic History Review* 72, no. 4 (2019): 1251–85; Emmet Larkin, 'Economic Growth, Capital Investment, and the Roman Catholic Church in Nineteenth Century Ireland', *American Historical Review* 72, no. 3 (1967): 852–84.

15 Maria Luddy, 'Magdalen Asylums in Ireland, 1880–1930: Welfare, Reform, Incarceration?', in *Armenfursorge und Wohltatigkeit. Landliche Gesellschaften in Europa, 1850–1930*, ed. Inga Brandes and Katrin Marx-Jaskulski (Berlin: Peter Lang, 2008), 293.

16 Maria Luddy, 'Unmarried Mothers in Ireland, 1880–1973', *Women's History Review* 20, no. 1 (2011): 110.

17 Olivier Coquelin, 'Politics in the Irish Free State: The Legacy of a Conservative Revolution', *The European Legacy*, 10, no. 1 (2005): 31.

18 Ibid., 29.

19 *Dáil Éireann Debate*, Thursday, 1 March 1923, vol. 2, no. 35, 1909.

20 Kwame Nkrumah, *Neo-Colonialism: The Last Stage of Imperialism* (London: Thomas Nelson & Sons, 1965), ix.

21 Walter Mignolo, 'Prophets Facing Sidewise: The Geopolitics of Knowledge and the Colonial Difference', *Social Epistemology* 19, no. 1 (2005): 112.

22 See A. A. Vallega, *Decoloniality and Philosophy, from a Latin American Perspective* (Eugene, OR: University of Oregon, 2010), 3.

23 N. Maldonado-Torres, 'On the Coloniality of Being: Contributions to the Development of a Concept', *Cultural Studies* 21, nos 2–3 (2007): 243.

24 John Banville, 'A Century of Looking the Other Way', *The New York Times*, 22 May 2009.

25 Dominick Murphy, *Sketches of Irish Nunneries* (Dublin: James Duffy, 1865), 165, quoted by Mark Coen Chapter 1, this volume.

26 James M. Smith, Maeve O'Rourke, Raymond Hill, Claire McGettrick et al., *JFM's Principal Submissions to the Inter-Departmental Committee to Establish the Facts of State Involvement with the Magdalene Laundries* (Dublin: Justice for Magdalenes, 18 September 2012, hereinafter *Principal Submission*), 105 ff., 123–5.

27 Paul Michael Garrett, '"Unmarried Mothers" in the Republic of Ireland', *Journal of Social Work* 16, no. 6 (2016): 708–25.

28 Smith, *Ireland's Magdalen Laundries*, 56.

29 Conditions of Employment Act, 1936, s. 62.

30 Department of Justice, *Report of the Inter-Departmental Committee to Establish the Facts of State Involvement with the Magdalen Laundries* (Dublin, January 2013, aka *McAleese Report*, hereinafter *IDC Report*), ch. 12, 522, 571, 573. Maeve O'Rourke, *Justice for Magdalenes Research NGO Submission to the UN Committee Against Torture in Respect of IRELAND (for the Session)*, July 2017, 13. See also *Principal Submission*, 117–31.

31 *Principal Submission*, 51–6; Smith, *Ireland's Magdalen Laundries*, 65.

32 *Principal Submission*, 58–9; Smith, *Ireland's Magdalen Laundries*, 75–6.

33 For example, see Gerry McNally, 'Probation in Ireland: A Brief History of the Early Years', *Irish Probation Journal* 4, no. 1 (2007): 5–24.

34 Lindsey Earner-Byrne, *Mother and Child, Maternity and Child Welfare in Dublin, 1922–60* (Manchester: Manchester University Press, 2007), 90–108, 123, 149.

35 Lindsey Earner Byrne, 'Mother and Child Scheme Controversy', History Hub Podcast, available online: http://historyhub.ie/mother-and-child-scheme-controversy (accessed 11 September 2022).

36 Eoin O'Sullivan and Ian O'Donnell (eds), *Coercive Confinement in Post-Independent Ireland: Patients, Prisoners and Penitents* (Manchester: Manchester University Press, 2012).

37 Paul Michael Garrett, 'Excavating the Past: Mother and Baby Homes in the Republic of Ireland', *British Journal of Social Work* 47, no. 2 (2017): 358–74.

38 O'Sullivan and O'Donnell, *Coercive Confinement in Post-Independent Ireland*, 7.

39 Harry Ferguson, 'Abused and Looked after Children as "Moral Dirt": Child Abuse and Institutional Care in Historical Perspective', *Journal of Social Policy* 36, no. 1 (2007): 132.

40 Lindsey Earner-Byrne, 'Child Sexual Abuse, History and the Pursuit of Blame in Modern Ireland', in *Exhuming Passions: The Pressure of the Past in Ireland and Australia*, ed. Katie Holmes and Stuart Ward (Dublin: Irish Academic Press, 2011): 52.

41 Ibid., 63–5.

42 Carole Holohan, *In Plain Sight: Responding to the Ferns, Ryan, Murphy and Cloyne Reports* (Dublin: Amnesty International, 2011), 32.

43 For examples, see ibid., 31, 108, 112–13, 140–1, 167, 188, 190, 199, 202, 291, 398.

44 See the testimonies Maeve O'Rourke gathered for the United Nations Committee Against Torture (CAT) in 2011, available online: http://jfmresearch.com/wpcontent/uploads/2017/03/jfm_comm_on_torture_210411.pdf (accessed 11 September 2022).

45 Available online: http://jfmresearch.com/home/restorative-justice/dublin-honours-magdalenes/ (accessed 11 September 2022).

46 Katherine O'Donnell, Sinead Pembroke and Claire McGettrick, *Magdalene Institutions: Recording an Oral and Archival History*, Government of Ireland Collaborative Research Project funded by Irish Research Council, 2012, available online: http://jfmresearch.com/home/oralhistoryproject/ (accessed 11 September 2022).

47 Katherine O'Donnell, Sinead Pembroke and Claire McGettrick, 'MAGOHP/88 Oral History of Molly Farrell': 49. The Oral Histories are available online: http://jfmresearch.com/home/oralhistoryproject/ (accessed 7 September 2022).

48 'Introduction by the Independent Chair Senator Martin McAleese', *IDC Report*, ii.

49 For some examples, see O'Donnell, Pembroke and McGettrick, 'MAGOHP/26 Oral History of Ellen Murphy'; ibid., 'MAGOHP/53 Oral History of Sinead'.

50 See Children Act, 1908 (as amended by the Children Act, 1941). Section 67 allowed for the placing out 'on licence' of a child in an industrial school; the wording of the statutory provision indicates strongly that the power to place a child out on licence was strictly *coterminous* with the childhood period during which a child 'is detained in a certified school'. According to section 67(1), the act of placing a child 'on license' was meant to 'permit the … child to live with any trustworthy and respectable person named in the license and willing to receive and take charge of him'. There is no mention of a child being detained while 'on licence'. Meanwhile, section 68 established a 'supervision' period following the *expiration* of the period of a child's lawful detention in an industrial school. It appears from the distinction between being granted a 'licence' during the supervision period, versus being 'recalled' and 'detained' again in the industrial school upon the licence being revoked, that the granting of a 'licence' during the supervision period was *not* intended to involve detention in an institution.

51 *IDC Report*, ch. 5, 70ff. As the Report puts it (70):

> The effect of this supervision [*sic*] was that until the age of 18 or 19 (until 1941) and until the age of 21 (after 1941), they remained under supervision and liable to recall. Release on licence and recall during post-discharge supervision were the basis in many cases for women [*sic*] being placed in the Magdalene Laundries either directly from or within a number of years of their discharge from an industrial or Reformatory School.

52 For examples of teenage girls who were incarcerated for decades, see O'Donnell, Pembroke and McGettrick, 'MAGOHP/9 Oral History of Maria': 55; Katherine O'Donnell and Claire McGettrick, 'MAGOHP/LE/4, Table 4: Danielle Petherbridge'. Magdalene Institutions: Recording an Oral and Archival History: 37. For examples of women who were incarcerated for their lifetimes, see Claire McGettrick, Chapter 11, in this volume and also O'Donnell, Pembroke and McGettrick, 'MAGOHP/67 Oral History of Mary and Kate Flood' and 'MAGOHP/80 Oral History of Sarah Williams'.

53 For indicative examples, see O'Donnell, Pembroke and McGettrick, 'MAGOHP/9 Oral History of Maria : 2; ibid., 'MAGOHP/85 Oral History of Nuala Lyons': 16ff.

54 Ibid., 'MAGOHP/30 Oral History of Nancy Shannon'.

55 See also *Principal Submission*, 13–16, for details on being held under lock and key.

56 O'Donnell, Pembroke and McGettrick, 'MAGOHP/30 Oral History of Nancy Shannon': 2.

57 Ibid.: 10.

58 Ibid., 'MAGOHP/80 Oral History of Sarah Williams': 3.

59 Ibid., 'MAGOHP/30 Oral History of Nancy Shannon': 13–14.

60 O'Donnell and McGettrick, 'MAGOHP/LE/7, Table 11: Fionna Fox': 4.

61 O'Donnell, Pembroke and McGettrick, 'MAGOHP/80 Oral History of Sarah Williams': 5.

62 Ibid.: 26.

63 Ibid.: 4.

64 Ibid., 'MAGOHP/30 Oral History of Nancy Shannon': 11.

65 Ibid.: 56.

66 Sr Stanislaus Kennedy, *But Where Can I Go? Homeless Women in Dublin* (Dublin: Arlen House, 1985), table 9.9, 132.

67 O'Donnell, Pembroke and McGettrick, 'MAGOHP/67 Oral History of Mary and Kate Flood': 6.

68 Ibid., 'MAGOHP/80 Oral History of Sarah Williams': 7, 27.

69 Ibid., 'MAGOHP/30 Oral History of Nancy Shannon': 16.

70 Ibid.

71 Ibid.: 3.

72 Ibid., 'MAGOHP/80 Oral History of Sarah Williams': 9, 13; 'MAGOHP/53 Oral History of Sinead: 9.

73 Ibid., 'MAGOHP/30 Oral History of Nancy Shannon': 8.

74 O'Donnell and McGettrick, 'MAGOHP/LE/7, Table 11: Fionna Fox': 78–9.

75 O'Donnell, Pembroke and McGettrick, 'MAGOHP/80 Oral History of Sarah Williams': 14.

76 For examples, see ibid., 'MAGOHP/30 Oral History of Nancy Shannon': 27–8; and Judith's testimony in O'Donnell and McGettrick, 'MAGOHP/LE/15, Table 15: Orla O'Connor': 8

77 O'Donnell, Pembroke and McGettrick, 'MAGOHP/85 Oral History of Nuala Lyons': 10.

78 For indicative examples of 'horizontal violence' by inmates, see ibid., 'MAGOHP/67 Oral History of Mary and Kate Flood': 11; ibid., 'MAGOHP/85 Oral History of Nuala Lyons': 9, 26; ibid., 'MAGOHP/80 Oral History of Sarah Williams': 8. Bridget O'Donnell reports that when she was moved to the Magdalene in Sean McDermott Street, she found that the violence by inmates there was much more terrifying than in DML: 48–9.

79 'Introduction by the Independent Chair, Senator Martin McAleese', *IDC Report*, vii.

80 Katherine O'Donnell, 'Official Ireland's Response to the Magdalene Laundries: An Epistemology of Ignorance', *REDRESS: Ireland's Institutions and Transitional Justice* (Dublin: University College Dublin Press, 2022), 282–303.

81 For indicative examples, see O'Donnell, Pembroke and McGettrick, 'MAGOHP/26 Oral History of Ellen Murphy': 13.

82 Ibid., 'MAGOHP/80 Oral History of Sarah Williams': 12.

83 Ibid., 'MAGOHP/30 Oral History of Nancy Shannon': 20–1.

84 Ibid., 'MAGOHP/80 Oral History of Sarah Williams': 12.

85 Ibid., 'MAGOHP/30 Oral History of Nancy Shannon': 56.

86 See also ibid., 'MAGOHP/26 Oral History of Ellen Murphy'. Sarah Williams reports that many girls aged 15 arrived at the RSC Magdalenes from the RSC 'orphanage' or industrial school in Ballaghaderreen, Co. Roscommon, 'MAGOHP/80 Oral History of Sarah Williams': 7.

87 O'Donnell, Pembroke and McGettrick, 'MAGOHP/45 Oral History of Bridget O'Donnell': 43.

88 Ibid., 'MAGOHP/80 Oral History of Sarah Williams': 12.

89 Ibid., 'MAGOHP/30 Oral History of Nancy Shannon': 13.

90 Ibid.

91 O'Donnell and McGettrick, 'MAGOHP/LE/1, Table 1: Aislinn O'Donnell': 6.

92 Ibid., 'MAGOHP/LE/13, Table 13: Lewis Mooney': 13–14.

93 Ibid., 'MAGOHP/LE/22, Table 22: Suzy Byrne': 12ff.

94 Ibid.: 13–14.
95 O'Donnell, Pembroke and McGettrick, 'MAGOHP/30 Oral History of Nancy Shannon': 31 ff.
96 Ibid., 'MAGOHP/45 Oral History of Bridget O'Donnell': 45.
97 Ibid.
98 O'Donnell and McGettrick, 'MAGOHP/LE/7, Table 11: Fionna Fox': 12–13.
99 O'Donnell, Pembroke and McGettrick, 'MAGOHP/45 Oral History of Bridget O'Donnell': 46.
100 Ibid., 'MAGOHP/30 Oral History of Nancy Shannon': 15.
101 Ibid., 'MAGOHP/30 Oral History of Nancy Shannon': 23.
102 Ibid., 'MAGOHP/85 Oral History of Nuala Lyons': 12. See also ibid., 'MAGOHP/30 Oral History of Nancy Shannon': 23.
103 Nancy Shannon knew of one inmate who successfully escaped to Cork: O'Donnell, Pembroke and McGettrick, 'MAGOHP/30 Oral History of Nancy Shannon': 52.
104 O'Donnell, Pembroke and McGettrick, 'MAGOHP/80 Oral History of Sarah Williams': 4.
105 Ibid., 'MAGOHP/26 Oral History of Ellen Murphy':15
106 Ibid., 'MAGOHP/30 Oral History of Nancy Shannon': 52.
107 O'Donnell and McGettrick, 'MAGOHP/LE/1, Table 1: Aislinn O'Donnell': 5.
108 O'Donnell, Pembroke and McGettrick, 'MAGOHP/80 Oral History of Sarah Williams': 27.
109 Ibid., 'MAGOHP/53 Oral History of Sinead': 8.
110 Ibid.
111 Ibid., 'MAGOHP/9 Oral History of Maria': 52.
112 Ibid.: 51.
113 Kennedy, *But Where Can I Go?*, 75, 88, 92, 123. See also Claire McGettrick, Katherine O'Donnell, Maeve O'Rourke, James M. Smith and Mari Steed, *Ireland and the Magdalene Laundries: A Campaign for Justice* (London: I.B. Tauris, 2021): 25–8.
114 Kennedy, *But Where Can I Go?*, 82, 123.
115 'Group 1' comprises 241 women (plus 3 other women who were resident in a long-term hostel that catered mainly for men) but analysis is based on information for only 220 of these women, with no explanation as to why that is the case. Kennedy, *But Where Can I Go?*, table 9.7, 132.
116 Ibid., 129.
117 Ibid.
118 Marie Griffin, 'Catholic Schools in Ireland Today – A Changing Sector in a Time of Change', *Studies An Irish Quarterly Review*, special issue, *Catholic Education in a New Ireland* 108, no. 429 (2019): 58.
119 Ibid.
120 Ibid., 56.
121 For a powerful fictional account of the precarity involved in making interventions resistant to religious congregations, see Claire Keegan *Small Things Like These* (London: Faber, 2021).
122 O'Donnell and McGettrick, 'MAGOHP/LE/23, Table 23: Vicky Conway': 53.

Social, Commercial and
Legal Significance of Donnybrook
Magdalene Laundry

5

Designing Donnybrook

Conceiving Ireland's 'Architecture of Containment'

Chris Hamill

In his 2007 'partial history' of Ireland's Magdalene Laundries, James Smith coins the term, 'the nation's architecture of containment' to refer to the network that connected and supported Ireland's Magdalene laundries together with other carceral institutions across the island.[1] But the use of the word 'architecture' also begs the question, what of the buildings themselves? To date, little has been written of the design and architectural features, nor of the experiential qualities of space within Ireland's Magdalene Laundries (with the notable exception of Jennifer O'Mahoney, Lorraine Bowman Grieve and Alison Torn[2] on the former Magdalene Laundry at Waterford). Yet the study of buildings and architectural history can provide a valuable insight into the cultural attitudes and social priorities of the past, and it is evident that the physical fabric of buildings themselves can act as invaluable historic artefacts.[3]

The evidential qualities of architecture

Architecture is never arbitrary. Buildings are commissioned by a client to serve particular purposes and are designed to meet these requirements and deal adequately with the constraints of site, structure, budget and taste. Therefore, the various iterations of design drawings and the eventual built reality represents a transcript of conversations, disagreements and compromises, which can be read either alone or in combination with other historic sources. Construction projects also tend to represent large investments of time, effort and money, with design decisions often carefully considered and indicative of not just the individual client's priorities, but also of broader institutional and societal attitudes.[4] This evidential quality of architecture, which results from the intentionality of its design, is one of the core concepts of architectural history.[5]

It is also important to remember that buildings are rarely static objects, and evolve and are changed throughout their (sometimes lengthy) lifespans. Thus, they provide evidence not only of design decisions made at the moment of their creation, but also a catalogue of changes made over decades and centuries, evident in revised design drawings[6] and the physical marks of change on the buildings themselves.[7]

Buildings, like all spaces, are also capable of being imbued with personal meaning and cultural significance.[8] Personal connections and associations are often made between the individual and a particular location and group identifications between communities and sites. Moreover, buildings have a noted ability to act as containers of memory, able to evoke and prompt the recall of memories long forgotten, merely by the act of returning to the location where the content of the memory originally occurred.[9]

Finally, buildings also possess another communicative dimension, one quite separate from their ability to act as repositories of design decisions or individual memories. That is the ability to speak to those people viewing the architecture from the outside, and drawing meaning from the form of the architecture. Martin Donougho reminds us that, 'a building's functions may be conveyed rather than just inferred. Buildings can signify or ... exemplify their uses and qualities. They can look like-and be made to look like-schools, prisons, or whatever ... buildings "speak" to us.'[10]

Sources

The ability of architectural remains to act as valid, and valuable, historic sources on their own merits is of increased importance when dealing with the Magdalene Laundries. This is because most 'traditional' historic sources (letters, ledgers, written records, financial documentation, etc.) remain within the private archives of the religious orders involved in the running of these sites, and these various orders have in recent years become extremely unwilling to allow researchers access to their materials.[11] Eva Urban has referred to this gatekeeping as 'a systemic prevention of access' by religious orders.[12] A similar lack of access to archival material is also encountered in relation to much of the written material that historical architectural work would have created (contracts, receipts, letters between client and architect, etc.).[13] Yet, critically, it is not the case for many original architectural drawings which were retained by the architect for reference and dispute resolution should issues with the building later arise. In the case of Donnybrook Magdalene Laundry (DML), the majority of the works on the site from 1877 onwards appear to have been carried out to the designs of architectural partnership O'Neill and Byrne (later W. H. Byrne Architect, c. 1883–1902, and W. H. Byrne & Son, 1902–). When the practice was dissolved in the latter quarter of the twentieth century, a large number of original drawings were deposited in the Irish Architectural Archive (IAA) in Dublin. Happily, due to the custom of dating architectural drawings at point of issue to the client, it is possible to construct a more accurate and fine-grained history of the buildings on site.

In addition to the surviving drawings, there are several other sources for DML from which the architectural researcher can draw. Perhaps most obviously, despite several phases of demolitions, large parts of the site remain standing as of 2021, including the original convent, the chapel and a large part of the laundry building (Figure 5.1, Blocks A, C and E, respectively). The chapel and convent buildings remain within the Sisters of Charity (RSC) Convent, and are not accessible to researchers, however the laundry (Block E) was sold in 1992 to a private laundry operator, and it closed in 2006.[14] The laundry building is now derelict and subject to reuse proposals which will see it

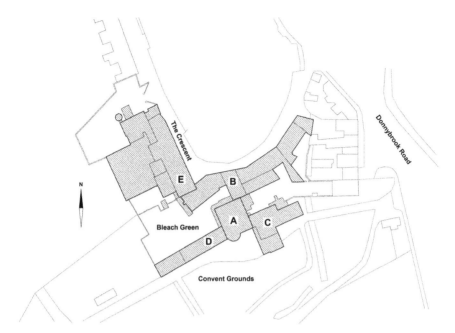

Figure 5.1 Block Plan showing the buildings constituting the Donnybrook Magdalene Laundry at its greatest extent (*c.* 1975–*c.* 1990), shaded. Not to scale. The complex has been classified into Blocks A–E, as mentioned in the text. Each block is bounded by a thick outline.

transformed into housing. The author visited this part of the site in October 2019. As part of the redevelopment process, several extensive drawn surveys and written reports on this discrete part of the site have been produced.[15] Critically, as part of the planning application for the site, these surveys and reports are part of the public record and available to view on Dublin City Council's online planning portal,[16] with older proposals, including 1990s demolitions, available to view in the Dublin Planning Archive. Although limited, several historic photos of the exterior of the site have also been uncovered, providing valuable information on window openings and elevational information. These multiple sources render the architecture of the Laundries (and DML in particular) as one of the best documented and accessible contemporaneous records of these sites and their operations.

Limitations of sources

The use of architectural drawings as a significant historical source is of course open to the critique that design drawings, however detailed, can only be firmly said to represent *proposals* and cannot be counted on to be a true record of what was actually built. This is certainly true, but there remains great value in looking at unbuilt designs, because serious proposals can be relied upon to contain significant insights into the client's needs, the architect's intentions and the overall priorities and influences on the design.[17] Moreover, the drawings contained in the W. H. Byrne collection do not *merely* contain proposal drawings, whose real-world impact is uncertain. Many drawings in the collection are in fact *contract* drawings, signed and dated by the client and the contractor and forming a binding part of the actual construction contract, and therefore a much more accurate indication of what was eventually built. Despite this, on-site variations and mistakes do on occasion mean that the contract set of drawings is not a complete and true reflection of the building which is constructed, however, the veracity of drawings can in many instances be checked against the surviving remnants on site. Furthermore, a great many of the proposal drawings in the collection adopt the standard architectural convention when drawing extensions to existing buildings of hatching the existing structure in grey, and the proposed additions in pink. Those parts of the drawing thereby marked as being 'existing' at the time of the proposals can be relied upon as being the result of survey work on site, and therefore an accurate documentary record, even if the proposed additions shown elsewhere on the same drawing were never realized. Furthermore, full site survey drawings exist from 1899 and 1935, showing in considerable detail the development of the site as it stood on these dates.

The primary limitation of the architectural sources is one of coverage. While some areas of the site are well documented in an ongoing series of drawings, others, such as the convent, are represented only by a single set of drawings, representing one discrete moment in time which allows for only a high-level interpretation of the evolution of the buildings' layouts in these areas. Some portions of the site may not ever have been documented, some additions may have been carried out by architects other than O'Neill and Byrne and their successors and are therefore missing from the IAA collection, and some O'Neill and Byrne drawings have been damaged, or may be missing from the collection entirely. The initial evolution of the site, dating between 1837 and the earliest architectural drawings from 1877, is ascertainable only from cross-comparison of Ordnance Survey (OS) maps from 1843 and 1865, and therefore internal layouts in these periods must be extrapolated from later layouts with more definitive documentation. These gaps in the record, and inconsistent documentary coverage of parts of the site in the available information, required a comparative analysis of the various fragments to piece together a fuller picture of the site's evolution.

General layout and evolution of the Donnybrook site

The following section details the history and evolution of St Mary's Magdalen's Asylum in Donnybrook through the buildings which made up the complex. Institutional histories of the site have been written previously[18] and indeed elsewhere within this volume, and the built heritage of the site has been investigated to an extent through a series of archaeological and architectural reports produced in relation to various planning applications on the site in recent years.[19] These reports have been limited only to that part of the site subject to redevelopment (Block E), using site survey and comparative analysis of historic Ordnance Survey maps at roughly 30-year intervals[20] to give a broad indication of the evolution of the site. These reports have not found or made use of the archival drawings held at the IAA, and as such, are mostly limited to discussions of the external layout of the site as revealed by the OS maps, with discussion of internal layouts and function not being possible. This is an area of research upon which this chapter, with its larger range of sources, expands.

The origins of the Magdalene 'Asylum' at Donnybrook lie in 1837 when after taking over the operation of a lay refuge for 'fallen women' in 1833, the RSC relocated this operation to Donnybrook.[21] The nuns occupied an eighteenth century Georgian villa built on the site of the former Donnybrook Castle.[22] From this core (Figure 5.1, Block A), which still stands today at the heart of the remaining convent, St Mary Magdalen's Asylum would grow. By 1843, the first stage of expansion was complete (Block B), a spur of buildings connected to, and due north of the original Georgian villa following the curved line of the road known today as The Crescent (then known as Church Lane; see Figure 5.2). This range of buildings would, in later years, be used as the receiving and work rooms of DML.

As of 1865, the site had expanded substantially, with the most notable extension being a chapel built adjoining the convent directly to its east (Block C). The curving range of work buildings along The Crescent was also extended eastwards, while a more rectilinear addition of similar floor area had been constructed on its western edge. Some time between 1865 and 1877, a three-storey spur containing sleeping quarters

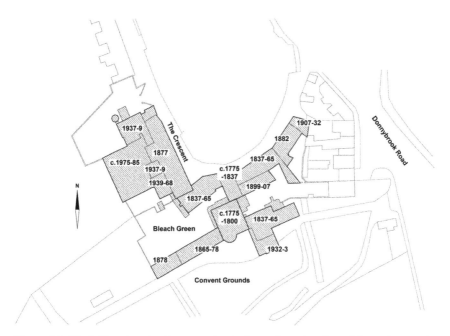

Figure 5.2 Block Plan showing the approximate dates of construction of the various parts of the Donnybrook Magdalene Laundry site. This plan is based off the laundry's greatest extent (*c.* 1975–90) and therefore does not show buildings on site that were demolished prior to this date, nor does it show the extent or dates of subsequent demolitions which took place *c.* 1990–1997.

(Block D) was constructed expanding the site towards the south-west. In 1877, the earliest surviving drawings by O'Neill and Byrne detail a significant two-storey expansion of the laundry facilities, which included a new washing room, steaming house, boiler room and associated chimney (not the one which stands on site today) (Block E).[23] These significant improvements to the industrial capacity of the site were complimented in the following year by a three-storey extension to Block D adding 24 additional women's cells on the upper floors.[24]

Further projects would see the extension of the laundry and dormitories[25] and new drainage systems to cope with the increased load from the enlarged laundry.[26] As can be seen in Figure 5.3, the period of rapid initial expansion of the complex slowed markedly after 1882, however numbers of women resident within the site are noted in the *Catholic Directory* as continuing to rise until the 1910s, when they similarly plateau at around 100–110 individuals.[27]

Between 1932 and 1935, the architect Ralph Byrne was engaged by the RSC to redesign and extend the existing chapel, ultimately settling on a proposal for a new southern choir and extensive exterior remodelling in austere neo-Gothic style, complete with crenelated aisles. The architect's drawings note that this extension is to be completed in a curious mix of granite and cement plaster scored to look like dressed masonry,[28] indicating a desire to keep costs under tight control.

Elsewhere on the site, the laundry was again extended, with designs produced between 1937 and 1939 for a sweeping upgrade to the institution's mechanical plant, including the procurement of two new industrial boilers from Glasgow, and the 90-metres-tall chimney which still stands today, and is the only part of the site designated as a historically 'protected structure'.[29]

Figure 5.3 reveals that although growth slowed post-1880, the site nevertheless expanded steadily throughout the twentieth century, with a significant addition some time between the late 1970s and early 1980s adding a large, flat-roofed block built over much of the former bleach green. At 590 m², this extension represented an increase of approximately 28 per cent to the floorspace of the complex dedicated to industrial laundry work. Records provided to the Committee to Establish the Facts of State Involvement with the Magdalen Laundries by the RSC revealed that the number of women housed in the site in the 1970s rose from 40 to 100 following 'renovations',[30] which very likely refers to this expansion. This move to significantly expand the site in terms of its built estate and numbers of inmates is notable both for its recency, but also because the *IDC Report* found that: 'Magdalen Laundries were operated on a subsistence or close to break-even basis rather than on a commercial or highly profitable basis.'[31] Therefore, this large-scale building project must either have represented a hugely risky outlay for the RSC given their supposedly limited financial means, or else it must call into question the official findings on the commercial nature of Magdalene Laundries such as DML.[32]

The Magdalene Laundry at Donnybrook closed in 1992, with Block E being sold to a private laundry business, which operated there until 2006. Since that time, this portion of the site, representing approximately 27 per cent of its total area, has lain derelict. The remainder of the site, including the convent and the women's residential quarters, was retained by the RSC. The period following the closure of the laundry and division of the site were marked by demolitions. Block D was demolished in 1994 and

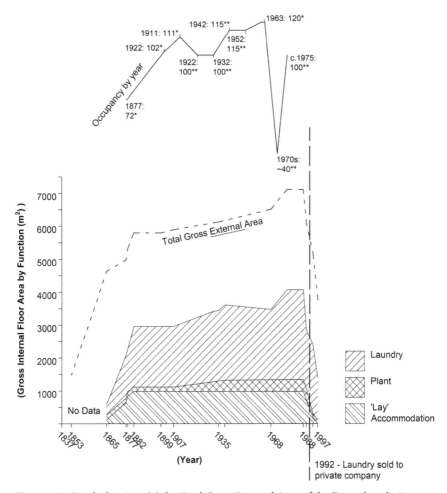

Figure 5.3 Graph showing: *(a)* the Total Gross External Area of the Donnybrook site 1843–1997; *(b)* the Gross Internal Floor Area by Room Function of the site 1865–1997; and *(c)* the numbers of Magdalene women recorded as being resident in Donnybrook 1872–mid-1970s. *Notes:* Gross External Area (GEA) is defined as: 'the area of a building measured externally (i.e. to the external face of the perimeter walls) at each floor level' (NRM1). Gross Internal Floor Area (GIFA) is defined as: 'the area of a building measured to the internal face of the perimeter walls at each floor level' (NRM1). *Sources:* * *The Catholic Directory.* ** *IDC Report* (**2013**) p. 27, citing *Annals of the Religious Sisters of Charity, Donnybrook.*

replaced with a new residential facility for the nuns and the women remaining in their care, and in stages between *c.* 1990 and 1997, the entirety of Block B was similarly demolished.[33] These latter demolitions were not replaced with any new construction, and the area once occupied by these buildings is now used for car parking and storage. The outer skin of these buildings, up to first floor level, still stands as an echo of the former elevation onto the crescent, which can be seen in Figure 5.4. Due to these demolitions, it is difficult today to read the site as the large, self-contained institution it once was. It is only when referring back to historic drawings of the DML complex (see Figure 5.5) that the true scale of the institution becomes apparent.

Figure 5.4 Photograph of the exterior of Donnybrook Magdalene Laundry taken from The Crescent, 1970. Original Photography by The Green Studio. *Source*: Irish Architectural Archive.

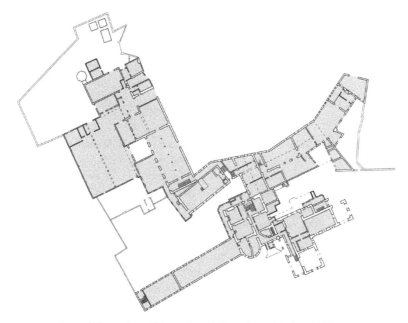

Figure 5.5a Ground floor plan of Donnybrook Laundry, *c.* 1975–*c.* 1990.

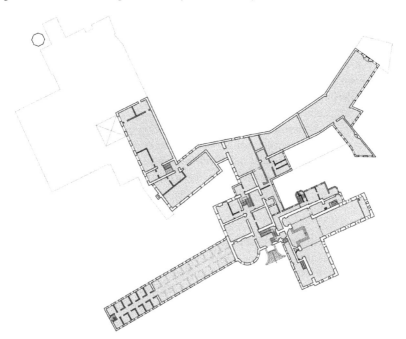

Figure 5.5b First floor plan of Donnybrook Laundry, *c.* 1975–*c.* 1990.

Figure 5.5 Internal layout plans of Donnybrook Laundry at its greatest physical extent, *c.* 1975–*c.* 1990 (third and fourth floors not shown). Internal areas shaded. Not to scale.

Recently, in 2016 and 2019, planning applications for the redevelopment of Block E have been lodged, with the latter being approved. These development proposals, and the reuse of Ireland's institutional heritage sites more generally, are however outside the scope of this chapter, but represent a potentially interesting avenue for further study.

Architectural analysis

An overall analysis of the Donnybrook site reveals a roughly 'X-shaped' plan (Figure 5.5), with various additions in the late nineteenth and twentieth centuries radiating outwards from the central form of the original convent. From above, these growth patterns give the site a superficial resemblance to Victorian prisons in the Pentonville model, whereby various wings are connected back to a central hub structure to maximize surveillance and security. Although a tempting analogy to draw, especially in the case of accommodation Block D, which is laid out internally in a very recognizable institutional pattern with small cells arranged off a central hallway, it is unlikely that the overall site was designed with such ordered, regulating geometries as seen in contemporaneous prisons[34] and mental asylums.[35] It is clear that growth was agglomerative over time, and certainly not centrally planned from the outset. The radial pattern of the plan likely owes more to the fact that the central convent building was the oldest on site, and extensions took place from there outwards, constrained to the north by the boundary of The Crescent. This ad hoc growth is supported by the 1935 survey plans which reveal that the layout of the laundry works was not particularly efficient, with arriving and departing laundry crossing paths and clashing in several areas.[36] Nevertheless, it is certainly arguable that this hub-and-spoke layout greatly aided in security and the control of occupants' movements, and indeed, several of the women interviewed in the Magdalene Oral History Project (2013) specifically describe the site as feeling 'like a prison'.[37]

The architecture of the site was clearly designed to be insular, with solid, impermeable walls facing out to the streetscape beyond, whilst being relatively more open to the enclosed grounds of the convent. Laundry rooms were arranged along the outer edge of the site, forming a 'buffer zone' of actively surveilled space.[38] This inward-looking design of the site is seen most vividly in the architectural drawings,[39] for example Figure 5.6, where the large sash windows facing inwards into the convent grounds contrast starkly with the blank walls facing onto the exterior world, still visible from The Crescent today.

It should be stressed that, whilst the architecture of DML very likely made the task of confining, surveilling and forcing the Magdalene women to work an easier one, this does not *necessarily* mean that the site was designed with these goals in mind. Buildings are constantly used in ways their designers did not envisage or intend, and indeed, much of the preceding analysis could be fairly applied to any convent, or 'total institution',[40] without the suggestion of malicious purpose. Despite this, MESH Architects writing about the site in 2019 were firmly of the view that:

> The largely blind external facades along The Crescent and the insular nature of the Asylum complex at large represent the imprisonment intended by these

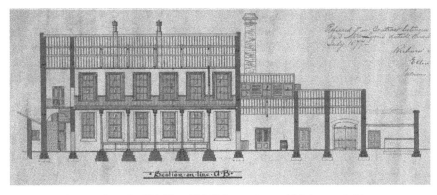

Figure 5.6 Extract from R. O'Neill and W. H. Byrne. 1877. *Additions to St Mary Magdalen's Asylum Donnybrook. Sheet No. 3. Note*: This cross section through the laundry buildings clearly shows the inward-looking nature of the site. Those windows looking to the interior of the convent ground are large, with lower cills permitting views out, and present on both ground- and first-floor level. Conversely, there are no windows on the opposite side of the building, which faces out onto The Crescent and the outside world beyond. *Source*: W. H. Byrne & Son Collection, Irish Architectural Archive.

structures … The lack of amenities and the larger landscape of control noted throughout the complex is indicative of the cultural trends towards persecution of unwed mothers during the height of the Magdalen Laundry era.'[41]

The immediate urban context of DML is also noteworthy. At the time of its foundation, the site was on the rural periphery of Dublin city, but was still a desirable and prosperous area, home to several large, demesne houses.[42] Following the construction of the local chapel to designs by Pugin and Ashworth in 1866 and the end of the annual medieval Donnybrook Fair in 1868,[43] the area became increasingly built-up and suburban in character whilst still retaining its prosperous aura. This growth surrounded and enveloped DML, bringing some of the city's wealthiest and most influential denizens into close physical proximity with the women held as Magdalenes within the convent. The development of and investment in the area would only continue in the twentieth century with the construction of the nearby University College Dublin and RTÉ (state broadcaster) campuses. As Emilie Pine notes, media depictions, and the broader public perception of the Magdalene Laundries, tend to illustrate isolated, rural institutions,[44] whereas in fact, these sites were almost exclusively located within major towns and cities, surrounded by large numbers of free-citizens living their lives in view of the convents' high walls. In the case of DML, these walls were 3.7 m tall on average,[45] and whilst obscuring the activities within the convent and laundry, acted as an unavoidable signifier of the presence of the institution. Indeed, as Nancy Shannon attests, during her time in DML in the 1960s, the local residents knew of the presence of the Magdalenes in their midst, even expressing sympathy for their plight.[46] It is however worth noting that this sympathy was not universal among local residents; Sara W. recalls that after a successful escape attempt, she and two fellow Magdalenes were taken in for the night by a local women, who then summoned the local Gardaí while the girls were sleeping. All three were returned to DML by the police.[47] The police officers in question would not have had to travel far. Donnybrook Garda Station was, and remains, less than 200 m from the entrance to the Magdalene Laundry; a potent metaphor for the links between the State and the religious orders which allowed for the perpetration and continuation of the Magdalene system for as long as it did.

The women's spaces

It is noteworthy that those spaces predominantly inhabited by the Magdalene women, the residential quarters and the laundry facilities, have been almost entirely demolished following the laundry's sale in 1992. Figure 5.3 shows that the maximum extent of residential provision for the women in Donnybrook was achieved around 1880, and remained relatively static until the site's closure more than a century later. This contrasts sharply with the laundry facilities, which grew and were extended (presumably at considerable expense) throughout the period. Of course, the lack of expansion of residential space during this same period does not mean that the bedroom spaces were neglected in terms of investment, and were likely refurbished, subdivided and maintained to an extent during this period. However, the architect's written submission to the planning authority for permission to demolish Block D reveals that, 'this building over the years become [*sic*] infected with dry and wet rot',[48] suggesting a lack of adequate maintenance during the last decades of its existence.

In the nineteenth century, residential quarters appear to have comprised a mix of individual cells[49] and dormitories;[50] however, it seems that by the 1950s, all dormitories had been subdivided into cells, as attested to in the oral history of Sara W. who was resident in Donnybrook 1954–6.[51] These cells were located on the uppermost floors of Block B and the first and second storeys of Block D. Block B contained laundry facilities on its lower two floors,[52] and Block D, at least initially, had a linen room on its ground floor.[53] This would seem to contradict the submission of the religious congregations to the Interdepartmental Committee of inquiry that, 'women who were admitted to the Magdalen Laundries never lived in the laundry premises, but rather in attached living quarters'.[54]

Rooms for the women were small, averaging 5–6 m², with those in Block D as small as 2.2 m × 2.2 m in dimension. Rooms within the main convent were substantially larger at 10–14 m², and it is suggested that these larger rooms were for the nuns, revealing a clear spatial hierarchy in the architectural layout. That the nuns lived and dined separately from the women is also stated in the oral histories.[55] Specifically, Bridget O'Donnell notes that the nuns lived separately from the women except for three who ran the laundry operations and lived 'over the laundry'.[56] This corresponds with the architectural investigation, which reveals three larger bedrooms on the second floor of Block B, in the oldest part of the block, very possibly the rooms for these nuns, and speaks to the accuracy and level of spatial specificity in the oral testimonies, which can only be revealed when the reader is familiar with the site's layout.

Sara W.'s testimony on the sleeping quarters for the Magdalene women is powerful: 'we were put up in those cells up in the corridors . . . we all had cells and you were put in there then and that was your sleep. The doors were locked every night. The room door was locked ...'[57] The locking of cell doors from the outside is also attested to by Nancy Shannon[58] and the control of electric lighting by the nuns outside the locked rooms[59] would no doubt have added to the carceral nature of the space, as well as raising troubling implications in terms of fire safety.

Views to the outside world would also have been obscured in at least some of the cells. The St Mary Magdalen's Donnybrook Annals of 1909–15 note: 'The shutters on the outside of the Penitents cells which gave the place a very gloomy aspect have been removed, and replaced by ribbed glass, which still shut out the view of the road, but give more light and brightness to the cells.'[60] It is however uncertain whether the cell windows were barred from the outside. Sara W. states clearly that they were,[61] but available photographs of the exterior of the site do not show bars on the high-level windows where the bedrooms are, although it should be stated that not all bedroom areas are visible in the surviving photographs. Escape from the rooms above Block B in particular would have been exceedingly difficult, with the cell doors locked and the small, high-level windows into the rooms visible in Figure 5.4 clearly showing bottom-hung, inward-opening hopper windows which would have been a significant impediment to escape. Even if escape through the window was possible, the women would have been confronted with a sheer, 11 m (36 ft) drop to the hard-surfaced road below. Figure 5.7 illustrates the following quote from Sara W., and is accurately drawn to scale from the surviving architectural records of the site, clearly showing the difficulty women would have had not only in escaping, but also in simply gaining a view of the world outside: '[T]he windows used to be up very high, like a small little window ... and I used to climb up the top of the bed to look out the window.'[62]

The chapel

It is in the chapel, however, that the fact that Donnybrook was deliberately designed with a regime of segregation and control in mind becomes most evident. In a series of design proposals to expand the chapel produced by architect Ralph Byrne during 1932, it is clear that the architect understands that there are two communities co-resident within this site, with the religious sisters being the senior party. For example, in the earliest proposal, Drawing 2806[63] (Figure 5.8), the architect proposes a new southern choir for the nuns. This is accompanied by a reorientation of the altar to face south and towards the nuns' seating in the extension, and away from the girls and women held as Magdalenes, despite the usual orientation of the altar and nave in a Catholic church being east/west. Later proposals, including the one actually constructed, returned the altar to its more usual orientation.

It is of course far from uncommon to find chapels shared between members of religious orders and laity, but spatially segregated between the two, though in the case of Donnybrook, this separation certainly emphasizes the power imbalance and subordination inherent within the Magdalene system.[64] However, the degree to which the architect understood the true workings of the site is revealed when one considers

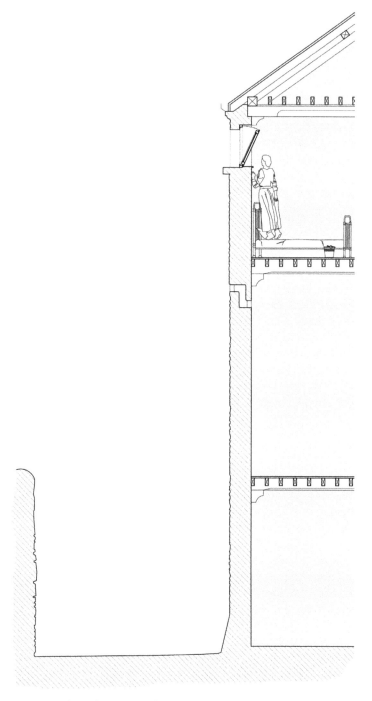

Figure 5.7 Section through accommodations in Block B, illustrating the testimony of Sara W.

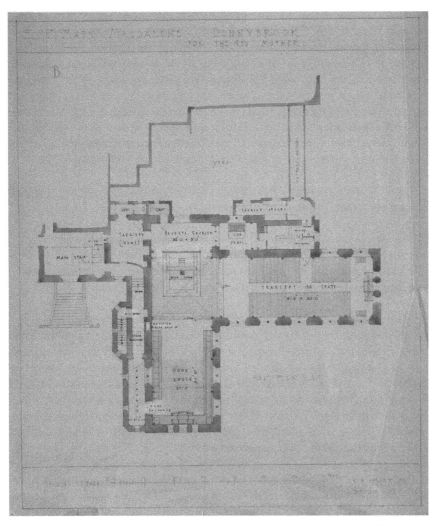

Figure 5.8 W. H. Byrne & Son Architects. 1932a. *Drawing 2806. St Mary Magdalene. Donnybrook. Note*: Early proposals for the expansion of the chapel at Donnybrook Magdalene Laundry in the 1930s. Note the orientation of the altar towards the nun's choir, rather than east/west as is traditional. The transept for the women and girls held as Magdalenes contains 156 seats and connects to the laundry buildings via an umbilical link noted as a 'Covered Bridge' in this drawing (upper right of the drawing). *Source*: W. H. Byrne & Son Collection, Irish Architectural Archive.

the circulation spaces proposed to connect the new extension back to the rest of the institution. Common to all the various proposals for the chapel renovations is a system of separate corridors; one leading to the nun's choir, and one leading to the Magdalene girls' and women's seating, clearly showing that the nuns and the women designated Magdalenes entered and exited the chapel separately. Following these respective corridors to their destinations elsewhere on site reveals that the corridor leading to the nun's choir returns to the main convent building, whereas the 'covered way' connecting to the seating area for the Magdalene girls and women leads directly back to the laundry, rather than to their accommodation. The implication being that, after Mass, the nuns returned to the convent, while the girls and women held as Magdalenes were sent back to work.

Again, this understanding of this part of the site, now demolished, reveals the spatial accuracy of survivor testimony. Sara W. recalls:

> We had two Masses every morning, one was at six o'clock and that was out kneeling in the corridor ... You'd come down then and you'd get porridge again for your breakfast, a cup of tea and a slice of bread, that was your breakfast, and you went back up to Mass then again and then you went straight to the laundry room.[65]

This phrasing is accurate to the spatial layout to the site; the refectory was on the ground floor, so the women would physically have to 'come down' to breakfast, and the chapel was positioned directly above the refectory, so they would indeed have gone 'back up' to attend Mass. Note also that Sara W. clearly states, 'then you went straight to the laundry ..', as does Bridget O'Donnell, attesting, 'Then from Mass, you went into the laundry and straight away it was non-stop work, work, work, work, work ...'[66] These are not just summarized accounts of these girls and women's daily routines; they are literal and accurate descriptions of the space. They did go 'straight' to the laundry from Mass, because the architect had designed a covered corridor linking these spaces, for that very purpose.

This architectural umbilical which funnelled the Magdalenes back to their place of labour was a common feature of the architecture of Magdalene Laundries. Similar structures existed at Sean McDermott Street in Dublin, Waterford[67] and Limerick,[68] and the existence of a similar structure connecting St Aiden's Industrial School and St Mary's Magdalene Laundry in New Ross Co. Wexford, was a critical feature in the testimony of Maureen Sullivan in her campaign for inclusion within the Industrial Schools Redress Scheme.[69] Notably, this arrangement appears to be relatively unique to O'Neill and Byrne's Magdalene Asylum churches as, even in other institutional settings, such as St Mary's Asylum for the Blind (also operated by the RSC) it is clearly recorded that, 'nuns and the blind use the same entrance [to the chapel]'.[70] This poses the inevitable question: why were the Magdalene women treated differently through the designs of the same architect?

It is clear from the architect's drawings and the very purposeful way in which the circulation of various occupant groups was directed by the site's architecture, that the person at the drafting table knew, at a minimum, that there was a subordinate class of women within this complex, and that this group were required to work in the laundry.

Indeed, it was such an imperative, that a direct link between the chapel and the laundry was envisaged and provided. To what extent the architect approved of the regimen of punitive control, confinement and coercive labour practices occurring within the site they were designing may never be known, and certainly not without access to private letters and correspondence which, if they exist at all, are in the restricted archives of the RSC. Nevertheless, it is clear that the architect knew a considerable amount about the operations and purpose of DML, and whilst they may never have considered the ethical implications of *why* such a place should exist, who the occupants were and whether they were volunteers or prisoners, the architect certainly had the *opportunity* to ask these questions should they have cared to do so. The work of architects evident in the DML site may also be read as a proxy for the male, Catholic and middle-class-dominated hierarchy of Irish society at the time. That the religious orders and government knew what went on in sites like Donnybrook is, since the *IDC Report* of 2013, beyond any doubt, but the degree to which the public at large knew of what occurred behind the convent walls remains a subject of debate.[71]

Conclusion

This chapter has made use of novel architectural and archival sources to add detail to our understanding of how the Donnybrook site evolved over time, and has analysed the architecture which was produced, in order to gain an insight into the experiences of the Magdalene women residing within those spaces, and the knowledge and intent behind those commissioning and designing the buildings. The level to which the testimony of former Magdalene women has been demonstrably accurate to the spatial qualities and layout of the site, even nearly 60 years later in some cases, is remarkable. It was not the author's intention that this architectural study should be used as a 'fact check' on survivor testimony (nor is this viewed as an appropriate use of any such study)[72] but the simple fact that the transcripts have proved verifiably accurate in terms of spatial recall, must give pause to those who have, in recent years, sought to dismiss such testimony out of hand as being somehow 'less reliable' than other sources.

Following the summary of the evidence laid out in this chapter, it seems very likely that, although initially, 'these institutions were in general established as refuges and that the laundry operations attached … provided their means of financial support',[73] the consciously designed additions to the Donnybrook site in subsequent years exhibit clear tendencies towards imprisonment, segregation, surveillance and control, to a much greater degree than would be expected of voluntary refuges or more standard monastic architectures.

For architects to carry out this introspection on what the immediately prior generations might have facilitated and colluded with, is to ask two fundamental questions. Knowing that the Magdalene Laundries, like all architectural creations, were designed to serve particular purposes: (a) how much did the architects know of the abuses perpetrated with and enabled by their designs; and (b) to what extent could or indeed should they have known? Whilst the question of intentionality may never be fully or even satisfactorily resolved, there are clues within the architecture of Magdalene sites which provoke difficult but necessary conversations about the ethics of architectural practice and the role of wider Irish society in the enabling and maintenance of the nation's architecture of containment.

Notes

1   James Smith, *Ireland's Magdalen Laundries and the Nation's Architecture of Containment* (Notre Dame, IN: University of Notre Dame Press, 2007).
2   Jennifer O'Mahoney, Lorraine Bowman Grieve and Alison Torn, 'Ireland's Magdalene Laundries and the Psychological Architecture of Surveillance', in *Surveillance, Architecture and Control: Discourses on Spatial Culture*, ed. Susan Flynn and Antonia Mackay (London: Palgrave Macmillan, 2019), 187–208.
3   Andrew Ballantyne, 'Architecture as Evidence', in *Rethinking Architectural Historiography*, ed. Dana Arnold, Elvan Altan Ergut and Belgin Turan Özkaya (London: Routledge, 2006), 36–49.
4   Leland Roth, 'Architecture, Memory, and Economics', in *Understanding Architecture: Its Elements, History, and Meaning*, ed. Leland Roth and Amanda C. Roth Clark (New York: Routledge, 2014), 153–60.
5   Hazel Conway and Rowan Roenisch, *Understanding Architecture: An Introduction to Architecture and Architectural History* (London: Routledge, 2004), 5.
6   William Whyte, 'How Do Buildings Mean? Some Issues of Interpretation in the History of Architecture', *History and Theory* 45, no. 2 (2006): 171.
7   Andrew Herscher and Eyal Weizman, 'Conversation: Architecture, Violence, Evidence', *Future Anterior: Journal of Historic Preservation, History, Theory, and Criticism* 8, no. 1 (2011): 115.
8   Doreen Massey, *For Space* (London: Sage, 2005).
9   Charles Fernyhough, *Pieces of Light: The New Science of Memory* (London: Profile, 2013); Laura McAtackney, 'Materials and Memory: Archaeology and Heritage as Tools of Transitional Justice at a Former Magdalen Laundry', *Éire-Ireland* 55, nos 1–2, (2020): 231–2.
10   Martin Donougho, 'The Language of Architecture', *Journal of Aesthetic Education* 21, no. 3 (1987): 54; Robert G. Hershberger, 'Architecture and Meaning', special issue, *Journal of Aesthetic Education* 4, no. 4 (1970): 9.
11   Catherine Cox, 'Institutional Space and the Geography of Confinement in Ireland, 1750–2000', in *The Cambridge History of Ireland*, ed. Thomas Bartlett (Cambridge: Cambridge University Press, 2018): 700; Maria Luddy, *Prostitution and Irish Society, 1800–1940*, (Cambridge: Cambridge University Press, 2007): 107.
12   Eva Urban, 'The Condition of Female Laundry Workers in Ireland 1922–1996: A Case of Labour Camps on Trial', *Études Irlandaises* no. 37-2 (2012): 52.
13   During the course of the research for this chapter, the Archives of the RSC were contacted (14 June 2021) regarding the availability of any records relating to the design, construction, maintenance and upkeep of the buildings at the Donnybrook site. A polite, but categorical reply was received on 15 June 2021 via email that no such records have been kept within the archive.
14   Department of Justice, *Report of the Inter-Departmental Committee to Establish the Facts of State Involvement with the Magdalen Laundries* (Dublin, January 2013, aka *McAleese Report*, hereinafter *IDC Report*), 27.

15 MESH Architects, *Architectural Heritage Impact Assessment, Proposed Development at the Former Donnybrook Laundry, The Crescent, Donnybrook, Dublin 4*, 2019, available online: https://webapps.dublincity.ie/AnitePublicDocs/00761085.pdf (accessed 3 August 2021).

16 Planning Ref: 3621-16 (2016; withdrawn); and 2412-19 (2019; approved).

17 Jonathan Glancey, *Lost Buildings* (London: Carlton Books, 2008), 218–51.

18 *IDC Report*, 18; Luddy, *Prostitution and Irish Society*, 94.

19 Historic Building Consultants, *Donnybrook Laundry, The Crescent, Donnybrook, Dublin 4, Built Heritage Assessment*, 2016; Faith Bailey, *Archaeological Assessment at The Crescent, Donnybrook, Dublin 4 on Behalf of: Pembroke Partnership*, 2019, available online: https://webapps.dublincity.ie/AnitePublicDocs/00761067.pdf (accessed 03.08.21); MESH Architects, *Architectural Heritage Impact Assessment, Proposed Development at the Former Donnybrook Laundry*, 2019, available online: https://webapps.dublincity.ie/AnitePublicDocs/00761085.pdf (accessed 03.08.21).

20 OS maps of the site date from 1843, 1865, 1907, 1935–6 and 1968.

21 *IDC Report*, 27. See further, Mark Coen, Chapter 3, this volume.

22 Historic Building Consultants, *Donnybrook Laundry*, 5.

23 John O'Neill and W. H. Byrne, 'Additions to St Mary Magdal ... [Damaged]', 1877.

24 John O'Neill and W. H. Byrne, 'Additions St Mary Magdalen's Asylum, Donnybrook', 1878.

25 John O'Neill and W. H. Byrne, 'Additions to St Mary's Asylum, Donnybrook. No. 2', 1882.

26 William H. Byrne, 'Block Plan Showing Proposed New Drains', 1899.

27 *Irish Catholic Directory, 1913*, 197.

28 W. H. Byrne & Son Architects, 'Proposed Alterations to Chapel' 1932b.

29 Planning Ref: 8713.

30 *IDC Report*, 27.

31 Ibid., 993.

32 The surviving financial records of DML also demonstrate that large surpluses were generated by the laundry. See Brid Murphy and Martin Quinn, Chapter 7, this volume.

33 Planning Ref: 1729/97.

34 Richard Butler, *Building the Irish Courthouse and Prison: A Political History, 1750–1850* (Cork: Cork University Press, 2020).

35 Patrick Quinlan, *Walls of Containment* (Dublin: University College Dublin Press, 2021).

36 W. H. Byrne & Son, 'Site Plan Showing Existing Laundry', 1935.

37 Katherine O'Donnell, Sinead Pembroke and Claire McGettrick, 'Oral History of Nancy Shannon', Magdalene Institutions: Recording an Oral and Archival History (Government of Ireland Collaborative Research Project, Irish Research Council, 2013), 16; Katherine O'Donnell, Sinead Pembroke and Claire McGettrick, 'Oral History of Sara W.', Magdalene Institutions: Recording an Oral and Archival History (Government of Ireland Collaborative Research Project, Irish Research Council, 2013), 19.

38 O'Mahoney, Bowman Grieve and Torn, 'Psychological Architecture of Surveillance', 198.

39 O'Neill and Byrne, 'Additions', 1877.

40 In 1961, Erving Goffman defined the concept of a 'total institution' as one which completely controls its inmates, 'symbolized by the barrier to social intercourse with the outside and to departure that is often built right into the physical plant such as

locked doors, high walls, [and] barbed wire . . .' See Irving Goffman, *Asylums: Essays on the Social Situation of Mental Patients and Other Inmates* (New York: Anchor Books, 1961), 4.

41 MESH Architects, *Proposed Development at the Former Donnybrook Laundry*, 14.

42 Bailey, *Archaeological Assessment at The Crescent*, 6.

43 See further Katherine O'Donnell, Chapter 4, this volume.

44 Emilie Pine, 'Coming Clean? Remembering the Magdalen Laundries', in *Memory Ireland: History and Modernity*, vol. 1, ed. Oona Frawley (Syracuse, NY: Syracuse University Press, 2011), 157–71.

45 William H. Byrne, 'Additions to St Mary's Asylum, Donnybrook, No. 3', 1882.

46 O'Donnell, Pembroke and McGettrick, 'Oral History of Nancy Shannon' (2013b), 54–5.

47 Ibid., 'Oral History of Sara W.' (2013c), 4–5.

48 Pamela Kennedy, Letter to Mr. R. Deegan, Dublin Corporation, Re: St Mary's, Brookvale Road, Donnybrook, Dublin, 'New Kitchen, Dining Room and Sitting Room', 23 March 1994. Ref: 2212/93, Dublin City Council Planning Archive.

49 O'Neill and Byrne, 'Additions', 1878.

50 Ibid., 1882.

51 O'Donnell, Pembroke and McGettrick, 'Oral History of Sara W.' (2013c), 6.

52 O'Neill and Byrne, 'Additions', 1882; W. H. Byrne & Son Architects, 'Site Plan', 1935.

53 O'Neill and Byrne, 'Additions', 1878.

54 *IDC Report*, 2.

55 O'Donnell, Pembroke and McGettrick, 'Oral History of Nancy Shannon' (2013b), 24.

56 Katherine O'Donnell, Sinead Pembroke and Claire McGettrick, 'Oral History of Bridget O'Donnell', Magdalene Institutions: Recording an Oral and Archival History, Government of Ireland Collaborative Research Project (Irish Research Council, 2013a), 46.

57 O'Donnell, Pembroke and McGettrick, 'Oral History of Sara W.' (2013c), 6.

58 Ibid., 'Oral History of Nancy Shannon' (2013b), 45.

59 Ibid., 'Oral History of Sara W.' (2013c), 25.

60 This excerpt from the House Annals of St Mary Magdalen's 1909 to 1915, RSC Archives, was shared with the author by Mark Coen on 8 October 2021. See the Introduction to this volume for further information on access to the House Annals.

61 See above.

62 Ibid., 6.

63 W. H. Byrne & Son Architects, 'Drawing 2806. St Mary Magdalene. Donnybrook', 1932a.

64 See, for example, the Chapel of the Sacred Heart in Strabane, also by O'Neill & Byrne.

65 O'Donnell, Pembroke and McGettrick, 'Oral History of Nancy Shannon' (2013b), 4.

66 Ibid., 'Oral History of Bridget O'Donnell' (2013a), 43.

67 O'Mahoney, Bowman Grieve and Torn, 'Psychological Architecture of Surveillance', 198.

68 Evelyn Glynn, '"Left Holding the Baby": Remembering and Forgetting the Magdalen Laundry' (BA thesis, Limerick Institute of Technology, 2009), 76.

69 See Steven O'Riordan's 2009 documentary *The Forgotten Maggies* at 4 minutes 50 seconds. The documentary is available online at: www.youtube.com/watch?v=Y4VAdN7HaxQ (accessed 10 September 2022).

70 J. J. Tracey, 'A Dissertation on the Buildings of John O'Neill and O'Neill and Byrne Architects 1862–1883' (MA thesis, Queen's University Belfast, 1987), 72. This thesis may be consulted at the Irish Architectural Archive.

71 Auxiliadora Pérez-Vides, 'Gender, Deviance and Institutional Violence in Ireland's Magdalene Laundries: An Analysis of Two Filmic Representations of Abuse', in *Teaching against Violence: The Reassessing Toolbox*, ed. Ines Testoni, Michael Wieser, Angelika Groterath and Maria Silvia Guglielmin (Utrecht: ATGENDER, The European Association for Gender Research, Education and Documentation, and Budapest and New York: Central European University Press, 2013), 78.
72 Robert Jan van Pelt, *The Case for Auschwitz: Evidence from the Irving Trial* (Bloomington, IN: Indiana University Press, 2002).
73 *IDC Report*, 2.

6

'Benefactors and Friends'

Charitable Bequests, Reparation and the Donnybrook Laundry[1]

Máiréad Enright

Magdalene orders' requests for public financial support were once a mundane part of Irish life. Raidió Éireann's listeners, tuning in on Halloween evening, 1970,[2] would have heard Fr Phillip O'Driscoll's appeal for donations to Donnybrook Magdalene Laundry (DML), in a five-minute slot between the Angelus and Sports Time.[3] That ordinariness was mirrored in the law. Focusing on charitable bequests, this chapter uses DML to explore the concepts of charity central to the laundries' operation. The first section explores how bequests both normalized and funded abuses in DML in the period 1922–72.[4] The second examines how concepts of charity operating during this period are inherited in contemporary efforts at 'redress' and 'restorative justice'. The chapter closes by showing how religious charity's uses are revealed and refracted in the controversy over Ireland's new National Maternity Hospital.

Past: Charity against abuse

DML, like other Magdalene Laundries and religious institutions, solicited and obtained bequests from Irish benefactors throughout the twentieth century. As discussed elsewhere in this collection,[5] DML's archives are not ordinarily open to researchers. This makes it difficult to analyse individual motivations for leaving money to the laundry, or to understand how bequests were treated once received. However, newspaper notices of these bequests give a sense of those leaving larger amounts. Some were priests. Most were lay people. They were generally men of the merchant, professional and landlord classes, their widows and their surviving daughters, who prospered as Ireland settled into independence. Some were strong farmers. Many lived in wealthier Dublin suburbs such as Rathgar, Dún Laoghaire, Terenure, Ballsbridge and Donnybrook itself. They include well-known Dubliners such as nationalist politician and industrialist Sir Joseph Downes,[6] publican Davy Byrne,[7] banker Thomas Patrick Morrissey,[8] Senator George Nesbitt[9] and his wife Enid[10] and Kate Ellen

Malone,[11] widow of the brewer and distiller Laurence Malone. Testators tended to leave several charitable bequests to several religious institutions, rather than a single large donation. In 1924, for example, one John Dowling left his money to over thirty religious organizations.[12] Some left money to more than one Magdalene or rescue institution. Generally, bequests were in cash, but other gifts were possible. William James Devereux, a retired merchant from Wexford, bequeathed the Mother Superioress at Donnybrook £200 worth of 'guaranteed stock' in the Great Southern and Western Railway Company of Ireland.[13] The Dublin grocer Philip Joseph Doyle directed that his properties at 73–77 Church Street should be sold and the proceeds divided equally between a number of religious organizations, including DML.[14] Most testators included a gift in exchange for Masses for the repose of their souls, and some included gifts to their parishes of origin.[15]

In leaving money to DML, some testators may have been honouring care obligations.[16] For instance, some widows who left such bequests had themselves lived in old age in the fee-paying institutions of the Religious Sisters of Charity (RSC), including St Monica's Widows' Home, Belvedere Place and St Mary's Home on Merrion Road.[17] Others may have had relatives who were RSC sisters. For example, in 1934, the Wexford stockbroker James John Keating[18] left £1,000 to DML 'for the charitable purposes of the convent as the superioress shall think fit'. He separately left £500 to the superioress of the Donnybrook convent at Floraville Road, where his sister, Ellen Mary, was a nun. Most people, however, left money for the laundry's charitable purposes.

Charitable bequests featured in discourses normalizing women's confinement in the Magdalene Laundries and legitimating their punishment. Although couched in the language of benevolence, charity rarely takes the form of pure gift.[19] Mary Douglas cautions that: '[t]here are no free gifts: gift cycles engage persons in permanent commitments that articulate the dominant institutions'.[20] Critical scholars emphasize that giving charitably is an opportunity[21] to cultivate compassion, good judgement and generosity, in the selection of favoured causes.[22] As Nancy Goldfarb puts it, charity is a means both to assuage one's guilt and 'purchase a delicious self-approval'.[23] It is also an exercise of power; it affirms one's status as one of those able to give; a member of a charitable elite.[24] John H. Hanson explains the status compensations of charitable donation:

> Charity is enacted through scripted activities, rituals, and social signals that co-opt class conflicts by the seeming surrender of resources. Gift giving, while overtly an act of voluntary loss, occurs within a covert framework of cultural compensation in which recognition, status affirmation, and other emoluments offset or negate that loss.[25]

These motivations are especially powerful in the context of bequests, when testators think about the legacy they would like to leave after their deaths. A bequest carries an element of generativity; 'a desire to invest one's substance in forms that outlive the self'.[26] Bequests can ensure the continuity of important institutions, and communicate moral lessons to those left behind.[27] Intentions to mobilize these ambitions are apparent in the fundraising materials employed by the RSC and their advocates to provoke the consciences of wealthy readers: encouraging potential benefactors to imagine themselves as agents of rescue.[28] They use hierarchical language, reinforcing moral and class divisions between benefactors and their imagined women beneficiaries.[29] In a Christmas newspaper appeal in 1916, the Donnybrook RSC wrote that:

> Those who help in the salvation of souls will, undoubtedly get a rich reward from Him, Who, in the great accounting day will use these consoling words. 'Amen I say to you, Whatsoever who did to the least of My brethren, you did it unto Me.'[30]

In a 1932 charity sermon, a Fr Harnett told listeners that 'the charitable public should show their love for Jesus by helping these poor lowly ones back to His feet.'[31] Charity was understood as a tool of social reform; given subject to conditions related to character, deservingness and accountability. Because charity, by definition, is exceptional giving to those in need, charitable organizations like DML produced and reproduced theories of the origins of that need, whether of individual failing or social injustice. References here to the 'least' and the 'lowly ones' distinguish the 'fallen' women and girls in DML from their morally upstanding benefactors.

Many testators will have understood that the laundry's work would cease without their donations. In 1938, in a charity sermon on behalf of DML, Fr Simon Hayes told his audience that:

> The main support of the institution was from the laundry work of the inmates but it was wholly inadequate and there were moments of gloom and almost despair in the lives of those who controlled the destinies of the refuge at the heartrending thoughts that after all their sacrifice they would have worked in vain. Worse still, that owing to the lack of material resources they might have to refuse some poor penitent whose only hope of salvation lay in such a home of innocence, and to whom the only other awful and appalling alternative was the certainty of perishing in sin in former haunts of shame.[32]

This theme of institutional poverty as an obstacle to essential welfare work echoes across appeals for donations. In October 1947, Fr Colman O'Driscoll told radio listeners that:

> [D]espite the spiritual importance of the social work done by the nuns in charge of the home, they received no assistance from the State and were dependent on the donations and legacies of the charitable and the small income derived from the laundry work. The home, however, even with the charity of the faithful and the industry of the penitents was under a heavy debt owing to the high cost of living.[33]

One radio appeal informed listeners that improvements to the Donnybrook complex had strained the nuns' financial resources: 'The nuns had no grants and depended for their income on work done by the sisters and the girls and on voluntary donations. It was no easy task to provide for over 100 people.'[34] These claims reinforced the sense of the sisters' goodness and their honour and stature as charitable workers,[35] while allowing testators to establish themselves as key patrons of their essential work.

Some testators will have received their sense of purpose from advertisements and sermons. Others who gave to DML likely had intimate knowledge of its work and of the kinds of women affected. Here are three Dubliners who left money to DML. Con Kennedy was the owner of Kennedy's (later Kiely's) pub, a minute's walk from the laundry.[36] From 1899, he served as an elected Poor Law Guardian of the South Dublin Union at Pembroke West. He was also a councillor on Pembroke District Council. The barrister Lawrence William Raymond Murphy[37] was Registrar of the High Court for twenty-five years, only retiring shortly before his death, aged 72. He was a prominent member of the Society of St Vincent de Paul.[38] His obituary noted that he made seventy-five pilgrimages to Lough Derg and fifty-eight to Croagh Patrick.[39] Genevieve McDermott was an unmarried member of the Third Order of St Francis, attached to the Capuchin Friary on Church Street where members also included Frank Duff (founder of the Legion of Mary) and Matt Talbot (who is now a candidate for canonization).[40] These people were active in organizations having responsibility for the poor, and in Dublin Catholic charities. All would have had a clear sense of how DML would use their money.

Past: Gift economies?

Although the charitable bequest is formally a kind of gift, it is simultaneously rooted in a transaction. In medieval Catholic teaching, it was understood that a testator who did not fund 'works of great mercy' on his death placed his salvation at risk.[41] This teaching remains at the root of charity law: one origin of the *cy-près* doctrine lies in the power of the Church authorities, and later the King, to correct a failed bequest, so that the testator's wealth would go to some suitable cause and his eternal reward would be assured.[42] This idea was still at work in twentieth-century Dublin. A 1928 advertisement in the *Irish Times* promised that: 'These Souls, so dear to Christ, pray DAILY for their BENEFACTORS AND FRIENDS.'[43] At a 1922 charity sermon for DML, Fr Malachy Cranfield assured the congregation that:

> By giving generously in aid of this most deserving charity they would be earning for themselves that reward which was promised to those who helped in such good works.[44]

As Olivia Frehill has written, faithful Catholics living in Ireland at the time would have understood that giving to the poor in exchange for prayer was an investment in their own salvation. Indeed, the prayers of the poor purchased through charity were especially valuable, since the poor were closer to God.[45] Without this religious underpinning, the transaction made little sense. Testators made charitable gifts to DML. Women working in the laundry could not reciprocate their benefactors' 'gift' in ordinary financial terms. Within the 'divine economy', however, gift-giving produced symbolic capital for the benefactor; capital rooted in concepts of faith, gratitude and women's sinfulness and redemption.[46] The law on charitable giving, in turn, enabled religious congregations to convert religious belief and associated symbolic capital into material resources.

Charity inevitably involves something of the secular as well as the supernatural.[47] Bequests were a redistribution of community wealth. The MP Jeremiah McVeagh once said of Joseph Downes, who left a generous bequest to DML, that:

> he posed as a philanthropist and from time to time gave generous subscriptions to charitable institutions; but ... he should henceforth credit his subscriptions to his unfortunate tenants.[48]

Through the bequests of wealthy citizens, the income of Dublin's lower-middle and working classes – the very classes regulated by institutions like DML – became part of its funding engine. Joseph Downes' tenants and those who bought his Butterkrust bread, those who drank pints at Davy Byrne's or Con Kennedy's pubs, those who kept accounts with the National Bank, indirectly funded the Magdalene institutions who benefited from the wills of these wealthy men.[49] That said, although their customers participated indirectly in the Magdalene economy, it was wealthy testators who directed this share of the city's wealth towards DML. The bequest was much more than an intimate spiritual transaction. It also demonstrated political commitment to the place of charity in the wider economic order. The benefits of charity can be bought cheaply; only token-giving is required.[50] As Maria Brenton wrote, charities enabled the 'control and patronage of the poor by the wealthy classes, for whom any more radical changes in the distribution of wealth would have been unthinkable'.[51] At the same time, those who might give enough to direct the flow of charity might 'multiply their influence, guide the destiny of others, and co-opt redistribution'.[52]

In the early decades of the State, papal encyclicals and the Irish Catholic hierarchy encouraged subsidiarity in welfare policy, with serious consequences for the poor.[53] Whereas socialists aim to change the hegemonic social structures which have made charity seem necessary, charity itself preserves those structures by making them bearable, or survivable for those who suffer most under capitalism. Charity establishes, reinscribes and naturalizes a hierarchical relationship between rich and poor. Hanson writes:

> It sanctifies inequality by providing the ritual space in which ceremonial loss can take place without redistribution, allowing affluent chieftains, circumscribed with tribute gifts and alliances, to seemingly surrender wealth without the fear of direct expropriation, noblesse oblige preserving loss of face and loss of wealth.[54]

There is also a clear sense in which, throughout the early life of the Irish state, private charity was a preferred mode of governing stigmatized people.[55] Each bequest and each donation to DML depended on the understanding that the women held in the Laundries would otherwise be destitute or put in danger, but that, at the same time, they deserved, not income or economic independence, but privately funded and inexpensive reformation. Reformation did not always mean a return to society. Claire McGettrick has shown that many women remained in DML for decades, ultimately dying there.[56]

By and large, Irish charity law supported this mode of governing the poor within institutions such as DML. Charity law is 'power-conferring'; its purpose is to harness individual autonomy and wealth towards preferred public and collective ends.[57] Charity law begins in the thirteenth century as the law of gifts given for 'pious causes'.[58] Pious causes honoured God and the Church.[59] As well as gifts funding acts of worship, they included gifts to organizations working with the poor and destitute.[60] In Britain and Ireland following the Reformation in the sixteenth century, as the state began to assume more responsibility for welfare, legally supported charity became secularized, and greater emphasis was placed on charity as a means of alleviating poverty.[61] This is reflected in the Statute of Uses, 1601, which encouraged private contributions to purposes believed to be of general benefit to society.[62] Charity law in twentieth-century Ireland was not concerned with how the subjects of charity experienced the activities funded by their 'benefactors'. Under Irish law, in the past as today, advancement of religion is recognized as a charitable purpose,[63] and a gift for the benefit of a religious organization is presumed to be for the public benefit.[64] This legal association of religious purposes and public benefit is deeply political. In Ireland it has a distinctive nationalist history. The right to channel money to religious orders was bound up with anti-Catholic laws in force before Ireland gained independence.[65] The Free State and its judiciary worked to ensure that the last remainders of these restraints were removed from Irish law.[66]

Magdalene Laundries were rarely the subject of litigation under charity (or any other) law in the twentieth century. The few cases where bequests to Magdalene Laundries generated controversy concerned, not the legitimacy of funding a Magdalene institution per se, but questions around whether the testator's intention had been properly respected.[67] For instance, in a 1942 unreported High Court case, Mr Justice Gavan Duffy had to decide whether a solicitor's bequest 'for the Magdalen Asylum, Dublin' should go to Donnybrook or Gloucester Street, eventually determining that it should be split between them.[68] That Magdalene Laundries were brutal places did not affect the legality of transfers of property to their congregations. Where the law on donations to religious charities associated gender with vulnerability, it tended to focus on wealthy donors' autonomy and decision-making, rather than on how the power generated by their money would be applied to female 'beneficiaries'.[69] This inattention to the lived impact of charitable redistribution of wealth was reflected elsewhere in the law. In particular, the law on inspection of factories distinguished sharply between the state power to determine working conditions[70] and the religious orders' moral and charitable jurisdiction over living conditions.[71] Similarly, in *Good Shepherd Nuns* v. *Commissioner of Valuation*,[72] the High Court confirmed the state's power to charge rates on property used for a Magdalene laundry's profit-making[73] activities,[74] but did not interrogate how this profit derived from unpaid labour.[75]

Before and after independence, Irish charity law supported flows of income to laundries like DML not only by permitting bequests without any substantive regard to the activities they would fund, but also by enabling laundries to receive them tax free, and by exempting them from the requirement to pay women who were confined to Magdalene Laundries for their work.[76] The Finance Act, 1921, exempted charities from income tax on the profits of trade 'if the work in connection with the trade is mainly carried on by the beneficiaries of the charity and the profits are applied solely to the purposes of the charity'.[77] Paid non-resident employees of a charity were not considered 'beneficiaries' but women confined to a Magdalene laundry were.[78] The Donnybrook laundry was first formally recognized for this purpose in 1921.[79] Here the law on income tax reinforced the exploitation of unpaid labour.

Present: Echoes of charity in responses to 'historical' abuse

Charity remains essential to our understanding of the wealth still held by the RSC in Ireland today and their entitlement to retain it. Bequests and small donations were not the only income generated by the DML's 'charitable' work, or by the RSC's wider activities. The RSC were generally free to invest funds raised, particularly in property, amassing significant wealth over time.[80] Today, much of their money is held in charitable trusts. Apart from direct income, the congregation's involvement in charity afforded them significant social capital that could later be put to work for other purposes. Today, although DML is closed, the RSC retain roles as providers of health and 'welfare' services and the congregation retains its charitable status. Its portfolio of charitable work includes, not only activities connected to survivors of abusive religious-run institutions in Ireland, but projects relating to sex work (Ruhama), immigration (Immigrant Council of Ireland), healthcare (St Vincent's University Hospital) and homelessness (Focus Ireland).[81] These echo the congregation's participation in older 'destitution economies'[82] and allows it to retain outsize influence over matters of social policy.

To some extent, the state now recognizes that laundries like DML were sites of human rights abuse. However, the notion that the RSC were, and are, engaged in charitable work dramatically curtails responsibility – theirs and the state's – to survivors of that abuse. The sense that religious-owned property is the fruit of charitable endeavour may immunize it from demands for redistribution via state-administered redress.[83] There are traces of this in the *Report of the Inter-Departmental Committee to Establish the Facts of State Involvement with the Magdalen Laundries* (*IDC Report*, 2013). For example, the Report constructs the income from women's unpaid laundry work as an essential support to the Magdalen Laundries' operations when charitable funding waned.[84] In correspondence with the IDC Inquiry on behalf of the Sisters of Mercy, a representative of the financial services firm L&P Cantor Fitzgerald notes that the orders' accounts did not impose charges for the 'services provided by [religious sisters] in the management and operation of the Home and Laundry and the use of its premises'.[85] The implication here is that it would be unjust to expect the congregation to part with assets derived from voluntary and charitable labour. The congregations are still positioned, not only as altruists, but as authoritative, prudent managers of collective wealth, entitled to prioritize other projects over survivors' claims. The state's continuing dependence on private charity and individual reform in addressing deprivation means that it can be difficult to unsettle that hierarchy. In recent years, some congregations have also argued that there is a tension between contributing to compensation schemes for victims of institutional abuse and pursuing their contemporary charitable mission.[86] In 2013, the then Minister for Justice, Alan Shatter, said that he could not strip orders formerly involved in running Magdalene Laundries of their charitable status to punish their refusal to contribute to redress funds because they were still involved in charitable work. In practical terms, charitable work today insulates the orders from responsibility for the harms of charity yesterday.[87]

Charity also continues to shape state understanding of survivors as legal subjects; they remain, to some extent, objects for generosity rather than rights-bearing subjects entitled to full reparations.[88] The state's redress schemes do not alter that position. Funds are administered on an *ex gratia* basis.[89] Stephen Winters argues that *ex gratia* payments and charity have much in common. Like charity, an *ex gratia* scheme does not recognize any right of relief; whether a right to compensation for a specific wrong, or a more general right as a citizen to healthcare, housing or social support.[90] Like charity, the Irish *ex gratia* redress scheme for women formerly held in Magdalene Laundries did not acknowledge liability for harms suffered in the laundry. It did not acknowledge that these women were entitled as citizens to financial supports other than the private provision they had received from the RSC via their benefactors and funders. *Ex gratia* schemes keep applicants in a subordinate position both to the state and to the religious orders.[91] Women were required to waive any right of action against the state or any other public or statutory body, as a condition of participation in the scheme. In determining how much money each applicant deserved, the state relied on the religious orders' records, even where those were contradicted by women's oral testimony or witness evidence. Many applicants to the scheme were living in the poverty and deprivation which commonly followed time in a laundry. Some were still living in institutions run by the orders. For these women in particular, the marginalization and exclusion that legitimated their abuse in the first place now determined how that abuse could be redressed.[92] There is, perhaps, a hint of testators past in shaping the purposes of the redress scheme. The Ombudsman described it as an effort 'to reflect the shame of the nation'.[93] Unlike charitable bequests, *ex gratia* redress does not promise a place in heaven, but it may promise the relief of quick release from our obligations to those once held in places like Donnybrook.

Politicizing charity

The state's approach to redress repeats aspects of an older politics of charity in three ways. It leaves the RSC's essential 'ownership' of long-held wealth unquestioned. It excuses (even if it can no longer normalize) the harms women suffered under the guise of charity. It reinscribes unequal social relationships between religious congregations and the women confined in their institutions, privileging private respectability over the public good. However, recent struggles over the RSC's properties in Dublin city, including in Donnybrook,[94] suggest the emergence of new, and potentially transformative, Irish politics of reparation, underpinned by a different account of charity. The best known is the ongoing dispute over the new state-funded National Maternity Hospital (NMH), planned for a site near the RSC's existing St Vincent's University Hospital complex at Elm Park.[95]

Following merger negotiations, the NMH[96] will become part of St Vincent's Healthcare Group (SVHG), currently owned by the RSC. The RSC's holdings in

SVHG were valued at €661 million in October 2018. They also own the land on which the new hospital is proposed to be built. In May 2017 and October 2018, reproductive rights activists and campaigners for survivors of institutional abuse[97] organized a mass petition and protest against this deal, which they characterized as 'gifting' a state-funded hospital to the RSC.[98] They objected to the deal because the RSC had refused to contribute to a redress fund for women who had been in institutions like DML, and because they had not met their redress obligations to survivors of abuse in their industrial schools. Campaigners argued that the RSC's autonomy in dealing with their property was constrained by their duty to atone for their past actions. They should not benefit financially from a new hospital because they had not made adequate reparation for the harm done in places like DML.[99]

The RSC eventually responded by removing its members from all formal involvement in governing St Vincent's and promising to 'gift' both the hospital land and the RSC's shareholdings in SVHG to the Irish people.[100] The government welcomed this decision as 'historic'.[101] However, the 'gifts' were never made. Instead, the shares and the land were transferred to a new charity, St Vincent's Holdings. The taxpayer will pay the NMH's running costs, in perpetuity. The state did not attempt to purchase the hospital land compulsorily, agreeing to enter into a long-term lease instead.[102] This would be nothing new; Irish governments have often gifted assets to voluntary hospitals run by private boards, and private owners have been permitted to profit from those assets. Speaking on a private members' motion on the National Maternity Hospital in 2018, Deputy Róisín Shortall reminded Dáil Éireann that:

> When the sisters built St. Vincent's University Hospital at Elm Park, they did so with public money. Not only did they use public money for it, they negotiated a deal whereby the State would have no involvement in the control and management of the hospital, despite the more than £5 million the order received between 1934 and 1969 when Elm Park opened. There was also another proviso, that if the sisters sold their old hospital at St. Stephen's Green, the proceeds would be given to the State via the hospital trust fund. Predictably, that never happened. The sisters sold the old hospital, but the proceeds were never handed over.[103]

The RSC subsequently used the state-funded St Vincent's building to secure loans to fund construction of a private hospital. The hospital rents land from the RSC, and this is an important source of income for the congregation, totalling millions of euro.[104] Feminist campaigners still reject the NMH deal, demanding that a publicly funded hospital should be publicly owned.

Since the 2017 protests, Ireland has partially legalized abortion. More recent campaigning has centred on concerns that a new NMH, forming part of the SVHG, will not be free to perform medical procedures, including abortion, which are contrary to the RSC ethos. In many ways, this emphasis on abortion is a continuation of the earlier argument about redress; both abortion restrictions and Magdalene Laundries symbolize religious control of women's reproductive and sexual lives.[105] The argument about property and reparation was now overlaid with a more explicit argument about institutional power in the present. St Vincent's University Hospital has required its employees to practice in accordance with an ethical code that prohibits abortion,[106] and there is concern that this arrangement may extend to the new NMH. Campaigners insist that the governance arrangements for the NMH are ambiguous on religious ethos.[107] Advocates for the transfer of the NMH to St Vincent's insist that the NMH will preserve its 'clinical independence', ensuring that abortions can be provided there in accordance with Irish law. Here, they point to the 'triple lock' within the draft 'legal framework' proposed to govern the hospital.[108] This consists of: (i) the constitutions of the St Vincent's charities which have been drafted to avoid direct reference to Catholic medical ethics, (ii) the new NMH constitution and the 'reserved powers' it confers on the Minister for Health and (iii) the hospital's agreement with the Irish health service (the HSE).[109] We do not know how useful these documents will be to individual abortion-seeking patients. Neither do we know whether the state can compel a Catholic hospital to provide healthcare incompatible with its ethos.[110] Key St Vincent's directors, though lay people, were appointed because of their commitment to continuing the congregation's religious mission.[111] Opaque references to that mission persist in the constitutions of St Vincent's charities. Campaigners are also adamant that the Vatican would not have permitted the RSC to transfer their shares, and associated governance powers,[112] if it meant abortions were going to be permitted in the new NMH.[113] At best, in cases where the law allows for exercise of medical discretion in the provision of abortion services, there is a real risk that they will not be provided at the new NMH.

Prominent public advocates for the deal included Nicholas Kearns (former President of the High Court and former Chairman of the NMH), Rhona Mahony (first woman Master of the NMH) and James Menton (businessman, Chair and Director of SVHG). They present the deal as an instrument of transition, from a religious past to a secular, charitable and commercial present. To campaigners, however, the deal is more akin to a bequest; intended to secure the RSC's legacy now they no longer govern the hospital. In ensuring that legacy, in this dispute as elsewhere, charity is used to distract from the RSC's accountability for past harm.

Conclusion

Many of those defending the proposed arrangements for the NMH respond by insisting again that the RSC's history of charitable endeavour should shield them from critique, just as it preserved them from obligations to pay redress.[114] For example, confirming that the RSC would profit from the hospital deal through the sale of land, James Menton said the profit was 'a very modest amount when you think of the number of religious sisters who worked without remuneration'.[115] Equally striking, however, is the continuing claim to collectively generated wealth. Exploring the history of individual bequests as it appeared in the public archive of DML allowed us to foreground old relationships between wealth, law, charity and gender. This inquiry unsettles charity as a static legal form, showing it instead as part of a web of ongoing secular and religious relations, redistributing and determining the inheritance of the privately controlled wealth of Dublin city and its hinterland. Thinking of the NMH dispute through the lens of bequest draws us back to those same issues. The campaign for public ownership of the NMH asks questions about the role of a new generation of wealthy and influential Dubliners in buttressing dwindling religious institutional power, enabling the RSC's gradual transformation into a plainly commercial, if charitable, entity[116] and protecting it against demands to divest itself of publicly generated assets. Part of the RSC's legacy in Dublin is its insistence that the state must compromise with religious interests, rather than disentangle itself from old charitable expectations.[117]

Charity is sometimes presented as a form of struggle against exploitative capitalism. Indeed, within Catholic social teaching, charity can be a dual concept; a loving relationship with God performed in a loving relationship with others.[118] Antonio Negri writes that charity can be 'a praxis that, in the communion of goods and wealth, struggles for the appropriation of the common and against the expropriation of work and production'.[119] Some liberation theologians[120] argue that whatever is given in charity to exploited people was already their property – challenging the exclusive entitlement of those who control available wealth to determine how it should be used. In Ireland, disputes around the NMH may disrupt established legacies of charity, interrogating the RSC's entangled capitalist and religious roles in Irish society, exposing class hierarchy behind the language of charity.

Notes

1 My thanks to Sheila Killian, Mary Cosgrove, Sonia McEntee, Mary Gaynor (Law Society of Ireland Library), Mark Coen, Katherine O'Donnell and Lisa Godson for their research advice and assistance. This chapter was written while I was a Leverhulme Research Fellow, 2020–2.

2 In the 1940s, Radio Éireann would accept public donations intended for the laundry. See 'Appeal on Behalf of Dublin Asylum', *Irish Independent*, 27 October 1947, 5.

3 See radio schedule in *Irish Press*, 31 October 1970, 19.

4 The requirement to publish advertisements of charitable devises and bequests was amended by s. 16 of the Charities Act, 1973, which exempted most bequests from this requirement.

5 See the Introduction to this volume.

6 'Will of Sir Joseph Downes', *Irish Times*, 6 February 1926, 15.

7 Byrne left £500 to Donnybrook from a total estate of £48,520. He left similar amounts to his cousins and for Masses for the repose of his soul. See 'Dublin Vintner's Bequests', *Irish Independent*, 10 May 1939, 12.

8 Morrissey died in Dún Laoghaire in August 1928, leaving money to a range of charitable causes, including £200 to the Magdalene Asylum Donnybrook, 'Recent Will', *Cork Examiner*, 11 December 1928, 8. John Farrelly, the former manager of the Hibernian Bank on College Green, died in 1949, leaving a large estate, including £1,000 to the Superioress of Donnybrook, 'Legal Notices', *Irish Independent*, 4 November 1949, 2.

9 'Legal Notices', *Irish Independent*, 15 September 1955, 13.

10 'Notice of Charitable Donations and Bequests', *Irish Independent*, 4 October 1963, 22.

11 'Bequests to Charities', *Irish Press*, 14 March 1938, 5.

12 *Dublin Evening Telegraph*, 28 April 1924, 4.

13	Ibid., 10 January 1920, 7.

14	'Legal Notices', *Irish Press*, 22 June 1935, 2.

15	See, for example, Isabella Kelly McDonnell, Dún Laoghaire, from a Roscommon horse-racing family (Lacken House); *Westmeath Independent*, 5 March 1938, 2.

16	On testamentary intention in sociolegal studies, see Daniel Monk, 'EM Forster's Will: An Overlooked Posthumous Publication', *Legal Studies* 33, no. 4 (2013): 572.

17	For example, see Elizabeth Nealon, the widow of Michael Peter Nealon, formerly of the National Bank, Drumcondra; 'Legal Notices', *Irish Times*, 5 February 1957, 6. Bequests also came from women living in religious nursing homes in London; for example, Anna Kane, who died in Eastbourne; *Irish Times*, 20 December 1922, 14. Anna Kane's executor was Sir George Roche, a former President of the Law Society.

18	'Notice of Charitable Bequests', *Irish Times*, 15 March 1934, 1.

19	Scott Cutler Shershow, *The Work and the Gift* (Chicago, IL: University of Chicago Press, 2005), 133.

20	Cited in John H. Hanson, 'The Anthropology of Giving: Toward a Cultural Logic of Charity', *Journal of Cultural Economy* 8, no. 4 (23 September 2014): 507. She is writing here about the work of Marcel Mauss.

21	On the agency of those donating to the Catholic Church in nineteenth- and twentieth-century Ireland, see Patrick Doyle and Sarah Roddy, 'Money, Death, and Agency in Catholic Ireland, 1850–1921', *Journal of Social History* 54, no. 3 (2021): 799.

22	See Bernard Harris, 'Charity and Poor Relief in England and Wales, *circa* 1750–1914', in *Charity and Mutual Aid in Europe and North America Since 1800*, ed. Bernard Harris and Paul Bridgen (New York: Routledge, 2007), 31, discussing the nineteenth century.

23	Nancy D. Goldfarb, 'Charity as Purchase', *Nineteenth-Century Literature* 69, no. 2 (1 September 2014): 247, 257, 259.

24	Hanson, 'The Anthropology', 507.

25	Ibid.

26	John N. Kotre, *Outliving the Self: How to Live on in Future Generations* (New York: W. W. Norton, 1996), 10.

27	Claire Routley and Adrian Sargeant, 'Leaving a Bequest', *Nonprofit and Voluntary Sector Quarterly* 44, no. 5 (2014): 881–2.

28	Sarah Brouillette, 'Human Rights Markets and Born into Brothels', *Third Text* 25, no. 2 (March 2011): 169.

29	Daniel Siegel, *Charity and Condescension: Victorian Literature and the Dilemmas of Philanthropy* (Athens, OH: Ohio University Press, 2012), 32.

30	*Freeman's Journal*, 23 December 1916, 1.

31	'A Deserving Charity', *Evening Herald*, 8 February 1932, 4.

32	*The Standard*, 4 March 1938, 1.

33	'Appeal on Behalf', *Irish Independent*, 5.

34	'Depends Entirely on Charity', *Irish Independent*, 25 May 1961, 10.

35	For an overview of women and the history of charitable work, see Maria Luddy, 'Women and Charitable Organisations in Nineteenth Century Ireland', *Women's Studies International Forum* 11, no. 4 (1988): 301.

36	'Notice of Charitable Bequests', *Irish Independent*, 22 November 1932. For examples of other Donnybrook residents who made bequests to DML, Mary Fitz-Gibbon of Eglington Road in Ballsbridge left £300 to the Superioress of Donnybrook, 'Recent Irish Wills', *Irish Press*, 24 July 1937, 3; Kathleen Barker of Anglesea Road left the Superioress £25, 'Legal Notices', *Irish Times*, 29 August 1949, 7.

37 'Legal Notices', *Irish Times*, 10 December 1962.
38 There are strong connections between the Dublin legal community and the Society of St Vincent de Paul, which was founded in St Michan's parish. It was (and remains) customary for many court-ordered payments to the court poor box to go to St Vincent de Paul.
39 'Obituary', *Irish Press*, 28 July 1961, 5.
40 'Dublin Woman Leaves £68,788', *Sunday Independent*, 19 May 1968. Her will included multiple charitable bequests, and she revised it five times.
41 Michael Jones (ed.), *Gentry and Lesser Nobility in Late Medieval Europe* (New York: St. Martin's Press, 1986) 3.
42 Edith L. Fisch, 'The Cy Pres Doctrine and Changing Philosophies', *Michigan Law Review* 51, no. 3 (1953): 375, 377. The power applies where a gift is made without designating an appropriate trustee, or where a gift is made for an illegal purpose, or a purpose contrary to public policy. The latter power was historically important in voiding gifts made for Catholic charitable purposes. See further Caroline R. Sherman, *The Uses of the Dead: The Early Modern Development of Cy-Près Doctrine* (Washington, DC: Catholic University of America Press, 2018).
43 *Irish Times*, 17 December 1928, 16.
44 'Will You Help?', *Evening Telegraph*, 27 February 1922, 1.
45 Olivia Frehill, 'Serving the "Divine Economy": St Joseph's Asylum for Aged and Virtuous Females, Dublin, 1836–1922', *Irish Economic and Social History* 48, no. 1 (September 17, 2020): 78.
46 Julie McGonegal, 'The Tyranny of Gift Giving: The Politics of Generosity in Sarah Scott's Millenium Hall and Sir George Ellison', *Eighteenth-Century Fiction* 19, no. 3 (2007): 294–7, 304–5.
47 Joanne E. Myers, '"Supernatural Charity": Astell, Shaftesbury and the Problem of Enthusiasm', *Journal for Eighteenth-Century Studies* 37, no. 3 (23 May 2014): 299–314.
48 Town Tenants, (Ireland) Bill, Second Reading, 4 March 1904, Hansard, vol. 134, col. 212.
49 A similar argument could be made about the funding of religious healthcare premises (and mother and baby 'homes') through the Hospitals Sweepstakes. See generally Marie Coleman, *The Irish Sweep : A History of the Irish Hospitals Sweepstake, 1930–87* (Dublin: University College Dublin Press, 2009).
50 Hanson, 'The Anthropology', 514.
51 Maria Brenton, *The Voluntary Sector in British Social Services* (Harlow: Longman Publishing, 1985), 16.
52 Hanson, 'The Anthropology', 516.
53 See more broadly Fred Powell, *The Political Economy of the Irish Welfare State: Church, State and Capital* (Bristol: Policy Press, 2017).
54 Hanson, 'The Anthropology', 516; see similarly Steven Engler, 'Modern Times: Religion, Consecration and the State in Bourdieu', *Cultural Studies* 17, no. 3–4 (2003): 445, 459, writing about early modern charity as a 'paradigmatic act of consecration' which 'invested social hierarchy with the cachet of eternal order'.
55 See, for example, Department of Justice, *Report of the Inter-Departmental Committee to Establish the Facts of State Involvement with the Magdalen Laundries* (Dublin, January 2013, aka *McAleese Report*, hereinafter *IDC Report*), 367, quoting a 1942 Department of Education memorandum describing arrangements for the committal of girls to Limerick Magdalene Laundry as 'a fortuitous arrangement made possible by the good will and charitable disposition of the Religious Order concerned'. See similarly *IDC*

Report, 404, quoting the Minister for Education in 1940, describing the religious orders as 'animated by a spirit of Christian charity'.

56 See Claire McGettrick, Chapter 11, this volume.

57 Nancy Harding, *On Being at Work: The Social Construction of the Employee* (New York: Routledge, 2013), 22–3, 47–8, 119–20, 188.

58 Jones, *Gentry and Lesser Nobility*, 3.

59 Ibid.

60 Ibid., 4.

61 Ann O'Connell and Joyce Chia, 'The Advancement (or Retreat?) of Religion as a Head of Charity: A Historical Perspective', in *Studies in the History of Tax Law, Volume 6*, ed. John Tiley (London: Bloomsbury Publishing, 2013), 367.

62 Ibid., 374.

63 In the case of *Pemsel* [1891] AC 531, Lord Macnaghten recognized 'the advancement of religion' as a charitable purpose. In Ireland, the testator's subjective view of whether an activity is for a recognized 'public benefit' is definitive (*In re Worth Library* [1994] 1 ILRM 161). On related debates in law, see Matthew Harding, 'Trusts for Religious Purposes and the Question of Public Benefit', *Modern Law Review* 71, no. 2 (2008): 159.

64 In Ireland, according to Keane J. (*Campaign to Separate Church and State* [1998] 3 IR 321, 362), religion is so central to public life that a presumption of public benefit applies in relation to religious charities. This is reinforced by s. 45 of the Charities Act, 1961. Gifts for religious purposes that might not have passed the public benefit test in England could be treated as charitable gifts in Ireland (*In re Howley*, [1940] I. R. 109; *Maguire v AG* [1943] 1 IR 238; *Bank of Ireland* v. *Attorney General* [1957] IR 257; *O'Hanlon* v. *Logue* [1906] 1 IR 247. Contrast *Gilmour* v. *Coats* [1949] AC 426).

65 Kerry O'Halloran, *Human Rights and Charity Law: International Perspectives* (Abingdon: Routledge, 2016) notes that Irish charity law, unlike that of other common law jurisdictions, originates with the Statute of Pious Uses, rather than with the Statute of Charitable Uses. As such, the link with religion is fundamental to Irish charity law.

66 Leaving donations in wills to male religious orders was specifically void from the passage of the Catholic Emancipation Act in 1829. Although restrictions on bequests to the Catholic clergy were largely lifted when Robert Peel introduced the Charitable Donations and Bequests (Ireland) Act, 1844, the issue of bequests to male religious orders was not fully addressed in Ireland until the Emancipation Act was repealed in 1922. Donations to religious communities of women were never void outright, and indeed were often essential to the foundation of the institutions of congregations. However, they had to be made to fund specific charitable works or to benefit individual members of the order, or those members of the order inhabiting a particular convent at the time of the testator's death. See Vincent Delany, 'The Development of the Law of Charities in Ireland', *International & Comparative Law Quarterly* 4, no.1 (1955): 30, 41.

67 For example, Our Lady's Home, Henrietta Street, was the subject of litigation around the will of Eliza Walsh. Miss Walsh's will directed that the proceeds of her estate should be used to construct a church. The executor, a priest, had attempted to use the bulk of the estate to fund what became Our Lady's Home. He was not permitted to do so, 'In the Law Courts', *Evening Herald*, 10 July 1899, 3.

68 'Cavan Solicitor's Will', *Irish Times*, 26 March 1942, 3. This is an application of the *cy-près* doctrine, discussed further within. Gloucester Street is now called Sean McDermott Street.

69 See, for example, *Allcard* v. *Skinner* (1887) 36 Ch D 145, discussed in Richard Hedlund, 'Undue Influence and the Religious Cases that Shaped the Law', *Oxford Journal of Law and Religion* 5, no. 2 (2016) 298.

70 Institutions performing 'charitable or reformatory purposes' but offering laundry services to the public were subject to regulation under the Conditions of Employment Act, 1936, and the Factories Act, 1955, as discussed in the *IDC Report*. Until 1907, compliance with inspection regimes was voluntary, albeit several laundries formally agreed to be inspected. After 1907, institutional laundries carried on for the purposes of trade were included in the mandatory inspection regime. See *IDC Report*, 129, 531, 534, 545.

71 Ibid., 552, 555. Charitable institutions could also apply for modifications to the applicable regulations, but these modifications were not intended to lead to worse conditions than applied to factories under the default regime.

72 [1930] 1 I.R. 646. This issue is now regulated by s. 49 of the Charities Act, 1961. This case is discussed in *IDC Report*, 758–62. Unlike the law on income tax, the law on rates allowed the state to levy some charges on the income of Magdalene laundries.

73 The emphasis on profit comes from section 63 of the Poor Relief (Ireland) Act, 1838.

74 DML was subject to rates on this basis, from 1910 onwards. See *IDC Report*, 760.

75 For a more complete analysis of this failure to account for women's unpaid labour, see Sheila Killian, '"For lack of accountability": The Logic of the Price in Ireland's Magdalene Laundries', *Accounting, Organizations and Society* 43 (2015): 17–32, 26.

76 The British Ministry of Labour considered that women working in a Magdalene laundry, though unpaid, could 'determine their relationship' with the order 'at will', just as the order could determine its relationship with them. See *IDC Report*, 589.

77 Section 30 remains in place via s. 208 of the Taxes Consolidation Act, 1997. Prior to October 1996, there was no formal process for seeking a tax exemption, unless an organization applied for repayment of tax. The *IDC Report* cites the Office of the Revenue Commissioners asserting that the risk of tax evasion by charities was perceived to be minimal. See *IDC Report*, 750, 752.

78 Ibid., 753–4.

79 Ibid., 751.

80 Claire O'Sullivan and Conor Ryan, 'Substantial Assets, but No More Cash for Redress', *Irish Examiner*, 7 February 2013.

81 Sr Stanislaus Kennedy (RSC) is 'Founder and Life President' of Focus Ireland, one of the largest and most respected housing organizations in the country. Focus Ireland receives approximately 50 per cent of its funding from the Irish Exchequer and the rest from charitable donations. In 2018, Focus Ireland had funds in excess of €25 million to spend on its activities and properties, estimated to be worth over €102 million; Claire McGettrick, Katherine O'Donnell, Maeve O'Rourke, James M. Smith and Mari Steed, *Ireland and the Magdalene Laundries: A Campaign for Justice* (London: I.B. Tauris, 2021), 29–30.

82 This phrase is from Kate Coddington, Deirdre Conlon and Lauren L. Martin, 'Destitution Economies: Circuits of Value in Asylum, Refugee, and Migration Control', *Annals of the American Association of Geographers* 110, no. 5 (2020): 1425.

83 This is a wider theme in Irish politics; see, for example, Leo Vardakar, 'Speech of An Taoiseach, Leo Varadkar, on the Occasion of the Visit of Pope Francis', juxtaposing the history of Church provision of social services in early-twentieth-century Ireland with histories of institutional abuse, but never suggesting that one enabled the other, 25 August 2018, available online: https://www.merrionstreet.ie/en/news-room/

speeches/speech_of_an_taoiseach_leo_varadkar_on_the_occasion_of_the_visit_of_
pope_francis.html (accessed 1 August 2022).

84 *IDC Report*, 40, citing Maria Luddy's work.

85 *IDC Report*, 1014.

86 The question of whether a contribution to funding payments made by the Residential
Institutions Redress Board is consistent with the purposes of a charitable trust (as
required by s. 3 of the Charities Act 2009) was dealt with in section 42 of the
Residential Institutions Statutory Fund Act 2012. No similar provision has been made
in respect of Magdalene laundries because the relevant orders refused to contribute to
the scheme.

87 Christina Finn, 'Shatter: Religious Orders Have a Moral and Ethical Obligation to
Contribute to Magdalene Survivors', *The Journal.ie*, 17 July 2013.

88 Maeve O'Rourke, 'The Manipulation of "Vulnerability": State Responses to So-Called
"Historical" Abuses in Ireland', *Human Rights Quarterly* 43, no. 3 (2021): 435, 436.

89 *Ex gratia* schemes and charity law are indirectly connected via the royal prerogative,
including the powers which the Crown enjoys as *parens patriae*. The power to establish
ex gratia schemes is originally a prerogative power; Margit Cohn, 'Medieval Chains,
Invisible Inks: On Non-Statutory Powers of the Executive', *Oxford Journal of Legal
Studies* 25, no. 1 (2005): 97. The same is true of the power to alter the purpose of
charitable property (*cy-près*); Fisch, 'The Cy Pres Doctrine and Changing
Philosophies'.

90 Stephen Winter, 'Australia's *Ex Gratia* Redress', *Australian Indigenous Law Review* 13,
no. 1 (2009): 49.

91 McGettrick et al., *Ireland and the Magdalene Laundries*, 127.

92 Máiréad Enright and Sinéad Ring, 'State Legal Responses to Historical Institutional Abuse:
Shame, Sovereignty and Epistemic Injustice', *Éire-Ireland* 55, nos 1–2 (2020): 68, 80.

93 *Opportunity Lost: An Investigation by the Ombudsman into the Administration of the
Magdalen Restorative Justice Scheme* (Dublin: Office of the Ombudsman, November
2017), 4.

94 In 2020, the RSC suddenly began proceedings to liquidate St Monica's home in Dublin
city centre, and St Mary's Home and the Caritas convalescent centre near the former
DML. St Mary's is on land adjoining the proposed NMH site. All were run by
charitable bodies created by the RSC to ensure their legacy in healthcare provision.
Residents were required to move, and staff were not guaranteed statutory redundancy
payments. See Shamim Malekmian, 'The Controversial Closure of St Mary's (Telford):
New Allegations of Abuse Levelled at Sisters of Charity', *Hotpress*, 20 October 2020;
Shamim Malekmian, 'Examinership Controversy: Firm Owned by the Sisters of
Charity Forces Residents Out of St Mary's Nursing Home', *Hotpress*, 26 September
2020.

95 The St Vincent's Healthcare Group Memorandum of Association opens with the
statement that the original building for St Vincent's, then in Dublin city centre, was
purchased with the dowry of an early member. The sister concerned was Letita
More-O'Ferrell (later Sister M. Teresa), the daughter of an aristocratic land-owning
family. See Mary Peckham Magray, *The Transforming Power of the Nuns* (Oxford:
Oxford University Press, 1998), 30.

96 Run by a new, designated activity company; NMH DAC. The NMH and St Vincent's
are independent voluntary hospitals, state-funded but with private governance
arrangements.

97   Known as 'Our Maternity Hospital' or the 'Campaign Against Church Ownership of Women's Healthcare'.

98   Ellen Coyne, 'Nuns Who Owe Millions in Abuse Reparations Given Hospital', *The Times*, 24 March 2017. The state's commercial interests would be protected by maintaining a lien over the property.

99   Although this argument emphasizes the RSC, the NMH is not innocent of involvement in abuses of women and children; its history includes obstetric violence and illegal adoption. Marie O'Connor, 'Rolling Back the Eighth Amendment: The Church's Power Grab for the New National Maternity Hospital – Backed by Government', *Village Magazine*, 5 December 2021.

100 Ailbhe Conneely, 'Sisters of Charity "Gift" St Vincent's to Irish Public', RTÉ News, 8 May 2020.

101 Ibid.

102 A compulsory purchase order is unattractive because it would further delay the project's progress. There are commercial reasons for refusing to give the land outright to the state. Doing so might diminish the value of the remainder of the campus; the land may be tied up in borrowing; another owner might object to future efforts to obtain planning permission. Campaigners, however, associate ownership with practical control of the property and the activities on it, and SVHG has said that it must own the property in order to guarantee continuity of care. Church property can be acquired by the state for 'necessary works of public utility' with full compensation but the scope of that power is unclear; Rachael Walsh, 'There is Legal Room for CPO of the National Maternity Hospital Site by the Government', *The Journal.ie*, 24 June 2021.

103 Houses of the Oireachtas, 'National Maternity Hospital: Motion [Private Members]', *Dáil Éireann Debate*, Wednesday, 23 June 2021, vol. 1009, no. 2, available online: www.oireachtas.ie/en/debates/debate/dail/2021-06-23/8/ (accessed 1 August 2022). See further Elizabeth Fitzgerald, 'There is a Long History of Intermingling of Church and State funds with Respect to St Vincent's', *The Journal.ie*, 4 May 2017. For a survey of the role of Catholicism in preserving the autonomy of religious hospitals, see Geraldine Robbins and Irvine Lapsley, 'Irish Voluntary Hospitals: an Examination of a Theory of Voluntary Failure', *Accounting, Business & Financial History* 18, no. 1 (2008): 61.

104 Eilish O'Regan and Cormac McQuinn, 'Nuns Will Get Millions from Sale of Former Hospital Land', *Irish Independent*, 30 May 2017.

105 For other invocations of religion and women's history in Ireland in the context of this debate, see Houses of the Oireachtas, 'National Maternity', *Dáil Éireann Debate*, Wednesday, 23 June 2021, vol. 1009, no. 2.

106 O'Connor, 'Rolling Back the Eighth Amendment'.

107 Ibid.

108 Kieran Mulvey, *Report to the Minister for Health Simon Harris, T.D. on the Terms of Agreement between the National Maternity Hospital (Holles St.) and St. Vincent's Hospital Group Regarding the Future Operation of the New Maternity Hospital – 'The National Maternity Hospital at Elm Park DAC'* (21 November 2016).

109 St Vincent's Hospital Group, *Briefing Paper – NMH Project*, 2021.

110 *Report of the Independent Review Group Established to Examine the Role of Voluntary Organisations in Publicly Funded Health and Personal Social Services* (2018), 81, available online: https://assets.gov.ie/9386/6d02f4a9fb554e30adbebb3eec5091d9.pdf (accessed 1 August 2022).

111 Some Catholic voluntary hospitals in Ireland are run by companies which are also public juridic persons (PJP) under Canon Law. Public juridic persons are companies in civil law, with a 'sponsoring' religious congregation, or diocese, which may 'reserve' certain governance powers to itself, so that it can discharge key faith-based responsibilities. Healthcare is considered an apostolic activity, and public juridic persons have been used across the world to ensure that the Catholic legacy of a hospital's religious founders persists, even when lay people come to manage the hospital. Juridic status is sometimes granted by the Vatican and sometimes by diocesan bishops, and public juridic persons are ultimately under the control of the relevant diocesan bishop. In the United States, juridic persons have been associated with denial of women's healthcare; Brooke Raunig, 'Is this Hospital Catholic? Assessing the Legality of Merger Contracts that Demand Adherence to Religious Doctrine', *California Western Law Review* 54, no. 1 (2018): 152. The St John of God hospitals and community services in Ireland are part of the St John of God Hospitaller Services Group. This is a company in civil law. All members of the company are also part of St John of God Hospitaller Ministries, which is a PJP. The Mercy University Hospital in Cork is a wholly owned subsidary of a holding company called Mercy Care South. The members of the company are also all members of a PJP, also called Mercy Care South. St Vincent's Hospital Group is not, in itself, a PJP; Paul Cullen, 'National Maternity Hospital: Has Threat of Church Influence Been Removed?', *Irish Times*, 2 June 2020.

112 In May 2020, the RSC received approval from the Vatican Congregation for the Doctrine of the Faith to transfer their shareholding in SVHG. Permission is given subject to the observance of Canon Law. For a detailed account of the approval process see Sharon Holland, 'Vatican Expert Unpacks Canonical PJP Process', available online: https://www.chausa.org/publications/health-progress/article/september-october-2011/vatican-expert-unpacks-canonical-pjp-process (accessed 1 August 2022). The Vatican approved the transfer in accordance with Canons 638–9 and 1292–4. Canon 1293 requires the RSC to avoid harm to the Church and its teachings.

113 In 2020, the Congregation for the Doctrine of the Faith ruled that the hospitals of the Brothers of Charity in Belgium could no longer be considered Catholic, when their (largely lay) governing body permitted patients to access euthanasia in accordance with Belgian law, but against the teachings of their founding religious congregation; Luis Ladaria, 'Letter to the Superior General of the Congregation of the "Brothers of Charity", Regarding the Accompaniment of Patients in Psychiatric Hospitals of the Congregation's Belgian Branch', March 2020, available online: https://www.vatican.va/roman_curia/congregations/cfaith/documents/rc_con_cfaith_doc_20200330_lettera-fratellidellacarita-belgio_en.html (accessed 1 August 2022).

114 Breda O'Brien, 'Time to Defy Mob Mentality Over Religious Orders', *Irish Times*, 6 May 2017; Victoria White, 'Modern Habit of Blaming Nuns is Completely Counter to the Facts', *Irish Examiner*, 4 June 2017; John Scally, 'Rite & Reason: Is Ireland No Country for Old Nuns?', *Irish Times*, 12 October 2021; Sarah McDonald, 'National Maternity Hospital: Nuns are Being "Bullied" Over Land for New National Maternity Hospital, Says Prominent Priest', *Irish Independent*, 19 July 2021; David Quinn, 'Uncharitable to Attack Sisters for Hospital Gift', *Sunday Times*, 17 June 2021.

115 O'Regan and McQuinn, 'Nuns Will Get Millions'.

116 The congregation began the process of transferring its assets and social functions to corporations in the 1990s.

117 Fintan O'Toole, 'A Real Republic Should Not Have Charity Delivering Public Welfare', *Irish Times*, 14 December 2021.

118 Matthew S. Holland, *Bonds of Affection: Civic Charity and the Making of America: Winthrop, Jefferson, and Lincoln* (Washington, DC: Georgetown University Press, 2007) 7; Andrea Muehlebach, 'The Catholicization of Neoliberalism: On Love and Welfare in Lombardy, Italy', *American Anthropologist* 115, no. 3 (2013): 452.

119 Antonio Negri and Gabriele Fadini, 'Materialism and Theology: A Conversation', *Rethinking Marxism* 20, no. 4 (2008): 665, 669.

120 Cihan Tuğal, 'Faiths with a Heart and Heartless Religions: Devout Alternatives to the Merciless Rationalization of Charity', *Rethinking Marxism* 28, nos 3–4 (2016): 418.

7

Accounting at the Donnybrook Magdalene Laundry

Brid Murphy and Martin Quinn

Until recently, Irish legislation on the accounting of charitable organizations, including religious ones, was scarce. Yet, all organizations – including not-for-profits and charities – are required to maintain accounting records to comply with tax law if they trade, in addition to ensuring that appropriate financial information is available to assist in decision-making. Canon Law, that is the ecclesiastical set of laws, ordinances and regulations which govern the Catholic Church, also includes provisions on how religious organizations should be administered. These include the rendering of an account of the financial administration of each religious institute to the Vatican. Some financial records of Donnybrook Magdalene Laundry (DML) have survived from the 1960s to the 1990s, with broken periods. During this time, DML was considered a religious entity and was not required to publish financial information, file accounts with a regulator of charities or otherwise publicly disclose financial data. DML was, however, subject to Canon Law and laws which required accounts be held to record the activities of a trade. The available financial records of the Laundry provide evidence of detailed record-keeping throughout this period, supporting its operation as a trade. These records present some factual insights into the financial state of DML and the financial procedures followed and on the cost structure of the operation. Through some reconstructive efforts, this chapter reveals that DML generated a good financial surplus annually. However, this surplus excludes an obvious cost omission in the cost structure – the labour cost of the women working there.

The Laundry accounting in context

The *Report of the Inter-Departmental Committee to establish the Facts of State involvement with the Magdalen Laundries* (*IDC Report*, 2013) states that the financial records of the DML did not survive.[1] However, some records have in fact survived. The records were donated by the owners of the DML site to the University of Galway Archives and are available for public inspection. The accounting records span the period from 1962 to 1987. There are also some sporadic records after this time into the early 1990s.

During this time, from a business and accounting perspective, there was much change in Ireland, which experienced decimalization (1971), joined the European Economic Community (EEC, 1973) and had a period of economic 'gloom and doom' from 1979 to 1985.[2] In relation to accountancy, this era witnessed increased regulation through both legislation and professional accounting standards. Legislation during this time included the passing of the Companies Act, 1963, with the *Irish Times* of 9 October 1962, noting that 'for the first time [it] makes it obligatory on a company to keep books and accounts'.[3] This Act, and a later Companies (Amendment) Act, 1986, also prescribed details of the format of financial statements to be produced by companies. The Income Tax Act, 1967, was Ireland's first statute to legislate for income taxes since independence and formed the basis of the income tax system as we know it today. Another important piece of legislation was the Value-Added Tax Act, 1972, which was driven mainly by Ireland's entry to the EEC. This legislation imposed Value Added Tax (VAT) on goods and services in the State and was (and is) relevant to any religious and/or charitable bodies that provided goods or services as a commercial activity during the period covered by the accounting records described in this chapter.

The professional regulation of accounting also developed during this time. The first Statement of Standard Accounting Practice (SSAP) – which covered accounting in Ireland and the United Kingdom – was issued in 1971. A total of 34 SSAPs (or revisions thereof) were released between 1971 and 1990. These SSAPs detailed how specific transactions/events should be accounted for. The standards typically applied to companies, but their content and spirit was followed by accountants for most entity types. An accounting standard specifically focusing on charities – known as the Charities SORP – was first issued in 1988 and has been updated several times since.[4] Use of the SORP is not compulsory in Ireland, although many larger charities voluntarily adopt it. It was not until the Charities Act 2009 that a specific piece of legislation stated that charities, whether trading or not, were required to keep proper accounts and issue annual reports.

DML was an unincorporated entity, and part of a larger unincorporated entity – the Religious Sisters of Charity (RSC). The RSC was registered as a charity with the Revenue Commissioners and, as noted by the *IDC Report*,[5] the laundries themselves were first granted charitable status in 1921.[6] As DML was an unincorporated entity, both in its own right and as part of the larger RSC, company law did not apply to it during the period of the analysis here. Thus, there was no requirement from company law that accounting records be maintained or financial statements (for example, profit and loss account, balance sheet) prepared therefrom. This also meant that the Laundry was not required to prepare and present audited financial statements. While the RSC was (and is) a registered charity, during the period of our analysis, there were no requirements to file or publish charity financial information, unlike today. The Income Tax Act, 1967 (s. 413), required that any entity 'produce to the authorized officer all such invoices, accounts, books and other documents and records'. This implies accounting records should be maintained by an entity or person to determine liability to pay taxes. However, s. 334 of the same Act exempted charities from income taxes arising from sales of land/property or from any profits from trade once profits were applied to the purposes of the charity. Thus, as the RSC was a registered charity, no income taxes were accrued and arguably no accounting records were required to be maintained. As Sheila Killian notes, 'laundries, unlike many other trades operated by the religious orders, were granted charitable status by the Revenue Commissioners, effectively exempting the profits from income tax'.[7] Indeed, Rebecca Lea McCarthy observes that throughout the nineteenth and twentieth centuries, 'convents in England and Ireland were not legally bound to keep records [...] of their financial transactions'.[8]

However, it is known from the *IDC Report* that accounting records were maintained by the Laundries. In the case of Donnybrook (and others), this was because the Laundry was registered for VAT and the activities of the Laundry constituted a trade as per the VAT Act, 1972. Under s. 16(3) of this Act, an entity which traded was required to 'keep full and true records of all transactions which affect or may affect his liability to tax', the tax in this case being VAT. While the *IDC Report* tended to focus on exemption from income taxes, there was little mention of VAT. There was no similar exemption from VAT for the Magdalene Laundries (or other charities with trades) after 1972, and thus they were bound by VAT rules and required to keep records. Moreover, the RSC were (and are) subject to Canon Law and the keeping of financial records has been required by Canon Law and rules of various Congregations for centuries.[9] For example, the Jesuits – noted as avid record keepers[10] – first published instructions on administration (including finances) in 1647.[11] During the period of analysis here, two Codes of Canon Law were applicable, that of 1917 and of 1983. For example, Canons 1522 and 1523 of the 1917 Code stated the need for an administrator to record incomes, expenses and assets such as 'immovable property [and] movable objects' and to 'observe the provisions of canon and civil law'. The 1983 Code is clearer, with Canon 636 requiring that 'at the time and in the manner established by proper law, Finance officers and other administrators are to render an account of their administration to the competent civil authority'. Canon 636 also states: 'insofar as possible, a Finance officer distinct from the local superior is to be designated even in local communities'. The implications of these Canons are twofold for the period of analysis covered in this chapter: (i) the Laundry (as a community) was obliged to keep financial records and, (ii) civil law had to be followed. For the latter, this implied the Laundry was also obliged under Canon Law (at least from 1983) to comply with the record-keeping requirements of the VAT Act, 1972.

Apart from legal obligations, there is of course another crucial reason for keeping accounting records in any organization, and that is as a basis for the provision of decision-making information. Religious orders have over time utilized income sources other than alms and donations to support their work and upkeep. Many orders have, for example, engaged in educational activities and others in trades. While such activities may serve some objectives of a religious order (e.g. an education with a religious ethos), they can also be an important source of income to sustain orders. Thus, from the view of the order, it is useful if not imperative, to maintain accounting records for activities to ensure they are not a drain on finances.[12] This use of accounting is akin to how merchants ensured their capital was not decreased for the financial year, and more detailed information for day-to-day decision-making was not required.[13] Accounting information can be used as a basis for more regular decision-making. This use of accounting information is termed management accounting, whereby managers of a business are provided with accounting information to help make decisions on, for example, the price of a product/service or whether to invest in new equipment, and it seems that such decisions, informed by accounting records, were made at DML.

Accounting records, income and costs

Available records

The available records relate to the period 1962 to 1987, with some broken periods. It is worth noting that the records described here relate solely to the Donnybrook Laundry. In accounting, the *entity concept* describes how each separate entity should maintain accounting records. Thus, the Donnybrook Laundry was one accounting entity while the RSC was another entity – similar to group and subsidiary companies. It is not possible to determine if the Laundry applied the double entry accounting method (the normal accounting method applied in business) and, similarly, there is no evidence that any form of financial statements (such as a profit and loss account or balance sheet) was prepared. The significant financial records available facilitate a strong understanding of the financial workings of the Laundry throughout these years. The records physically consist of handwritten hardback analysis books in the main – with numerous analysis columns to capture expenditure types, for example. Such books were commonplace in small Irish businesses until computerized accounting became the norm from the mid-1990s. There are also some supporting documents and cheque stubs.

While limited, the 1960s records relate to expenditure and provide an itemized account of Laundry spending from 1962 onwards, describing dates, details and categories of spending monthly. The available 1970s records are more comprehensive and, in addition to expenditure records, comprise invoices for routine expenditure including utilities, laundry supplies, laundry maintenance, as well as VAT records (first accounted for in February 1973, in line with the application of the VAT Act, 1972).[14] The 1970s financial records also contain individual contract account files for larger contract business customers where van collections and deliveries of laundry were facilitated; sundry customer account records of smaller household customers whose laundry was dropped into the laundry; and a record of receipts for customer monies. The 1980s records similarly comprise expenditure records, invoices for routine expenditure, VAT records, contract account records, sundry account records and more detailed cash receipts records for customer monies. In addition, some cheque-book stubs and bank-lodgement stubs are available, as well as some detailed correspondence, including with contract account customers and other larger customers, providing greater insights into the Laundry interactions with its client base. The 1990s records (up to 1992) comprise cash receipts records for customer monies, customer account lists, price lists (detailing different pricing for different customer categories), the number of articles laundered on a weekly basis (approximately 877,000 items per year), as well as some correspondence with account customers and suppliers.

Customer accounts

According to available records, there were over 900 customer accounts across four broad categories, ranging from 'hall door collections' to large business customers.[15] Customers documented were varied, including hospitals, nursing homes, hotels, guest houses, schools, colleges, churches, clergy, sporting organizations, businesses and private households. Each customer was given a unique reference number and for customers other than 'hall door' customers, a specified van driver was also generally assigned to each account and noted in the individual customer account record. Contract and business customers represented about one-third of the overall customer base (in terms of numbers of customers). However, in aggregate, they represented about two-thirds of the total revenues of the laundry. Some customers accounted for substantial revenues: for example, a review of customers for a sample year, 1981, reveals one large hospital comprised one-third of the total revenue recorded in that year.

Contract customers were largely repeat clientele, and comprised a number of semi-state companies, third-level institutions, hotels, restaurants, hospitals, retail businesses, sports clubs and professional services companies (including accounting and legal firms). The records indicate that this diversity and scale of customers existed across all three decades and these customers received formal price lists regularly. Correspondence with customers highlights that the Laundry was conscious of providing a quality service to customers. For large customers, clear procedures were outlined, emphasizing matters such as pricing, issuing invoices and credit notes. Where any items were lost or damaged, DML reimbursed the customer (typically as a credit in the next billing invoice) for the full replacement value of the items or alternatively organized for replacement of the item. A detailed listing of suppliers for common items laundered was maintained so that damaged items could be replaced. Detailed records were maintained for individual customers, where individual sales and subsequent cash receipts were meticulously documented: sales were recorded in either blue or black pen and payments were duly offset against these in red pen. Further records entitled 'Laundry Daily Sales' contain what today would be termed an accounts receivable ledger, the purpose of which was to keep account of credit sales to customers and cash receipts from them. These made it possible to keep track of amounts owed by customers. In addition, DML maintained a 'Laundry Cash Book' which recorded all cash amounts received by the Laundry on a daily basis. An analysis of these two sets of records highlights that the majority of sales, over 90 per cent, were credit (not cash) sales, i.e. the laundry work was completed, customers billed with payment received later. In a small number of instances, minor bad debts amounts were recorded; however, in almost all cases, amounts were ultimately received in full. Where some accounts were slow to render payment, correspondence highlights that, on occasion, the Laundry engaged the services of the Irish Trade Protection Association (ITPA). For example, the ITPA was used to assist in the recovery of a debt in excess of £3,000 from a hotel customer in 1981.

Cash receipts

Cash amounts from customers were lodged to the Laundry bank account on a weekly basis, usually on a Wednesday. A reconciliation of cash lodged versus cash from sales revenues per VAT records for two sample years (1981 and 1984) highlighted additional cash amounts were lodged over and above the amounts recorded for VAT purposes. This is not uncommon as organizations can receive cash from other sources which is not subject to VAT. An analysis of the cash receipts records that the Laundry received amounts from the RSC on a monthly basis to cover some expenses, including fuel, interest, repairs and maintenance and stationery items. In 1992, the Laundry also received monies from the RSC to cover payments to an accounting firm, suggesting that the RSC provided some financial support to the Laundry in relation to the imminent sale of the Laundry as a going commercial concern to a private entity at that time. While it is known there were activities to promote bequests to the Laundry (see Chapter 6), and it was registered as a separate charitable organization, there are no available accounting records to evidence that any such amounts were received and lodged directly to the Laundry bank account.

Based on available records, an indication of the annual revenue generated by the Laundry activities is reflected in Table 7.1. The figures are shown for each year from 1975 to 1984 (£, Actual) and as index-adjusted values to reflect the values in present-day terms (€ as of December 2021). As can be seen, the average income per annum was over €826,000 in 2021 values. For comparison, this level of income equates the Laundry to a micro-enterprise (income less than €2m per EU criteria).[16] If it were a present-day limited company, it could likely obtain an audit exemption, not have to prepare audited financial statements and be amongst 92 per cent of all enterprises in Ireland.[17] Thus, in simple terms, the size of the Laundry based on its revenues was equivalent to a large proportion of Irish business. The *IDC Report* provided revenue figures for some other Magdalene Laundries. The revenues at Donnybrook were higher than the laundry at Sean McDermott Street, Dublin, where the *IDC Report* reported average annual revenue of €603,147 in 2011 values, or about €653,000 in 2021 values.[18]

Costs

Costs itemized throughout the period of the available records include running costs, comprising laundry supplies, machine repairs/maintenance and utilities (power, water and fuel oil). From the 1970s onwards, wages and associated payroll taxes were specifically itemized. It is not clear from the records to what or to whom the wages relate in all instances, but 'van men' are mentioned in some months which suggests the

Table 7.1 Annual revenues for sample years – cash receipts basis

	1975	1976	1977	1978	1979	1980	1981	1982	1983	1984	Average
£, Actual	89,616	118,935	138,856	154,102	142,456	164,291	217,832	224,982	254,227	266,135	177,143
€, 2021	817,639	899,798	948,316	975,122	777,411	758,274	815,215	749,748	768,092	753,510	826,312

drivers of the vans which transported the laundry were employees. Additional cost items recorded included new machinery/vans/plant costs from 1973 onwards, building repairs/maintenance costs from 1983 onwards, while a reserve fund for 'building' was created in 1979. Other items such as 'donations' were also recorded. In addition, a category labelled 'laundry girls' was recorded from May 1974 onwards. The precise nature and recipients of these amounts are not clear. There were also amounts described as 'Institutional maintenance', 'Mother Rectress', 'Institution', 'Convent' or 'Maintenance' transferred to the RSC on a monthly basis.

Reconstructed revenues and expenditure

Sufficient details of both revenues and costs were available for several periods and a reconstruction of aspects of revenues and expenditure was completed for three sample years. The years 1975, 1981 and 1984 were randomly selected from the available records. Table 7.2 shows the revenue and expenses[19] for each of these years and the resulting surplus on activities, as well as indexed values to present day (December 2021, €) amounts (in *italics*).

Table 7.2 Reconstructed revenue and expenditures for 1975, 1981 and 1984

	1975	*2021*	1981	*2021*	1984	*2021*
Indexation factor		*7.186*		*2.947*		*2.230*
	£	*€*	£	*€*	£	*€*
Revenue	89,616	*817,639*	217,832	*815,215*	266,135	*753,510*
Expenses						
Machine maintenance	4,510	*41,148*	21,448	*80,267*	21,090	*59,712*
Fuel oil	12,563	*114,622*	45,219	*169,228*	66,899	*189,412*
Power	4,037	*36,833*	11,100	*41,541*	15,122	*42,815*
Water	324	*2,956*	941	*3,522*	1,821	*5,156*
Laundry supplies & chemicals	4,041	*36,869*	6,699	*25,070*	7,123	*20,167*
Office expenses	261	*2,381*	637	*2,384*	437	*1,237*
Motor van expenses	1,541	*14,060*	3,065	*11,470*	2,994	*8,477*
Wages	1,685	*15,374*	20,774	*77,745*	32,829	*92,949*
Rates & Insurance	1,322	*12,062*	1,977	*7,399*	3,915	*11,085*
	30,284	*276,305*	111,860	*418,625*	152,230	*431,010*
Surplus on trade	59,332	*541,334*	105,972	*396,590*	113,905	*322,500*
Surplus used for						
Contribution to RSC	31,000		48,000		60,000	
Laundry girls	6,156		14,340		19,140	
Building			25,152		18,264	
Reserve fund					54,000	
Equipment/Vans/Plant	30,859		12,080			
Donations			3,000		8,100	
	68,015		102,572		159,504	

Note: The £ amounts are converted to € at £1 = €0.787564 before being indexed.

To give an idea of the purchasing power of the surplus in the particular years, in 1975 a bungalow in Bray, Co. Wicklow, 'beside train and shops' was on sale for £13,250;[20] in 1981, a four-bedroom Georgian house in Blackrock, Co. Dublin, was on sale for offers in excess of £40,000;[21] one year later, a seafront house in Clontarf, Dublin, was on sale for £50,000.[22]

While Table 7.2 reveals that the bookkeeping records maintained by the Laundry provide a relatively comprehensive account of all activities, there is no evidence that any statement like that shown in Table 7.2 was prepared. However, it is quite likely some end-of-year summary was produced. In preparing Table 7.2, it must be noted that, first, we cannot be certain they are fully accurate as we have no way to verify the receipts or payments. Normally, verification against bank statements would be undertaken, but no such statements are available in this instance. Second, all amounts are shown net of VAT, as is standard regulated practice in accounting. While the actual records of payments are inclusive of VAT, we have made assumptions on the applicable VAT type and deducted it in our calculations.[23] This reduces the accuracy of the expense figures, but it is the best outcome given the records available.

Table 7.2 shows that revenue was relatively consistent throughout the periods examined and comprised revenue from a number of different customer categories. As outlined above, expense items recorded largely relate to the running costs of the laundry operations and comprise machine-running costs, utilities, motor-van costs, office expense, rates, insurance and wages. There are some marked differences in spend levels in some expense items. One notable area is 'fuel oil', where expenditure increased considerably during the periods depicted in Table 7.2. Fuel oil referred to a heavy kerosene-like fuel used to run boilers to generate the steam needed in the Laundry. The increased fuel oil cost is likely not reflective of increased capacity but may be best understood against the backdrop of the 1970s oil crisis and the quadrupling of oil prices at the latter end of the 1970s and into the early 1980s. Further items which recorded significant increases were machine maintenance and wages. On machine maintenance, the cost increases are more than the cost-of-living increase (about 3.2 times) over the period covered in Table 7.2. Two possible reasons for increased costs may be: (i) increased mechanization of laundry operations necessitating greater expenditure on machine maintenance, or (ii) ageing equipment necessitated more spend on maintenance. On wages, the increase is more in line with the general cost of living increase over the period. We should note that one obvious expense is excluded from Table 7.2, that of depreciation – the gradual write-off of capital expenditure over its useful life – as dictated by accounting practice and regulations. The depreciation amount cannot be estimated with any reasonable accuracy from the records available, but typically the cost of plant and machinery would be depreciated over a period of 10 to 15 years, by equal amounts each year. The actual life of plant and machinery could be shorter or longer as depreciation is an accounting estimate. Thus, the surplus on trade presented per Table 7.2 is higher than it would have been in reality. To put the surplus amounts in context is difficult as small Irish companies were not required to publish detailed accounting information until the late 1980s.

Table 7.2 also reveals how generated surpluses were used. The amounts shown in Table 7.2 are amounts spent in the year and do not necessarily match the surplus for the year – excess funds would be from accumulated surplus as there is no evidence of any debt or bank loans. 'Institutional maintenance' was a very significant component, typically between one-third and one-half of the total surplus in a given year (and even higher in 1975). Each month, an amount so described was transferred to a specific RSC bank account, often denoted in the records as the 'Sisters of Charity No 1 A/c' or 'Convent' account. This fixed monthly amount appears to have been determined at the beginning of each year. In some months, an additional amount was also transferred to a second RSC account, sometimes labelled as the 'Sisters of Charity No 2 A/c' or as the 'Institution' account. This amount was generally not a standard amount and, in the absence of bank statements or further supporting records, it is not possible to determine why these transfers took place at specific times or for the amounts recorded. Indeed, it could be that the policy was simply to take excess funds from the Laundry to the RSC. These amounts for 'Institutional maintenance' were most likely a contribution to the ongoing expenses of the RSC in general, or contributions towards their charitable purposes. It is not uncommon for religious orders to raise surpluses through trade or other activities (for example, schools/colleges) to fund their own upkeep or related purpose. Of course, here it could be argued that any surplus was generated (at least partially) through the unpaid labour of the women in DML.

Amounts labelled as 'Laundry girls' were also documented in the records. The precise nature/recipients of these amounts is not clear. These amounts were first recorded as 'wages' in May 1974 and described as 'girls premium'. However, these were subsequently separately recorded (i.e. not as wages) from November 1974 and described as a further RSC item in respect of 'Sisters of Charity (Girls)', 'Sisters of Charity L. Girls' or 'Laundry Girls'. It is possible that this was pocket money paid to the women in the institution. The narrative within the records sometimes referred to the name of a particular Sister, i.e. the cheques were paid to a named Sister, for example from November 1976, 'Sr T. Bernadine', was referenced. The initial monthly amount, £513, remained fixed for the first four years (with one exception in July 1976, when it was only £400) until October 1977, at which point it increased to a higher fixed amount, £668. This amount was in turn increased at other intervals, for example March 1979 (£895), January 1981 (£1,195), December 1983 (£1,595), April 1986 (£2,000). In 1987, alternating amounts of £2,600 and £3,100 were recorded in every other month. This suggests that some decisions were made in relation to the extent/appropriateness of this amount at regular intervals.

Surpluses generated were also allocated to capital expenditure, as shown in Table 7.2. Records highlight that various amounts were transferred to a building reserve fund over a number of years. However, it is not clear from the records if this reserve fund was actually utilized by the time the Laundry was sold in 1992. Another key area of capital expenditure was on substantial operational assets such as equipment, machines, and vans required to maintain laundry operations. Some examples include: (i) in 1975, more than £23,000 was allocated for the purchase of a new calendar – a machine used to dry/iron items such as bed sheets, pillowcases and table cloths to produce a high-quality finish, and (ii) in 1981, two new vans were purchased at a cost of just over £12,000. In addition, monies were allocated to maintenance costs of the actual laundry facility itself (as distinguished from machine maintenance costs which were part of the running costs of the laundry operations). In 1984, such maintenance expenditure comprised a burglar alarm in the laundry building at a cost of £2,300, ducting costing £2,100, electrical work costing £5,500, roof repairs costing £3,100 and painting costing £5,200. Subsequent periods detail different such expenditure, for example monies allocated toward the installation of gas in the laundry (1985 and 1986). Other, more ad hoc, expenditure items were also periodically documented. 'Donations' were one such item and would have been part of the charitable remit of the RSC. It is not clear how the amounts were determined or who decided the amounts. Different individual amounts were recorded at various times, ranging from individual donations of £100 to £4,000. The largest aggregate annual donations, in excess of £9,000, were recorded in 1985. The donations were mainly to international development organizations.

Overall, we can see that the records provided sufficient detail to ensure compliance with the VAT record-keeping requirements of the time. VAT was first recorded by the Laundry in February 1973 and was completed on a cash receipts basis, which was not in strict compliance with the legislation. However, the cash receipts basis of records preparation is consistent with that across the religious orders more generally.[24] Accounting for VAT on this basis means a trader pays VAT due when the customer pays, not when the customer is invoiced (which is the norm). The VAT Act, 1972 (s. 14), stipulated that the cash receipts basis could only be used where at least 90 per cent of sales were made to customers not registered for VAT, for example when sales are made to the general public. The larger VAT-registered contract customer accounts represented about two-thirds of the total revenue of the Laundry, and as noted these contract accounts were invoiced for services. Therefore, the application of the cash receipts basis was not correct. However, mindful that the bookkeeping clerk(s) – possibly one of the RSC sisters – most likely did not have much professional accounting or tax education, it is probable that the selection of method of calculation was not an intentional misrepresentation. Incorrectly applying the cash receipts basis of accounting for VAT did not in any way reduce the amount of VAT paid, nor result in any incorrect payments. Its application did however mean VAT amounts were paid to the Revenue Commissioners later than stipulated by law.

Accounting and decision-making

An important reason for maintaining accounting records is so that the resulting information can be used as a basis for decision-making. This could include decisions regarding, for example, what prices to charge, whether a product or service is profitable or whether capital investments should be made. As shown in Table 7.2, the Laundry did invest in the ongoing maintenance and renewal of equipment (capital). Surviving records (from the 1990s) show that pricing decisions did occur at the Laundry. The records highlight different prices for different items as might be expected: different prices were set for different laundry items, for example sheets, pillowcases, different size towels, different clothing garments, etc.

However, different prices were also charged to different customers. This may have been on the basis of volume of activities, with larger customers charged a lesser price per item than smaller customers. Records from 1992 show pricing for the laundry of a pillowcase across a wide range, from 17 pence to 42 pence per item. Detailed price lists document that particular prices were also charged in respect of different categories of business to large customers. For example, a price list was generated for an RSC-owned hospital which catered for adults and children, both public and private patients, and also maintained staff residences. In this case, different prices were charged for adult bedding versus children's bedding, bedding for its public hospital element versus bedding for its private hospital element, and patient bedding versus staff bedding. Some interesting examples are documented in this price list, for instance sheets and pillowcases for private bedding were priced more than 40 per cent higher than public bedding and 70 per cent higher than staff bedding. Further documentation highlights that specific wash, rinse and dry cycles were scheduled for different items – specific numbers, durations and temperatures of wash and rinse cycles, and specific detergents at each cycle stage.

This suggests that key operational and pricing strategy decisions were made as differing prices were being charged, although we have no direct evidence of such decision-making in the surviving records. However, with the accounting records maintained, the RSC at least knew the various costs each month (and year) and could use this as a basis to know the overall revenues needed to cover costs. Again, while we have no evidence from the records, it is likely that a target costing approach may have been applied. This approach looks at the price the market will pay (for example, large versus small customers) and works back to determine if the product/service can be delivered at a cost which will yield a profit. In the Laundry, it is possible that volumes and prices were estimated and once these could exceed cost, then the price could be set according to a particular customer. While this is speculation, the fact that price lists existed and varied according to customer and laundry type implies information-based pricing decisions were made – and accounting records would without doubt have been drawn upon for such decisions.

The *IDC Report* reported on the finances of several laundries, giving the general impression that they were not commercially viable or operating on a break-even basis. From a decision-making point of view, it is highly likely that the RSC would have intended their Magdalene Laundries to generate a surplus or at least break even. As outlined in Table 7.2 – even though it is incomplete in terms of costs – the Donnybrook Laundry almost certainly generated a reasonable surplus. As shown, this surplus was used to reinvest in new equipment and contribute to the overall running of the RSC.

The information reported by the *IDC Report* is less detailed than that presented in Table 7.2, and with this more detailed breakdown, we can explore the viability of the Donnybrook Laundry. Viability is considered from two aspects – its viability to the RSC and commercially. The Laundry's viability to the RSC would likely have been an ongoing decision, particularly from the view of its contribution to the Order overall. In this case, as highlighted earlier, the surplus over the years increased and the amounts contributed to the RSC likewise increased. Thus, from the perspective of the RSC, the Donnybrook Laundry was viable and contributed funds over the years to the Order in pursuit of its charitable/religious objectives.

To assess its commercial viability is more difficult. We can reflect on the cost structure of the Laundry as shown in Table 7.2 and how this would (or would not)

Table 7.3 Imputed wage cost effect on surplus/RSC contribution

	1975	1981	1984
Average weekly manufacturing wage £ (incl. employer costs)[29]	43.13	125.70	177.81
50-week cost at 50% of average wage £	1,228	3,142	4,445
Staff no. equivalent to consume surplus	50	38	35
Staff no. equivalent to consume surplus and RSC contribution	75	53	49

equate to a commercial operation. The cost structure as per Table 7.2 is clearly missing a substantial cost, that of paid workers. The staff costs would be of two types. First, the girls and women who worked in the Laundry were unpaid from an accounting perspective – the records of payments show no evidence of any regular payroll/wages other than van drivers. Second, although likely a smaller segment of cost, any members of the RSC involved in the administration and operation of the Laundry were likely unpaid. It could be argued that the surplus transfer to the RSC included payment for the nuns' work in the laundry, however accounting norms would not recognize this unless it is classified as payroll per se. As noted above, the Laundry was viable from the perspective of the RSC, which of course excluded these two substantial costs.

An assessment of the commercial viability of the Laundry requires consideration of these costs. We have attempted in Table 7.3[25] to illustrate that the surplus as per Table 7.2 would effectively be consumed by 'real' wage costs. Table 7.3 shows the average weekly manufacturing wage for the same years described earlier. Assuming that laundry staff were paid even 50 per cent of this rate, Table 7.3 shows how many staff could have been paid from surplus, and how many staff could have been paid from the surplus plus the contributions made to the RSC. According to the *IDC Report*,[26] the maximum capacity at Donnybrook was 120 women. The number of women entering annually averaged 30–40[27] until the 1980s. While we cannot be certain how many women actually worked in the Laundry in a given timeframe, it seems reasonable to infer that the surplus and contribution to the RSC were in a large part due to the lack of labour costs.[28]

Conclusion

The *IDC Report* stated that financial records of the Donnybrook Magdalene Laundry had not survived and was therefore unable to provide any understanding of its financial operations. However, the financial records used as a source for this chapter, while incomplete and with some broken periods, provide detailed documentary evidence, and are an important testimony of the financial workings of the Laundry. These detailed records, spanning the early 1960s to the early 1990s, have enabled the reconstruction of the income and expenditure of multiple years and provide a greater understanding of the financial operating model of the Laundry within this time period.

It is important to note that these reconstructed accounts have been prepared on the basis of cash income from customers and cash expenditure on operating activities only, as per the available records. While some charitable entities such as the RSC and their laundries may also have benefitted from other charitable sources of income, for example bequests and donations, no accounting records have been recovered to indicate how DML fared in this regard. Similarly, the reconstructed accounts do not incorporate some typical business costs which would have been necessary to ensure the running of a commercial laundry activity. Such costs include wages for all those who worked in the Laundry and appropriate costs of relevant capital expenditure items such as machinery and equipment (that is, depreciation). In addition, while 'Institutional maintenance' is recorded in the accounts, the precise nature of this is not clear from an accounting perspective. It is quite likely that the RSC provided services and support for the management of the laundry; however, no cost of this activity per se is recognized in the Laundry financial records. This may be explained by the fact that the RSC was a charitable undertaking, and while receiving monthly amounts from DML, the RSC did not invoice it for what would be described as a management fee in a commercial organization. Thus, although it likely did generate a surplus as shown earlier, from a purely commercial perspective, the Laundry would have been less viable than indicated if all costs were to be appropriately considered. As shown in Table 7.3, any surplus and contribution to the RSC may be approximated to a projected number of staff who could have been paid. Of course, the women and girls in DML were unpaid, and it can be reasonably argued that the surplus and RSC contribution were earned as a result of their efforts.

Reflecting on the accounting records maintained at Donnybrook over the time frame of this chapter, it is clear – to paraphrase Killian[30] – that there was little or no external reporting of accounting information by the Laundry. Indeed, little or none was required. While the maintenance of accounting records was required for VAT purposes, the VAT rules only needed records of transactions and no accounting summaries were necessary. This was a clear lack of accountability, as, for example, year end statements similar to those in Table 7.2 were not required by any external party. However, as detailed here, accounting information is likely to have been used to support the decision-making needs of the RSC and the Laundry itself, as well as address Canon Law requirements on reporting of finances. While there is no direct evidence of this, the fact that prices for laundry services existed at varying levels and that a surplus was typically generated suggests accounting information must have been an input to decision-making. Killian noted a 'removal of accounting ways of thinking from relationships between the state and private bodies to which pivotal services have been outsourced'[31] and also referred to how official tax records did not capture the cost of labour at the Magdalene Laundries. The records here support this, and one can only ponder if questions would have arisen if annual accounting statements were part of the accountability relationship with the State and others. A low, or near absent, wage cost may have raised some flags. Killian[32] also highlighted Maeve O'Rourke's claim that contemporaneous legal norms should have resulted in intervention by the State. Unfortunately, this logic did not apply to accounting norms, and as noted earlier, it was not until after 2009 that any charity specific legislation required publication of accounting information.

Notes

1 Department of Justice, *Report of the Inter-Departmental Committee to Establish the Facts of State Involvement with the Magdalen Laundries* (Dublin, 2013, hereinafter *IDC Report*), 997.

2 Cormac O'Gráda, *Rocky Road: Irish Economy since the 1920s* (Manchester: Manchester University Press, 1997), 31.

3 'Companies Bill is Not Radical', *Irish Times*, 9 October 1962, 4.

4 Noel Hyndman, 'The Charities SORP: An "Engine" for Good?', *Public Money & Management* 38, no. 4 (2018): 247–50.

5 *IDC Report*, 754.

6 Today, all registered charitable organizations must file an annual report with the Charities Regulator. This report includes financial data. Those with an income in excess of €100,000 must also prepare full audited accounts.

7 Sheila Killian, '"For Lack of Accountability": The Logic of the Price in Ireland's Magdalen Laundries', *Accounting, Organizations and Society* 43 (2015): 17–32.

8 Rebecca Lea McCarthy, O*rigins of the Magdalene Laundries: An Analytical History* (Jefferson, NC: McFarland, 2010), xii.

9 The first to write about the double-entry system of accounting used to the present day was a Franciscan friar, Luca Pacioli, in 1494.

10 John W. O'Malley, *The Jesuits: A History from Ignatius to the Present* (Lanham, MD: Rowman & Littlefield, 2014).

11 On their establishment, the RSC initially followed the Rules of the Constitution of the Society of Jesus. However, they were not suited to their type of apostolic life and new rules were drafted in 1824. See *Final Report of the Commission to Inquire into Child Abuse* (Dublin: Stationery Office, 2009), vol. 2, 473. It is possible this initial connection with Jesuit rules influenced their approach to record-keeping.

12 As an example, in the 1500s, Jesuit colleges ran up debts which led to a decree in 1646 imposing penalties on colleges with excess debt. For more detail, see Dauril Alden, *The Making of an Enterprise: The Society of Jesus in Portugal, Its Empire, and Beyond, 1540–1750* (Stanford, CA: Stanford University Press, 1996).

13 Pierre Gervais and Martin Quinn, 'Costing in the Early Industrial Revolution: Gradual Change to Cost Calculations at US Cloth Mills in the 1820s', *Accounting History Review* 26, no. 3 (2016): 191–217.

14 The VAT rates in force during the period 1972 to 1987 range from 6.25% to 23%, with 10% being the typical rate. All income figures reported here exclude VAT.

15 The listings are not dated and it is possible that this may not represent all customers.

16 European Commission, 'SME Definition', Internal Market, Industry, Entrepreneurship and SMEs, available online: www.ec.europa.eu/growth/smes/sme-definition_en (accessed 9 December 2021).

17 Central Statistics Office, 'Business in Ireland 2018', Statistics, available online: www.cso. ie/en/releasesandpublications/ep/p-bii/businessinireland2018/ (accessed 9 December 2021).

18 *IDC Report*, 1002.

19 Income and expenses in Table 7.2 are net of VAT. See more detail later.

20 *Irish Times*, 8 January 1975, 18.

21 Ibid., 9 January 1981, 23.

22 Ibid., 6 January 1984, 17.

23 Machine maintenance, fuel oil and power are assumed as reduced rate VAT items (6.75%, 15% and 23%, in order from the earliest year); laundry supplies, office supplies and motor expenses are assumed at the standard rate (19.5%, 25% and 35%, in order).

24 *IDC Report*, 998.

25 Average manufacturing wage + 12% estimated employers Pay Related Social Insurance (PRSI). See, Central Statistics Office, 'Historical Earnings 1938–2015: Sectoral Earnings', available online: www.cso.ie/en/releasesandpublications/ep/p-hes/hes2015/se/ (accessed 10 January 2022).

26 *IDC Report*, 157–203.

27 Ibid., Appendix 4.

28 It is worth noting that under the Conditions of Employment Act, 1936, s. 62, industrial work carried on in institutions for charitable or reformatory purposes could be unpaid. This 1936 Act was not repealed until the Organisation of Working Time Act, 1997. This poses an interesting conflict with the fact that the DML was regarded as a trade for VAT purposes from 1976.

29 Central Statistics Office, 'Historical Earnings 1938–2015'.

30 Killian, '"For Lack of Accountability"'.

31 Ibid., 17.

32 Ibid., 17–32.

8

'Women of Evil Life'

Donnybrook Magdalene and the Criminal Justice System

Lynsey Black

This chapter explores cases of women who entered Donnybrook Magdalene Laundry (DML) from the criminal justice system.[1] After independence, state deference to the role of the Catholic Church became, effectively, Irish Free State policy.[2] As Gerry McNally[3] and Katherine O'Donnell in Chapter 4 in this collection, have outlined, the acceptance of the Catholic principle of subsidiarity by the Irish state ensured that much social policy was within the domain of Catholic Church organizations. This policy extended to education and health services, as well as to the state's use of religious institutions such as laundries for women within the justice system. This principle, originally espoused in the Papal encyclical *Rerum Novarum*, preached caution on the ills of an overweening state, advocating instead for voluntary organizations to take up those roles most suited to them in the delivery of education, healthcare and social services.[4] As a result, female offenders were regularly subject to religious rather than state control. While prisons for women remained, fewer women were admitted to them.[5] Instead, certain offending women were sent to religious detention in sites such as Magdalene Laundries and other religiously run institutions.[6] The provision of this 'service' by religious sisters was considered complementary to their mission, as women who entered Magdalene institutions from the criminal justice system were often deemed suitable cases for religious instruction and penitential atonement rather than prison, their wrongdoing more explicable as 'sin' than 'crime'.

Drawing on the archival files of the Central Criminal Court, government departments and press reporting, the case studies in this chapter explore the use of the Donnybrook Magdalene as a site of punishment within this penal landscape. As the Religious Sisters of Charity (RSC) proclaimed in a Christmas appeal, St Mary Magdalen's was 'the oldest penitentiary in Dublin'.[7] The statement was accurate, both in the carceral functions of the institution and in its literal translation as a place of penitence. The cases discussed below elaborate DML's use under the Probation Acts and as a component of suspended sentences, as well as for women serving life sentences who were transferred to DML from prison. The cases are a sample of those women who were prosecuted for the murder of an infant in the decades after independence.[8] Some of the women discussed herein who were prosecuted for murder were ultimately convicted of lesser offences, such as manslaughter and concealment of birth, and their sentences included a requirement to enter DML. Two women were actually convicted of murder and were sentenced to penal servitude for life following reprieve of the capital sentence. These two women were later released from prison on the condition that they enter the Donnybrook Magdalene. One central theme of the cases discussed is the disproportionate number of prosecutions for the murder of an infant born outside of wedlock. The status of 'illegitimacy', when a baby was born to an unmarried mother, shaped the profile of women prosecuted for murder.[9] While laundries were often branded as more humane sites of punishment for young women (a frequent refrain from judges and barristers who compared them favourably to prison), it was occasionally noted that time spent in a Magdalene institution carried with it much greater stigma. This stigma related to the moral blameworthiness associated with entry to a Magdalene. The appropriateness of Magdalene institutions as sites of punishment for women deemed to have 'fallen' is explored below.

Any discussion of DML as a site of punishment must grapple with the difficulty of reconstructing the archive for women whose lives intersected with both the criminal justice system and the system of Magdalene institutions, without access to the archives held by the RSC. That the Magdalenes functioned as places of punishment has been documented by scholars such as James M. Smith and Clíona Rattigan.[10] Smith records that of all known entries to DML through the nineteenth century, only 2.52 per cent entered via the police or prison.[11] In contrast, the 2013 *Report of the Inter-Departmental Committee to Establish the Facts of State Involvement with the Magdalen Laundries* (*IDC Report*, 2013) found that post-1922, 8.1 per cent of entries to all laundries came via the criminal justice system (although this figure is very unreliable).[12] Therefore, although the evidence suggests their increasing use through the post-1922 decades, without access to the records of the religious organizations who ran the laundries, only a partial impression can be gleaned. The case studies below have been pieced together from the state archival material and the press reporting, something which varied according to the particular features of the case. As Ryan found, reporting in such cases was often perfunctory, suggesting the quotidian nature of infanticide-related offences.[13] Newspapers sometimes published that a woman had been discharged from court while omitting that her sentence stipulated confinement in a Magdalene laundry.[14] Just as some women's admittance to laundries could be obscured, so details on women's release (for those who were released) is often lacking. For women admitted by the courts or from prison, the sudden disappearance of the paper trail is jarring. It means that for many of the women, the length of time spent in laundries is unknown. The lack of access to the archives of religious organizations renders investigation of the fates of these women difficult.[15] While the lack of documentary record is a significant issue for *all* women who entered the laundries, for those who entered by the criminal justice system it is particularly troubling and speaks to the state's failure in its duty of care to those women within its custody. This is evident throughout the cases explored below. The nuns' expectations that inmates would remain in Magdalene laundries for life renders this particularly galling, compounding the women's invisibility and the state's failure in its duty. While the archives available do not record specific references of payment to the nuns for the women accepted to the laundries, it seems payment could be sought under section 35 of the Public Assistance Act, 1939.[16]

Crucially also, such sites presented very different expectations of transparency compared to the prison. Women prisoners had occasional visits from Prison Visiting Committees, could petition the Minister for Justice and write letters. Such oversight was absent once women entered religious institutions, and were particularly stark in the case of Magdalene Laundries. There are few traces in the state archives of any ongoing oversight of women in the Magdalene institutions. Occasional correspondence from probation officers being one of the few pieces of evidence which suggests that even cursory follow-up was undertaken.[17] In practice, many women relied on the conscientiousness of individual probation officers to remember and advocate their cases for eventual release. As the cases demonstrate, some women entered laundries via the criminal justice system and remained there for the rest of their lives.

Entry from the courts under sentence

Women entered the Magdalene Laundries from the courts under sentence, on probation and on remand.[18] There was a legislative basis for some of these pathways, but they remained ad hoc and highly discretionary. The case studies in this section centre on women who entered DML under a suspended sentence or probation. For women entering by suspended sentence, the sentence included a period of imprisonment, for instance two years' imprisonment, which was suspended on the convicted woman agreeing to enter a religious institution – in this case, DML.[19] The Irish Human Rights Commission suggested that in these cases, an apparent element of 'choice' smoothed over the lack of statutory underpinning: 'Using this approach of providing an "option", was most likely employed by the Courts to avoid any legal infirmity that might arise from detaining such women in laundries without legal authority.'[20] Women were also sent to Magdalene institutions on foot of probation orders. The consolidation of probation had occurred with the Probation of Offenders Act, 1907, and the Criminal Justice Administration Act, 1914. These acts provided for probation to be used in lieu of imprisonment. As with suspended sentences, probation orders often required women's committal to a religious institution.

There was occasional unease at the informal processes by which women entered religious detention from the courts. The *Cussen Report*, reporting in 1936 primarily on the Industrial and Reformatory School system, notes that the situation was 'undesirable' due to the 'absence of specific power' which allowed judges to commit women and girls to religious sites.[21] Probation officer E. M. Carroll also expressed her disquiet at committals to Magdalene Laundries in particular, noting that these institutions often expected 'permanent denunciation' and lifelong confinement.[22]

In all cases, chaplains, religious prison visitors and probation officers acted as essential links between criminal justice personnel, the women and the religious sisters, negotiating entry to the Magdalene institutions. In his memoirs, Father J. Anthony Gaughan recalls his experience of this while serving as chaplain at DML:

I attended the proceedings in Green Street Criminal Court and brought a message to the judge from the Sisters that the young woman who had taken refuge with them had her best chance of being rehabilitated in St Mary's rather than in prison ... without exception they, as well as the Sisters, were very reluctant to see women in prison.[23]

Below, a sample of case studies illustrate how entry to the Magdalene institution worked in practice, and elaborate on some of the central themes of Donnybrook as a site of punishment.

Lucy Byrne

On 21 November 1929, 23-year-old Lucy Byrne was tried for the murder of her newborn baby. In her statement, she recalled that the labour pains had come at night when she was in bed:

I went to bed at about 10.30pm. I was about 5 or 10 minutes in bed when I got sick. I got up out of bed and went out into the shed and I was only a few minutes in the shed when the child was born . . .[24]

She left the body outside in a concealed place. The following day she stayed in bed, and when she was well enough to get up, she washed the bloodstains from her clothing. Lucy lived with her parents, her sister, her three brothers and her 4-year-old daughter. Sergeant Higgins Myshall, after receiving information about Lucy, called to the Byrne residence and cautioned her. He reported her saying, 'They'll kill me. I will show you where it is.'[25] The sergeant soon found the body of the infant in a ditch. Although Lucy told police that the baby had been dead at birth, examination showed that death was due to asphyxiation.[26] Lucy pleaded guilty to concealment of birth. She was sentenced to six months' imprisonment, suspended on the condition that she enter DML for two years.[27] There is little press reporting on the case. The fact that Lucy was already a mother to an older child out of wedlock, compounded by the evidence of her second 'illegitimate' pregnancy, may have informed the decision to send her to DML. Lucy remained in DML for decades and died in hospital in 1978; the available records suggest that at the very least, she remained in Donnybrook for 49 years.[28]

Mary Tobin

The following year, 17-year-old Mary Tobin was also tried for the murder of her newborn baby and was found guilty of concealment of birth. The body of the infant was discovered with a stocking tied around the neck and with pieces of paper in the mouth. When arrested on 27 January 1930, she replied, 'I have nothing to say,'[29] and on discovery of the body, Mary claimed the baby had not stirred from the moment of birth. Mary's mother had died after three years of illness when Mary was just 9 years of age, and, 'From that time she had no one to guide her or give her any knowledge of life.'[30]

Cecil Lavery, QC, prosecuting, referred to infanticide as 'a most serious problem', but argued that the jurors could not rely on their sympathy to protect Mary from the law.[31] Mary was sentenced to 12 months' imprisonment, suspended on the condition that she enter DML for 18 months.[32] The *Irish Times* reported the suspended sentence, and stated that Mary had been discharged on entering into a bond to keep the peace, omitting her detention in DML.[33] Mary disappears from the records available to us. We do not know how long she spent in DML.

Nora Hannigan

Nora Hannigan was tried for the murder of her newborn baby on 18 June 1931. Nora was unmarried and lived in Waterford with her father, James Hannigan, a widower with 12 children. Gardaí first arrested James, but the murder charge against him was subsequently dropped, and Nora herself was charged. An investigating guard said that when they arrived at the house, Nora had told them: 'My father carried the child downstairs and threw it in a tub of water in the backyard. I looked through the window and saw him throwing the baby in the tub. The child was alive when born.'[34] In her statement, Nora claimed she had been made pregnant by her father.[35] The *Evening Herald* reported this allegation with little sympathy:

> She made a very abominable charge as to the paternity of the child, and suggested that her father had an interest in its destruction quite apart from the shame that would fall on him as her father.[36]

Mary pleaded guilty to concealment of birth and on 19 June was sentenced to spend two years in the Donnybrook Magdalene.[37] Unlike the case of Mary Tobin, Nora's disposal to a religious institution was remarked on in the newspapers, and the *Evening Herald* headline following sentencing was: 'Concealment of Birth – Waterford Girl to be Committed to an Institution.'[38]

Nora's case demonstrates the limits of religious detention as sites of punishment for convicted women. Some months into her sentence, Nora appeared before Mr Justice Meredith. She had broken the terms of her sentence while in Donnybrook. A letter from the RSC to the County Registrar, outlined the issue:

> I regret to say, Nora Halligan [sic] . . . has broken the 'orders and regulations' of this Asylum, she has also broken the peace by endangering the life of one of its inmates – on more than one occasion. We cannot be accountable for the said Nora Halligan [sic], and would deem it a favour on your part to have her removed without delay.[39]

When no response was forthcoming, the RSC again wrote:

> It is unreasonable that we should be expected to keep the woman, in question, under the circumstances – She has to be kept apart from the other inmates of the Institution. The strain is pretty great for both sides and we cannot be accountable for what may happen.[40]

Nora was transferred from DML to the Magdalene at Gloucester Street (later known as Sean McDermott Street), and ordered to remain there for a period of two years from the new date of transfer, rather than from the date of sentence in June 1931. Effectively, the court had increased Nora's sentence by approximately nine months. At this juncture, Mr Justice Meredith also imposed a suspended sentence of two years' imprisonment. When Nora appeared before the courts again accused of breaching the terms of her sentence on 13 June 1932, Mr Justice O'Byrne made the order that she be imprisoned for this two-year period, but stipulated that the sentence would run from the original sentencing in June 1931. The courts were willing to extend her period of confinement in a Magdalene institution but not if her place of confinement was instead the state-run prison.

Kate Reilly

As a married woman, 35-year-old Kate Reilly was an unlikely inmate of the Magdalene system. On 4 November 1937, she pleaded guilty to the manslaughter of her 2-year-old child. When she appeared for sentencing, she was ordered to enter the Donnybrook Magdalene for two years. It was alleged that Kate had poisoned her daughter, and when police called to her residence, Kate produced a packet of strychnine powder that she claimed to have put in the children's morning meal. When asked why, she replied, 'Ah! I am discontented; they are like no other children. My head is not right. I know I am not right.'[41] Kate added that her intention had been to then take the strychnine herself. A neighbour gave evidence that for some time prior to the killing, she had noticed Kate 'very changed in her manner'.[42] Giving evidence, her husband revealed that his wife's behaviour had become peculiar the year before, following the death of their son, after which she increasingly had delusions that something was wrong with the children. Rather than pursue a defence of legal insanity, Kate was convicted of manslaughter. Sentencing her, Mr Justice Gavan Duffy noted that the offence had been committed 'at a time when she was not herself'.[43] The defence barrister urged that her sentence should reflect this, arguing that 'it was evident that Mrs Reilly would have to be placed under some restriction on her liberty for some time until the disorder which affected her mind had been cleared up'.[44] The *Anglo-Celt* reported that a 'suitable institution' would be found in which Kate would be detained.[45] The decision to send her to DML appears to have been viewed as an intermediary solution, between imprisonment and absolute release. The Magdalene institution, again, is ambiguous in its nature and its capacity. There are cases of other women in similar situations who are instead confined for a period of time in psychiatric institutions. In this particular case, Donnybrook was accepted as a suitable institution in which to confine a woman suffering from mental illness.

Mary Reilly

Mary Reilly, aged 23 and unmarried, pleaded guilty to the manslaughter of her newborn baby at her trial on 31 May 1940. Mary had previously worked as a domestic servant, but for the past number of years she had remained at home where she helped her mother with duties in the house. Mary gave birth in her bed at home. She recalled in her statement:

> The child was born in the bed and I broke the cord with my hand. The child did not cry when it was born, but I found it breathing after it was born. About five minutes after the child was born, I put a piece of cloth that I tore off a flower bag, around its neck, and held it tight around the neck for about a minute.[46]

Mr Justice Conor Maguire sentenced Mary to 18 months' imprisonment, suspended on entering DML for three years.[47] This disposal was noted in the press, such as in the *Evening Echo* which relayed that the judge 'imposed a sentence of 18 months imprisonment, not to be enforced if she enters St Mary's Convent, Donnybrook.'[48] An anonymized case presented in the *IDC Report* has strong similarities to Mary's case. If it is Mary, it seems that she died of consumption (tuberculosis) while still an inmate at Donnybrook.[49]

Conditional release from prison

The chapter now turns to explore the cases of two women convicted of the murder of their infants who were transferred from Mountjoy Prison to DML – Mary Anne Keane and Margaret Finn. These women had been sentenced to death following their murder convictions, and this sentence had subsequently been commuted to penal servitude for life. After some time in prison, both were released from prison on licence on the condition that they enter DML. The procedures were vague for women who entered religious institutions such as DML on conditional release from prison.[50] Licences were issued under the Penal Servitude Acts, 1853 to 1891. Women were given to understand that their release from prison was conditional only on their agreeing to enter a named institution. However, in practice, the licence was never made explicitly conditional on this 'agreement' as to add such conditions would have required raising the issue in the Oireachtas (Parliament). Such a resort was considered unduly burdensome, and fear was expressed that airing individual cases in such a forum would attract 'harsh, tyrannical or absurd conditions'.[51] While it was a condition of their release that women could be returned to prison if they did not abide by the terms of the licence, this was not availed of in practice. As the Department of Justice noted, should women leave their designated institutions, there was little that could be done beyond admitting them again to prison – and it was stated that this course of action had not been taken in decades.[52] Nevertheless, the Department of Justice held that it was 'unlikely' women would leave. In the case of women transferred from prison to laundries, this was very much the case.

While in prison, women sometimes expressed a willingness to enter religious institutions such as Donnybrook, articulated in their petitioning to the Minister for Justice. Such petitions cannot be read straightforwardly as many women first asked to be released to their families, and when this was refused, petitioned instead for some form of amelioration such as by transfer elsewhere. Petitions were encouraged by religious visitors to Mountjoy. Nuns visited women reprieved from sentence of death while they were in prison. Priests working as chaplains in the prisons similarly urged women to petition to be released to religious institutions and many chaplains worked behind the scenes to negotiate these transfers, providing a point of liaison between the prison governor, the Department of Justice, probation officers and the religious organizations.[53]

While the religious sisters who ran the laundries may have harboured hopes of the lifelong detention of women, probation officers were generally of the view that holding out some hope of release was beneficial. This view was communicated to the Minister for Justice in 1930:

> It does seem desirable that the Rev Mother of Convents to which prisoners undergoing a life sentence are sent should be in a position to hold out some tangible hope of release. It is perhaps difficult to bind yourself at this stage to any very short term, but I think the prisoner could be assured that there was no question of holding her for life, and that if she were well conducted and showed definite signs of reform she might expect to be released at the end of a few years.[54]

Women were told that their eventual release was contingent on their own conduct. Probation officer Sullivan was quick to remind the Department of Justice that women were informed of this when leaving prison. These assurances were occasionally brought up by the women themselves. Probation officers reported that Mary Anne Keane reminded them that her eventual release from DML had been promised by the governor of Mountjoy Prison.[55] In Margaret Finn's records, there is also an example of explicit commitments being made to Keane which are documented in correspondence from the Department of Justice to the governor of Mountjoy Prison:

> The convict should be informed that while she is liable to be detained in the Institution named, she may, if her conduct is satisfactory, be released in a few years, the period being largely dependent on her good behaviour.[56]

Mary Anne Keane

Mary Anne Keane was capitally convicted of the murder of her male infant. Unlike most women prosecuted for infanticide-related offences, 23-year-old Mary Anne Keane was married. However, despite her marital status, she had been living apart from her husband prior to the birth of her child. Like so many other women, Keane was confronted with a crisis pregnancy and the prospect of raising her child alone in a hostile society. While married, Keane had left her husband and gone into domestic service, before returning home in July 1928. As a result of her husband's suspicions that she had returned home pregnant, he had sent her to the Roscommon County Home in November, and her child had been born there on 11 February. Following her release from this institution on 27 February, Keane was destitute. She made her way on foot to her husband's home in rural Roscommon. Witnesses who saw her on this day gave evidence that she was carrying a parcel which they supposed was the child. That night, she was found lying outdoors in a weakened condition, without her infant, whose body was found in a nearby bog-hole. The defence argued that Keane had walked 16 miles carrying her infant, a substantial exertion so soon after confinement and something that could have led to an imbalance of the mind.

Mary Anne was convicted of murder and sentenced to death on 10 June 1929 before Mr Justice O'Byrne. She was recommended to mercy by the jury and her sentence was commuted to penal servitude for life. Keane spent little time in Mountjoy Prison and was conditionally discharged to DML on 4 November 1930.[57] Her release to DML came after sustained but unsuccessful efforts to persuade her husband to allow her to return home. Her eventual fate is unknown. In 1932, it was noted in a Department of Justice document that there was 'no definite proposal of any sort for her future'.[58] In July 1936, following further unsuccessful pleas to her husband, Keane was still in DML. When her husband refused to accept her home, it was viewed that there were no further options for her absolute release. Keane was considered 'safer' in Donnybrook, and not 'fit to face the world'.[59] She was also viewed to be 'of low mentality', incapable of domestic work, and would 'very likely get into trouble' if released.[60] A letter from the Sacred Heart Home to a probation officer asked: 'Why cannot she remain with the nuns there, and try to be happy under the circumstances.'[61] It seems most likely that Keane remained in DML for a considerable period of time.

Margaret Finn

Margaret Finn was also capitally convicted of the murder of her infant. Finn was 25 years old and unmarried; until just prior to the birth of her child she had worked as a domestic servant. The birth had occurred in a field beside Margaret's house; she gave evidence that she had felt pains for some time before the birth, and had confided in her cousin Brigid that she was to have a baby. When the pains did not slacken, both women went outside, and labour was over in ten minutes:

> The child started to cry and she told me to catch it by the neck and choke it. She then took a lace out of her boot and gave it to me. I tied it around the child's neck and she lifted up the stones and I took it over and she fixed the stones down herself and then we went in home.[62]

Margaret was convicted on 3 March 1931 and her death sentence was commuted to penal servitude for life. Margaret was conditionally discharged to DML on 3 October 1933 after spending over two years in prison.[63]

For women entering the laundries from either the courts or prison, religious sisters could accept or decline women according to their preferences. It was arranged that Donnybrook would first be approached in the case of Margaret Finn, and if rebuffed, High Park Magdalene in Drumcondra would then be approached.[64] In deciding the best 'fit' for women, judgements were made about their moral blameworthiness. For instance, Our Lady's Home on Dublin's Henrietta Street, was considered an appropriate place for women who had not 'fallen', hence its stated inappropriateness for Margaret Finn who had given birth to a baby while unmarried. Probation officer Kathleen

Sullivan wrote to the Department of Justice in 1930 outlining that Our Lady's Home was 'open to girls who have erred in other directions, but who have not led a life of vice'.[65] Probation Officer E. M. Carroll made a similar assessment in 1941 when she reported that Our Lady's Home was for the 'better types'.[66] Illustrating this hierarchy of moral blameworthiness is the case of Mary Moynihan. Moynihan was convicted of the murder of her employer Nora Horgan in 1922, but was nonetheless considered a 'respectable' young woman. Women who killed adults were often considered less morally culpable than those who killed their 'illegitimate' infants. Mary Moynihan also benefitted from the view that her family was respectable. Moynihan was first accepted into DML, but probation officer Sullivan viewed this as most inappropriate:

> This latter Convent is a Home for Penitents, and I should not like a girl, who was under twenty when [she went] to Mountjoy, and who had not associated with women of evil life, to be placed among such women, if a convent of a different type is willing to receive her. The Convent in Henrietta Street does not receive women of the unfortunate class, and for this reason is, in my opinion, more likely to have a reformative effect on Mary Moynihan than a Magdalen Home would have.[67]

Many women who entered the Magdalene institution from the criminal justice system spent very lengthy periods there, sometimes the rest of their lives. Often, their prolonged confinement was associated with judgements of them as incapable of caring for themselves, or fears that they had inadequate (or inappropriate) family support. Margaret Finn's lifelong detention was informed in part by moral judgements made about her mother, whose character was described as 'not very exemplary'. This stood against Finn, notwithstanding the fact that her mother had petitioned the Department of Justice for her daughter's release when Margaret was in prison. Despite these overtures, Finn's family was considered unsuitable for her absolute release.[68] It did not help that Finn's mother was reported to be poor: 'not in possession of any land save two small gardens'.[69] Following her conditional release to DML, Margaret never again had freedom and remained held at the DML for the rest of her life.[70]

Conclusion

Taking a sample of women who made their way through the criminal justice system to DML, the chapter has explored that institution as a site of state-ordered punishment. Drawing together case histories of women who had been prosecuted for infant murder, the preceding sections have presented key themes which characterized the use of laundries as carceral spaces. In the decades post-independence, the numbers of women entering state-run prisons declined while increasing use was made of laundries. There were stark disparities between the prison and the laundries. Women in the prison system remained visible and the regimes in which they lived were subject to oversight. Prisoners could petition the Minister for Justice and they remain present in the state archives. In contrast, women who were punished in the laundries were rendered largely invisible. The paper trail invariably stops on their entry to a Magdalene institution.

Oversight dwindled as authority for their custody was transferred to private, religious bodies. For women ostensibly in the custody of the state, this represents a particular abrogation of its duty to these vulnerable women.

This failure is exacerbated by the nature of the laundries, and the religious sisters' intentions that women entering would remain there for life. A Department of Justice document made the admission:

> Going back as far as 1928 I can trace only one case in which a convict released on licence to a 'Home' was afterwards allowed to leave the 'Home' and take up a situation outside. In the other cases the women were sent to other Homes or Convents as domestic servants, etc.[71]

Women disappeared into a shadow penal system in which the lack of access to the records of religious organizations renders their fates unknowable. While it was occasionally viewed as a more humane disposal than prison, the existing records such as those which outline the views of probation officers, leave no doubt that the Magdalene institutions maintained a punitive regime. As Probation Officer Carroll noted, the laundries were also possessed of considerable stigma, to the extent that girls known to have been in Magdalene Laundries were not accepted into the Catholic Girls' Hostels in Dublin and could also be refused by Reformatory Schools.[72]

It is clear that the religious sisters actively sought out women from the courts and from prison, while exercising their right to refuse admission. From the discussions of the most appropriate 'fit' for certain women, the Donnybrook Magdalene emerges as an institution at the bottom rung of a respectability hierarchy. It held very different meanings compared to a religious institution such as Our Lady's Home. Magdalene institutions were considered suitable for a particular 'type' of woman. The particular calibration of culpability meant that women who had killed adults were often considered more amenable to rehabilitation and less deserving of harsh punishment than unmarried women who had killed their infants, suggesting that sex outside marriage was the graver crime than murder. Women convicted of infanticide-related offences were considered less 'criminal', but more sinful and hence more morally culpable. As Earner-Byrne remarks: 'The notion of moral criminality was ingrained in most public debates on the issue of illegitimacy.'[73]

While the cases overviewed in this chapter demonstrate the use of laundries for women deemed to have offended against morality, the cases also demonstrate that their use was wider than this purpose. Kate Reilly's case, for instance, provides an example of a woman admitted to the DML because of her mental ill health. The Magdalene institutions were ambiguous in their functions, and were used for a range of discrete and ad hoc needs. While they were an essential component of the Irish criminal justice system post-1922, the case of Nora Hannigan illustrates that Magdalene institutions were not prisons – they were under no obligation to hold onto women they found to be refractory and they were never prevailed on by state authorities to release women once their court sentences had expired. They were carceral institutions that remained key to criminal justice disposals for decades following independence.

Notes

1   The chapter examines cases of women who entered the Donnybrook Laundry following infant murder prosecutions. However, while these serious and atypical cases leave behind a more substantial archival record, they represent just one facet of the use of laundries by the criminal justice system. A fuller profile of the women who entered laundries from the justice system is less clear and is difficult to reconstruct without access to the records of the religious sisters.

2   Katherine O'Donnell, 'A Certain Class of Justice: Ireland's Magdalenes', in *Histories of Punishment and Social Control in Ireland: Perspectives from a Periphery*, ed. Lynsey Black, Louise Brangan and Deirdre Healy (Bingley: Emerald Publishing, 2022), 79–106.

3   Gerry McNally, 'Probation in Ireland: A Brief History of the Early Years', *Irish Probation Journal* 4, no. 1 (2007): 5–24.

4   See further, Katherine O'Donnell, Chapter 4, this volume.

5   Christina Quinlan, *Inside: Ireland's Women's Prisons Past and Present* (Dublin: Irish Academic Press, 2011).

6   Such as mother and baby 'homes' and Our Lady's Home in Dublin, see Lynsey Black, *Gender and Punishment in Ireland: Women, Murder and the Death Penalty, 1922–64* (Manchester: Manchester University Press, 2022), 106–39.

7   'Advertisement', *Sunday Independent*, 21 December 1930, 3.

8   Until the Infanticide Act, 1949, women prosecuted for the intentional killing of an infant were prosecuted for murder. As murder carried a mandatory sentence of death, this meant that women convicted of murdering infants were sentenced to death. Infant murder was, however, understood as an offence apart and was often referred to simply as 'infanticide' even before the creation of this offence in 1949.

9   Clíona Rattigan, *'What Else Could I Do?' Single Mothers and Infanticide, Ireland 1900–1950* (Dublin: Irish Academic Press, 2012).

10 James M. Smith, *Ireland's Magdalen Laundries and the Nation's Architecture of Containment* (Manchester: Manchester University Press, 2008), see, for example, table 2.9, 196–7; Rattigan, *'What Else Could I Do?'*.

11 Smith, *Ireland's Magdalen Laundries*, table 1.2, 191.

12 Department of Justice, *Report of the Inter-Departmental Committee to Establish the Facts of State Involvement with the Magdalen Laundries* (Dublin, January 2013, aka *McAleese Report*, hereinafter *IDC Report*), 207. For critique, see Claire McGettrick, Katherine O'Donnell, Maeve O'Rourke, James M. Smith and Mari Steed 'Chapter 6: Never Tell, Never Acknowledge (. . . everyone knew, but no one said)', in *Ireland and the Magdalene Laundries: A Campaign for Justice* (London: I.B. Tauris, 2021).

13 Louise Ryan, 'The Press, the Police and Prosecution Perspectives on Infanticide in the 1920s', in *Irish Women's History*, ed. Diane Urquhart and Alan Hayes (Dublin: Irish Academic Press, 2004), 137–51.

14 Black, *Gender and Punishment*, 106.

15 Maeve O'Rourke, 'Ireland's "Historical" Abuse Inquiries and the Secrecy of Records and Archives', in *Histories of Punishment*, ed. Black, Brangan and Healy, ch. 5.

16 There is correspondence to this effect relating to Jane Middleton's detention in the Bethany Home. Middleton, from Sligo, was convicted of the manslaughter of her infant in 1945 and was sentenced to spend two years at this institution. NAI, State Books Central Criminal Court (SBCCC), 1941–1945.

17 Black, *Gender and Punishment*, 161.

18 *IHRC Assessment of the Human Rights Issues Arising in Relation to the 'Magdalen Laundries', Nov 2010* (Dublin: Irish Human Rights and Equality Commission, IHREC, 2010), 9–10.

19 Religious institutions such as laundries, mother and baby 'homes', Legion of Mary hostels, and Our Lady's Home on Henrietta Street were all named in the sentences of convicted women.

20 *IHRC Assessment*, 15.

21 'The Cussen Report', *Commission of Inquiry into the Reformatory and Industrial School System, 1934–1936* (Dublin: Stationery Office, 1936), 48, para. 183.

22 Dublin Diocesan Archives, Archbishop John Charles McQuaid AB8/b/XXVIII/983, Memorandum prepared by EM Carroll, Probation Officer at Dublin Metropolitan Courthouse, forwarded in a letter of 9 July 1941.

23 J. Anthony Gaughan, *At the Coalface: Recollections of a City and Country Priest 1950–2000* (Dublin: Columba Press, 2000), 73.

24 National Archives of Ireland (NAI), State Files Central Criminal Court (SFCCC), Carlow 1929. Statement of Lucy Byrne.

25 NAI, SFCCC, Carlow, 1929, Statement of Sergeant Higgins Myshall.

26 'Carlow Child Murder Charge', *Irish Times*, 27 August 1929, 3.

27 NAI, SBCCC, November 1927 to June 1935.

28 I am very grateful to Claire McGettrick and her work on the Magdalene Names Project for this information.

29 'Charge of Infanticide', *Kilkenny People*, 1 February 1930, 11.

30 'Young Girl Put Back', *Irish Independent*, 25 February 1930, 10.

31 'Murder Charge', *Irish Examiner*, 25 February 1930, 2.

32 NAI, SBCCC. November 1927 to June 1935.

33 'Concealment of Birth', *Irish Times*, 4 March 1930, 3.

34 'Young Woman Charged with Murder', *Waterford News and Star*, 1 May 1931, 5.

35 NAI, SBCCC, November 1927 to June 1935.

36 'Concealment of Birth', *Evening Herald*, 18 June 1931, 5.

37 NAI, SBCCC, November 1927 to June 1935.

38 'Concealment of Birth', *Evening Herald*, 18 June 1931, 5.

39 NAI, SBCCC, November 1927 to June 1935, Letter from the RSC, Donnybrook, to County Registrar, 17 February 1932.

40 NAI, SBCCC, November 1927 to June 1935, Letter from the RSC, Donnybrook, to County Registrar, 22 February 1932.

41 'Cavan Mother Remanded', *Irish Press*, 14 August 1937, 9.

42 'Sent for Trial', *Irish Examiner*, 27 August 1937, 2.

43 'Butlersbridge Tragedy', *Anglo-Celt*, 6 November 1937, 12.

44 Ibid.

45 Ibid.

46 NAI, SFCCC, Cavan, 1940, Statement of Mary Reilly.

47 NAI, SBCCC, November 1933 to 22 April 1941.

48 'Dead Infants', *Evening Echo*, 31 May 1930, 5.

49 *IDC Report*, 283. With thanks to Claire McGettrick and the Magdalen Names Project, whose research suggests that Mary died there on 18 June 1941.

50 Black, *Gender and Punishment*, ch. 5.

51 NAI, Department of Justice 234/1744.

52 NAI, Department of Justice 234/259, Minute sheet, 29 October 1929.

53 Black, *Gender and Punishment*, chs 4 and 5.

54 NAI, Department of Justice 234/2016, Note to the Minister for Justice, 27 June 1930.
55 NAI, Department of Justice 18/3540, Letter from probation officer Mary O'Brien, 7 May 1936.
56 NAI, Department of Justice 234/3118A, Letter from the Department of Justice to the Governor of Mountjoy Prison, 26 September 1933.
57 NAI, Department of An Taoiseach S.5884; Department of Justice 18/3540.
58 NAI, Department of Justice 18/3540, Note, 20 May 1936.
59 NAI, Department of Justice 234/1744, Memorandum prepared by Stephen Roche, 15 April 1932.
60 NAI, Department of Justice 18/3540, Note, 14 June 1929.
61 NAI, Department of Justice 18/3540, Letter from Sacred Heart Home Roscommon to Probation Officer, 23 July 1936.
62 NAI, SFCCC, Clare 1931, Statement of Margaret Finn, 30 June 1930.
63 NAI, Department of Justice 234/3118A.
64 See discussion on the suitability of various institutions in NAI, Department of Justice 234/3118A and NAI, Department of Justice 234/1744.
65 NAI, Department of Justice 234/1744, Letter from Kathleen Sullivan to Department of Justice, 21 June 1930.
66 Dublin Diocesan Archives, Archbishop John Charles McQuaid, AB8/b/XXVIII/983, Memorandum prepared by EM Carroll, Probation Officer at Dublin Metropolitan Courthouse, forwarded in a letter of 9 July 1941.
67 NAI, Department of Justice 234/1744, Letter from Kathleen Sullivan, 21 June 1930.
68 NAI, Department of Justice 234/3118A, Garda Report, 31 July 1933.
69 NAI, Department of Justice 234/3118A, Garda Report, 31 July 1933.
70 *IDC Report*, 297–300. This anonymized case study is of Margaret Finn.
71 NAI, Department of Justice 18/3540, 20 May 1936.
72 Dublin Diocesan Archives, Archbishop John Charles McQuaid, AB8/b/XXVIII/983, Memorandum prepared by EM Carroll, Probation Officer at Dublin Metropolitan Courthouse, forwarded in a letter of 9 July 1941.
73 Lindsey Earner-Byrne, 'Reinforcing the Family: The Role of Gender, Morality and Sexuality in Irish Welfare Policy, 1922–1944', *History of the Family* 13, no. 4 (2008): 364.

Heritage and Memory

9

Contemporary Archaeology and Donnybrook Magdalene Laundry

Working with the Material Remnants of an Institutionalized Recent Past

Laura McAtackney

The subdisciplines of historical and contemporary archaeology have expanded greatly in the past four decades in terms of subject matter, theoretical framing and endpoint so that to complete an archaeology of a Magdalene laundry is not considered an unusual or outlandish task. Focusing on how we can use archaeological methods and concepts to retrieve the experiences of the overlooked, marginalized and disenfranchised – including from institutional settings – have been important topics from both historical and contemporary perspectives, with prisons[1] and mental institutions[2] proving especially popular. There are a number of reasons that archaeological perspectives can provide important insights into institutional experiences. First, they prioritize material rather than documentary sources, which means they are not unduly influenced by the perspectives of those who ran the institutions. Second, they can work with different forms of material culture and so can explore how the more personal artefacts can relate to built structures and exist within a wider landscape setting rather than fixate on only one source. Last, archaeology is the only humanities discipline that is built into the planning process of most Global North countries (including Ireland), which means that those who wish to develop or demolish former Magdalene Laundries must employ archaeological consultants to mitigate any potential damage. It is through the role of archaeology in the planning process that I was first introduced to Donnybrook Magdalene Laundry (DML) as a consequence of a failed planning application.[3]

Due to the nature of Ireland's heritage laws and policies, archaeology is generally defined through the planning process as subterranean or above ground materials that predate 1700.[4] In a global context, to have archaeological heritage defined by an end date over 300 years ago is an old-fashioned idea of what 'archaeological' is – defined by age rather than material nature. In heritage practice in the Republic of Ireland, it appears this discrepancy is being partially addressed; there are a select number of post-1700 entries on the national Sites and Monuments Record (SMR), 'for example, industrial and military sites'.[5] The role of archaeology in the planning process is to protect archaeological heritage alongside facilitating construction and development. This is primarily done through mitigation – with the aim of preserving subterranean archaeological remains *in situ* – but if this is not possible there must be preservation by record, that is excavation, recording of material remains and deposition of excavated materials with a museum.[6] Magdalene Laundries would not usually be required to receive archaeological attention in the Irish planning process because the structures and contents are not usually subterraneous, they do not predate 1700 and, generally, they have been considered too unexceptional to be assigned any inherent value. As of 2021, no Magdalene Laundries are included on the SMR database, which holds the records of over 138,800 archaeological monuments, although the convent and monastery associated with the Magdalene Laundry at Sean McDermott Street are both included on the National Inventory of Architectural Heritage.[7]

In practice, it has been notable that, following the publication of the report by the *Inter-Departmental Committee to Establish the Facts of State Involvement with the Magdalen Laundries* (*IDC Report*, 2013)[8] some council planning departments have been reluctant to allow the redevelopment of Magdalene Laundries and associated institutions such as mother and baby 'homes' without extensive archaeological inquiry taking place. In relation to DML, a planning application submitted by developers who owned the site in 2016 was rejected in 2017 due to 'the potential for burials to be uncovered'[9] and a lack of sufficient engagement with the historical and social significance of the site by the archaeological work commissioned to date. This decision was undoubtedly prompted not only by the ongoing ramifications of the *IDC Report* but also because of public scandals surrounding the discovery of unconsecrated, unmarked mass graves at both the former Magdalene laundry at High Park in Dublin in 1993[10] and, even more infamously, Catherine Corless's work in uncovering the presumed burial site of 796 babies and children in a septic tank in the grounds of the Bon Secours Mother and Baby Home at Tuam in Co. Galway.[11] But legislation has not been introduced to specifically deal with the social relevance of these sites, so decisions as to how to develop them are not uniform. The implicit premise of any archaeological work in a construction and development context in Ireland is that the remaining archaeological remains will be mitigated, removed or demolished and so it is nearly always about facilitating change. The understanding that engaging with developer-funded archaeology would almost certainly allow fundamental alterations to the site at Donnybrook was important in considering how to creatively record the site. But it also brought me to reflect on how a contemporary archaeology perspective might approach the site differently than a more traditional archaeological approach.

Contemporary archaeology at Donnybrook Magdalene Laundry

The relationship between contemporary and historical archaeology is a difficult one to clearly delineate. In many ways, contemporary and historical archaeology are aligned in having a number of shared trajectories: the focus on the modern world and especially a concern with marginalized experiences that are often absent from official documentary records. But in many cases, contemporary archaeology has deviated into areas that have emerged from the specific, contemporary context of the societies we work in and often employs creative methodologies in order to better understand the messy and entangled material world that exists around us. This approach contrasts with the traditional format of retrieving and recording the past as a detached, scientific exercise. James Dixon has argued that historical archaeologies, even if they are of the 'recent past', are not the same as archaeologies that are conceived of the 'present day',[12] particularly because working in and of the contemporary means 'we have a different responsibility to the world we study when the world we study is our own'.[13] My own archaeological practice has moved between being historical and contemporary archaeology by intermingling different sources and methods to provide a range of insights into the operation and experience of the material world. In particular, my work at Long Kesh / Maze Prison in Northern Ireland included documentary, artefactual, structural, landscape and oral testimonies to better understand how the prison functioned in the past and continued to be understood into the present.[14]

In approaching DML as an archaeological site I decided to be consciously directed by the social justice imperatives of the social significance of the site, that is, as a place of forced incarceration of girls and women with many survivors who were able to speak of their experiences. I was conscious that a focus solely on the material world of the Magdalene laundry – as is the norm in developer-funded archaeology – would skew the investigations to recording it primarily as an industrial site. Rather, I wanted to ensure that while the archaeological methodologies would include traditional excavation and recording techniques – expected for planning applications – it would be supplemented by more creative and responsive approaches that would bring together memory and material to provide people-orientated perspectives. I was also inspired by the work of Lucas Lixinski who has convincingly argued for the inclusion of cultural heritage as a facet of transitional justice due to the need to consider how we can 'write and rewrite history in the nomination and selection of heritage items'[15] in the aftermath of major societal traumas. I wanted to consider how a selective sample of the material world of Donnybrook could be transitioned into national heritage. To do all of this, there was a need to collaborate. At a very early point in the consultation process, I made contact with my archaeology colleague Franc Myles to request him to complete an inventory of the artefactual remains of the site, and I also contacted Brenda Malone, National Museum of Ireland curator, to ask her to visit the site with me with the aim of selecting some of the material world of the Magdalene Laundry for the national collection.[16] My own contribution to the archaeological work was: (i) to complete a standing brief, which entailed monitoring and recording what was being disposed from the site by contractors to ensure nothing of social significance was removed and (ii) to complete small-scale and experimental site-responsive oral testimonies, which would allow a small number of survivors to record their reactions to the site in its current post-operative and pre-development state. My two contributions were conceived as being appropriate, contemporary archaeology responses as they were engaging with the site in what Rodney Harrison has called, a 'surface-survey'[17] approach that viewed the site as an active assemblage in the present and explicitly included survivors as central to the recording exercise.

The rest of this chapter will discuss four aspects that were revealed by the contemporary archaeology approaches utilized at the site. First, I will discuss some of the findings from working with the material world of DML as a messy, multilayered, contemporary place. Second, I will posit the importance of *not* engaging with the material world but rather focusing on 'presencing absence',[18] and how being conscious of absences is central to contemporary archaeology. Third, I will reflect on insights I gained from working with survivors as part of the recording process. Last, there will be a short concluding discussion regarding the future and especially the heritage implications of this work.

Some insights from Donnybrook Magdalene Laundry

The convoluted material world of Donnybrook Magdalene Laundry

A contemporary archaeology approach to DML involves moving beyond our traditional training as archaeologists – to focus on the material traces of the distant past – to instead include all the materials that coexist in the places we are investigating in the present. Following Laurent Olivier,[19] it is about acknowledging that all archaeology is essentially 'contemporary' because we can only work with what materially survives at that point in time. The aim of such a contemporary archaeology approach is to allow for coexistence, messiness and following Rodney Harrison, 'to identify both relationships of functional flow and more volatile relationships of friction and conflict'.[20] Such an approach allows us to understand how the past and present are both entwined and constitutive. Indeed, it is by conceptualizing archaeologies of and in the present, as a palimpsest in the process of assembling and reassembling[21] that a more creative and responsive approach can be undertaken. In this conception of archaeology, the past is not dead and awaiting our 'excavation', rather it is active and networked with seemingly disparate material elements in making our world. By examining the material world of a Magdalene laundry through such a lens we can reveal how the past remains meaningful in the present and thereby how it makes our world rather than reflects an irretrievable past. This approach to Donnybrook is especially compelling as one of the issues we face as a society is that of downplaying and disregarding[22] what happened in these institutions even though it occurred in the very recent past. Highlighting the ongoing nature of these places as abusive institutions is a significant act in Ireland, as the society continues to exhibit features of 'denial and minimization'[23] even after (flawed) government reports and state apologies.

It is important to acknowledge when working with the material world of DML that it functioned as an industrial laundry until the very recent past. Interestingly, there are discrepancies between the historical and archaeological evidence on the longevity of its operative life. The *IDC Report* indicates that the site was sold to a private laundry in 1992 and continued to function until 2006.[24] While the exchange of ownership in 1992 appears to be correct, the material evidence from the laundry indicates that it was in use for many years after 2006. There were multiple calendars on the site dating from 2013 and significant paper records – mainly in the form of letters but also business records – dating up to 2014. It is unclear in what capacity the site was operating post-2006 but it is certain that it continued to be utilized in some capacity for many years after the date provided in The *IDC Report*. The jumbled, messy material world of the site, as it has been from 2018 onwards, reveals that it was a functional laundry materially constituted by its Magdalene precursor that still maintained and structured how it operated up to its final closure. The laundry was a composite of structures, including a nineteenth-century accommodation block and a range of purpose-built industrial buildings that were added to as required. The second last addition was one of the biggest changes with more open-plan elements – the packing room and new reception area – being added in between 1968 and 1988.[25] All the buildings that make up the current site relate to its industrial usage and there are no religious or accommodation buildings within its current walls. Some accommodation and religious buildings remain on the adjoining convent land but they are currently inaccessible to researchers.

A description of Donnybrook from a 2018 architecture report created for the current owners described it as: 'a building which was simply locked and abandoned ... Although there is debris, dirt and bird droppings throughout, the previous history of the building is fully legible.'[26] Starting with the most obvious material remains, the machines, it is clear from the size and date of many of these machines – including substantial calendar machines and a range of washing and pressing machines – that many are from the Magdalene period and were still being used and serviced up to the closure of the site. Of those machines that were definitively dated to the private laundry period – including some of the washing machines – it was apparent that they were still situated within a layout that had been set and maintained while a Magdalene laundry. Extending the lens of view from the machines to their surroundings, the laundry had many remnants of a religious character that clearly still persisted into, and shaped the experience of, the private laundry. There were many empty – and just as many still occupied – plinths dotted around the buildings that had clearly been used to hold religious statues and objects. These were often placed in strategic locations – over doorways or at eye-level beside work stations – and in many ways dominated how the forced and unforced workers experienced the laundry. There were smaller religious items such as a photograph of Pope John Paul II (1978–2005) placed near the entrance of the packing room and many small religious medals and crucifixes were still *in situ* round around the laundry rooms. One of the most compelling examples is a collection of two steam presses from 1937 and 1951 that were placed strategically below a large, ornate plinth (with shamrock detail) that contained a substantial Sacred Heart statue precariously balancing alongside a small fan. They were located to the left of the only doorway to the upstairs space, which also had a clock and a large crucifix placed above. Everywhere, the deliberate entanglement of religion with industry, time and movement was clear. The shamrock plinth had a number of drawing pins still *in situ* and even more pin pricks apparent around the front and side of the plinth, which had evidently been used to pin notices (Figure 9.1). This scene compellingly revealed not only how the religious nature of the laundry continued long after its supposed transfer in 1992 but that there was a certain pragmatism to how this hybrid religious-industrial space functioned.

Figure 9.1 Ornate plinth with shamrock detail positioned above industrial ironing machines. Detail of drawing pins, and holes from previous drawing pins, that had been used to attach notices to the front. Photo by Laura McAtackney, August 2018.

While relatively old and comparatively new material culture has clearly been intermixed at Donnybrook, what is less easy to ignore – but traditional archaeological approaches would have done so – is the more disruptive changes that have been made to the material world since the final closure of the site in *c.* 2014. It was not difficult to ascertain that the site continued to be active and accessed up to the present day through both official and unofficial means. When I first accessed the site in June 2018, it was evident that much of the furniture and moveable material culture had been recently displaced – with tables upended and collected at the sides and in the corners of the packing room and the calendar room – due to archaeologists using ground penetrating radar (GPR) to scan for unexpected disruptions under the floor of the laundry (essentially looking for evidence of illicit burials; they found none).[27] While it is understandable why furniture and machines needed to be moved, the arrangement of the larger items spoke to pragmatic moves with the aim of making the floor accessible but not a reciprocal process of returning the objects back to their original positions. Likewise, there were a number of large excavation pits with associated debris left to the side that disrupted the space and also made it difficult to visualize how the operational laundry looked on closure. Other illicit activities had left material traces due to unknown persons breaking into the site who have added – graffiti, paint splashes and even a small fire (Figure 9.2) – and taken away – all the old ceramic sinks, many metal

Figure 9.2 Evidence of a small fire that had been recently lit inside the Packing Room at Donnybrook. Photo by Laura McAtackney, August 2021.

components and religious statues were removed over the summer of 2018 – from the site. At every new introduction to Donnybrook, it has been evidently a continually altering, ever-changing material world.

The importance of absence in contemporary archaeology

While archaeology is primarily a discipline of things,[28] there is a particular need to presence absence when examining contemporary sites. This fundamental idea has been articulated on a number of occasions but most clearly by Victor Buchli and Gavin Lucas in their groundbreaking study from 2001 of what they called 'archaeologies of the contemporary past'[29] when they called for the need to acknowledge 'the absent present' and also 'presencing absence'. This understanding of the relationship between absence and presence – and especially how some absences can be presenced if we view the material world as assemblages rather than individual artefacts – is even more important when we are working with sites that have extensive material worlds but not all of it is of equal importance in understanding those structures. All archaeologies are skewed by the fact that not everything survives and the larger and more durable items tend to be retained. But in sites that are especially loaded or active in the presence then survival can be deliberately altered. In the case of derelict Magdalene Laundries, especially as DML had a long post-Magdalene operational life, a wide range of modern material culture coexists with the material world of the Magdalene Laundry. Sometimes it is easy to locate the materials that were linked to its original operation, other times it is not so clear. Modern material worlds are complex and messy due to the overwhelming array of 'stuff'[30] and it is not easy, or necessarily important, to try to disentangle them completely. In general, contemporary archaeologists aim to include the ephemeral and mundane material culture but I was mindful of the need to utilize a range of specific methodologies at DML in order to better understand the experiences – not just the extant contents – of this industrial complex.

The most important absence that must be recognized is the changes made to the site on its sale in 1992. The structures that were sold to a private operator in 1992 – and that survive and are accessible via the developers today – were almost exclusively connected to the industrial operation of the site. When the laundry was sold in 1992, the sale did not include any religious or accommodation buildings (although the adjoining convent still exists and is in operation). In comparison, Sean McDermott Street, the last Magdalene laundry to close in 1996, was retained by the religious order before it was transferred to Dublin City Council as part of a property exchange.[31] Demolitions occurred at the site after a fire in the old laundry buildings in 2006[32] and all the associated industrial structures and contents were removed, and presumably disposed of, at that time. The rest of the original structures – the convent, deconsecrated Church and women's living quarters – are structurally intact and in many places include some original contents. Donnybrook functioned as a contained private, industrial laundry about twenty years after its final use as a Magdalene laundry, with some survivors working in both manifestations.[33] Such a long post-Magdalene laundry operational life is atypical and means that its 'closure' date is much later than any of the other laundries. It has a more complete, surviving material world but that also prompts questions. In particular, one could debate how 'authentic' the site is now in comparison to its original operation, at least in materialist if not constructivist terms,[34] and how much we can represent the experiences of survivors or victims with what remains there today.

After detailed inspection of the contents of the material culture that remained at the site it was clear that the most glaring absence was of materials explicitly related to the lives of the women from the Magdalene period. While many of the industrial remains were datable to the period pre-1992, in the vast majority of cases their intimate connection to the forced workers did not leave a distinct trace. But there were a number of sporadic survivals that either definitely or probably related to the women which were not simply industrial survivals and were important to record. There were a large number of laundry carts that would have been used by workers to transport loads of washing around the industrial areas. Some of these carts were clearly more recent and some were older. Many of the carts had names added to them (there must have been a degree of ownership involved) and for the older carts we might assume that the women's names were Magdalene residents. Scattered around the building were a small number of religious artefacts – not simply the statues on plinths, crucifixes, etc. – but small medals and crosses that had been attached to various parts of the building. These are ambiguous finds but appear to have more connection to the religious-industrial site rather than being added in its later phase of operation (Figure 9.3).

Figure 9.3 Religious medal attached to a pipe in the Packing Room at Donnybrook. Photo by Laura McAtackney, June 2018.

There were also a small number of isolated objects that provide brief glimpses, rather than detailed insights, into the women's experiences of the site. Two examples: a plan of the laundry with a list of names and supervisors (the latter were nuns) associated with particular work areas was located attached to a pillar in the packing room when the site was examined in 2018 (Figure 9.4). This was an incredible find not just for giving a very specific insight into named women who were assigned to particular parts of the laundry but it was astonishing that such a document survived *in situ* for decades after the site had transitioned to a private laundry. Last, when I was conducting oral testimonies with a survivor, we had finished our recording when she pointed out a small, nondescript cabinet amongst assorted furniture pushed to the side of the packing room. She informed me that it was a bedside table that would have been placed between the women's beds. She was able to tell us that the large ring on the top of the cabinet was created by a metal water jug and dish that the women used to wash. This also felt like an important find as it was a significant connection to the otherwise absent domestic life of the women, but it was also an anomaly. We do not know how the cabinet transitioned from domestic to industrial space and also how it survived on the site to the present day. When contextualized alongside the fact a small number of Magdalene women continued to work in the private laundry,[35] these seeming 'small things forgotten'[36] hint at how much the former Magdalene Laundry continued into the

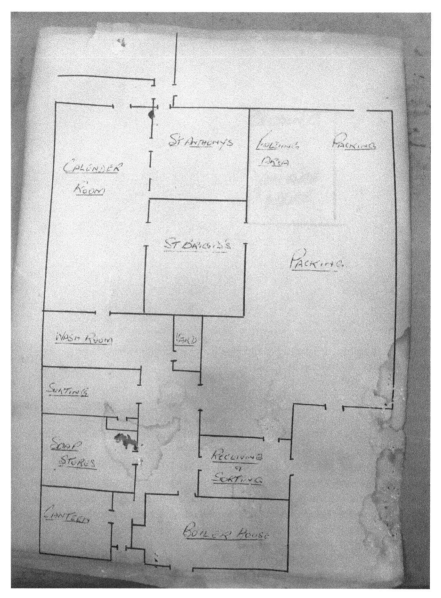

Figure 9.4 A plan of the laundry that was found attached to a pillar in the Packing Room at Donnybrook. By Laura McAtackney, September 2018.

private operation. This enduring material world made me wonder how much the post-1992 site operated independently from the adjoining convent.

Last, there is a future-orientated absence that we must consider with regard to DML: the existential threat to the structure itself. As already noted, the laundry is in the hands of developers with planning permission for its partial demolition and repurposing as private homes. Not only will the laundry almost certainly not survive for much longer in its current form, this stage in its life is associated with increasing ruination due to long-term dereliction. There has been a strong interest in the meaning and interpretation of modern ruins in contemporary archaeology in recent years with analysis veering from damning critiques of end point capitalism[37] to compelling claims for material afterlives to be valued in their posthuman state.[38] I do not believe we can make universal claims about the meaning of ruins, rather we need to understand the specific context of their ruination and interpret them accordingly

The ruination at Donnybrook is materially noticeable and active; this has both positive and negative implications. My experience as an Irish archaeologist who has worked on what could be euphemistically called 'difficult heritage'[39] for over twenty years is that there is a long and established trajectory in Ireland of derelicting and then demolishing sites that are uncomfortable 'material memory'[40] for those in power.[41] My interpretation of this form of conscious neglect – including leaving structures unheated, overventilated, under-weatherproofed and open to illicit entry – is that facilitated ruination acts as justification for the buildings' demolition because they are unnerving and uncomfortable presences to retain. Over the years I have been sporadically accessing DML there has been a clear lack of interest in preserving the material integrity of the site. It has no heating or electricity and has a number of broken windows that birds and sometimes humans have used to access the buildings (some of the windows have been boarded up when requested). Clearly, the more ruinous the structure becomes – as it slowly moves through the planning process (the current owners submitted their first planning application in 2016) – the less likely the final outcome will be for the site to be retained, despite formal objections throughout all stages of the planning process (there have been objections submitted from activist groups, neighbours and survivors).

On a positive note, the enduring materiality, especially when actively ruinous and derelict, has the potential to communicate the difficult nature of that past. As it becomes more noticeably decrepit, the past becomes more tangibly close and demands our attention. Following Bjørnar Olsen and Þóra Pétursdóttir's observations, on the unsettling nature of active, modern ruins,[42] these laundries are not quiet follies, prosaically persisting or imperceivably disintegrating. They are caught in the limbo of being 'inbetween and not belonging'.[43] It is in this state of active dereliction – when they are materially vulnerable, disintegrating and increasingly under threat – that we publicly question what is to become of them. It has been clear in the local media[44] and social media that public anxiety regarding what happens to them – including their possible role in government-mandated memorialization[45] – is heightened as they act as a monumental, material reminder of the mistreatment of marginalized women in our recent past. One of the roles of the contemporary archaeologist is to include the material fragility of what remains and ensure that we at least consciously note the ongoing nature of this process that will almost definitely lead to destruction and possible erasure.

Working with survivors and victims of the Magdalene Laundries

An underdeveloped element of contemporary archaeology relates to how we work with people with direct experience of the sites in recording and understanding them. While people are included in a number of interesting case-studies – including Gabriel Moshenka's intriguing study of (now) adults who were children during the Second World War while excavating a site destroyed during the London Blitz[46] – methods remain relatively undertheorized. Indeed, people are often consciously excluded from contemporary archaeologies by those who believe the focus on the material should be all-encompassing.[47] There are different reasons for the reticence of archaeologists to work with living people but in my experience, it arises either due to a lack of training and / or understanding from archaeologists who were originally trained in researching the distant past or it is a conscious theoretical standpoint that articulates including people as not *proper* archaeology. All of my contemporary archaeology projects (starting with Long Kesh / Maze Prison)[48] have considered people a significant part of the methodological process of exploring material places, but I have always done so with a focus on how we made people connect with their material environment. For me, this means including people who have an intimate connection with the places *as* they are engaging with the materiality of the site. Ideally this has been on site, as I have found that being physically immersed in the buildings and landscapes better ensures the interlocutor is more reactive to the experience and less practised or self-conscious in what they are communicating. But there are clear issues in following such an immersive process when working with survivors of institutions who were often more vulnerable than interlocutors I had previously worked with. This meant making amendments in conception and in practice from what I had done before.

The process of locating women who had been incarcerated at DML to be part of this recording exercise was facilitated by Justice for Magdalenes Research as they had an established relationship with many of the women who had been held in these institutions. A small number of women who had spent short periods at the site many decades ago were asked if they wished to contribute and I worked with two women over the summer of 2018. Both of the women flew from England (at the expense of the developers) to complete the task. The first change from my usual process was that I had ongoing prior contact with both of the women to answer any questions and talk through the process of what we were going to do. I met both women in a neutral space so we were able to talk about what would happen, I showed them some pictures of the site as it currently looked (as I knew the dereliction might be shocking to them otherwise) and we talked about the consent forms and resources for counselling for afterwards. Both women also brought a companion – one brought her husband; the other brought a female friend – and we went to the site together. I told both women that we would walk around the site and I would be taping our conversation and taking photographs of anything in particular the women pointed out but otherwise they would not be visually recorded. When they asked what I wanted them to talk about, I indicated that I did not want to direct their responses; they were to say whatever thoughts came into their head as we walked around the complex. It was emphasized that there was no detail too large or too small and they were under no pressure to talk about anything they were uncomfortable with. It was reiterated that we could stop at any stage and leave the site when they wished. In theory, I did not want to direct our discussion, but rather follow the ethics of Cahal McLaughlin's Prison Memory Archive project where 'leading questions were eschewed in order to return more agency to the participants'.[49]

In practice, this process was much more complicated than I had previously experienced with former political prisoners at Long Kesh / Maze Prison; the participants were physically much older than the men I had previously worked with and at times were clearly more physically and mentally vulnerable in responding to institutions they had been forced to inhabit. While my experiences with the two women were also quite different, I felt on both occasions that I needed to be more present than I had previously been and often I had to direct how we moved around the complex and what we discussed more than I had anticipated. This decision was made spontaneously soon after we entered the site and was due to variations in the women's responses to the openness of the process but I was also concerned about how retraumatizing the experience might be if they had little support to navigate the site. I had to reaffirm the aim of this oral testimony process: first, to complete site-responsive testimonies so survivors could add their narratives so it would not be dominated by factual interpretations of the machines and infrastructure of the industrial laundry. Of secondary importance was their potential ability to identify objects that otherwise would not have been included in our inventories or potentially offered to the National Museum. In essence, this process was what Homi Bhabha has called a 'right of narration'[50] rather than solely about gathering facts and details about the site.

Both of the women had different approaches to how they began their testimonies. One of the women wished to start outside the gates of the site and wanted to start with information about herself to frame her introduction to the site rather than allow for a fully site-responsive experience. I felt it was important that she was able to control how we engaged with the site and so I did not intervene to direct her back to the site. The second woman waited until we entered the site for the recording to start and she followed the process of responding to her physical reintroduction to the Laundry. What was not expected was quite how much the contemporary state of the site – and especially its tangible ruination – would shape and determine the initial responses. The active nature of the site's ruination made it an uncanny site to encounter and this was exacerbated by our entrance to the site. As we moved through the public entrance to the large packing area – both areas the women would not have encountered before as these were later additions to the laundry – they entered a large space derelict of previous furniture, filled with a variety of dirt and debris – including graffitied walls – and the floors were punctuated with large holes from recent excavations. The oral recording from the first survivor picks up her audible intake of breath – involuntary shock – at the disturbed state of the room. Such an entry to the site clearly disorientated the survivors to the extent that, for both women, the site-responsive intention of the oral testimonies quickly derailed as they silently tried to make sense of the material disruption in front of them. To enable some form of reconnection to the site, and to support them as they tried to make sense of it, I deviated from this being a solely site-responsive exercise. Rather, I proceeded to guide them to some of the oldest and most complete areas – where the large industrial laundry machines still remained – to allow them to refamiliarize themselves with the site.

Being reacquainted with the laundry machines brought back memories to the women of where they had worked and how the machines and associated infrastructure had been used by them. Short discussions about how one would use the machines were often used – by me and them – as a way to reset the conversations or insert some form of control back into the site-responsive engagement when it became difficult for them to verbalize reactions. But these deviations were also useful inclusions. The first woman was of small stature and she indicated how difficult it was for someone her size to navigate the industrial space by pointing out an otherwise anonymous blue pallet that she and others would have stood on to reach the back of the washing machine (Figure 9.5). She was also able to discuss the more intangible nature of their experiences as we stood at a sorting station (Figure 9.6) and she explained to me and my colleague Franc Myles – who was in the building recording the contents of the site – that the nuns would use the repetition of prayer and enforced silence to ensure the women were not verbally communicating with each other while sorting laundry. In contrast, the other woman punctuated her testimony with anxious exclamations about how little she could remember of the site due to how much it had changed and how little she

Figure 9.5 A blue pallet in the industrial laundry that was identified by a survivor as the type of apparatus that would be used by smaller girls and women to stand on to allow access to the insides of the washing machines. Photo by Laura McAtackney, August 2018.

Figure 9.6 A sorting table located in the Packing Room at Donnybrook. Photo by Laura McAtackney, August 2018.

could make sense of it. She could indicate how machines were used when requested but her strongest memories were of an intangible nature – of the heat, steam and noise of the busy laundry when it was operational. Although less factually informative, this oral testimony was also important in indicating how specific memory can be as well as its frailties in reconnecting with these uncanny spaces. What stuck in my mind after we had finished was how much being at the site prompted the second woman to reflect on her time in the laundry as a fracture point in her life – her memories more often focused on how her life led her to it and how it was shaped afterwards – rather than focus on her experiences *of* and *in* the laundry. This felt like an important insight into how her traumatized memory reacted to the disorientation of the site; rather than focus on the material world around her she abstracted to the impact of the laundry on her life biography. For various reasons all these insights were useful in understanding not only the place but its enduring, traumatic impact on lives.

Conclusion

This chapter aimed to present some insights into how contemporary archaeology can take a different approach from historical and oral sources to bring a material-centred understanding of the past that continues to the present. An emphasis on the material is important as there are currently few surviving structures that have not been demolished or drastically reconfigured and so we need to consider what we do with the few remaining former institutions. This does not necessarily mean that all the surviving laundries should be retained, but there should be serious consideration as to the potential role of these material spaces to remember the past. What we must not do is let all the sites disappear through conscious and unconscious neglect. If we do retain all of the extant sites then we need to consider what types of experiences the partial material remains can reveal – whether it is the industrial nature of Donnybrook or the religious and accommodation aspects of Sean McDermott Street. Despite the impact of dereliction and ruination, we are still in an enviable position of having significant survivals of buildings and artefactual contents that, when read together, have the potential to reveal absences as well as presences in terms of how architecture and artefacts constitute each other.[51]

Looking to the future, this chapter argues that we should consider how we incorporate material remains as part of the memory of institutional abuse. This can be through incorporating survivors into the archaeological recording process but also more broadly by considering how we engage with the social significance of places. Lixinski has argued, in the context of South Africa, that we should consciously change our definitions and forms of cultural heritage to allow meaningful objects from our difficult recent past to be included in our most significant heritage institutions as a form of transitional justice.[52] While in Ireland we need to deal with a different form of societal trauma it is increasingly clear that there is a need to accept the vast impact of institutionalization and to take meaningful steps to acknowledge the harm that has been done to significant groups of people by incorporating their experiences into public memory. While this may not include the retention of DML, it should include open and public discussions about where and how we remember this very recent past.

Notes

1   See, for example, Eleanor Conlin Casella, *The Archaeology of Institutional Confinement* (Tallahasse, FL: University Press of Florida, 2007); Laura McAtackney, *An Archaeology of the Troubles: The Dark Heritage of Long Kesh/Maze Prison* (Oxford: Oxford University Press, 2014).

2   Casella, *The Archaeology of Institutional Confinement*; McAtackney, *An Archaeology of the Troubles*.

3   Planning and Property Development Department, Dublin City Council, 'Permission for Development on this Site of approximately 0.247 ha, Site of the Former Donnybrook Laundry, The Crescent, Donnybrook Dublin 4, D04 R856'.

4   Ibid.

5   Department of Housing, Local Government and Heritage Office of the Planning Regulator, *A Guide to Planning Permission*, Planning Leaflet 3 (Dublin, 2021), 3.

6   Department of Housing, Local Government and Heritage Office of the Planning Regulator, *Archaeology in the Planning Process*, Planning Leaflet 13 (Dublin, 2021), 6.

7   Crinan Youth Project (former convent / nunnery), National Inventory of Architectural Heritage Reg. No. 50011149; Monastery of Our Lady of Charity of the Refuge (Church / Chapel), National Inventory of Architectural Heritage Reg. No. 50060466.

8   Department of Justice, *Report of the Inter-Departmental Committee to Establish the Facts of State Involvement with the Magdalen Laundries* (Dublin, 2013, aka *McAleese Report*, hereinafter *IDC Report*).

9   Ibid.

10 Joe Humphreys, 'Magdalen Plot had Remains of 155 Women', *Irish Times*, 21 August 2003.

11 Catherine Corless, *Belonging: A Memoir of Place, Beginnings and One Woman's Search for Truth and Justice for the Tuam Babies* (Castleknock: Hachette Books Ireland, 2021).

12 James R. Dixon, 'Is the Present Day Post-Medieval?', *Post-Medieval Archaeology* 45, no. 2 (2011): 313–21.

13 Ibid., 319.

14 McAtackney, *An Archaeology of the Troubles*.

15 Lucas Lixinski, 'Cultural Heritage Law and Transitional Justice: Lessons from South Africa', *International Journal of Transitional Justice* 9, no. 2 (9 April 2015): 279.

16 See Brenda Malone, Chapter 10, this volume.

17 Rodney Harrison, 'Surface Assemblages: Towards an Archaeology in and of the Present', *Archaeological Dialogues* 18, no. 2 (26 October 2011): 157.

18 Victor Buchli and Gavin Lucas, *Archaeologies of the Contemporary Past* (London: Routledge, 2001).

19 Laurent Olivier, *The Dark Abyss of Time: Archaeology and Memory* (London: AltaMira Press, 2011).

20 Harrison, 'Surface Assemblages', 156.

21 Ibid., 154–6.

22 Claire McGettrick, 'Chapter 6: Never Tell, Never Acknowledge (. . .everyone knew, but no one said)', in *Ireland and the Magdalene Laundries: A Campaign for Justice*, by Claire McGettrick, Katherine O'Donnell, Maeve O'Rourke, James M. Smith and Mari Steed (London: I.B. Tauris, 2021).

23 Anne-Marie McAlinden, 'An Inconvenient Truth: Barriers to Truth Recovery in the Aftermath of Institutional Child Abuse in Ireland', *Legal Studies* 33, no. 2 (2013).

24 *IDC Report*.

25 MESH Architects, 'Preliminary Historic Structure Report' (Dublin: unpublished report, 2018).

26 Ibid., 10.

27 Irish Archaeological Consultancy Limited (IAC), 'Archaeological Assessment at the Crescent, Donnybrook, Dublin 4' (Dublin: unpublished report, 2018).

28 Bjørnar Olsen, Michael Shanks, Timothy Webmoor and Christopher Witmore, *Archaeology: The Discipline of Things* (Berkeley, CA: University of California Press, 2012).

29 Buchli and Lucas, *Archaeologies of the Contemporary*.

30 Daniel Miller, *Stuff* (London: Polity Press, 2010).

31 Conor Ryan, 'Site by Laundry Grave Sold for €61.8m', *Irish Examiner*, 5 July 2011.

32 'Laundry Room', Atlas of Lost Rooms, last modified 2020, available online: www.atlasoflostrooms.com/laundry/ (accessed 15 December 2021).

33 *IDC Report*, 27.

34 Siân Jones, 'Experiencing Authenticity at Heritage Sites: Some Implications for Heritage Management and Conservation', *Conservation and Management of Archaeological Sites* 11, no. 2 (2009): 133–47.

35 *IDC Report*, 27.
36 James Deetz, *In Small Things Forgotten* (New York: Doubleday, 1977).
37 Alfredo González-Ruibal, 'Time to Destroy: An Archaeology of Supermodernity', *Current Anthropology* 49, no. 2 (2008): 247–79.
38 Þóra Pétursdóttir, 'Concrete Matters: Ruins of Modernity and the Things Called Heritage', *Journal of Social Archaeology* 13, no. 1 (2013): 31–53.
39 Following Sharon Macdonald, *Difficult Heritage: Negotiating the Nazi Past in Nuremberg and Beyond* (Abingdon: Routledge, 2009).
40 A term coined by the French archaeologist Laurent Olivier, *The Dark Abyss of Time: Archaeology and Memory* (London: AltaMira Press, 2011).
41 McAtackney, *An Archaeology of the Troubles*.
42 Bjørnar Olsen and Þóra Pétursdóttir, *Ruin Memories: Materialities, Aesthetics and the Archaeology of the Recent Past* (Abingdon: Routledge, 2014).
43 Ibid., 7.
44 Including Louisa McGrath, 'In Donnybrook, Future of Crumbling Magdalene Laundry is Uncertain', *Dublin Inquirer*, 9 March 2016; Gráinne Ní Aodha, '"Burn It to the Ground": What Should Be Done with Magdalene Laundry Buildings?", *TheJournal. ie*, 25 August 2017.
45 *The Magdalen Commission Report: Report of Mr Justice John Quirke on the Establishment of an* ex gratia *Scheme and Related Matters for the Benefit of Those Women Who were Admitted to and Worked in the Magdalen Laundries* (Dublin, 2013, aka *Quirke Report*), available online: www.justice.ie/en/JELR/THE%20Quirke%20 report.pdf/Files/THE%20Quirke%20report.pdf (accessed 15 December 2021).
46 Gabriel Moshenska, 'A Hard Rain: Children's Shrapnel Collections in the Second World War', *Journal of Material Culture* 13, no. 1 (2008): 107–25.
47 See, for example, Olsen et al., *Archaeology: The Discipline*.
48 McAtackney, *An Archaeology of the Troubles*.
49 Cahal McLaughlin, 'A Documentary Archive of Prison Experience: Introduction to the PMA', Prisons Memory Archive, accessed November 2021, available online: www. prisonsmemoryarchive.com/illustrated_ essay/a-documentary-archive-of-prison-experience-introduction-to-the-pma/ (accessed 15 December 2021).
50 Homi K. Bhabha, 'Democracy De-realized', *Diogenes* 50, no. 1 (1 February 2003): 27–35.
51 Victor Buchli, *An Archaeology of Socialism* (London: Routledge, 1999), 1.
52 Lixinski, 'Cultural Heritage'.

10

The Material Evidence of Donnybrook Magdalene Laundry

Brenda Malone and Barry Houlihan

This chapter considers the material culture and archival documents that survive from Donnybrook Magdalene Laundry (DML). It evaluates their significance in the preservation of history and their importance in the delivery of social justice to survivors of the Irish Magdalene system. While the importance of the surviving material is patently clear today, it will assume even greater importance in the future, when survivors are no longer able to relay their stories. Both research and education will benefit from its preservation and display. The gathering and preservation of evidence is also essential in light of the information denied to the survivors of the institutions, and the refusal of the Religious Sisters of Charity (RSC) to engage with academic researchers investigating and seeking to understand our institutional past.

(i) Museum Display and Interpretation as an Act of Social Justice

Brenda Malone

Introduction

The National Museum of Ireland (NMI) is the national cultural institution charged with the collection and preservation of Ireland's portable material heritage. Its galleries display the island's cultural and natural histories, while behind the scenes its stores are filled with millions of artefacts and specimens, documented and preserved for further research and future exhibition. Museum displays, particularly those in national museums, very often reflect a national identity; the way in which a society sees itself, and even contribute to or consolidate the creation of that identity. The NMI reflects the importance that our archaeological and natural heritage, traditional crafts and modern design have in Irish culture. The centuries' long fight for independence plays a central role in our history displays, to explain the emergence of the Irish state not only to our citizens and newer communities, but also to our non-Irish visitors. However, the collecting, study and display of more marginalized and difficult histories, such as systems of discrimination and the institutionalization of people on the edge of Irish society's norms, did not happen during the twentieth century. These histories have only recently been actively collected and curated. National museums, through careful display and interpretation, can be a critical vehicle by which a society can play a part in delivering justice to those affected by past traumas and abuses. This chapter looks at the importance of the acquisition of the Donnybrook Magdalene Laundry (DML) machinery and equipment to the national collections. It examines how their presence in the collections can represent the history of the Laundry system, the histories of survivors of this and other systems of institutional incarceration in Ireland, and how addressing this history through its material culture in a museum space can benefit Irish society as a whole.

Twentieth-century Irish history at the National Museum of Ireland

The struggle for independence during the first two decades of the twentieth century have been thoroughly examined and exhibited, with eight exhibitions (from 1932 to 2016) dedicated to the fight for Irish freedom, all of which were centred around the 1916 Rising and its direct aftermath. Recent exhibitions have also examined how these events have been remembered and commemorated throughout the twentieth century. It was not until 2006, with the opening of *Soldiers and Chiefs: The Irish at War at Home and Abroad from 1550 to the Present Day*, that an NMI history exhibition examined events occurring in post-independence Ireland. Independent Ireland has been under-represented in the NMI's galleries until very recently, despite being extremely relevant to the creation of modern Irish society. This society, formed in the aftermath of war against a colonizing nation and a subsequent, bloody civil war, endeavoured to demonstrate its own unique Irish identity. The National Museum played its part in this visualizing and defining of 'Irishness' by displaying its ancient history, heritage, art and culture as its central exhibitions, showcasing the finest examples of Celtic art while relegating Irish decorative arts (which were visually similar to British decorative arts to enable Irish craftspeople and manufacturers to effectively compete in the market with British-made wares) to its basements, away from public view. In the 1930s, the museum built on this expression of high culture and civilization by displaying the resilience of Irish people through its displays of traditional folklife and crafts, alongside the many battles and uprisings (always with a focus on the 1916 Rising), to gain independence from British rule.

Simultaneously, the 1930s was to see a cementing of the relationship between Catholic teaching and Irish nationalism in politics and society, leading to the establishment of a close relationship between the Catholic Church in Ireland and the Irish state's legal and policy systems. It was this which created a conservative religious society in which Church-run institutions, with the compliance of the Irish government and society, could form a nationwide institutional system to remove and process those who it perceived, for any reason, as a threat to Catholic Irish society. Institutions such as Magdalene Laundries, Mother and Baby Homes and Industrial and Reformatory Schools subjected whole sections of Irish society, usually those in the lower socioeconomic groups, to incarceration and abuse. The last reformatory school closed in 1973 and the last Magdalene Laundry in 1996, with survivors and their descendants still suffering its multigenerational damage.

The recent and raw nature of this experience, and the effect it has on both survivors and their families, makes this topic a contemporary history, and one that is very contentious and difficult. It is also one which would not normally be considered subject to museum preservation and display according to traditional acquisition policies and exhibition practice. However, museums worldwide now recognize that they have an important part to play in the examination of the society they represent, and can play a critical role in the healing process for survivors through the activity of truth-telling of difficult histories. Recognizing that museums play this role makes it imperative that these histories are integrated into national collections, and therefore the national narrative.

Collecting difficult histories in the National Museum of Ireland

Though the absence of difficult histories in the NMI can seem conspicuous to the visitor, much work has happened over the last two decades in the curatorial areas of examining the collections. This work has identified their weaknesses and issues which will negatively impact the museum's ability to tell the story of the first century of the independent Irish state. Knowledge of these gaps has encouraged a new focus on collecting objects which tell the stories of the Irish state, outside of the military and political arena, or objects which provoke discussion and an increase in the understanding of how our past influences our contemporary social landscape. Most of this work, which includes the collection of recent civil rights referenda material, has not yet reached the point of full interpretation and public exhibition. However, there have been moves towards the display of objects collected as part of this effort, such as the temporary display of referenda material in the *Exhibiting the Nation* space.

The most visible example of this work of expanding the collections and displays into social issues is the exhibiting of Alison Lowry's artwork in glass *(A) Dressing Our Hidden Truths* at the NMI's Decorative Arts and History Museum at Collins Barracks in 2019. Lowry's work was in response to the revelations at the Tuam Mother and Baby Home in the aftermath of historian Catherine Corless's research and the publication of her findings in 2012.[1] The multimedia exhibition consisted of works in glass, sound pieces with survivor testimony, visual elements such as a filmed piece commenting on rape culture, consent and domestic violence, historical artefacts and a commemoration of lost lives. The central section holds a series of sand-cast *pâte de verre* christening robes, each delicately and discreetly suspended from above, free to slowly revolve themselves in the space, while the names of the children who died at Tuam are read aloud with the complete list of 802 dead babies and infants printed on a nearby wall. The traumatic nature of the topic was fully recognized by the museum, which understood that visitors, in particular survivors and their families, might react very strongly in the space. Information on counselling supports and other help that is available to survivors was made available in the exhibition, as well as a space to write a response to the exhibition and deposit it privately. Front-of-house staff also received training to inform them of the history of the institutions, and how to provide any help necessary to visitors experiencing difficulties should the situation arise in the galleries. The work provoked a strong public reaction when it opened, with both positive and negative responses, and has subsequently remained one of the most visited exhibitions within the Museum.

Lowry's exhibition was the first public display of the history of women and children's institutions in the NMI, and the art works have since been acquired into the collection as an important work for the NMI to hold both as an example of modern craftsmanship and a work commenting on a difficult history. The Minister for Tourism, Culture, Arts, Gaeltacht, Sport and Media Catherine Martin said of the acquisition:

> The issues that Alison Lowry touches on in this exhibition are a part of our history and culture that we are not proud of and, for that reason, it is all the more important that we never forget them. I am glad that they will now take a deserved place in the permanent collection of our national museum.[2]

The display of this history informed the public that the NMI collects this story, and there has since been contact between survivors of the institutions and the NMI, that has in turn led to donations of artefacts to tell their stories.

While Lowry's was the first display, the first instance of the NMI collecting the history of the institutional incarceration of women and children in the Irish state happened between 2008 and 2010, with the salvage and acquisition of the remaining material culture of the reformatory system found in St Conleth's Reformatory School in Daingean, Co. Offaly, one of the institutions included in the 2009 *Report of the Commission to Inquire into Child Abuse* (*The Ryan Report*). The site and its complex of buildings (originally the site of the county courthouse, prison and British army cavalry barracks) had housed an extensive reformatory school run by the Oblates of Mary Immaculate in Ireland from 1940 until its eventual closure in 1973. This closure came about as a result of findings of neglect and abuse in the 1970 Kennedy Commission report and the subsequent financial disagreement between the Oblate Brothers and the Department of Education, which funded the school.

The site remained empty until 1979 when it was designated as a storage site for the NMI, which was also under the jurisdiction of the Department of Education at that time. The large objects of the collections, such as agricultural machinery and transport vehicles, were transferred to the Daingean complex. Few refurbishment works were carried out to fundamentally change the buildings from the time they were vacated by the Oblate Brothers, unlike other institutions such as Letterfrack Industrial School in County Galway, which was fully refurbished for reuse. Because of this, many of the older areas at Daingean retained some material remains of its former life. I was assigned to manage the complex and curate the Irish Folklife collections held there between 2008 and 2012, during which time I examined and recorded the buildings and site as they were used as a reformatory, and salvaged and acquired a number of artefacts to represent the history of the industrial and reformatory school system in Ireland. Artefacts such as clerical clothing found in the Priests' House accommodation, religious relics such as holy water fonts and images, items such as a wooden cross, sewing-machine needles (for the tailoring workshop), prayer books and dormitory name plates such as 'St Stephen' all evoke the religious and industrial ritual that dictated life in the school. However, as with much material culture, the objects that survived (or perhaps all that existed in the first place) were those of the people who held status and power on the site.

The presence of the boys was less obvious in the objects. However, the publication of the *Ryan Report* in 2009 brought many survivors back to visit the site, as the publication had raised more public awareness of the abuses within the system and had retraumatized many former residents. In meeting and listening to those who came to Daingean to try to access the site as a coping mechanism for their trauma, I learned much about the lives and experiences of the boys who were sent there, and their personal histories informed the collection of artefacts as much, if not more, than the general known history of the complex could. Objects found in areas connected to the stories they told became meaningful objects, as they became witnesses and carriers of individual stories which represented the experience of many.[3] A scrap of a faded crêpe-paper Christmas decoration in one room tells how this room, the only room shown to the boys' visitors, was decorated for the season. A showerhead and soap dish evoke the sexual abuse and rape so often spoken of in the Commission's reports. The graffiti on the inside of the toilet doors displays the numbers given to the boys as they entered the reformatory system (rather than their names) and groupings of numbers denote the relationships between groups of friends. 'No Fish' appears very frequently, and has many meanings according to those who were there, the most prominent being a statement that they are not new, and therefore should not be considered a target for abuse. Walls also bear warnings about particularly violent or abusive priests. The stories that were told by survivors when viewing the artefacts *in situ* illustrate the vital importance of the testimony and voice of the survivors in informing the collection of such histories in order for the objects to accurately represent their stories and to continue telling them.

The collecting of the material culture of the Daingean site came about primarily through the fortunate timing of a curatorial posting coinciding with the publication of the *Ryan Report*, and the opportunity that gave to preserve a history which does not survive materially in other such sites. Future collecting, though also very much reliant on opportunity, should be more proactive and deliberate in order to widen the representation of this history in the collections and pave the way for future interpretation and exhibition.

The Donnybrook Laundry Collection

An opportunity to engage in more structured collecting of material relating to Ireland's institutional past arose in 2018, when the laundry formerly attached to St Mary Magdalen's Convent at Donnybrook was being assessed by heritage professionals, having been sold to a private owner who sought planning permission to demolish the buildings and build an apartment complex. Contemporary archaeologists Laura McAtackney of Aarhus University and Franc Myles of Archaeology and Built Heritage were engaged by the owner to carry out archaeological surveys of the site, its buildings and contents, including any evidence of on-site burials of women who had died there, as part of the requirement for archaeological assessments in planning applications. During this process, McAtackney contacted me to ask if NMI would be interested in collecting items from the site, in the knowledge that the museum was embarking on new collecting of contemporary histories as seen in the collecting of the 'Repeal the 8th' abortion referendum.[4]

This convent was situated on the site from 1837 and had operated a Magdalene laundry through the twentieth century until 1992 when it was sold as a going concern to a private company.[5] This long-running Magdalene laundry was one of the last to close, and because it had continued as a non-religious commercial laundry for some years afterwards it had retained many of the machines which had been in use during its Magdalene era. These machines are an essential part of the story of the women incarcerated under the Magdalene system, and it became crucial for the NMI to collect and preserve them as the industrial material culture of a laundry site. In order to collect this history, the NMI enacted some updates to its acquisition policy to reflect current collecting practice and allow such collecting to happen. Colleagues in the NMI Conservation Department joined me in carrying out further investigations and assessments of the objects in the laundry, and a short list was made of which machinery to acquire. This assessment was to be informed by a number of overall curatorial criteria, but was initially based on the authenticity of the object (i.e. that it was in use during the Magdalene era), and condition (some machines had been exposed to the elements for a number of years due to broken roofs and were now unsalvageable). Due to the poor conditions in the buildings, which had been subject to break–ins, robberies, vandalism and general neglect, it was imperative to take action immediately to salvage whatever material was possible and process them for either acquisition or disposal once the material was safe.

Many small items, such as statues and religious objects, were removed from the site for safe-keeping elsewhere, as well as smaller items representing the work carried out by the women in the laundry. Larger objects of organic materials such as folding tables, drying racks, laundry trollies and baskets were removed to NMI storage to dry out and be re-assessed before formal acquisition. The large machinery remained on site until June 2022, its removal delayed by the discovery of asbestos in the laundry rooms and the subsequent need for specialist hazardous waste removal, as well as lockdown restrictions due to the Covid-19 pandemic. The machinery selected for acquisition has now been removed, and work is ongoing to ensure its preservation.

As the convent area and accommodations of the nuns and the Magdalene women had been separated from the laundry during its 1992 sale, the site at Donnybrook provides us only with the opportunity to preserve the industrial element of the history of the Magdalene Laundry system and not the personal dimension. However, oral testimonies of the survivors were recorded by the Justice for Magdalenes Research (JFMR) group and by McAtackney during her work on the site, and, like in the collecting at Daingean, these were critical to the process of deciding on the initial salvage of the material.

The oral histories carried by the survivors, with their descriptions of their lives and work in such institutions, when combined with the physicality of the material objects of the laundry, bring the reality of manual laundry work to life. An element that strongly stands out in their oral histories is that of process, control and repetition in the work. The process of carrying out this work is very structured, with a strict system to be followed; first sorting, then washing, spinning, drying, pressing, folding and packing. Each part of the system had a physically defined area within the laundry, with the specific machine or equipment required for that work, which also had its own system of operation. The laundry process was also highly controlled, with the supervising nun making the decisions as to who worked in which area, the hours worked, the quantity of tasks to be carried out and when breaks could be taken. The repetitive nature of the work is also evident in the machines; the calender machine evokes a seemingly endless supply of wet bed sheets to be steamrolled and folded for return to hospitals and hotels, the steam burning the women's hands as they are handled for packing, or causing more serious injuries. This brings us to the physicality of the machines and what they elicit; the heat of the laundry room filled with steam, the smell of wet textiles, their weight when moving them from machine to machine and from one part of the process to the next. The size of the machines, so much larger than domestic versions, would have dwarfed the average-sized woman during the laundry's operation, and add to the visual recognition that such work was extremely physically arduous and, in many cases being forced labour, would have amounted to a form of physical torture.

The careful selection of machines to be collected to represent this system of labour which dominated the women's lives was critical for the carrying forward of the survivors' experiences. The artefacts themselves also speak of the religious ideals permeating through the laundry space; the drying racks and folding tables are painted Marian blue, and the walls adorned with crucifixes and papal photographs; all reminders to those who worked in the space that they were being watched over by God and Church at all times. However, the Donnybrook material represents only part of the women's lives in the system, and objects that represent their personal lives and losses are yet to be secured for preservation.

Sean McDermott Street: A vision for a new museum

During the period of assessment of the Donnybrook Laundry, the question of the future of the site of the Sisters of Our Lady of Charity convent and laundry at Sean McDermott Street came into public focus. The site was the last Magdalene Laundry to close in 1996, and remained mostly unused for the following two decades. The laundry area to the rear was demolished, and the living accommodations for the nuns and the women were left to deteriorate. It was due to be sold to a hotel group by its current owners Dublin City Council in 2018, although this sale was halted as a result of campaigning by a number of collectives such as JFMR and Open Heart City. With the future of the site again contested, it has become imperative that a strong argument be put forward to Dublin City Council and the Irish Government that the complex be retained in public ownership, especially in light of the fact that the majority of the built heritage of this part of Irish history and the material culture within is held in private ownership and has therefore already been destroyed or is under serious threat of imminent destruction.

The aim of the argument is, however, not just to retain the site but to develop it into a Site of Conscience. The International Coalition of Sites of Conscience states that Sites of Conscience: 'interpret history through site; engage the public in programmes that stimulate dialogue on pressing social issues; share opportunities for public involvement and positive actions on issues raised at the site; and promote justice and universal cultures of human rights'.[6] The International Coalition defines a Site of Conscience as: 'any memorial, museum, historic site, memory initiative or non-governmental organization that commits to these defining operating principles'.[7]

The Sean McDermott Street site is ideally situated to become Ireland's Site of Conscience to address the history of institutional abuse on the island of Ireland. While the state of the building is not ideal, what remains (the chapel, convent and, most crucially, the women's dormitories) is the physical evidence of how the women in such institutions lived. In addition, though access is very limited at the time of writing due to safety concerns in the buildings, preliminary assessments by McAtackney and myself confirmed that it contains some material which represents the more personal lives of those incarcerated there, including items such as hospital beds and babies' cots, which when joined on-site with the industrial material from Donnybrook could become a minimalist but very powerful illustration of institutional life within an authentic space. When also joined with the material from the Daingean Reformatory School already in the NMI collections we would have the foundations of a Site of Conscience (by being able to interpret this history on an authentic site) using the buildings as a universal form to begin to explore Ireland's history of the institutionalization and abuse of both socially and economically marginalized women and their children, engaging with all survivor groups from across the whole island.

Sean McDermott Street is also a large site with much potential for the development of education and social spaces in line with the needs of the area, which is historically and culturally rich but with a large proportion of residents defined as economically deprived and living with the loss of opportunity which comes with that status. One of the uses for the site, suggested by JFMR, is a repository building to hold the archives created by both the system (where they survive) and by the recent enquiries and commissions. This would form part of a centre for survivors, their families and researchers.

However, this is also a unique opportunity to create a space with survivors which can be used as part of the healing process. The wonderfully user-centred Danmarks Forsorgsmuseum (Danish Welfare Museum) in Svendborg[8] can be seen as a model for such an activity. Of particular importance is its programme with survivors of the Danish Care System which explores and recognizes that when survivors finally see their official files they very often do not recognize themselves in them, leading to retraumatization. This led the Welfare Museum to become a safe space for survivors to create their personal files and control their deposit in an official institution; a very challenging but positive outcome for the survivor. By applying similar methods Sean McDermott Street could become not only a holder of historic records, but a depository for those created by survivors as part of the healing process of finding and taking ownership of their histories. The significance of this interaction, and the impact that it can have on a survivor of institutional abuse in Ireland, must make the Irish Government consider its responsibilities and what can be provided to survivors in this area. In order to provide this important function the proposed museum and archive should be established as a National Cultural Institution (NCI) and resourced appropriately, including full-time counselling and community outreach staff.

The vision of Sean McDermott Street as a museum and archive leads to a consideration of a further function which should be carried out by the proposed museum; that of a badly needed repository for oral histories, which have required a central repository in Ireland for some decades, and a properly resourced museum and archive which is sustainably funded by government can provide a solution to this long-standing problem, essentially creating an NCI which functions as a research centre for Irish oral histories.

In planning for museum display on a site of such significant heritage value, a number of considerations need to be incorporated into the planning from the earliest stages. The building site itself is part of the museum's message, and therefore must be preserved and respected, with any development integrated into the fabric of the museum site. It will need to be designed with an eye to being fully sustainable and controllable in terms of the environment and external light to ensure the care of collections or objects on display. At the same time it is imperative that it be a space that is comfortable and inviting for users, with the flexibility to create private spaces for personal reflection and group discussion, as well as open spaces for larger groups, such as a conference or seminar space. The space design will also need to be sensitive to the need to provide the individual with choices of experience as they enter and move through the space. For example, providing a choice in public access and visitor flow allows for personal decisions on what to experience, mindful of the fact that the physicality of the site and how the sensitive materials are displayed can be triggers for trauma. Visitor flow should be professionally planned in conjunction with survivor representatives, without risking changing or sanitizing the message that the site and exhibitions communicate.

Conclusion

Duffy categorizes museums which exhibit human rights as: museums of remembrance, Holocaust and genocide museums, museums of slavery and the 'slave trade', museums of African-American civil rights, prison museums and museums of torture.[9] In his examination of the types of museums, he concludes:

> It is encouraging that there is an emerging group of museums of human rights that might be the custodians of what one could term a 'human rights culture' ... It is certainly the privilege of these museums of 'human suffering' to show the worst

moments in the experiences of peoples in the hope that such portrayals will contribute to the advancement of human rights worldwide.[10]

In fully acknowledging what positives such museums of human rights gives us, we must also be cognizant of the fact that sites of difficult histories are traumatic, and we will need to find the balance between teaching this history and remembering and supporting the survivors while avoiding the retraumatizing of them and their families. We must also remember that there are many different opinions on what a museum is; many see it as a class-based institution discussing something that happened in the past. For others, such a 'memorial' site can be seen as an indication that the problem is resolved while not taking into account that the survivors and their families are still affected by the historic system and its legacy. For others still, a memorial fails to acknowledge the failings of the systems which replaced them.

Any new museum exploring Ireland's institutions will inevitably be a museum of human sorrow and suffering in its reflection on this difficult and painful history. The museum must also be a genuine examination and acknowledgement of human rights failures in Ireland, both historic and current (such as Direct Provision and state child protection and welfare); an aid in educating people about these systems to help end them. However, the museum must also be part of the healing process for survivors through their collaboration in its development, and play an active part in the social life of its participatory communities to help ensure those in need now receive assistance and skills to succeed in their goals. This goal is a tall order for any museum, and it will take time and effort to achieve it. However, the very act of making this site, whether it be called a museum, a memorial or a Site of Conscience, is in itself an act of social justice that is desperately needed in Ireland for all its people.

(ii) Archival Legacies

Barry Houlihan

This section examines the contemporary archival legacy of DML. The surviving archives and records of the DML comprise material evidence of the Magdalene Laundry system of incarceration and of the coercive labour of the women detained within the Laundry's walls at Donnybrook, as well as commercial arrangements and contracts with public and private sectors of Irish society through the latter half of the twentieth century. The records of DML that have survived are certainly incomplete and detail the finances, operation and business operations of the Laundry from the early 1960s through to the mid-1990s.

As an archivist at the University of Galway, I have worked on an increasing number of archives that engage with Irish and international human rights practice, activism, legal advocacy and research, including the Professor Kevin Boyle Archive[11] and the Tuam Mother and Baby Home Oral History Project.[12] Dialogue, discussion and a survivor-centred approach to archival appraisal and acquisition has enabled University of Galway to progress partnerships to facilitate and expand the archival record of

Ireland's institutional histories, from mother and baby 'homes' to Magdalene Laundries. I was first approached about the records of Donnybrook Magdalene Laundry by Brenda Malone, curator at the National Museum of Ireland, and Maeve O'Rourke, lecturer at the Irish Centre for Human Rights at University of Galway. The fact that a tranche of records was recovered from the original laundry site was highly significant. It was also a reminder of how scarce any operational Laundry records are, from any of the other nine such Magdalene Laundries which operated in Ireland. Ahead of their transfer to the University of Galway Library, it was clear that such records provided a detailed account of the running of the DML, as well as revealing the commercial and personal exploitation of the women within the Magdalene Laundry system. The records of DML consist of numerous administrative and financial ledgers and related record books which reflect the operation and administration of the laundry. Client lists, cheque stubs and correspondence with large institutional customers are included.

Documentary remains

Richard Ovenden has outlined how truth, information and transparency of social governance is under attack within contemporary society. 'Archives,' Ovenden writes, 'are at the heart of the rights of citizens and at the heart of contentious debates.'[13] Archival records provide viewpoints into the construction of memory and of accountability within a culture and society. Such archival memory interrogates the record beyond its evidential process – it contributes to a wider social memory, which can enable a process of truth-telling that pushes against the grain of silencing and closures of official records.

The DML, run by the Sisters of Charity (RSC), kept detailed organizational and administrative records, outlining the operation of a profitable and established commercial business. Irish law does not require religious congregations that operated large public institutions to open their records to public scrutiny. Catriona Crowe has previously called for the religious orders to voluntarily open their records to researchers.[14] The refusal of the four religious orders who operated Magdalene Laundries to do this makes the Donnybrook archival documents now in the custody of University of Galway extremely important.

Patterns emerge within the client and customer accounts and financial ledgers of DML: for example, the client base is predominantly drawn from the elite and professional classes. The outsourcing of laundry services by the State and its semi-state bodies, international embassies, as well as private schools of the children of the professional classes to DML, as evidenced in the account and customer books, underscores the class politics of the history of DML. The recovery of these records from the site at DML works against the veiling and silencing of memory, the class-driven (as well as gendered) segregation of Irish society. As Laura McAtackney has outlined, the abandonment, destruction and/or ruin of Magdalen Laundries reveals a pervasive discomfort in contemporary Ireland in dealing with a past that many would rather forget.[15] The records list hundreds of regular clients, from private individuals, public services, leading commercial retailers, financial companies, hospitals, local authority services, among many others. These documents reveal the volume of materials which passed through the laundry, and the extent of unpaid labour carried by the women of the laundry, as the RSC accumulated profits from the various companies and organizations contracted to DML. A file is present for the National Maternity Hospital, Holles Street, Dublin. In December 1988, a quotation was issued by Donnybrook to the hospital for the next twelve months. Items listed include sheets, pillow slips, blankets, towels, gowns, aprons, babywear, baby blankets, baby gowns, baby sheets, among many others. Over 75,000 individual pieces were quoted for processing by Donnybrook from Holles Street alone. Materials from private rooms were priced higher per item for laundering, indicating a higher profit for the Laundry for patients who could afford a private room. Materials from doctors, nurses' residence, matron and sacristy were also included, as well as the range of clerical vestments such as amices and albs.

In August 1992, the headed paper used in correspondence from the National Maternity Hospital indicated a new patron for the hospital – President of Ireland, Mary Robinson. Robinson's presidency was a significant moment for Irish women and for the status and influence of the office of President. The material evidence of the records highlight the connection between Church and State in more symbolic but also visible terms. As Ireland embraced its first woman president in the early 1990s, we still see the National Maternity Hospital in a financial contract to the Magdalene Laundry in Donnybrook. For the women working in the laundry who processed the thousands of laundry items from baby wards of Holles Street and sent to the Laundry at Donnybrook each year, it must have been an intensely emotional experience. Other records outline the extent of items laundered each week, month and year at DML. From January to March 1992, for example, 220,746 items were processed. In 1991, the total number of items processed was 876,915. An exhaustive level of detail breaking down this near 1 million number of items of laundry is documented in the records. Households that engaged the Laundry services were understood to have forty-six potential categories of laundry, hospitals could have twenty-four categories of material, while sacristy laundry is listed under thirteen different categories.

The Department of Justice, *Report of the Inter-Departmental Committee to Establish the Facts of State Involvement with the Magdalen Laundries* (*IDC Report*, 2013) cited a Report on the Policy of Hospital Linen Services, produced in 1984 by Craig Gardner on behalf of the Hospital Joint Services Board, and which outlined the disquiet among hospital workers and fears from hospital management within Dublin and regional hospitals regarding the lack of resources for provision of laundry services by hospitals. The Report was prepared at a time when deteriorating industrial relations were regarded as a threat to the reliable supply of emergency and surgical linen for hospitals.[16] While the Craig Gardner report confirmed the extensive and established commercial relationship between state hospitals and the religious-run laundries, at Donnybrook, High Park, and Sean McDermott Street by the mid-1980s, the subsequent ledgers and customer/account books of Donnybrook Laundry, and of correspondence between the laundry and the hospital, reveal the extent that the RSC went to gain new and large-scale hospital laundry contracts. For example, in May 1983, arrangements were being discussed to increase the volume of laundry processed from St. Vincent's Hospital.

Conclusion

The records of DML demonstrate that the Laundry was a very well organized, industrial and profitable enterprise that was connected to the highest echelons of the Irish state, from government departments and hospitals to private schools and third-level colleges and religious organizations. Even a cursory review of the documents reveal much not merely of the profitable business of the DML but that it will be a rich resource for considering the politics of class in twentieth-century Ireland.

Notes

1 Catherine Corless, 'The Home', *Journal of the Old Tuam Society* 9 (2012): 75.
2 National Museum of Ireland, 'National Museum of Ireland Acquires Works from Alison Lowry: (A) Dressing Our Hidden Truths for the National Collection', News Release, 9 December 2020, available online: www.museum.ie/en-IE/Press-and-Media-Information/Latest-Media-Releases/09-December-2020-National-Museum-of-Ireland-acquir (accessed 10 September 2022).
3 National Museum of Ireland, Irish Folklife Register of Collections, 2012. Collections registers list every object acquired formally into a museum's collection for that year with a unique number to identify it and link it to its associated information.
4 See Brenda Malone, 'Recording Change: Collecting the Irish Abortion Rights Referendum, 2018', in *Museums, Sexuality, and Gender Activism*, ed. Joshua G. Adair and Amy K. Levin (London: Routledge, 2020), 120–9.
5 See further, Mark Coen, Chapter 3, this volume.
6 'FAQs', International Coalition of Sites of Conscience, available online: www.sitesofconscience.org/en/who-we-are/faqs/ (accessed 10 September 2022).
7 Ibid.
8 See Adele Chynoweth, Bernadette Lynch, Klaus Petersen and Sarah Smed (eds), *Museums and Social Change: Challenging the Unhelpful Museum* (Abingdon: Routledge, 2020).
9 Ibid.
10 Ibid., 15–16.
11 From Newry, Co. Down, Kevin Boyle was appointed the first full-time Professor of Law at the University of Galway (then University College Galway) in 1977. Boyle was instrumental in developing the disciplines of law and human rights teaching and research at the University of Galway. As a practicing barrister, he represented cases at the European Court of Human Rights, Strasbourg, through the 1980s and 1990s. Boyle was the founding director of the international NGO for freedom of expression, 'Article 19' in 1987 and was later the Director of the Human Rights Centre, Essex, until he died in 2010.
12 The Tuam Mother and Baby Home Oral History Project is based at the University of Galway and run by co-principle investigators, Dr Sarah-Anne Buckley and Dr John Cunningham. For more information on the project, see University of Galway, 'About the Project', Tuam Oral History Project, available online: www.nuigalway.ie/tuam-oral-history/about/ (accessed 11 September 2022).
13 Richard Ovenden, *Burning the Books: A History of Knowledge Under Attack* (London: John Murray Press, 2020). 14.

14 Caitriona Crowe, 'Guilt, Shame, Acknowledgement and Redress: Some Reflections on Ireland's Institutional Treatment of Women and Children', in *Producing Knowledge, Reproducing Gender: Power, Production, Practice in Contemporary Ireland*, ed. Mary Corcoran and Pauline Cullen (Dublin: University College Dublin Press, 2020), 235–51.

15 Laura McAtackney, 'Materials and Memory: Archaeology and Heritage as Tools of Transitional Justice at a Former Magdalen Laundry', *Éire-Ireland* 55, nos 1–2 (2020): 232.

16 Department of Justice, *Report of the Inter-Departmental Committee to Establish the Facts of State Involvement with the Magdalen Laundries* (Dublin, January 2013, aka *McAleese Report*, or *IDC Report*), 656–743.

11

Guerrilla Archive

Donnybrook and the Magdalene Names Project

Claire McGettrick

Introduction

Successive Irish governments have failed to initiate a Transitional Justice (TJ) process in response to the historic and ongoing human rights violations associated with the State's twentieth-century system of institutionalization, forced labour and forced family separation. In the absence of such a process, the Magdalene Names Project (MNP) acts as an accountability mechanism, providing evidence, documents and resources to survivors, relatives and advocates who are denied access to the records of both Church and State. This chapter discusses the MNP's work in relation to Donnybrook Magdalene Laundry (DML). It begins on a somewhat personal note, setting the scene behind the motivations, methodologies and instincts that drive the work of the MNP. The MNP's findings lay bare the inequities in death between the former Magdalene women and the nuns buried at Donnybrook.[1] In honour of those most affected by the Magdalene institutions, the chapter closes with five case studies of women who died while they were confined in DML.[2]

Adoption and the Magdalene Names Project

In August 2003, I co-founded Justice for Magdalenes (JFM, now JFM Research, JFMR) with Angela Newsome and Mari Steed.[3] All three of us are adopted people. We were spurred into action by Mary Raftery's investigation into the anomalies surrounding the exhumation in 1993 of 155 women at the Sisters of Our Lady of Charity of Refuge (OLC) Magdalene Laundry at High Park in Drumcondra. The Sisters were in debt and wanted to sell a portion of their lands at High Park. The land being sold included a communal Magdalene grave and the Order applied to the Department of the Environment (DoEnv) for a licence to exhume the women buried there. Between 23 August and 2 September 1993, 155 women were exhumed from High Park, 154 of whom were immediately cremated and then reinterred in a private ceremony at

Glasnevin Cemetery. Ten years after the exhumations took place, Raftery's investigation revealed significant issues: in 1993, unbeknownst to the public, the undertakers had found 22 additional human remains in the graveyard. Moreover, in their application to the DoEnv, OLC could not produce legal names for 23 women or death certificates for 58 women. Worryingly, many of the names on the exhumation licence did not match the names inscribed on the grave at Glasnevin Cemetery.[4]

As adopted people, JFM's founders felt we had no choice but to act; we understood all too well that the Magdalene Laundries were part and parcel of the same system that severed us from our original families and obliterated our identities. Mari and Angela were shocked to discover during their adoption searches that both their mothers had been sent to Magdalene Laundries. Mari's mother Josie was confined for ten years in the Good Shepherd Magdalene Laundry at Sundays Well in Cork, and Angela's mother Mary was incarcerated in both High Park and Donnybrook laundries for a total of approximately fifty years.[5] Worse still, Angela was devastated to learn that her mother did not have a life beyond the Magdalene Laundry system: Mary had never left Donnybrook. Mary Newsome died in St Margaret's Centre, a Religious Sisters of Charity (RSC) facility on the former DML campus, just one year after she and Angela reunited with each other.

Reading Raftery's article, Angela, Mari and I were particularly troubled by the absence of legal names and the inaccuracies on the High Park grave.[6] We were reminded of the events of Spring 1997 when Sr Gabriel Murphy resigned from her position as Director of St Patrick's Guild (SPG), an adoption society run by the RSC.[7] A year earlier in RTÉ's *Dear Daughter* documentary, Sr Gabriel had been accused of giving misleading information to industrial school survivor Christine Buckley, who was searching for her parents. In April 1997, SPG's new director, Sr Francis Ignatius Fahy, admitted that the agency had indeed deliberately misled several adopted people.[8] This led to one woman grieving at the wrong graveside because SPG had given her an incorrect year of death for her mother.[9] We wondered what would happen if a son, a daughter or another family member of a woman exhumed from High Park wished to visit Glasnevin to pay their respects. Might they, too, end up laying flowers on the wrong grave?

I do not have a direct personal connection to the Magdalene Laundries. I was born in Dublin in 1973 and adopted through SPG, having spent most of my first six weeks in St Patrick's Infant Dietetic Hospital in Temple Hill, Blackrock, an institution also run by the RSC. Irish adopted people have no automatic right to their birth certificates or adoption files, and thus I grew up with no knowledge of my origins. In October 1992, at the age of 19, I arrived unannounced to the offices of SPG on Haddington Road, seeking information regarding my parents and about my own identity. Sr Gabriel Murphy answered the door and expressed her bemusement that I had not sought an appointment prior to my arrival. Once I provided identification, Sr Gabriel gave me a small piece of paper with what is known in the adoption field as 'non-identifying information': my parents' ages, religion, occupations, build and hair colour. Though the information was just twenty words in length, for me it was like treasure – the importance of such seemingly minor facts is usually only discernible to an adopted person. I reunited with my mother on 25 May 1993; we met in an SPG meeting room at their Haddington Road offices. That same day, on the other side of the city, the Assistant

Secretary of the DoEnv was signing the exhumation licence that permitted OLC to disinter and cremate the Magdalene women buried at High Park.[10]

Although Irish adopted people have no automatic right to their birth certificates, these documents have been public records since 1864.[11] In the early 1990s, adoption activist and researcher Enda Pyne developed a methodology to assist adopted people in navigating the civil registration system to obtain their birth certificates.[12] The methodology entails searching the Register of Births for all non-marital births on the adopted person's date of birth, and then carefully using one's non-identifying information to narrow down the results. Thousands of Irish adopted people have used this research method to obtain their birth certificates and they have proven themselves adept at the task. Adopted people intuitively appreciate the significance of tiny fragments of information that might be taken for granted or ignored by others. They are highly proficient at stitching these slivers of data together to discover their original identities and construct their narratives. These skills, methodologies and instincts are at the forefront of my work in the MNP.

Transitional justice

I established the MNP in 2003 after Angela and I visited Glasnevin Cemetery and photographed the grave which contained the cremated remains of the women exhumed from High Park. The MNP began as a tribute, but in the years since its formation, it has become a vehicle through which survivors, relatives and advocates can speak truth to power. In his account of the development of access to archives, Michel Duchein argues that 'the preservation of archives has always been linked to the exercise of power, since the possession of memory is essential to governing and administering. Accessibility to archives was therefore a privilege, not a right.'[13] This rings true in the Irish case; the Department of the Taoiseach refuses to provide access to the archive of the Inter-Departmental Committee to Establish the Facts of State Involvement with the Magdalen Laundries (IDC), and the four Magdalene orders have repeatedly refused to open their records. In the face of State and Church secrecy, the MNP has become a 'guerrilla archive', facilitating accountability and truth-telling.

The work of the MNP is guided by the four core principles of TJ: the right to know the truth and the fate of the disappeared; the State's obligation to investigate and prosecute against human rights violations; the right to reparations and measures of restorative justice; and the State's obligation to prevent these human rights violations from reoccurring.[14] The records held in the MNP's repository serve as a human rights archive. Such archives are defined by Anna Ferrara as: 'those created and owned by civil society groups ... that systematically monitor and collect evidence of human rights violations'.[15] Over the past two decades, I have developed the MNP archive by gathering and cataloguing publicly available records, including gravestones, census and electoral registers, cemetery registers, death certificates, inquest records, Freedom of Information requests, prison records, workhouse records, *Catholic Directories* and newspaper archives. The MNP archive is predominantly digital in format and plans are underway to make it freely available online, with the necessary measures to protect the women's privacy. As demonstrated in the following examples, the MNP puts TJ principles into practice; its findings lay bare human rights violations and throw into sharp relief the State's refusal to engage in a meaningful TJ process.

The right to know the truth and the fate of the disappeared

The MNP's primary objective is to determine the fate of the Magdalene disappeared, that is, to establish the identities and whereabouts of women who died while incarcerated in the laundries. Relatives of women who died in these institutions frequently approach JFMR, seeking the truth about what happened to their kin. Where documents are available in the MNP archive, these are provided, and I also advise family members on how to obtain records from religious orders. The *Report of the Inter-Departmental Committee to Establish the Facts of State Involvement with the Magdalen Laundries* (*IDC Report*, 2013) is of minimal assistance to family members searching for burial locations. The *IDC Report* merely lists the cemeteries with Magdalene plots without any further information and omits the graveyards used by the orders after the closure of the laundries.[16] To aid family members in determining their relative's final resting place, I maintain a record of all locations where former Magdalene women are buried.

The *IDC Report* contends that 879 women died within the laundries between 1922 and 1996.[17] Yet, my research thus far has recorded the details of 1,838 women who died while in Magdalene Laundries or while institutionalized in religious-run nursing homes after the closure of the laundries, which suggests that the IDC ignored or failed to identify more than half of the women who died.[18] Inexplicably, the IDC disregarded '[d]eaths occurring in nursing homes after the closure of the Magdalen Laundries, of women who had in their earlier lives been admitted to a Magdalen Laundry.[19] However, this only partly accounts for the number of deaths omitted by the IDC, and without access to the Committee's archive, there is no way of knowing how or why it came to its conclusions. Thus much of my MNP research involves pursuing fragments of data in the hope that they yield further information on the women who died while incarcerated.

The obligation to investigate and prosecute

JFM made numerous submissions to the IDC in an effort to ensure the Committee's investigation would be as thorough as possible. The MNP's findings played an important role in these submissions. For example, JFM drew the IDC's attention to 141 women, most of whom endured lengthy periods of confinement of between 11 and 74 years in the laundries. Nevertheless, the *IDC Report* claims that the median duration of stay of women and girls confined in the laundries was approximately seven months and that the average stay was 3.2 years.[20] To counter this finding, after the publication of the *IDC Report*, I began gathering electoral register records and used these to demonstrate that, in stark contrast with the IDC's conclusions, over half the women named in the 1954–64 registers for High Park and DML remained in the institutions until their deaths. In the case of the Good Shepherd Magdalene Laundry in Limerick, an average of 60.4 per cent of women named in the electoral register between 1961 and 1983 died while confined in the institution.

The right to reparations

The MNP archive is an effective resource for survivors applying to the Irish government's *ex gratia* redress scheme, particularly for women who have difficulty proving the length of time they were detained in the laundries. For example, 'Caitríona' was confined in a Magdalene Laundry for seven years from the age of 11. However, in considering her application for redress, the Department of Justice (DoJ) accepted the religious order's contention that she had been in the institution for just two years. In her correspondence with the DoJ, Caitríona had provided the names of nuns who were in the Magdalene Laundry while she was confined. I analysed extracts from the electoral registers contained in the MNP archive and compiled the names of nuns who were in the laundry during Caitríona's time there and demonstrated that at least two (and possibly four) of the nuns identified by Caitríona were in the institution only during years when the DoJ claimed she was not. Ultimately, JFMR members made a total of 254 pages of submissions, legal analysis and exhibits in support of Caitríona's case. In September 2019, Mary O'Toole SC, who had been appointed by then Minister Charlie Flanagan to review disputed applications, recommended that Caitríona's length of stay be increased to seven years.[21]

The obligation to prevent recurrence

As part of my work on the MNP, I engage with local authorities, developers and others involved in demolishing and developing former Magdalene Laundry sites, including Donnybrook.[22] In early 2016, JFMR learned that a property developer was planning to demolish the DML building to facilitate the construction of an apartment complex.[23] In October 2016, JFMR sent a submission to Dublin City Council requesting that, in the event the proposed development proceeded, a condition would be added 'whereby if any human remains are discovered, that all demolition works will be immediately stopped and suitable experts are brought in to examine the site and ascertain the identity of those who are interred there and what became of them.'[24] A geophysical survey confirmed that no additional burials were present at Donnybrook; however, the development is nonetheless subject to several planning conditions, including a requirement for archaeological monitoring.[25]

Donnybrook and the MNP

The graveyard at Donnybrook Magdalene Laundry

The graveyard at DML is situated at the rear of the convent campus. The cemetery was established after the RSC moved their Magdalene Laundry from Townsend Street to Donnybrook in 1837. It was the Order's first dedicated burial ground.[26] There are 657 burial plots at the cemetery, 201 of which contain the remains of former Magdalene women and 456 in which the religious sisters are interred.[27] Most graves are marked with black iron crosses. Along a wall to the south of the cemetery there are six headstones which seem to relate to individuals who were not confined in DML. Three of these appear to be graves of women who may have worked in St Vincent's Hospital. It is unclear whether the other three headstones are cenotaphs or if the deceased are interred at Donnybrook. One relates to Anne Mary C., a possible benefactor of the institution. Another is dedicated to Mary B., the infant daughter of a bank inspector and a niece of one of the RSC nuns. Mary died in 1871 at the age of two.[28] I have been unable to obtain further information on M. Ellen D., whose death in 1867 does not appear to have been registered.

The graveyard at DML is unusual in several respects. First, whereas at other Magdalene burial locations (where graves are marked) the women's names are generally engraved together on a small number of large headstones, at Donnybrook most of the women's graves have individual markers with up to three names signifying who is buried in that plot. The exception is a large headstone bearing the names of seventy-eight women which is adjacent to an unmarked area at the south-west of the site. Although these women appear to be among the first who died at Donnybrook between 1841 and 1907, the headstone appears to have been erected retrospectively. This suggests that up until 1907, most Magdalene women confined in DML were buried in unmarked graves. Three women who died in this period have graves with individual markers that seem to have been erected at the time of their death.[29]

A further unusual feature of the graveyard at DML is that it contains the tomb of the RSC foundress Mary Aikenhead. While other Magdalene institutions have memorial crosses honouring their founders, Aikenhead's tomb is by far the most opulent.[30] This may be related to the RSC's efforts to have their founder canonized as a saint. Aikenhead died in 1858 and was initially laid to rest in 'a crypt, under a beautiful limestone cross'.[31] The cause for her canonization was commenced by the RSC's Australian congregation in 1908.[32] By 1910, the Archbishop of Dublin William Walsh had opened a file containing correspondence relating to the campaign.[33] In 1912, Aikenhead's coffin was opened; RSC Superior General Sr Mary Christian told the attendees at a celebration of the Order's bicentenary: 'From the archives we learn: "On 15 March 1912, the grave of Mary Aikenhead was opened in Donnybrook: the skeleton was practically intact."'[34] It is perplexing that the Sisters thought this to be of significance, as the incorruptibility associated with sainthood concerns *corpses* that do not putrefy and not 'intact' skeletal remains, though such incorruptibility is not a requirement for sainthood.[35] After the disinterment in 1912, Aikenhead's remains and the original coffin were placed into a new casket and returned to the tomb.[36] In 1921, Pope Benedict XV signed a decree for the 'Introduction of the Cause of Mary Aikenhead', which is the first step towards canonization.[37] In subsequent years, 'special novenas' were held to 'hasten the cause' of Aikenhead's beatification, and 1933 saw the commencement of annual pilgrimages to her tomb, with 3,000 in attendance at the first.[38] The RSC would have to wait until 2015 for their efforts to pay off. In March of that year, the Vatican declared Aikenhead to be 'venerable', which is the second of four steps towards becoming a saint.[39] The Order is currently campaigning for Aikenhead to be declared 'blessed', which, according to the Sisters: 'requires a miracle and so we continue to make her more known and we pray for the healing of people through her intercession'.[40] Today, Aikenhead's tomb is well maintained. Photographs taken by Angela Newsome of JFMR during a visit to see her mother Mary in 2002 show flower beds on each side of the steps that led to the entrance. The tomb has seen further refurbishment in the years since; a lit passageway descends to the crypt where Mary Aikenhead's oak coffin is now visible through the window of the door.

A final distinctive characteristic of the graveyard at DML is the fact that the Magdalene graves are located adjacent to those of Mary Aikenhead and the other religious sisters. Conversely, in other Magdalene Laundries, when a girl or woman died, in most instances, she was buried in a public cemetery. At the OLC Laundry at High Park, the Sisters of Mercy Laundry in Galway and the Good Shepherd Laundry at Sundays Well, 'auxiliaries' or 'consecrated Magdalenes', that is, those women and girls who vowed to remain in the laundry for life in exchange for a quasi-religious status, were buried in their own graveyard on the institutional campus. However, in all three locations, the auxiliaries' graveyards are at the opposite end of the campus to those of the religious sisters.[41]

During the late nineteenth and early twentieth centuries at least, the significance of the graveyard at DML was such that it was held up as a symbol of the redemptive work of the RSC in 'saving' the Magdalene women from dangers of the outside world:

> in the cemetery of St Mary Magdalen's lies a woman in her last sleep … Other women lie there, too, spiritual daughters of the mother, Mary Aikenhead. Nearby sleep yet others – drawn by the spirit of Charity out of the world's great snare into the peace and healing that breathe where Mary Magdalen, the saint of penitence, is the chosen patron.[42]

In December 1891, Rev. Daniel Downing delivered a charity sermon which romanticized the lives and deaths of the Sisters and the Magdalenes at Donnybrook:

> Side by side with the penitents lie the graves of Mary Aikenhead … and her devoted sisters, working side by side, hand in hand with the penitents, in death they are not separated. The dust of their loving hearts lies co-mingled beneath the same green Irish sod.[43]

This idyllic image persisted in the discourses surrounding the graveyard at DML. For example, in 1907, Rev. Dowling's words were repeated almost word for word in an obituary for Rev. Sylvester Bourke, who was a regular visitor to Donnybrook.[44]

Religious sisters' graves

Although the former Magdalene women are buried adjacent to members of the RSC congregation at Donnybrook, their graves are not so close in proximity that it is plausible their dust has 'co-mingled'.[45] Indeed, there are stark differences between the women's graves and those of the nuns. At the time of writing, there are 810 religious sisters buried at Donnybrook; these deaths occurred between 1818 and 2021 and include nuns from other RSC institutions, such as the Stanhope Street Training Centre, Lakelands Industrial School and Temple Street Children's Hospital.[46] The Magdalene crosses are plain and are set out in straight lines. In contrast, the religious sisters' crosses are more decorative, and are positioned to face the more elaborate graves of deceased RSC superior generals, with 127 crosses facing Mary Aikenhead's tomb.

Most of the religious sisters who died from 2003 onwards are buried in a newer area of the cemetery with black headstones in lieu of the iron crosses. However, up until 2015, Magdalene survivors who died at Donnybrook continued to be interred in the old part of the cemetery, except for those women who were taken home for burial with their families. To date, I have been unable to establish the names and burial locations of Donnybrook survivors who died after 2015. The burial location of some religious sisters suggests that their personal wishes regarding their final resting place were taken into account. For example, one nun who died in 2012 is buried in a plot facing Mary Aikenhead's tomb rather than the new section of the cemetery. Moreover, there are twenty-four instances where two nuns of the same surname are buried in the same plot together or in adjacent plots. In at least five cases, these are the graves of familial sisters who were buried together, including one nun who died in 2014 and is buried in the old part of the graveyard with her sister.

The RSC appear to place great emphasis on honouring their dead. In 2015, at an event celebrating the Order's bicentenary, scrolls bearing the names of 'all the deceased members' of the congregation were carried to the tomb of Mary Aikenhead'.[47] Furthermore, a large plaque at the entrance to the cemetery bears the names of the first eleven deceased members of the congregation who are buried in James Street Cemetery and the Pro Cathedral Vaults. Significantly, many of the RSC graves at Donnybrook are numbered to facilitate ease of access for friends and family who wish to visit their final resting place. No such finding aids are visible on the Magdalene crosses.

Most of the Magdalene graves simply record the women's names and year of death, with no further details on their age or length of confinement. By contrast, the nuns' crosses state when they were born, when they entered religion and when they died. This data reveals that the average age at death of the RSC members buried and memorialized at DML is 72, while the median is 80.[48] The average age on entering the convent is 24.6 years, while the median is 23 years.[49] Twenty-five sisters (3.1%) were under the age of 18 when they entered, whereas over 40% of the 8,852 cases of Magdalene women and girls analysed by the IDC were 18 or under when they were sent to a laundry.[50] Sara W. told the Magdalene Oral History Project that she was just 15 when she was 'kidnapped' by the Legion of Mary and sent to DML.[51]

Graves of former Magdalene women

Thus far, I have located the names of 315 women who died while they were confined in the DML campus.[52] These women died between 1841 and 2015, and most deaths (61.9%) occurred after the foundation of the State. After the closure of the laundry, 41 women (13.1%) died. Most of the 315 women are buried at Donnybrook; 3 women are buried in family plots, and to date I have been unable to determine the burial location of 3 other women. The grave markers of 5 women indicate that they were 'jubilarians', a term generally used to refer to a special anniversary marking a significant number of years in religious life, which suggests that these women may have been auxiliaries. One visitor to Donnybrook in 1897 remarked that in the infirmary there was: 'a distinguished jubilarian, who has just celebrated her *diamond* jubilee, that is the *sixtieth* anniversary of her entrance into penitential life'.[53]

Some of the women's crosses contain errors.[54] Twelve crosses have an incorrect date of death and there is no date of death at all on Bridget C.'s marker. Four women's names are spelled incorrectly. One woman, Mary C., has a grave marker at Donnybrook but according to Glasnevin Cemetery's records, she was buried there.[55] Mary is the only person named at that particular burial plot in Donnybrook, which begs the question: if Mary C. is not buried at that location, then who is?

There are twenty-two crosses at Donnybrook with no names or dates inscribed. These crosses are located between other graves that do have names and dates of death. In most cases, the graves before and after the unmarked crosses are in chronological order; for example, an unmarked cross is situated between Lily Q. (died 1934) and Mary Anne L. (died 1934). In most instances, the plots adjacent to unmarked crosses have two women buried in them. Moreover, many of the unmarked crosses are interspersed between the graves: one cross is located between Annie B. (died 1927) and Teresa F. (died 1931), while further along this row there is another unmarked cross between the same Annie B. and Maggie T. (died 1932). If the unmarked plots are empty, it is perplexing that the adjacent graves have two women buried in them. In the case of Gretta D., her name is inscribed on an additional piece of iron that is welded onto the cross, which may imply that she is buried with another woman whose name is not inscribed on the marker. Furthermore, through searches of the Registers of Deaths, I found the names of three women who died while they were in Donnybrook but whose names are not on any of the markers. Elizabeth C. died at the Richmond District Lunatic Asylum (RDLA) in 1914. Her death was registered by the RDLA so it is possible that she was buried by that institution. However, the deaths of the other two women, Agnes D. (died 1922) and Teresa G. (died 1925) both took place at Donnybrook and were registered by the RSC yet their names do not appear on any of the grave markers at Donnybrook. Approximately half of the unmarked crosses are located adjacent to women who died in the 1920s, which raises the question of whether Agnes and Teresa are buried in unmarked plots. Taking the above factors into account, I contend that the twenty-two crosses may in fact be unmarked graves, each containing the remains of women who died at Donnybrook. Without access to the RSC's registers it is impossible to verify the situation any further.

Duration of stay

According to the *IDC Report*, the median duration of stay of women and girls confined in the laundries was approximately seven months and the average stay was 3.22 years.[56]

Just over half of the 315 Donnybrook women I have identified are recorded in the census returns and/or electoral register extracts in the MNP archive.[57] An analysis of these records indicates that at minimum, these 166 women spent between nine months and 61 years in DML. The average period of confinement is 23.8 years, while the median is 22 years. The census returns for Donnybrook reveal that the number of women incarcerated in Donnybrook was 102 in 1901, and 111 in 1911.[58] Of the women detained at DML in 1901, 45 (44.1%) were still there in 1911. A comparison between the census returns and the names of the women on the grave markers indicates that 61.8% of the women registered in 1901 remained in the institution until they died, while 69.4% of the women confined in 1911 remained at Donnybrook for life.

The available electoral registers between 1937 and 1964 show that the RSC were registering the Donnybrook women to vote from as early as 1954. An analysis of the electoral registers between 1954 and 1964 reveals that 63.1% of the women in the 1954–5 register were incarcerated for a minimum of nine years and 67.9% of those in the 1955–6 register were incarcerated for a minimum of eight years. When the electoral registers and the grave markers are compared, the results show that an average of 55.2% of the women confined between 1954 and 1964 died in the institution.

Death certificates

I have located death certificates for 252 of the 315 Donnybrook women whose details are recorded in the MNP archive. No death certificates could be found for forty-one women, one woman's grave marker had no date of death, and twenty-one women died before civil registration began in 1864.[59] An analysis of the 252 available certificates indicates that the average age at death for these women is 63.9 years, while the median is 69 years. This suggests that the RSC sisters buried at Donnybrook lived an average of 8.1 years longer than the women confined in their Magdalene Laundry. The 'occupation' inserted on most women's death certificates is 'laundress' or 'laundry worker' (36.1%). Forty women (15.9%) are described as 'inmates' and seventeen women (6.7%) were seamstresses. Forty-six women (18.3%) are recorded as 'retired' laundresses, laundry workers or seamstresses.

Half of the women's death certificates (52%) state that they suffered from a heart condition or that they had a heart attack.[60] A quarter of the certificates (25.8%) reported respiratory illnesses or diseases. Instances of heart and respiratory conditions remained constant over time. Thirty-eight women (15.1%) had cancer. 'Debility' was stated as a cause of death in thirty-two instances. Seventeen women's death certificates said they had Alzheimer's disease, 'senile decay', dementia, schizophrenia, 'cognitive impairment' or an intellectual disability. Most women (71%) died in Donnybrook, while 20.6% died in Dublin-area hospitals. Most deaths in Dublin hospitals took place during the latter half of the twentieth century, predominantly from the 1970s onwards. Prior to this time, the majority of women died at Donnybrook. Notably, Margaret C. died at the age of twenty-two in the National Maternity Hospital (NMH) on Holles Street in September 1924. Margaret died from a cerebral tumour and a cardiac syncope. The information provided on her death certificate does not explain whether she was pregnant or why she was admitted to the NMH. Another woman, Teresa T. was forty-one and unmarried when she died at Donnybrook. Teresa died from TB, a cardiac syncope and toxaemia, also known as preeclampsia, a condition which occurs in pregnant people. The records offer no information about when Teresa became pregnant, and it is of note that women and girls who were pregnant outside of marriage were sent to Mother and Baby Homes and not Magdalene Laundries before they gave birth.[61] However, records from Mountjoy Prison indicate that in 1924 Teresa was a sex worker, which may explain why she was in Donnybrook and not in a Mother and Baby Home.[62]

Death notices

Whereas the RSC were publishing death notices for deceased members of their congregation from as early as the 1920s, this did not happen when a Magdalene woman died at Donnybrook. A search for announcements yielded just seventeen death notices and one acknowledgement from the family of a deceased woman.[63] On closer examination, six of these announcements appear to relate to women who are buried at Donnybrook but who may not have been Magdalenes. For example, Mary F., Brigid M. and Mary C. (who, as discussed above, is buried in Glasnevin) all died in the 1970s. While most women who died at DML during the 1970s can be found in the available electoral registers for Donnybrook, these three women are not recorded. This, along with the presence of death notices indicates that these women may have been buried at Donnybrook in an agreed arrangement with the Order. It is possible they may have been amongst the women described by the RSC as 'shabby genteels' – 'refined lonely old ladies' who were invited to occupy 'vacant' bedrooms at Donnybrook from the 1970s.[64] In some instances, the occupation recorded on the women's death certificates betrayed a difference. According to Fidelma M.'s death certificate, she was an 'accounts clerk' when she died in 1989. Vera T. was a retired nurse at the time of her death in a private nursing home in 2002, while Brigid M. was a 'retired linen supervisor' in 1975. Mary G. was a 'retired housekeeper', and her death certificate signals that she was married when she died in 1996. In the absence of access to RSC archives, it is not possible to establish the situation conclusively, however the evidence is pointing towards these women *not* being Magdalenes. In the interests of accuracy, these six women are not counted in the statistics for Magdalene women in this chapter. The eleven death notices that relate to former Magdalene women date from the 1990s onwards. Notably, all eleven notices appear to have been organized by the women's families.

Case studies

Anne Enright argues that in the *IDC Report,* the women's testimonies 'are turned into a kind of chorus'.[65] In contrast, the case studies constructed from MNP data demonstrate that even working solely from documentary evidence, it is possible to afford former

Magdalene women the dignity of being acknowledged as individuals with a range of experiences. Although the publicly available information on the women themselves is often minimal, through these fragments of data we can nonetheless gain an insight into their suffering, often endured over decades behind convent walls. The following case studies of five women who were confined in Donnybrook are imparted to emphasize that behind the statistics in this chapter are over three hundred women who, through no fault of their own, were removed from the outside world and confined until death in a Magdalene institution.

Sarah B.

Sarah B. was 22 and unmarried when she was recorded in the 1911 census for Donnybrook. She was from County Wicklow and she was able to read and write. Sarah is also named in all the available electoral registers between 1954–64. In July 1966, Sarah died at the age of 78 from heart disease, cardiovascular disease and anaemia at the Royal City of Dublin Hospital. These records indicate that Sarah spent almost her entire adult life (at least 55 years) at Donnybrook.

Elizabeth/Frances C.

Elizabeth/Frances C. was 81 when she died at Donnybrook in 1963.[66] Like Sarah, she died from heart disease, cardiovascular disease and anaemia, as well as 'debility'. The 1911 census return for Donnybrook indicates that Elizabeth was 24 at the time, but no further details are recorded. Elizabeth is named in all the available electoral registers between 1954 and 1963, suggesting that she was confined for at least fifty-two years at Donnybrook.

Winifred D.

Some women ended up in Donnybrook after the death of their husbands. For example, Winifred D., also known as Winnie, is named in the 1901 census return; she was 37 years of age. Winnie was still at Donnybrook when the 1911 census was taken; her age was recorded as 48 and the return states that she was from Kilkenny, she could read and write, and that she was a seamstress. According to the census return, Winnie was married for fourteen years and had given birth to five children, four of whom were living; however, civil registration records show that Winnie was married in 1884, and that her husband Nicholas died in 1889. No records relating to children born to the couple could be found. I was unable to locate a death certificate for Winnie. Her grave marker states that she died in 1940, indicating that she spent at least thirty-nine years at Donnybrook.

Kate V.

Kate V. was born in the early 1870s near Duleek in County Meath.[67] The records are conflicted regarding Kate's religion, with some reporting her as Protestant and others stating she was Catholic. According to the 1911 census return, Kate had been married for seven years and she had three children with one still living. I could not locate a marriage certificate for Kate or birth certificates for her children. In 1897, Kate was sentenced to fourteen days in Grangegorman Female Prison for begging.[68] According to the Grangegorman record, at that point Kate was a 'char', i.e. a charwoman. Two years later, in 1899, Kate was sentenced to seven days in Mountjoy Prison for 'soliciting'. This time her occupation is recorded as 'pros' (prostitute). According to Mountjoy, Kate was 5'1" in height with black/brown hair, blue eyes and she had a fresh or fair complexion.

When the census was taken in March 1901, Kate was in a 'home for fallen women' at 2 Northcote Avenue, Kingstown (now Dún Laoghaire).[69] The institution's income was derived from laundry work, and thus Kate's occupation was recorded as 'laundress'. In October 1901, Kate was admitted to the North Dublin Union (NDU) Workhouse for just over a week. Her address was given as Benburb Street, indicating that by then she had left the institution in Kingstown.[70] Just two days after her discharge, on 6 November 1901, Kate was admitted to the South Dublin Union (SDU) Workhouse with a broken ankle, where she stayed until 27 January 1902.[71] Two days later, Kate was readmitted to the NDU Workhouse for a further two days.[72] In February 1904, Kate was back in the NDU Workhouse, where she stayed until the end of April.[73] According to the census return, Kate was confined at DML by 1911. Kate had been institutionalized multiple times prior to 1911 and she appears to have had freedom of movement. However, Kate would never leave Donnybrook. A grave marker shows that she died there thirty years later in 1941. Thus far, no death certificate has been located for Kate.

Frances D.

The final case study, that of Frances D., is an account of what became of Frances and one of her daughters in the aftermath of the death of her husband Patrick, a police constable. At the time of their marriage in 1879, Frances and Patrick were living on Dorset Street in Dublin. Although the 1911 Donnybrook census return indicates that Frances had five children, four of whom were still living at the time, only two daughters could be found in the civil registration records: Mary born in 1880 and Bridget born in 1883. In 1893, Patrick died at the age of 42; Bridget and Mary were just 10 and 13 years of age. Patrick is buried at Glasnevin, with Frances named as the informant on the cemetery record.

It is unclear what became of Frances in the years immediately after Patrick's death, however, by 1899, her circumstances had declined to such an extent that she found herself in Mountjoy Prison.[74] The record states that she was a prisoner, but no details are available in relation to her alleged offence. By 1899, Frances' daughter Bridget's situation had also deteriorated and she was admitted to the NDU Workhouse from 14 to 19 June under her alias 'Anne'.[75] Two years later, in 1901, Frances was in the SDU Workhouse from 1 February until 16 March.[76] The workhouse record reports that her 'residence previous to admission' was the 'Magdalen Asylum' in Donnybrook, indicating that she had been confined in the laundry prior to her stay in the workhouse. The 1901 census was taken on 31 March 1901, and Frances is named in the Donnybrook return.

She is also recorded in the 1911 return. In 1919, Frances died in DML at the age of 53 from a 'malignant disease' of the breast. Unlike the RSC members who are interred with their relatives, Frances is buried not at Glasnevin with Patrick, but at Donnybrook with the other women; her name is misspelled as 'Francis' on the cross marking her grave.

Bridget's circumstances did not improve in the years after she was admitted to the workhouse. The records suggest that Bridget was in Mountjoy at least eighteen times between 1904 and 1910.[77] Where noted, her occupation was recorded as 'prostitute'. The offences with which Bridget was charged predominantly involved being drunk, drunk and disorderly, as well as soliciting, using profane and obscene language and threatening behaviour. Most of Bridget's records for Mountjoy state that her next of kin is Frances D. with an address at 'Donnybrook'. One record in 1905 names Bridget's sister Mary as her next of kin and infers that Mary had left Ireland to live in London. No further prison records are currently available for Bridget.[78]

In 1959, a Bridget D. died from cardiac failure and cancer in St Kevin's Hospital (now St James's Hospital). Bridget's death certificate states that she was 'late of St Mary's High Pk Convent'. A Bridget D. is named in the electoral registers for High Park between 1954-1956. Bridget's death certificate reports that she was seventy when she died, which suggests she was born in 1889. Frances D.'s daughter Bridget was born in 1883, however errors relating to dates were not uncommon. At present it is not possible to state categorically whether the Bridget D. who died at High Park in 1959 is the same woman born to Frances D. in 1883. However, given that it was not unusual for women in Bridget's situation to find themselves confined in a Magdalene Laundry, it is not beyond the realms of possibility that this is the case.

Conclusion

Inspired by the research methodologies adopted people use to obtain their information, the MNP empowers relatives and advocates to execute acts of resistance against church and State authorities. The MNP's findings reveal how the RSC and other orders discriminate against former Magdalene women even in death. The contentions of the *IDC Report* about the duration of stay of women and girls confined in the laundries no longer hold water in the face of the data compiled via the MNP. The case studies constructed using MNP data afford a measure of dignity to former Magdalene women and bring to light the myriad circumstances behind some women's confinement and the decades of suffering they endured. By compiling and analysing sources that are routinely ignored or undervalued, the MNP penetrates the veil of secrecy that hangs over Magdalene Laundry abuses. In doing so, it exposes human rights violations and ensures that the women confined in Donnybrook and the other Magdalene Laundries are not forgotten. It will be impossible to account for all women who were confined at DML and the other laundries until such a time as the State engages in a meaningful TJ process that includes the opening of all records relating to the laundries and related 'historical' injustices. In the meantime, the MNP's work continues.

Notes

1 Most of the women buried in Donnybrook died while the laundry was in operation. Forty-one women died after the closure of the institution. In recognition of the fact that many survivors object to being referred to as 'Magdalenes', where possible, I use the collective term 'former Magdalene women' to refer to both cohorts.

2 I am very grateful to the editors for their helpful comments and for the research materials they shared which were immensely helpful in ensuring this chapter did justice to the women confined in Donnybrook.

3 See Claire McGettrick, Katherine O'Donnell, Maeve O'Rourke, James M. Smith and Mari Steed, *Ireland and the Magdalene Laundries: A Campaign for Justice* (London: I.B. Tauris, 2021).

4 Mary Raftery, 'Restoring Dignity to Magdalens', *Irish Times*, 21 August 2003, 14. See also McGettrick et al., 'Bringing up the Dead: Burials and Land Deals at High Park', in *Ireland and the Magdalene Laundries*, 163–80.

5 See Mari Steed, 'Foreword', in McGettrick et al., *Ireland and the Magdalene Laundries*, xii–xv.

6 Raftery, 'Restoring Dignity', 14.

7 Padraig O'Morain, 'Adoption Society Admits Supplying False Information to Shield Mothers' Identities', *Irish Times*, 7 April 1997. See also Religious Sisters of Charity, available online: www.rsccaritas.com/ (accessed 7 September 2022).

8 Ibid.

9 Padraig O'Morain, 'Adoption Agency's Misinformation is Blamed for Years of Fruitless Searching', *Irish Times*, 8 April 1997.

10 McGettrick et al., *Ireland and the Magdalene Laundries*, 168.

11 Registration of Births and Deaths (Ireland) Act, 1863.

12 See also, 'How to Get Your Birth Certificate and Adoption Records', Adoption Rights Alliance, available online: www.adoption.ie/records/ (accessed 7 September 2022).

13 Michel Duchein, *Obstacles to the Access, Use, and Transfer of Information from Archives: RAMP Study* (Paris: United Nations Educational, Scientific, and Cultural Organization, 1983), 2.

14 Office of the United Nations High Commissioner for Human Rights, *Transitional Justice and Economic, Social and Cultural Rights* (Geneva: Office of the United Nations High Commissioner for Human Rights, 2014), 5.

15 Anna Ferrara, 'Archives and Transitional Justice in Chile: A Crucial Relationship', *Human Rights Review* 22 (2021): 254.

16 Department of Justice, *Report of the Inter-Departmental Committee to Establish the Facts of State Involvement with the Magdalen Laundries* (Dublin, January 2013, aka *McAleese Report*, hereinafter *IDC Report*), 789–90.

17 Ibid., 791.

18 This figure does not include unmarked plots or women whose legal identities have not yet been ascertained. As new information is constantly coming to light, the total number of deaths is always in flux.

19 *IDC Report*, 791.

20 'Executive Summary', *IDC Report*, XIII; *IDC Report*, 170 (3.2 years = 167.5 weeks).

21 See McGettrick et al., *Ireland and the Magdalene Laundries*, 143–4.

22 See 'JMFR Planning Submissions', Justice for Magdalenes Research, available online: www.jfmresearch.com/publications/jfmr-planning-submissions/ (accessed 7 September 2022).

23 Justice for Magdalenes Research, 'March 2016: JFMR Statement Re: Donnybrook Magdalene Laundry', 2016 Press Releases, available online: www.jfmresearch.com/press-releases/ (accessed 7 September 2022).

24 Justice for Magdalenes Research, *Submission to Dublin City Council Regarding the Proposed Property Development at the Former Magdalene Laundry at Donnybrook, Dublin 4*, 4 October 2016, available online: www.jfmresearch.com/wp-content/uploads/2017/02/JFMR-Submission-to-DCC-Re-Donnybrook.pdf (accessed 7 September 2022).

25 Heather Gimson and Ursula Garner, Earthsound Archaeological Geophysics, *Archaeological Geophysical Survey*, Detection Licence No. 17R0085, 8 June 2017; Stephen Bohan, An Bord Pleanála, *Board Order*, ABP-305475-19, 30 January 2020.

26 Maria Nethercott, *The Story of Mary Aikenhead: Foundress of the Irish Sisters of Charity* (London: Burns & Oates and New York: Benziger Bros, 1897), 140–1.

27 All data on the burial plots was generated by transcribing photographs of the graves.

28 Most deaths up to 1969 were located via searches of the civil registration records available online: IrishGenealogy.ie, www.irishgenealogy.ie/en/ (accessed 7 September 2022). Deaths after 1969 were located manually in the Research Room of the General Register Office. I am extremely grateful to Judy Campbell for her assistance in this work.

29 One of the four women from this period who have individual grave markers is Mary Gibbons. See further Mark Coen, Chapter 3, this volume.

30 For example, the Celtic cross erected by the Sisters of Our Lady of Charity to commemorate Sr Mary of the Sacred Heart Kelly, founder of High Park. Jacinta Prunty, *The Monasteries, Magdalen Asylums and Reformatory Schools of Our Lady of Charity in Ireland, 1853–1973* (Dublin: Columba Press, 2017), 169. There are seven other plots at Donnybrook with dedications to former superior generals of the order.

31 Nethercott, *The Story*, 194.

32 'The History of the Cause of Mary Aikenhead', Religious Sisters of Charity, available online: www.rsccaritas.com/96-uncategorised/487-history-of-the-cause (accessed 7 September 2022).

33 Dublin Diocesan Archives, Walsh Papers, Nuns 1910, 376/1, 'Re: M. M. Aikenhead Cause'.

34 Mary Christian, Sr, '200 Years Celebrations from Donnybook', Religious Sisters of Charity, Ireland, available online: www.sistersofcharity.org.au/wp-content/uploads/2017/02/200-years-celebrations-from-Donnybook.pdf (accessed 7 September 2022).

35 Robert Bartlett, *Why Can the Dead Do Such Great Things? Saints and Their Worshippers from the Martyrs to the Reformation* (Princeton, NJ: Princeton University Press, 2013), 100.

36 Christian, '200 Years', Religious Sisters of Charity, Ireland.

37 'The History', Religious Sisters of Charity.

38 'The Beatification of Mother Mary Aikenhead', *Irish Independent*, 13 May 1926, 3; 'Thousands Gather at Nun's Tomb', *Irish Press*, 11 September 1933, 7.

39 Kelly O'Brien, 'Cork's Mary Aikenhead is Two Steps Away from Sainthood', *Irish Examiner*, 19 March 2015.

40 'The History', Religious Sisters of Charity.

41 McGettrick et al., *Ireland and the Magdalene Laundries*, 166.

42 *The Irish Sisters of Charity: Giving a Brief Sketch of the Foundations of the Congregation* (Dublin: Anthonian Press, 1941), 26.

43 'The Magdalen Asylum, Donnybrook', *Freeman's Journal*, 28 December 1891, 6.

44 'Death of the Very Rev. Sylvester Bourke P.P., St. Laurence O'Toole's', *Freeman's Journal*, 27 December 1907, 15.

45 'The Magdalen Asylum, Donnybrook', *Freeman's Journal*.

46 The RSC own at least one other cemetery located in Sutton, County Dublin, where 312 sisters are buried. See 'Religious Sisters of Charity Cemetery', Find a Grave, available online: www.findagrave.com/cemetery/2579669/religious-sisters-of-charity-cemetery (accessed 7 September 2022).

47 Christian, '200 Years', Religious Sisters of Charity, Ireland.

48 Some grave markers were illegible. Data on age at death was available for 803 sisters. All percentages in this chapter are based on the total number for which data was available.

49 Data was available for 801 sisters.

50 *IDC Report*, 173.

51 Katherine O'Donnell, Sinead Pembroke and Claire McGettrick, 'Oral History of Sara W', Magdalene Institutions: Recording an Oral and Archival History (Government of Ireland Collaborative Research Project, Irish Research Council, 2012).

52 Most data was generated by transcribing photographs of the graves. A small number of women were identified through death certificates.

53 Mary Costello, 'The Sisterhood of Sorrow', *The Lady of the House*, 15 March 1897, 8, emphasis in original.

54 There are minor spelling and numerical errors on some religious sisters' graves.

55 Glasnevin burial locations in this chapter have been ascertained through searches of Glasnevin's genealogy service. See Dublin Cemeteries Trust, available online: www.dctrust.ie/genealogy/home.html (accessed 7 September 2022).

56 'Executive Summary', *IDC Report*; ibid., 169.

57 Census records were obtained via 'Census of Ireland 1901/1911 and Census Fragments and Substitutes, 1821–51', National Archives of Ireland, available online: www.census.nationalarchives.ie/ (accessed 7 September 2022); electoral registers were obtained from Dublin City Library.

58 For an analysis of the number of women confined over time, see Mark Coen, Chapter 3, this volume.

59 Registration of Births and Deaths (Ireland) Act, 1863.

60 Causes of death were simplified using medical dictionaries in order to put them into a general category for analysis. In many cases, it appears that causes of death were reported out of sequence, i.e. the underlying cause was reported as the immediate cause of death. This chapter reports the general categories of causes of death that appear on the death certificates; it does not purport to represent the conclusive cause of death for each woman.

61 McGettrick et al., *Ireland and the Magdalene Laundries*, 12.

62 Mountjoy Prison Index General Register Female, 1921–1927, Book No. 1/53/10, Item No. 1. Workhouse and prison records have been accessed via Find My Past, available online: www.findmypast.ie./ (accessed 7 September 2022).

63 Death notices were obtained via the *Irish Newspaper Archives* website, available online; https://www.irishnewsarchive.com/ (accessed 7 September 2022).

64 Dublin Diocesan Archives, McQuaid papers, religious orders (female), 1971.

65 Anne Enright, 'Antigone in Galway: Anne Enright on the Dishonoured Dead', *London Review of Books* 37, no. 24 (December 2015): 11–14.

66 Elizabeth was named as both Elizabeth and Frances/Fanny.

67 There are two women named Catherine V. who were born in the early 1870s in the same area. I have been unable to establish which of these women is the Kate V. who was confined in Donnybrook.

68 Grangegorman Female Prison General Register 1896–1897, Book No. 1/9/39, Item No. 2.

69 Rosa M. Barrett, *Guide to Dublin Charities Part III* (Dublin: Hodges, Figgis & Co., 1884), 4.

70 Poor Law Records of North Dublin Poor Law Union, 1840–1918, Book No. 13, Item No. 2.

71 Poor Law Records of South Dublin Poor Law Union, 1840–1918, Book No. 82, Item No. 5.

72 Poor Law Records of North Dublin Poor Law Union, 1840–1918, Book No. 110, Item No. 2.

73 Ibid., Book No. 64, Item No. 3.

74 Mountjoy Prison Index General Register Female, 1899, Book No. 1/48/1, Item No. 7.

75 Poor Law Records of North Dublin Poor Law Union, 1840–1918: Workhouse admission and discharge records, B.G. 78 v. G book 75 (14 April 1898, no. 3001) – v. G book 80 (18 November 1899, no. 840). Item No 4.

76 Poor Law Records of South Dublin Poor Law Union, 1840–1918: Workhouse admission and discharge records, v. G book 89 (25 January 1900, no. 361) – v. G book 94 (7 January 1902, no. 480), Folio 84, Item No. 3.

77 Mountjoy Prison Registers.

78 Find My Past holds records up to 1924.

Appendix

Women who occupied the office of Rectress/Superior of St Mary Magdalen's Convent, Donnybrook, as named in the Irish Catholic Directory

Mrs Ennis (possibly Mother Mary Patrick Ennis)	1836–7
Superior not listed in Directory	1838–40
Mother Elizabeth Knaresborough	1841–70
Mother M. Finbar Barden	1871–7
Mother M. F. Scholastica Lyons	1878–83
Mother M. Camillus Sallenave	1884
Mother M. Alphonsus Baker	1885–8
Mother M. Anne Aloysius Domitillo Farrell	1889–93
Mother Peter Synnott	1894–1906
Mother M. Gonzaga Keating	1907–19
Mother M. Francis Kennedy	1920–8
Mother M. Camillus Dalton	1929–32
Mother M. Lelia Butler	1933–5
Mother M. Joseph Eunan O'Neill	1936–41
Mother M. Frances Eucharia Greer	1942–6
Mother M. Josephine Cunningham	1947–52
Mother M. Frances Eucharia Greer	1953–7
Mother M. Senan Mulcahy	1958–63
Mother Joseph Martina Stafford	1964–9
Mother Joseph Christina Casey	1970–5
Directory unavailable; possibly not published	1976
Mother Agnes Dominic Quirke	1977–81
Sister Margaret Teresa Lowry	1982
Sister Joseph Austin Gahan	1983–8
Sister Teresa Emmanuel Rooney	1989–95
Sister Mary Malachy Tully	1996–2001

A note on methodology

The above list of Donnybrook Superiors was compiled from editions of the *Irish Catholic Directory* dating from 1836 to 2001 (when the Directory ceased naming the

Superiors of RSC convents; it is possible that the functions previously exercised by Superiors were replaced by 'Leadership Teams' at that time).

The dates provided for each Superior should be treated as rough estimates; it is possible that some Superiors took up office in the same year as their predecessor left office, but this is not reflected in the information provided in the Directory.

There may be other errors. For example, Mother M. Camillus Dalton is listed in the Directory as Superior of Donnybrook for the years 1929 to 1932, but newspapers published on 3 January 1929 refer to her recent death.

Select Bibliography

Articles and books

Aikenhead, Mary. *Letters of Mary Aikenhead.* Dublin: M. H. Gill & Son, 1914.

Atkinson, Sarah. *Mary Aikenhead: Her Life, Her Work and Her Friends.* Dublin: M. H. Gill & Son, 1879.

Bayley Butler, Margery. *A Candle was Lit: The Life of Mother M. Aikenhead.* Dublin: Clonmore & Reynolds, 1954.

Black, Lynsey. *Gender and Punishment in Ireland: Women, Murder and the Death Penalty, 1922–64.* Manchester: Manchester University Press, 2022.

Blake, Donal S. *Mary Aikenhead: Servant of the Poor.* Dublin: Caritas, 2001.

Buchli, Victor, and Gavin Lucas, *Archaeologies of the Contemporary Past.* London: Routledge, 2001.

Butler, Richard. *Building the Irish Courthouse and Prison: A Political History, 1750–1850.* Cork: Cork University Press, 2020.

Casella, Eleanor Conlin. *The Archaeology of Institutional Confinement.* Tallahassee, FL: University Press of Florida, 2007.

Catholic Emancipation Centenary Record. Dublin: Dublin, Literary Committee, 1929.

Clear, Caitriona. *Nuns in Nineteenth-Century Ireland.* Dublin: Gill and Macmillan, 1987.

Constitutions of the Pious Congregation of the Religious Sisters of Charity of Ireland. Dublin: Browne & Nolan, 1927.

Coquelin, Olivier. 'Politics in the Irish Free State: The Legacy of a Conservative Revolution'. *The European Legacy* 10, no. 1 (2005): 29–39.

Cox, Catherine. 'Institutional Space and the Geography of Confinement in Ireland, 1750–2000'. In *The Cambridge History of Ireland, Vol. 4*, edited by Thomas Bartlett, 673–707. Cambridge: Cambridge University Press, 2018.

Crossan, Rosaleen. *Friend of the Poor: Mary Aikenhead.* Dublin: Columba Press, 2016.

Crossman, Virginia. *Poverty and the Poor Law in Ireland, 1850–1914.* Liverpool: Liverpool University Press, 2013.

Crowe, Caitriona. 'Guilt, Shame, Acknowledgement and Redress: Some Reflections on Ireland's Institutional Treatment of Women and Children'. In *Producing Knowledge, Reproducing Gender: Power, Production, Practice in Contemporary Ireland*, edited by Mary P. Corcoran and Pauline Cullen, 235–51. Dublin: University College Dublin Press, 2020.

Cullen, John Hugh. *The Australian Daughters of Mary Aikenhead.* Sydney: Pellegrini & Co., 1938.

D'Arcy, Fergus A. 'The Decline and Fall of Donnybrook Fair: Moral Reform and Social Control in Nineteenth Century Dublin'. *Saothar* 13 (1988): 7–21.

Delay, Cara. *Irish Women and the Creation of Modern Catholicism, 1850–1950.* Manchester: Manchester University Press, 2019.

Diver, Cara. *Marital Violence in Post-Independence Ireland, 1922–96: 'A Living Tomb for Women'.* Manchester: Manchester University Press, 2019.

Donovan, Margaret. *Apostolate of Love: Mary Aikenhead 1787–1858*. Melbourne: The Polding Press, 1979.

Earner-Byrne, Lindsey. 'Child Sexual Abuse, History and the Pursuit of Blame in Modern Ireland'. In *Exhuming Passions: The Pressure of the Past in Ireland and Australia*, edited by Katie Holmes and Stuart Ward, 51–70. Dublin: Irish Academic Press, 2011.

Earner-Byrne, Lindsey. *Mother and Child: Maternity and Child Welfare in Dublin, 1922–60*. Manchester: Manchester University Press, 2017.

Earner-Byrne, Lindsey. 'The Rape of Mary M.: A Microhistory of Sexual Violence and Moral Redemption in 1920s Ireland'. *Journal of the History of Sexuality* 24, no. 1. (2015): 75–98.

Earner-Byrne, Lindsey. 'Reinforcing the Family: The Role of Gender, Morality and Sexuality in Irish Welfare Policy, 1922–1944'. *History of the Family* 13, no. 4 (2008): 360–9.

Enright, Máiréad, and Sinéad Ring. 'State Legal Responses to Historical Institutional Abuse: Shame, Sovereignty and Epistemic Injustice'. *Éire-Ireland* 55, nos 1–2 (2020): 68–99.

Gaughan, J. Anthony. *The Archbishops, Bishops and Priests Who Served in the Archdiocese of Dublin 1900 to 2011*. Dublin: Kingdom Books, 2012.

Gaughan, J. Anthony. *At the Coalface: Recollections of a City and Country Priest*. Dublin: Columba Press, 2000.

Gott, Chloe K. *Experience, Identity & Epistemic Injustice within Ireland's Magdalene Laundries*. London: Bloomsbury, 2022.

Hanson, John H. 'The Anthropology of Giving: Toward a Cultural Logic of Charity'. *Journal of Cultural Economy* 8, no. 4. (2014): 501–20.

Harrison, Rodney. 'Surface Assemblages: Towards an Archaeology in and of the Present'. *Archaeological Dialogues* 18, no. 2. (2011): 141–61.

Hatfield, Mary, and Ciaran O'Neill. 'Education and Empowerment: Cosmopolitan Education and Irish Women in the Early Nineteenth Century'. *Gender and History* 30, no. 1 (2018): 93–109.

Haughton, Miriam, Mary McAuliffe and Emilie Pine, eds. *Legacies of the Magdalen Laundries*. Manchester: Manchester University Press, 2021.

Holohan, Carole. *In Plain Sight: Responding to the Ferns, Ryan, Murphy and Cloyne Reports*. Dublin: Amnesty International, 2011.

Irish Sisters of Charity 1843–1943: Souvenir Book. Dublin: Annesley Press, 1943.

Jones, Mary. *These Obstreperous Lassies: A History of the Irish Women Workers' Union*. Dublin: Gill & Macmillan, 1988.

Kennedy, Stanislaus. *But Where Can I Go? Homeless Women in Dublin*. Dublin: Arlen House, 1985.

Kennedy, Stanislaus. *The Road Home*. Dublin: Transworld Ireland, 2011.

Killian, Sheila. '"For Lack of accountability": The Logic of the Price in Ireland's Magdalene Laundries'. *Accounting, Organizations and Society* 43 (2015): 17–32.

Lally, Anne. *History of the Religious Sisters of Charity in Nigeria (1961–2011)*. Dublin: Speciality Printing, 2011.

Lixinski, Lucas. 'Cultural Heritage Law and Transitional Justice: Lessons from South Africa'. *International Journal of Transitional Justice* 9, no. 2 (9 April 2015): 278–96.

Luddy, Maria. 'Convent Archives as Sources for Irish History'. In *Religious Women and their History: Breaking the Silence*, edited by Rosemary Raughter, 98–115. Dublin: Irish Academic Press, 2005.

Luddy, Maria. 'Moral Rescue and Unmarried Mothers in Ireland in the 1920s'. *Women's Studies: An Interdisciplinary Journal*. 30, no. 6 (2001): 797–817.

Luddy, Maria. *Prostitution in Irish Society 1800–1940.* Cambridge: Cambridge University Press, 2007.

Luddy, Maria. 'Prostitution and Rescue Work in Nineteenth-Century Ireland'. In *Studies in Irish Women's History in the 19th and 20th Centuries*, edited by Maria Luddy and Clíona Murphy, 51–84. Swords, Co. Dublin: Poolbeg, 1989.

Luddy, Maria. *Women and Philanthropy in Nineteenth-Century Ireland.* Cambridge: Cambridge University Press, 1995.

Magray, Mary Peckham. *The Transforming Power of the Nuns.* Oxford: Oxford University Press, 1998.

McAtackney, Laura. *An Archaeology of the Troubles: The Dark Heritage of Long Kesh/Maze Prison.* Oxford: Oxford University Press, 2014.

McAtackney, Laura. 'Materials and Memory: Archaeology and Heritage as Tools of Transitional Justice at a Former Magdalen Laundry'. *Éire-Ireland* 55, nos 1–2. (2020): 221–44.

McCann, Catherine. *In Gratitude: The Story of a Gift-Filled Life.* Dublin: Orpen Press, 2015.

McCarthy, Michael John Fitzgerald. *Priests and People in Ireland.* Dublin: Hodges, Figgis & Co., 1902.

McGettrick, Claire, and Katherine O'Donnell, Maeve O'Rourke, James M. Smith and Mari Steed, *Ireland and the Magdalene Laundries: A Campaign for Justice.* London: I.B. Tauris, 2021.

McKenna, Yvonne. *Made Holy: Irish Women Religious at Home and Abroad.* Dublin: Irish Academic Press, 2006.

Member of the Congregation. *The Life and Work of Mary Aikenhead.* London: Longmans, Green & Co., 1924.

Milotte, Mike. *Banished Babies: The Secret History of Ireland's Baby Export Business.* Dublin: New Island 2012.

Mosse, George Lachmann. *Nationalism and Sexuality: Respectability and Abnormal Sexuality in Modern Europe.* New York: Howard Fertig, 1985.

Nethercott, Maria. *The Story of Mary Aikenhead.* London: Burns and Oates, 1897.

O'Donnell, Katherine. 'A Certain Class of Justice: Ireland's Magdalenes'. In *Histories of Punishment and Social Control in Ireland: Perspectives from a Periphery*, edited by Lynsey Black, Louise Brangan and Deirdre Healy, 79–106. Bingley: Emerald Publishing, 2022.

O'Donnell, Katherine, and Maeve O'Rourke and James M. Smith, eds. *Redress: Ireland's Institutions and Transitional Justice.* Dublin: University College Dublin Press, 2022.

O'Mahoney, Jennifer, Lorraine Bowman Grieve and Alison Torn. 'Ireland's Magdalene Laundries and the Psychological Architecture of Surveillance'. In *Surveillance, Architecture and Control: Discourses on Spatial Culture*, edited by Susan Flynn and Antonia Mackay, 187–208. Cham: Palgrave Macmillan, 2019.

O'Rourke, Maeve. 'Ireland's "Historical" Abuse Inquiries and the Secrecy of Records and Archives'. In *Histories of Punishment and Social Control in Ireland: Perspectives from a Periphery*, edited by Lynsey Black, Louise Brangan and Deirdre Healy, 107–38. Bingley: Emerald Publishing, 2022.

O'Sullivan, Eoin, and Ian O'Donnell, eds. *Coercive Confinement in Post-Independent Ireland: Patients, Prisoners and Penitents.* Manchester: Manchester University Press, 2012.

Pine, Emilie. 'Coming Clean? Remembering the Magdalen Laundries'. In *Memory Ireland: History and Modernity*, vol. 1, edited by Oona Frawley, 157–71. Syracuse: Syracuse University Press, 2011.

Prunty, Jacinta. *The Monasteries, Magdalen Asylums and Reformatory Schools of Our Lady of Charity in Ireland 1853–1973*. Dublin: Columba Press, 2017.

Rattigan, Clíona. *'What Else Could I Do?' Single Mothers and Infanticide, Ireland 1900–1950*. Dublin: Irish Academic Press, 2012.

Rules of the Religious Sisters of Charity. Dublin: Mount St Anne's Milltown, 1941.

Ryan, Louise. 'Sexualizing Emigration: Discourses of Irish Female Emigration in the 1930s'. *Women's Studies International Forum* 25, no. 1 (2002): 51–65.

Rynne, Catherine. *Mother Mary Aikenhead*. Dublin: Veritas Publications, 1980.

Sebbane, Nathalie. *Memorialising the Magdalene Laundries: From Story to History*. Oxford: Peter Lang, 2021.

Sisters of Charity. *St Mary Magdalen's Donnybrook: Yearbook*. Shannon Publication, 1961.

Smith, James M. *Ireland's Magdalen Laundries and the Nation's Architecture of Containment*. Manchester: Manchester University Press, 2007.

Taylor, Fanny. *Irish Homes and Irish Hearts*. London: Longmans, Green & Co., 1867.

The Irish Sisters of Charity: Centenary Brochure. Dublin: Mount Saint Anne's, 1958.

The Irish Sisters of Charity: Giving a Brief Sketch of the Foundations of the Congregation. Dublin: Anthonian Press, 1941.

Tweedy, Robert. *The Story of the Court Laundry*. Dublin: Wolfhound Press, 1999.

Government and NGO reports

Department of Health. *Report on the Inquiry into the Operation of Madonna House*. Dublin: Stationery Office, 1996.

Department of Justice. *Report of the Inter-Departmental Committee to Establish the Facts of State Involvement with the Magdalen Laundries*. Dublin: Government Publications, 2013.

Final Report of the Commission to Inquire into Child Abuse. Dublin: Stationery Office, 2009.

Final Report of the Commission of Investigation into Mother and Baby Homes and Certain Related Matters. Dublin: Department of Children, Equality, Disability, Integration and Youth, 2021.

IHRC Assessment of the Human Rights Issues Arising in Relation to the 'Magdalen Laundries', Nov 2010. Dublin: Irish Human Rights and Equality Commission (IHREC), 2010.

McCormick, Leanne, Sean O'Connell, Olivia Dee and John Privilege. *Mother and Baby Homes and Magdalene Laundries in Northern Ireland, 1922–1990: A Report for the Inter Departmental Working Group on Mother and Baby Homes, Magdalene Laundries and Historical Clerical Child Abuse*. Coleraine and Belfast: Ulster University and Queen's University Belfast, January 2021.

O'Rourke, Maeve, Claire McGettrick, Rod Baker, Raymond Hill et al. *Clann: Ireland's Unmarried Mothers and Their Children: Gathering the Data: Principal Submissions to the Commission of Investigation into Mother and Baby Homes*. Dublin: Justice for Magdalenes Research, Adoption Rights Alliance, Hogan Lovells, 15 October 2018.

Ombudsman. *Opportunity Lost: An Investigation by the Ombudsman into the Administration of the Magdalen Restorative Justice Scheme*. Dublin: Office of the Ombudsman, November 2017.

The Report of the Commission of Inquiry into the Reformatory and Industrial School System, 1934–1936. Dublin: Stationery Office, 1936.

Review of Child Safeguarding Practice in the Religious Congregation of the Religious Sisters of Charity. Maynooth, Co. Kildare: National Board for Safeguarding Children in the Catholic Church in Ireland, 2015.

Reynolds, Marion. *A Shadow Cast Long: Independent Review Report into Incorrect Birth Registrations.* Commissioned by the Minister for Children and Youth Affairs. 2019.

Newspapers

Anglo-Celt
Connacht Tribune
Cork Examiner
Donnybrook Review
Dublin Evening Telegraph
Evening Echo
Evening Freeman
Evening Herald
Evening Press
Freeman's Journal
Irish Independent
Irish Press
Irish Times
Kilkenny People
The Standard
Sunday Independent
Waterford News and Star
Westmeath Independent
Wicklow People

Periodicals

Blackrock College Annual
Capuchin Annual
Irish Catholic Directory
Irish Ecclesiastical Record
Irish Jesuit Directory
Irish Monthly
Irish Rosary
The Lady of the House
St Anthony's Annals
St Mary's College Annual

Websites

https://jfmresearch.com
https://jfmresearch.com/home/oralhistoryproject/

http://mappingdubliners.org
www.adoption.ie
www.cso.ie
www.dctrust.ie
www.findagrave.com
www.findmypast.ie
www.irishstatutebook.ie
www.justice.ie
www.museum.ie
www.nuigalway.ie/tuam-oral-history
www.oireachtas.ie
www.prisonsmemoryarchive.com
www.rsccaritas.com
www.rte.ie
www.safeguarding.ie
www.sistersofcharity.org.au
www.sitesofconscience.org
www.stmargaretsdonnybrook.ie
www.thejournal.ie
www.vatican.va

Archives

Dublin City Council Planning Archive, Dublin
Dublin Diocesan Archives, Dublin
General Register Office, Dublin
Irish Architectural Archive, Dublin
National Archives of Ireland, Dublin
Prisons Memory Archive (www.prisonsmemoryarchive.com)
Religious Sisters of Charity Archives, Sandymount
University of Galway Archives, Galway

Index

Plate 1 St Mary Magdalen's Convent, Donnybrook, *c.* 1970. Courtesy of the Irish Architectural Archive.

Plate 2 A box bearing the name of the official residence of the President of Ireland found in Donnybrook Magdalene Laundry in June 2018. Photo by Mark Coen.

⊲ THE SISTERHOOD OF SORROW. ⊳

No. II.—THE MAGDALENS.

"A rose poire—l'ombre et le silence."

THERE is no branch of state service for which religious communities are more especially fitted, and in which they succeed more notably, than in the rescue of fallen women.

Secular establishments, no matter how intelligently organized, or how ably conducted, must *a priori* lack that vital spark which animates ascetic life. A spark which, as we hope to show, has the power of not only keeping the fire of perseverance aglow, but of kindling the rare high flame

This mandate has to go forth to those over whom the Sisters have no legal control, who are in no way bound by vows, and, therefore, free to leave the institution at any moment they like.

In the absence of a religious atmosphere, what would be the likelihood of the success of such a task? Surely no sensible person would think of attempting it on mere worldly or non-sectarian lines?

What the fallen woman wants is not cut and dry reformatory discipline, but

of heroism in the breasts of those whom men call the frail daughters of earth.

Let us consider in a few words the task which the Sisters of Charity and of the Good Shepherd undertake in their various Homes of Rescue throughout the land.

They are given one, two, or three hundred souls, gathered in considerable majority from the lowest fields of licence; women of weak wills but strong appetites, initially, it may be assumed, of wayward, emotional, pleasure-craving temperaments, a great many of whom in the effort to make bearable the degradation into which they had fallen, have contracted habits of drink, and are, in fact, confirmed inebriates.

To such a gathering the Sisters have to say, "All you who pass our gates must abjure your former habits, you must not only lead lives of virtue and sobriety, but of restraint. You must practically look upon the joys of this world as at an end, and spend your remaining days in works of usefulness and abnegation."

a spiritual hospital, provided with an experienced staff, always by to lay a sympathetic hand on the patient's pulse, to comfort, to advise, to encourage, to cross and sustain. She wants an *entourage* which is a constant and all-pervading appeal to the commanding emotional parts of human nature, which creates a spirit of reverence, stimulates the yearning for perfection, "for the consolation of the life out of self," which makes holiness tangible, and gives it at the same time magisterial power and effect.

"What it takes three policemen of a Saturday night, one of them here can make me do, with the lifting of an eye," whispered a stalwart young woman to a friend who had halted beside her wash-tub. "I don't know how they manage it. We fret and sulks, and swears we must be off fifty times a day in the first month, the most of us; but we never give one of them—' with a glance at a veiled figure flitting past '—what we'd give outside to those that goes against us, faith, smart enough !"

"Yes, it's the first few weeks that is the struggle," said the Reverend Mother of the Sisters of Charity at Donnybrook, with an eloquent lifting of

Plate 3 Donnybrook Magdalene Laundry in the late nineteenth century. (*The Lady of the House*, 15 March 1897). Image reproduced courtesy of the British Library.

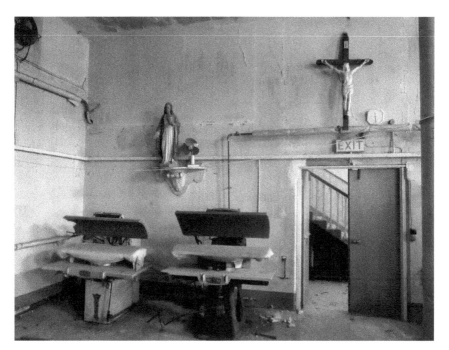

Plate 4 The interior of Donnybrook Magdalene Laundry in June 2018. Photo by Mark Coen.

Plate 5 Sinks in position at Donnybrook Magdalene Laundry in June 2018. These sinks were subsequently removed by persons unknown, according to the agents acting for the owners of the site. Photo by Mark Coen.

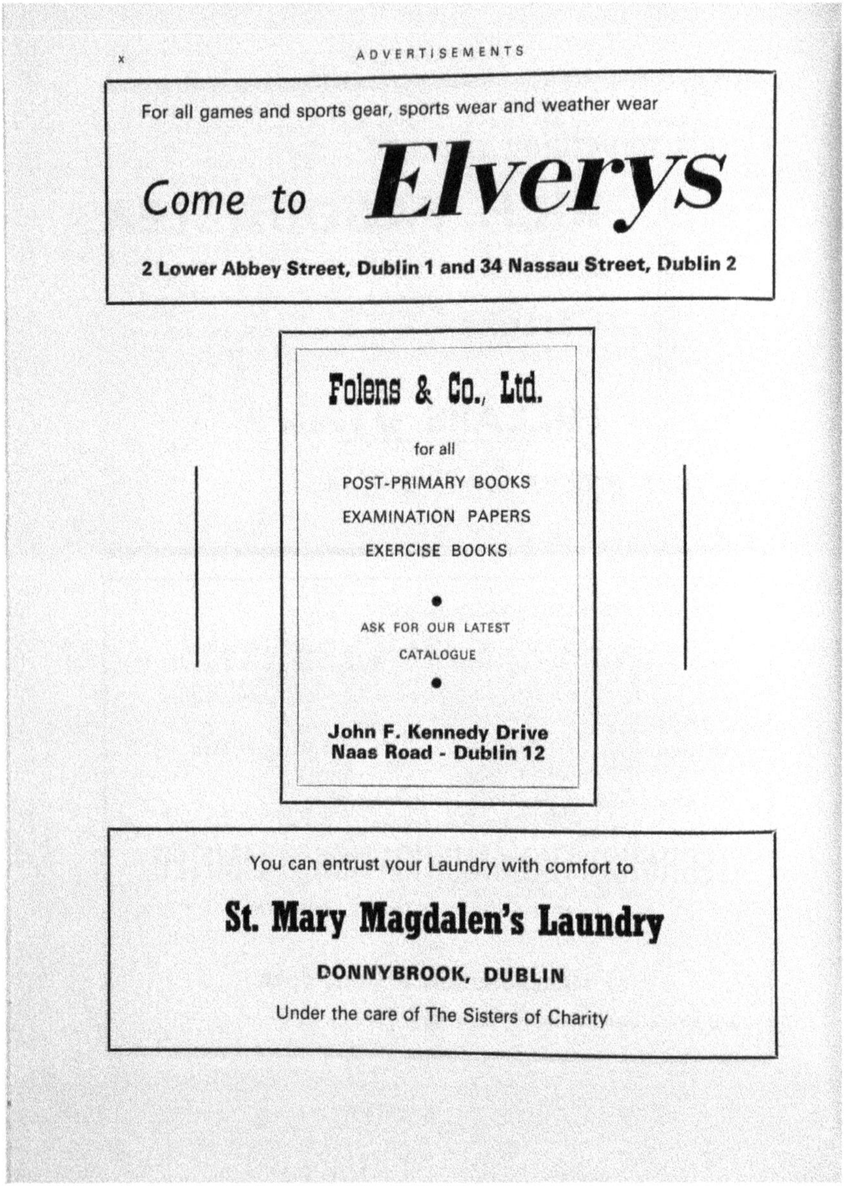

Plate 6 An advertisement for Donnybrook Magdalene Laundry, in the *Blackrock College Annual*, 1970. Blackrock College was established by the Holy Ghost Fathers in 1860 and is one of Dublin's most prestigious Catholic schools. Image courtesy of the National Library of Ireland.